# The Modern Liberal Theory of Man

GERALD F. GAUS

CROOM HELM
London & Canberra
ST. MARTIN'S PRESS
New York

© 1983 G.F. Gaus
Croom Helm Ltd, Provident House, Burrell Row,
Beckenham, Kent BR3 1AT

British Library Cataloguing in Publication Data

Gaus, Gerald F.
    The modern liberal theory of man.
    1. Liberalism
    I. Title
    320.5'1        HM276
    ISBN 0−7099−1127−0

All rights reserved. For information write:
St. Martin's Press, Inc., 175 Fifth Avenue, New York, N.Y. 10010
First published in the United States of America in 1983

Library of Congress Cataloging in Publication Data

Gaus, Gerald F.
    The modern liberal theory of man.

    Bibliography: p.
    Includes index.
    1. Liberalism. 2. Social psychology.
3. Political science.   I. Title.
HM276.G39    1983       320.5'1       82−25493
ISBN 0−312−54083−3

Printed and bound in Great Britain
by Billing and Sons Ltd, Worcester.

# CONTENTS

# Contents

## Contents

The ideas of every philosopher concerned with human affairs in the end rest on his conception of what man is and can be. To understand such thinkers, it is more important to grasp this central notion or image, which may be implicit, but determines their picture of the world, than even the most forceful arguments with which they defend their views and refute actual and possible objections.

ISAIAH BERLIN

# ACKNOWLEDGEMENTS

The roots of this book go back to 1975, when I participated in J. Roland Pennock's seminar on democratic theory at the University of Pittsburgh. Throughout the last seven years Professor Pennock has been kind enough to read and comment upon drafts from the various stages of my project. At the University of Pittsburgh, Kurt Baier, Bob Kocis, Irwin Schulman and Fred Whelan all were generous with their time in offering suggestions and counter-arguments. Bert Rockman also deserves my deep thanks. At the Australian National University, my good friend and colleague, Stanley Benn, has been a constant source of intellectual stimulation. His influence shows through in many more places than he might guess. Fred D'Agostino has tried his best to sort out my methodological problems; the argument of the book no doubt would have been clearer if I had taken his advice even more often. I am particularly grateful to John Kleinig for his detailed comments on a draft of Part One: I think I can even now forgive him for so damaging my ego. In general, though, I would like to extend my deepest thanks to the Research School of Social Sciences of the A.N.U. Not only has the school provided a perfect environment for research, but it also has been generous in providing funds without which the publication of this book would not have been possible.

In preparation of the manuscript I have been lucky enough to have had the best of editors, Harriet Halliday. We fought seldom but changed a great deal, which is surely the sign of excellent editor-author relations. Caroline McAlpin set the manuscript, using a less-than-perfect word-processing programme; her perseverance in the face of a maniacal technological adversary has been an inspiration to us all. For bringing the manuscript to its ultimate publishable form, I am indebted to Louise Hogden's expert typesetting. In the earlier stages of my research, Jenny Kerr was a great help, especially in compiling a preliminary bibliography. My thanks too to Brian Embury for tracking down some of my more obscure sources. I would also like to note my appreciation to Christopher Helm, whose early interest in the book was a great encouragement.

I first presented the outlines of my thesis in a paper presented to the 1978 meeting of the American Political Science Association. A revised version of that paper was published in the October 1981 issue of *Ethics*. I thank the University of Chicago Press for permission to use here material from that paper. I also wish to acknowledge the permissions of Harvard University Press and Oxford University Press to quote at length from *A Theory of Justice*. The University of Toronto Press and Routledge and Kegan Paul have provided permission to so quote from the University of Toronto Edition of *The Collected Works of John Stuart Mill.*

Last, but by no means least, I wish to thank John Chapman. Over the years he has been teacher, colleague and friend. Not only this book, but my whole approach to political theory shows his influence. Students cannot really repay their teachers; all they can do is show their appreciation. It is in order to do so that I dedicate this book to him.

G.F.G.

CANBERRA
JULY 1982

# INTRODUCTORY

## Modern Liberalism

It is generally agreed that sometime in the latter part of the nineteenth or early twentieth centuries liberal theory underwent a fundamental transformation. Some date its beginnings with John Stuart Mill, others with T.H. Green, while others have more recently emphasised such later liberals as L.T. Hobhouse and John Dewey.[1] Most typically, this transformation is seen, as Dicey put it, as a movement from an earlier laissez-faire 'individualism' to a socialistic 'collectivism'.[2] But that transition is essentially one regarding conclusions and prescriptions; if we are interested in the nature of this new liberal theory, we clearly want to go deeper and discover the theoretical underpinnings of these revised conclusions. As soon as we do look deeper, however, we are struck by the tremendous diversity of ethical and metaphysical views that 'new liberals' have put forward to support their prescriptions. For all his alleged departures from utilitarian ethics, J.S. Mill certainly believed that his political positions were endorsed by his utilitarianism. T.H. Green, however, launched what he saw as a fundamental attack on Mill's 'hedonistic' ethics, and yet, as he acknowledged, the practical differences between them were small.[3] In a similar way, Hobhouse undertook a reformulation of Mill's and Green's ethics and metaphysics with a view to better supporting their liberalism.[4] And in America John Dewey proclaimed a 'renascent liberalism' growing out of a pragmatic-experimental philosophy and faith in human intelligence.[5] Most recently, John Rawls has offered a new version of social contract/natural rights theory which, he believes, provides a firmer foundation for liberal liberties than does the hitherto dominant utilitarian philosophy. Once again it seems that we are witnessing an attack on the fundamentals of Mill's philosophy in order to better uphold his politics.[6]

To some extent, of course, the new liberals have overemphasised their differences. Green, Hobhouse and Dewey were much closer to Millian utilitarianism than they realised. And the influence of Green's idealism can be seen in Hobhouse, Dewey and even Rawls.[7] Granted all this, however, the philosophic diversity among such liberals remains impressive: utilitarianism, idealism (and the common good), harmony, instrumentalism and the social contract all have been offered as the

1

basis for a revised liberalism. Indeed, it seems reasonable to question whether 'modern liberal theory' is anything but a group of essentially different philosophies with converging political prescriptions. Does a modern liberal theory exist?

## The Thesis

The main thesis of this book is that a modern liberal theory does indeed exist. The core of all the theories mentioned above, I shall argue, lies in what a social psychologist, Zevedei Barbu, has called the balancing of two conceptions of individuality. According to Barbu, in the uniquely democratic personality the individual sees himself both as a unique manifestation of humanity, an end in himself, and as a member of a group. Such persons, he tells us, are both individualists and 'communists'; they combine individuality and sociability.[8] This theme of combining and reconciling individuality and sociability, I will try to show, is fundamental to the liberalisms of J.S. Mill, T.H. Green, L.T. Hobhouse, John Dewey, John Rawls and Bernard Bosanquet.

In itself this is not a particularly new or surprising idea. Although today the critical transformation in liberalism is often thought to turn on Dicey's distinction between economic individualism and collectivism, many, especially in the nineteenth century, saw the change in liberalism as centring around theories of man and society. Perhaps this is first signalled in Mill's pair of essays on 'Bentham' and 'Coleridge', which indicate a growing uneasiness with the narrow and one-sided picture of man upon which, at least to most liberals in the latter nineteenth and early twentieth centuries, traditional liberalism was thought to depend.[9] Certainly new liberals such as D.G. Ritchie were convinced that the debate between liberal collectivists and such proponents of laissez-faire as Spencer ultimately turned on opposing theories of man and society.[10] And yet a bit later, Dewey was very clear that, as he understood it, the earlier, ruggedly individualistic, liberalism rested upon a false antagonism between the individual and society that collectivistic liberalism overcomes.[11] Thus, not too surprisingly, it has often been said of liberals like Mill, Dewey, Hobhouse and Rawls that their aim is to reconcile or synthesise individuality and community.[12]

But if the only fundamental commonality of these modern liberal theories is a concern with something so broad and vague as reconciling individuality and community (or sociability), 'modern liberal theory' would still be a pretty thin thing. The purpose of Part One of the book is thus to demonstrate a wide-ranging consensus among modern liberals as to just what 'individuality' and 'sociability' involve. Chapters I, II and III deal with the main elements — what we might very roughly call the 'statics' — of personality while Chapter IV focuses on dynamics, i.e. processes by which personalities are formed. Basic to my thesis is the agreement of these modern liberals not only on the outlines of a healthy personality but also on the nature of the developmental process and the general consequences of its inhibition.

Part One alone, however, is not sufficient to uphold the claim that a modern liberal theory exists: although it demonstrates commonality among our modern liberals it does not link this agreement to their liberal positions. Hence Part Two is devoted to showing how this conception of man provides the foundation for modern liberal arguments concerning Liberty (Ch. V), Democracy (Ch. VI) and Economic Organisation (Ch. VII). Although these are not the only issues to which modern liberals have addressed themselves, questions of liberty, democracy and (domestic) economic organisation seem fundamental to the modern liberal programme in ways that do not seem true of, say, issues concerning conscientious objection or international economic justice. These latter matters are certainly important, and indeed may become increasingly so in the coming years, but thus far they have not been core elements of the modern liberal programme. My purpose here is not to examine what modern liberals ought to have said, or ought to be saying, but how they have justified that to which they are committed.

## Modern Liberalism and the New Liberalism

As I said, the modern liberals with whom I shall be dealing are Mill, Green, Bosanquet, Hobhouse, Dewey and Rawls. This list seems controversial in at least two respects. First, including Mill and Green appears to run against the trend of recent scholarship, which sets the advent of the 'new liberalism' closer to the time of Hobhouse. Secondly, and far more scandalously, it includes Bosanquet, who, as far as I know, has never been called a new liberal and, indeed, whose 'Toryism' has been contrasted to Green's 'Neo-Liberalism'.[13]

At this point we need to clearly distinguish 'modern liberalism' and the 'new liberalism'. My main concern in this book is with the attempt by our six modern liberals to develop a theory of man that reconciles the pursuit of individuality with sociality and membership

in a community. All of the six liberals in the above enumeration, I
will argue, seek such a reconciliation. In Part Two I try to show that
this conception of man provides the basis of what we might call 'typically modern liberal arguments' for liberty, democracy, and economic
reorganisation. When we come to economic questions in Chapter
VII, the 'typical modern liberal argument' is that this theory of man
supports the collectivistic economic prescriptions associated with the
new liberals. We may even wish to say that new liberal economics
is the most natural economics for a modern liberal. But, we shall see
that by adding extra assumptions to the core modern liberal theory of
man it is by no means impossible for a modern liberal to be an anti-
collectivist in economics. Consequently, it makes sense to say that
Bosanquet, who was certainly a 'liberal and a reformer',[14] embraced
the modern liberal theory of man but refused to endorse the new liberal,
i.e. 'collectivist', economics. Mill and Green too evince modern liberal
concerns with reconciling individuality and community but only go
part of the way towards the collectivism of the new liberalism. A
similar 'looseness' between the modern liberal theory of man and liberal
proposals for developmental-deliberative democracy will also be seen
to obtain in Chapter VI. In his classic work on *The Political Tradition
of the West*, Frederick Watkins held that the 'distinguishing feature'
of modern liberal thought was its emphasis on political deliberation.[15]
But as with the collectivism of new liberal economic proposals, I shall
argue that while modern liberals typically are proponents of the 'deliberative state', it is quite possible for a theorist like Bosanquet to
reconcile the modern liberal theory of human nature with a conception
of democracy which, while by no means denying the value of deliberation, puts more stress on underlying institutional structures and only
partially conscious communal sentiments and ideas.

I want to argue, then, that the general modern liberal theory of
human nature is connected to particular political and economic prescriptions in a 'loose' way. Although it provides the basis for such prescriptions, additional arguments are required to bring this general
theory to bear on particular issues. And it is because additional arguments are required that two theorists such as Hobhouse and Bosanquet
can embrace the general modern liberal theory of human nature but
disagree about its political applications. This is not to say that 'anything
goes' or that one political position is, in respect to the general modern
liberal theory of man, as good as any other. We can still judge the
cogency of the different ways the theory is applied to politics and so
may well conclude that some attempted applications are relatively

unconvincing or are not really in the spirit of the general theory of human nature. This, for example, may well be the case for the dispute concerning state provision of a social minimum (§VII.B.1): there are, I think, grounds for concluding that the new liberals present a convincing case that state provision of a minimum is necessary to further the development of human nature. But Bosanquet's rejoinders, insisting that such aid is harmful to development, cannot simply be rejected on logical grounds, i.e. for being inconsistent with the modern liberal theory of man. They can be rejected, but on the basis of the plausibility of their further psychological postulates, and the immense harm to development caused by poverty. To say that differing applications are logically consistent with the general theory is not to say that all are equally convincing.

I suspect that some will object to this account of political theorising. Those who believe that political philosophy must achieve a Euclidean-like deductive rigour will certainly be unhappy with it and will probably see it as an admission of the weakness of my thesis. And it is likely to confirm the conviction of those who insist that such political argument is mere ideology and not philosophy at all. But between these two extremes lies a conception of political philosophy as resting on genuine arguments, but these being judged more properly in terms of plausibility or reasonableness than logical entailment. Moreover, upon reflection this seems an eminently reasonable approach. For one of the modes of political argument is to show that the ideals or ultimate values that lie at the heart of a traditional theory, if 'properly understood', can be shown to lead to policies radically at variance with the traditional theory. (The case that comes to mind here is that of C.B. Macpherson in relation to liberal-democratic theory.) In such instances whether one accepts the traditional or revisionist account will depend on which seems to offer the most plausible story as to the proper implementation of these ideals. It is most unlikely one's decision will turn on an examination of the deductive validity of the argument. And it is to be hoped that it will not simply turn on one's prior ideological commitments.

## Modern Liberalism and Modern Thought

One might propose a *reductio* of this understanding of political thinking along the following lines: 'If modern liberal theory essentially concerns the attempt to reconcile individuality and community and only "typically" leads to liberal prescriptions, it seems that Marx and most anarchists might be called modern liberals who avoided the "typical" conclusions. For Marx and most anarchists, like modern liberals, can reasonably be said to aim at the synthesis of individuality and community.[16] But (it might be concluded) if Marx and the anarchists are modern liberals according to my thesis, something is clearly wrong.' To begin with, the conclusion is not at all as absurd as it might first appear. Marx and communal anarchists like Kropotkin do, I think, have much more in common with modern liberals than we are apt to think. The problem of reconciling individualised personalities with a yearning for a community of some sort informs a great deal of nineteenth-century European thinking, and both the modern liberal and Marxist-anarchist traditions arise during this era. But that does not mean that either modern liberals are closet Marxists or vice versa. As I said above, if all we could say about modern liberalism (and the same applies to Marxism and anarchism) is that it seeks to integrate individuality and community, it would be a pretty thin thing. Modern liberalism is not characterised here simply by the attempt to reconcile individuality and sociability but, in addition, by (i) the form that reconciliation takes and (ii) the way in which the theory of human nature is used to justify liberal-democratic institutions. Hence, Part One is devoted to examining just how the modern liberal theory of man attempts the reconciliation, while Part Two demonstrates how this theory of human nature leads to an endorsement of liberal-democracy. Now, while we shall also discover important disagreements among modern liberals on some points, I expect that their positions are all much closer to each other than any are to Marx. To take an important example: we will see in Chapter I that modern liberals look to occupations as a focus for organising one's individuality along specialised lines. Without attempting to offer any definitive interpretation of Marx on this score, it seems reasonable to hold that he would not have looked kindly on organising one's life around a vocation. Certainly the communal anarchists would not have endorsed such 'bourgeois individuality'. Moreover, we will see later (§III.E) that, unlike Marx and the anarchists, modern liberals ultimately stop short of the claim that individuality and community can be completely integrated. In the end, despite their aim of harmonisation, they believe that communal unity can be pushed too far and, hence, endanger individuality. Once this concession is made, the 'typical' liberal concerns with protecting the autonomy and freedom of the individual can get a foothold. In sum, then, although the modern liberals share some of the general hopes and aims of Marx and the communal anarchists, the specifics of their theory of human nature point to important differences between them and radical theorists, differences, moreover, that easily lead to typically liberal concerns.

However, even if we grant that Marx and the anarchists concur with some aspects of the modern liberal theory of man, it is indeed significant that they do not draw on this understanding of human nature to justify a liberal democracy based on a market economy. For as they read human nature liberal democracy is not the most fertile ground for its growth. In contrast Bosanquet is a modern liberal because he both endorses the modern liberal theory of man and provides many of the typical modern liberal arguments linking this theory to a liberal order. In sum, then, while my thesis recognises that the underlying concerns of modern liberal theory are by no means exclusively liberal concerns, and might plausibly be said to characterise most post-Rousseauian political thought, modern liberalism remains distinct from these other strains of modern thought by virtue of the specifics of its theory of human nature and the conviction that these provide a justification for those institutions characteristic of liberal democracy.

## Modern and Classical Liberalism

As I indicated above, modern liberals like Mill fairly explicitly saw their theory as an alternative to the overly individualistic theory of traditional liberalism. One of the assumptions underlying this book is that fundamental differences do indeed separate 'classical' and modern liberal theory. Although classical liberalism is itself very diffuse, I think that it is safe to say that the liberalisms articulated by Locke and James Mill, as different as they are, share a vision of men as essentially independent, private and competitive beings who see civil association mainly as a framework for the pursuit of their own interests. While I do not want to imply that these notions are entirely alien to modern liberalism, its conception of man is much more apt to stress mutual dependence over independence, co-operation over competition, and mutual appreciation over private enjoyment.

Some, who assert something like an analytic link between the notions of liberalism, individualism and competition, may want to insist that what I have called classical liberalism is the only true liberalism. Modern liberals like Mill, it might be charged, betray liberal ideas by embracing communitarian ideals hostile to liberal individualism: modern liberalism is not liberal at all. It is to be hoped that Chapter V provides an adequate reply to this sort of charge. The aim of Chapter V is not merely to show that modern liberals endorse equal liberty − including the traditional civil liberties − but that they do so on the basis of their 'revisionist' theory of man, drawing upon those communitarian elements which are sometimes said to be illiberal.

## Modern and Contemporary Liberalism

It is essential to realise that it is no part of my thesis that all post-Millian liberals are what I have called modern liberals. Most obviously, liberals such as F.A. Hayek and Robert Nozick (again, despite their significant differences) are no doubt much better understood as being in the classical tradition. But, more importantly, in the strictest sense my thesis applies only to the six liberal theorists I discuss. Throughout this book 'modern liberals' strictly denotes only Mill, Green, Hobhouse, Bosanquet, Dewey and Rawls. I add 'strictly' as it seems very probable indeed that most of what I say will apply to a good many others. If I can show, for example, that Green and Bosanquet share a similar theory of human nature, it would be most surprising if later liberal idealists such as A.D. Lindsay or Ernest Barker radically departed from it. The sort of 'Millian-Greenian' liberalism I discuss in this book, I believe, has been an important part of twentieth century liberal thought and, as evinced by the application of the thesis to Rawls, remains so to this day. But even if the reader disagrees and insists that the study centres around a unique group of six thinkers, the use of the general label (i.e. 'modern liberalism') seems justified. For I am not dealing here just with six political theorists but rather with some of the outstanding figures of the past 150 years of liberal theory. If it can be shown that Mill, Green, Bosanquet, Hobhouse, Dewey and Rawls argue their cases for liberal-democracy on essentially similar grounds, that in itself will establish an important strain of liberal political thought even if somehow they are the only six who argue in this way. I shall call that tradition 'modern liberalism'.

Describing this tradition as 'modern liberalism' seems appropriate for two reasons. First, and most obviously, it points to the fact that all our six liberals have written in the past 150 years, and most a good deal more recently than that. In comparison to the theories of Hobbes or Locke, all these liberals are making attempts to come to terms with a modern industrial society. Not only their concern with democracy, but also (as we will see) their attention to mass education and economic organisation are manifestations of this effort to apply liberalism to advanced industrial societies. I am not claiming that this is the only sort of liberal theory that has tried to come to terms with industrial society; certainly, albeit in a very different way, F.A. Hayek has sought to work out a liberal theory appropriate to modern society. But, I would hazard, much more than Hayek, our modern liberals have seen themselves as innovators and revisionists, consciously rejecting the older liberalism as inadequate for modern industrial societies. Another consideration also supports calling the liberalism of Mill, Green, Bosanquet, Hobhouse, Dewey and Rawls, rather than that of Hayek, 'modern'. For, as I have said, their aim of reconciling individuality and community seems one of the basic themes of modern European thought, including that of Marx and the communal anarchists. Calling our six liberals 'modern' thus draws attention to their relation to a much wider movement in post-Enlightenment European thought.

## Essentialism and Political Theory

The account of the modern liberal tradition defended in this book might be called 'essentialist' in the sense that it asserts that the essence of modern liberalism is a particular theory of human nature. (Although what characterises modern liberalism is this theory of human nature conjoined with arguments connecting it to liberal political prescriptions.) It might seem old fashioned nowadays to offer such an essentialist account. After all, Wittgenstein taught us not to search for a word's essential core meaning but instead to look for the family of meanings connecting its varied usages.[17] Cannot a similar account be given of a tradition in political theory? No doubt it can, but there is no *a priori* reason why a group of political theories cannot be characterised by a common essence rather than simply by 'family resemblances'. If we search for such an essence and it is not to be found, then we may have to resort to the looser sort of unity indicated by family resemblance. But I aim to show here that modern liberalism is characterised by the former sort of unity.

Although in this respect my thesis may be a radical one, it is important to distinguish it from another. I am not arguing that, as a matter of fact, modern liberals came to embrace liberal political prescriptions because they first assented to this theory of human nature and then saw its political implications. Why modern liberals came to embrace liberalism or, indeed, the modern liberal theory of man is a matter of biography — or perhaps the sociology of knowledge. It is not itself a part of political theory. My concern is with the structure of modern liberal political theories, and I shall argue that in that structure the theory of human nature is fundamental. But I leave it entirely open as to whether liberals first embraced liberalism and then were attracted to the modern liberal theory of man because it cohered with their politics or vice versa. (I suspect that both processes were involved.) In any event, my concern is with modern liberal theory and not with why modern liberals come to hold the views they do.

## Notes

1. For interpretations stressing Hobhouse's role, see Michael Freeden, *The New Liberalism: An Ideology of Social Reform* (Clarendon Press, Oxford, 1978); Peter Clarke, *Liberals and Social Democrats* (Cambridge University Press, Cambridge, 1978); Stefan Collini, *Liberalism and Sociology: L.T. Hobhouse and Political Argument in England, 1880-1914* (Cambridge University Press, Cambridge, 1979); on Dewey and the 'new liberalism', see Alfonso J. Damico, *Individuality and Community: The Social and Political Thought of John Dewey* (University Presses of Florida, Gainesville, 1978), Ch. 5. For traditional accounts focusing on the influence of Mill and Green, see D.G. Ritchie, *Principles of State Interference* (Allen and Unwin, London, 1902), Ch. IV, p. 82; John Rodman, 'Introduction' to his edited collection *The Political Theory of T.H. Green* (Appleton-Century-Crofts, New York, 1964); Thomas P. Neill, *The Rise and Decline of Liberalism* (Bruce Publishing Co., Milwaukee, 1953), pp. 255 ff; G.H. Sabine, *A History of Political Thought* (Harrap, London, 1937), pp. 673-80.

2. A.V. Dicey, *Lectures on the Relation Between Law and Public Opinion in England During the Nineteenth Century*, 2nd edn (Macmillan, London, 1919), Introduction, Lectures IV, VI-IX. See also Edward Shils, 'The Antinomies of Liberalism' in *The Relevance of Liberalism*, staff of the Research Institute on International Change (eds.) (Westview Press, Boulder, 1978), pp. 135-200.

3. T.H. Green, *Prolegomena to Ethics*, A.C. Bradley (ed.) (Clarendon Press, Oxford, 1890), p. 398.

4. See L.T. Hobhouse, *The Rational Good: A Study in the Logic of Practice* (Watts, London, 1947), Chs. VII-VIII; and his *Liberalism* (Oxford University Press, Oxford, 1964), Chs. V-VI.

5. John Dewey, *Problems of Men* (Philosophical Library, New York, 1946), pp. 126-40.

6. John Rawls, *A Theory of Justice* (The Belknap Press of Harvard University Press, Cambridge, 1971), pp. 209-11.

7. That Green greatly influenced Hobhouse is a commonplace. For Green's influences on Dewey see A.H. Somjee, *The Political Theory of John Dewey* (Teachers College Press, New York, 1968), pp. 72-79. Further, John A. Irving reports that Dewey was 'addicted' to Green; see his 'Comments' to Arthur E. Murphy, 'John Dewey and American Liberalism', *Journal of Philosophy*, LVII (1960), p. 447. See also below Ch. I, note 126, and, for general Hegelian influences on Dewey, see Ch. I, note 105. A number of writers have noted the 'idealist-organic' strain in Rawls; see C.B. Macpherson, 'Rawls' Models of Man and Society', *Philosophy of Social Sciences*, III (1973), pp. 341-47; Robert Paul Wolff, *Under-*

*standing Rawls* (Princeton University Press, Princeton, 1977), pp. 190-91; John Luther Hemingway, 'The Emergence of an Ethical Liberalism: A Study in Idealist Liberalism from Thomas Hill Green to the Present', unpublished PhD thesis, University of Iowa, 1979.

8.  Zevedei Barbu, *Democracy and Dictatorship: Their Psychology and Patterns of Life* (Routledge and Kegan Paul, London, 1956), p. 74.

9.  See especially Mill's comments on Bentham's conceptions of man and society. 'Bentham' in J.M. Robson (ed.), *The Collected Works of John Stuart Mill* (University of Toronto Press, Toronto, 1963), vol. X, pp. 94-100.

10.  Ritchie, *Principles of State Interference*, p. 22. What is interesting in this regard is that Spencer seemed to adopt so much of the 'organic' outlook of the new liberals but drew opposite conclusions; Ritchie's aim was thus to show that Spencer did not have a truly organic view of man and society. See Herbert Spencer, *Social Statics and Man Versus State* (Williams and Norgate, London, 1892), pp. 229-95. On the organic view of social life, see § II.D; see also Ch. III.

11.  Damico, *Individuality and Community*, p. 70.

12.  For Mill, see Abram L. Harris, 'John Stuart Mill's Theory of Progress', *Ethics*, LXVI (Apr. 1956), p. 172; Graeme Duncan, *Marx and Mill: Two Views of Social Conflict and Social Harmony* (Cambridge University Press, Cambridge, 1973), p. 237; John M. Robson, *The Improvement of Mankind: The Social and Political Thought of John Stuart Mill* (University of Toronto Press, Toronto, 1968), p. 135. For Hobhouse, see Freeden, *The New Liberalism*, pp. 48-49; Morris Ginsberg, 'The Work of L.T. Hobhouse' in J.A. Hobson and Morris Ginsberg (eds.), *L.T. Hobhouse: His Life and Work* (Allen and Unwin, London, 1931), p. 175; John E. Owen, *L.T. Hobhouse: Sociologist* (Nelson, London, 1974), p. 117; Peter Weiler, 'The New Liberalism of L.T. Hobhouse', *Victorian Studies*, XVI (Dec. 1971), pp. 141-61. For Dewey, see Damico, *Individuality and Community*, pp. 5, 73. For Rawls, see Macpherson, 'Rawls' Models of Man and Society', pp. 346-47; Allan Bloom, 'Justice: John Rawls Vs. The Tradition of Political Philosophy', *American Political Science Review*, LXIX (June 1975), p. 649.

13.  John Herman Randall, Jr., 'Idealistic Social Philosophy and Bernard Bosanquet', *Philosophy and Phenomenological Research*, XXVI (1965-66), pp. 473-502.

14.  Stefan Collini, 'Hobhouse, Bosanquet and the State: Philosophical Idealism and Political Argument in England, 1880-1918', *Past and Present*, LXXII (Aug. 1976), p. 87.

15.  Frederick Watkins, *The Political Tradition of the West: A Study in the Development of Modern Liberalism* (Harvard University Press, Cambridge, Mass., 1948), p. 244. See also John W. Chapman, *Rousseau – Totalitarian or Liberal?* (Columbia University Press, New York, 1956), Ch. 8.

16.  I have argued elsewhere that Marx and the anarchists aimed at such a synthesis. See Gerald F. Gaus and John W. Chapman, 'Anarchism and Political Philosophy: An Introduction', in J. Roland Pennock and John W. Chapman (eds.), *NOMOS XIX: Anarchism* (New York University Press, New York, 1978), pp. xvii-xlv.

17.  See Ludwig Wittgenstein, *Philosophical Investigations*, 3rd edn, G.E.M. Anscombe (trans.) (Macmillan, New York, 1958), pp. 31 ff. On essentialism and political theory see D.J. Manning, *Liberalism* (Dent, London, 1976), pp. 60-61, 139-40.

# PART ONE
# HUMAN NATURE

# I  INDIVIDUALITY

In Part One I explore the theory of human nature expounded by our six modern liberals — Mill, Green, Bosanquet, Hobhouse, Dewey and Rawls. The heart of this theory, I shall argue, is an attempt to show that sociability, properly understood, is essentially consistent with, indeed largely supportive of, individuality. This attempt at reconciliation is premised on a conception of individuality according to which, no matter how highly developed we might be, we need our fellows to complete our lives. The very nature of our individuality thus drives us into a co-operative, mutually enriching social life. However, social life is not the same as community; whereas the former is premised on interaction and association, community involves a sense of belongingness and some devotion to the group. Modern liberals have recognised this, believing not only that we are impelled into a co-operative social life, but also that we naturally manifest communal outlooks and sentiments. Although, as we will see, modern liberals exhibit less agreement on the nature of these communal ties than on individuality or social life, one important strain in their thinking is that these stronger communal ties arise out of the interactions and associations of social life. In this respect, then, their theory of human nature is a striking one: if we follow out the implications of individuality, we will see that social life and, to some extent, community, are its consequences, not inherent enemies. Although we will discover that some tensions persist in modern liberalism between individuality and community, the emphasis is on their continuity and harmony, not their opposition.

In this chapter I examine the foundation of the modern liberal theory of man, its conception of individuality. I turn in Chapter II to its theory of social life and in Chapter III to modern liberals' understandings of community. In the conclusion to the third chapter (§III.E) I briefly evaluate the success of the modern liberal attempt to reconcile individuality and sociability. Finally, after this analysis of the modern liberal ideal of personality, Chapter IV examines modern liberals' developmental account of the genesis of personality.

## A. Positive Individuality

It would seem that an uncontentious starting place for an analysis of modern liberal individuality is the idea that, at its very core, is the

15

tendency 'to be oneself'.[1] Certainly that is the theme of Mill's third chapter of *On Liberty*, 'Of Individuality, As One of the Elements of Well-Being'. 'Human nature', Mill writes in an oft-quoted passage, 'is not a machine to be built after a model, and set to do exactly the work prescribed for it, but a tree, which requires to grow and develope [*sic*] itself on all sides, according to the tendency of the inward forces which make it a living thing.'[2] Indeed, Mill so emphasises that individuality requires the development of one's own nature – to be oneself – that he sums up his thesis as '[h]aving said that Individuality is the same thing with development'.[3]

But the idea that individuality consists in being oneself does have a controversial history in modern liberal theory, for it lies at the heart of Bosanquet's distinction between 'positive' and 'negative' individuality. Bosanquet contrasted positive individuality, or being oneself, with a negative or 'formal' conception that sees the 'essence of Individuality not as the being oneself, but as the not being some one else'.[4] On this negative view, 'To realise our individuality is to absorb ourselves in our exclusiveness. The dim recesses of incommunicable feeling are the true shrine of our selfhood.'[5] By emphasising our exclusiveness and isolation – what we are not rather than what we are – Bosanquet believes the content of the self is emptied. Consequently, he argued that as in the case of Mill, if such individuals do have content, all that will matter is if they are unique and exclusive: individuality thus lapses into mere eccentricity.[6] In a similar vein, Dewey too contrasts the creative originality of true individuality with 'cranky eccentricity'.[7]

What makes all this controversial is that Hobhouse, in his classic (if polemical) critique of idealist political theory, *The Metaphysical Theory of the State*, specifically attacked Bosanquet's notion of 'positive individuality'. Charging that Bosanquet denied the distinction between persons, Hobhouse, apparently defending the liberal tradition, argues in favour of 'the element of isolation which, in contradiction to Bosanquet's dictum, is the true core of individuality.'[8] We meet here at the outset a characteristic of the Hobhouse-Bosanquet controversy that we shall encounter throughout: Hobhouse and Bosanquet commonly overstate the distinctiveness of their positions, thus greatly exaggerating their differences. To be sure, genuine disagreements exist, but these need to be understood in the context of extensive and fundamental commonality. The dispute about 'positive' and 'negative' individuality is a case in point. While we shall see in §II.D.2 that Bosanquet's theory may well have some difficulties along the lines Hobhouse suggests, underlying any disagreement on this score is a basic concurrence that individuality has both positive and negative dimensions. His assertions of negativity or exclusiveness as the essence of individuality notwithstanding, Hobhouse can be found to be repeatedly stressing that individuality consists in the positive development of capacities. In his *Mind in Evolution*, for example, he postulates a 'will to live' that 'persists in the various impulses tending not merely to the maintenance of life, but to the maintenance of the individual in his own character, the fulfilment of his impulses or desires, the realisation of his individuality'.[9] And, in expounding the liberal tradition, he tells us that '[m]anhood, and Mill would emphatically add womanhood too, rests on the spontaneous development of faculty. To find vent for the capacities of feeling, of emotion, of thought, of action, is to find oneself.'[10] This idea of 'finding oneself' in the positive development of capacities is the core of Bosanquet's conception of selfhood too. Although he would have us believe that his is very far indeed from the Millian understanding of individuality, Bosanquet's talk of our 'capacities for development' or our 'gifts' and 'powers' has a distinctly Millian ring to it.[11] And while true to his critique of 'negative individuality' he insists that we do not ultimately care about our 'bare personality' or 'separate destiny', he does insist that we care deeply about the development of our capacities to their highest pitch. 'We want to live out our life, to work out our self − a poor thing, but our own − and so all we have to give and create'.[12] Moreover, we shall see presently that even Bosanquet, the constant critic of 'negativity', recognises that the materials out of which each of us fashions our 'positive' development differ, thus introducing into his theory an element of uniqueness or exclusiveness.

I wish to suggest, then, that the very core of individuality for liberals as diverse as Mill, Bosanquet and Hobhouse (and, as we shall discover as we progress, Rawls and Dewey too) is the positive development of one's nature, 'to be oneself'. A basic theme of all modern liberal writings on personality is that we each possess a wide range of capacities, the cultivation of which constitutes the essence of individuality. Some dispute exists, however, whether this is true of Green. According to Sidgwick and Lamont,[13] Green vacillates between (i) a wide conception of self-realisation as the realisation of *human* capacities and (ii) self-realisation as the realisation of *moral* capacities, i.e. the Kantian Good Will. More radically, interpreters such as H.D. Lewis[14] have maintained that the realisation of a Kantian Good Will is the essential Greenian self-realisation. Now it is only this latter, more radical, interpretation that we need to consider here: even if Green swings between a wide and a narrow conception of capacity, the wider (i.e. human capacity) conception will still be available to him when arguing for liberty, democracy and economic reorganisation. But if the narrower (i.e. Kantian) view is Green's only, or fundamental, position, it may be doubted whether he entertains any Millian conception of individuality at all.

To begin with, it ought to be pointed out that reading Green as anything like a strict Kantian is problematic. In his own analysis of Kantian ethics, Green was led to the conclusion that one of the chief difficulties in Kant's theory was its liability to be interpreted in such a way as to render the notion of duty purely abstract.[15] And, significantly, he turns to the Greeks to overcome Kant's apparent formalism. In the early part of his discussion of Greek ethics in his *Prolegomena*, Green writes:

> The good will may be taken to mean a will possessed by some abstract idea of goodness or of moral law . . . But it is not thus that we understand the good will. The principle which it is here sought to maintain is that the perfection of human character — a perfection of individuals which is also that of society, and of society which is also that of individuals — is for man the only object of absolute or intrinsic value; that, this perfection . . . [consists] in a fulfilment of man's capabilities according to the divine idea or plan. [16]

This seems to support Ann R. Cacoullos's thesis that Green's ethics is more Aristotelian than Kantian. 'He finds that Aristotle has offered the best account of man's true good, which he reiterates as follows: "The full exercise or realization of the soul's faculties in accordance with its proper excellence, which [is] an excellence of thought, speculative and practical".'[17]

We need not insist, however, on accepting a thoroughgoing Aristotelian interpretation of Green's ethics. It is sufficient for my thesis that Green often talks of human capacities in ways inconsistent with their being simply moral capacities in any narrow sense. Thus, for example, Green describes the 'educated citizen of Christendom' as having developed a wider range of faculties 'than those which are directly exhibited in the specifically moral virtues'. Indeed, he tells us that the development of such capacities, which are manifested not only in social relations but in the arts and sciences as well, is a necessary constituent of a satisfactory life.[18] Moreover, Green maintains that we do not know the full range of our capacities (see §I.E) and that they differ from person to person (see §I.B). Neither of these seems to cohere well with an under-

standing of our capacities as being merely abilities to act from a Kantian
Good Will.

## B. Unique/Diverse Natures

The modern liberal conception of individuality is thus 'positive' in the
sense that it centres on the positive development of capacities. But
surely individuality is more than the development of faculties. Plato,
as Dewey pointed out, was deeply concerned with 'discovering and
developing personal capacities',[19] yet we hardly think of Plato as a
philosopher of individuality. As Dewey sees it, Plato's anti-individualism
stems from his inability to perceive the uniqueness of individuals. 'For
him they fall by nature into classes, and into a very small number of
classes at that.'[20] According to Dewey, it is Rousseau who first insists
upon the existence of natural psychological and physical differences
among individuals. 'Plato exercised a great influence upon Rousseau.
But the voice of nature now speaks for the diversity of individual
talents and for the need of free development of individuality in all its
variety.'[21]

The diversity of individual capacities and natures looms large in
Dewey's own writings, particularly those on education. In *Democracy
and Education* he observes that it is impossible to consider the natural
powers of humans without being struck by the diversity of individual
natures. 'The difference applies not merely to their intensity, but even
more to their quality and arrangement. As Rousseau said, "Each individual is born with a distinctive temperament".'[22] In his essay on
'Time and Individuality' Dewey takes a somewhat different — though
obviously related — approach. Here he concentrates on the uniqueness
and originality of individual lives; because we have such rich and varied
potentialities, Dewey argues, individual life is always 'pregnant with
new developments'.[23] Hobhouse agrees: life, he says, 'is individual,
and in each of its cases there is something unique and unseizable by the
intellect — creative of essentially novel, and therefore unpredictable,
developments'.[24]

Green, too, at least at times, sounds, if not precisely Rousseauistic,
romantic. In an early essay he wrote that 'true individuality [arises]
from the internal modifications of passion . . . These modifications are
as infinite and complex as the spirit of man itself.'[25] But the critical
statement of Green's theory of individual differences occurs in §191
of the *Prolegomena*:

But the function of society being the development of persons, the realisation of the human spirit in society can only be attained according to the measure in which that function is fulfilled. It does not follow from this that all persons must be developed in the same way. The very existence of mankind presupposes the distinction between the sexes; and as there is a necessary difference between their functions, there must be a corresponding difference between the modes in which the personality of men and women is developed. Again, though, we must avoid following the example of philosophers who have shown an *a priori* necessity for those class-distinctions of their time which after ages have dispensed with, it would certainly seem as if distinctions of social position and power were necessarily incidental to the development of personality. There cannot be this development without a recognised power of appropriating material things. This appropriation must vary in its effects according to talent and opportunity, and from that variation again must result differences in the form which personality takes in different men. Nor does it appear how those reciprocal services which elicit the feeling of mutual dependence, and thus promote the recognition by one man of another as an 'alter ego', would be possible without different limitations of function and ability, which determine the range within which each man's personality developes [*sic*], in other words, the scope of his personal interests.[26]

It is necessary to quote this long passage in full as it is the focus of David L. Norton's recent interpretation of the *Prolegomena*, which contends that Green did not uphold a conception of individuality based upon a diversity of individual natures. According to Norton, while it 'prima facie' suggests that Green believed individual natures to differ, 'closer examination' 'appears' to show that this is not the case. As Norton reads Green, 'The full context of *Prolegomena* makes clear [that] he rejects innatism altogether as an account of individuality.'[27] The key to the passage, he says, is Green's phrase 'necessarily incidental' — which he interprets as 'incidental necessity'. What Green really means, Norton tells us, 'is that it is fortunate that all persons need not be developed in the same way, for incidental necessity [e.g. the facts of place of birth, parentage, etc.] does not permit identical development'.[28]

Norton's interpretation involves two related, but distinct, claims: (i) that Green did not think individual natures differed and (ii) that he believed it merely 'fortunate' that we need not develop identically, since 'incidental necessity' precludes it. The first claim is the central one for our present purposes and, upon examination, Norton does not provide a great deal of evidence to support it, especially given that it seems to run counter to Green's explicit acknowledgement here of differences in abilities and talents. Norton's main foundation for the claim seems to be a reading of Green (following Sidgwick)[29] according to which the rational self − the self to be realised − is the same for all and is to be radically distinguished from the animal or bodily self (which does differ from one individual to another). But as Cacoullos points out, although our 'animal' self alone is not the subject of Green's theory of self-realisation, as a constituent of a 'self-as-a-whole' it does indeed enter into his theory:[30] self-realisation is of the whole self, not just the 'rational' any more than the 'animal self'. Green denies only that 'feeling' amounts to the '*full* individuality of man', not that it is a constituent of individuality.[31]

However, Norton's interpretation does highlight an important aspect of Green's theory to which I shall have occasion to return (§C.3). In an important sense, the development of men's (rational) nature is indeed unitary; whatever particular capacities and talents we possess, in so far as their cultivation is understood as the realisation of rational or intellectual faculty, all human 'perfection' (to use Green's language, see §I.E), is essentially the same. I will suggest later that Norton's error does not lie in thinking that Green sees all development as 'the same' in this way, but in concluding that such commonality is inconsistent with natural differences in talents and capacities.

(ii) Norton's second claim − that it is merely 'fortunate' that we need not exhibit identical development − is far more puzzling, for it seems to entirely miss the point of the last sentence of the passage. Green argues here that recognition of others and feelings of mutual dependence stem from differences in personalities which, at least in part, grow from differences in abilities. The implication is that the very nature of the social order − men living among others recognised as men − derives from the difference in personalities. *Pace* Norton, it thus does not seem that Green thinks it merely fortunate that we need not all be developed in the same way; rather, his conception of human society as based on an interconnectedness of diverse but mutually recognised personalities centrally depends upon differential development.

As Plamenatz has noted, this understanding of human society as premised on the diversity of personalities is also essential to Bosanquet's political theory.[32] 'It takes all sorts to make a world'[33] is, perhaps, Bosanquet's most important aphorism. We shall see in the next chapter that this conception of the social order is central to the modern liberal

theory of sociability, but for now what is relevant is the importance it
places on the differences of individualities as the very essence of social
life. Not surprisingly, then, Bosanquet reports: 'I see no reason for
being afraid of questions about our personal gifts and likings, so far as
they mean our special capacities.'[34] Moreover, he is very clear (and,
one must admit, much clearer than Green) that these differences are
natural. In a discussion of eugenicists' arguments for selective breeding,
Bosanquet (as does Hobhouse in a similar analysis) acknowledges that
we have no reason to doubt the existence of differential inborn qualities
— though (again like Hobhouse) he does dispute the equation of ' "inferior stocks" with the poorer classes'.[35]

In an important sense, though, Bosanquet's (and probably Green's)
notion of diverse individual natures departs from the Rousseauian
view as, for example, it is expressed by Mill:

> Human beings are not like sheep; and even sheep are not undisting-
> uishably alike. A man cannot get a coat or a pair of boots to fit him,
> unless they are either made to his measure, or he has a whole ware-
> houseful to choose from: and is it easier to fit him with a life than
> with a coat, or are human beings more like one another in their
> whole physical and spiritual conformation than in the shape of
> their feet?[36]

Humans are not only diverse, but infinitely so: their natures, theorists
like Mill and Dewey clearly insist, are distinctive. And because each is
distinctive, each has at least a potential to make an original contribution to human life. While Bosanquet agrees that individual capacities
and faculties are diverse, he more than once notes that '[i]t is possible
in various degrees for individuals to contain others, and to be identical
with them.'[37] Some people, he suggests, can make no original contribution to the world at all. All their capacities, aims, values, plans, etc.
have been anticipated, indeed manifested, by others. In this sense,
then, they do not seem capable of originality. Depending upon how
much is made of this possibility, two positions, both hostile to liberal
individuality, might emerge. (i) If some few individuals 'contained'
all others, Bosanquet's theory could easily lead to an exaltation of
great men and a corresponding disparagement of the masses. (ii) Alter-
natively, if many individual natures are 'identical', we seem to move
towards a Platonic view of classes of character types. And, unlike the
first possibility, Bosanquet seems sometimes attracted to this view. In
the *Philosophical Theory of the State*, for example, he tells us that

'[t] he individual, in short, is unique, or belongs to a unique class.'[38] This certainly seems to represent a departure from Dewey's and Mill's insistence on the essential uniqueness of persons. But we also ought to take note that Bosanquet obviously wishes to minimise the importance of the possibility of repetition of personalities. At one place, for example, after acknowledging the possibility, he quickly goes on to say that 'repetition and similarity' are only superficial features of the social order. 'What hold [*sic*] society together, we find, are its correlative differences; the relation which expresses itself on a large scale in the division of labour, or in Aristotle's axiom, "No State can be composed of similars".'[39]

Moreover, Bosanquet wants to argue that the 'repetition' need not preclude 'uniqueness': 'Originality, within finite conditions, is not in principle excluded by agreement or even by a large measure of repetition. Its essence lies in the richness and completeness of a self, not in the non-existence of any other self approximating to it.'[40] We shall see later in this chapter (§D.1) that stressing the complexity and richness of an individual's nature does indeed help support a claim to uniqueness; still, if some person's individuality is so rich that it 'includes' others (i.e. it manifests all their capacities, enduring aims and projects, cherished values, etc.), little room remains for originality on the part of the others. Everything thus depends on Bosanquet's notion of '*a large measure* of repetition'. Persons who are in many respects similar can certainly still be unique individuals. If all Bosanquet means is that unique individuality does not entail extreme eccentricities (and thereby exclude significant commonality), then he is without doubt correct. But if some person (Jones) generally does 'contain another' (Smith), i.e. they are not only in 'a large measure' similar but, in some sense, Smith is included in Jones, then any meaningful notion of unique individuality (at least for Smith) seems impossible. All things considered, it appears most reasonable to conclude that while Bosanquet acknowledges the possibility of 'repetition', his basic conception of society as composed of diverse but interconnected personalities leads him to insist that it is not the essential feature of the social order and, unless extreme, does not preclude uniqueness.

In so far, then, as Bosanquet's psychology allows that many may 'share' the same personality, we might well say that it entails a 'weaker' conception of individuality than do Dewey's or Mill's theories. But, typically, liberal critiques of Bosanquet's notion of individuality have gone a good deal further than this. Hobhouse, for example, stresses that Bosanquet maintains 'the likeness between individuals to a common self' and ultimately denies the reality of the distinction between persons altogether.[41] The 'idea of Personality', Hobhouse insists, is the 'ethical rock lying always in the track' of idealism.[42] Dewey, following James, held pretty much the same view, charging that a philosophy such as Bosanquet's has no room for individuality since 'according to absolute idealism . . . the individual is simply a part determined by the whole of which he is a part'.[43]

In evaluating such arguments it is of the utmost importance to determine in just what sense Bosanquet's philosophy is hostile to the individuality of persons. Certainly his metaphysics does not place individual persons in a pre-eminent position. 'Individuality', he argued, 'is the ultimate completeness of that character of wholeness and non-contradiction which we . . . generalised under the name logical stability.' And, Bosanquet argued, only that which is fully complete, 'a world self complete', i.e. a thoroughgoing individual, is 'ultimately real'.[44] Finite individuals (e.g. persons) are not, as we shall see, self-complete in this sense and so, he maintains, do not possess ultimate reality. Moreover, to add to this apparently damning (from a liberal perspective) case, Bosanquet attributes direct value to the Absolute — the only ultimate individual — and not to finite 'units' as such.[45]

Quite clearly, then, Bosanquet's idealism does not ascribe complete individuality (or, directly, value) to persons. But we ought to be wary of jumping too quickly from this to sweeping conclusions about the place of individuality (in the usual sense) in his psychology, ethics or politics.[46] We need to look at what he says about psychology, etc. to determine his positions rather than to infer everything from his general metaphysics. Let me quickly add that I am not claiming that Bosanquet's psychology is entirely divorced from his metaphysics: we will see, for example, that the themes of the incompleteness of 'units' and the integration and completion of 'units' into systematic wholes do indeed carry over from his metaphysics to his theories of individuality and social life. But we will also see that, in the context of an account of individual psychological organisation or of social life, these are typically modern liberal themes (certainly they are to be found in Hobhouse) and, indeed, form a central part of the modern liberal theory of man. My point, then, is that we must look at each issue involving individuality, social life and community in its own right and refrain from the temptation to read off all the answers from Bosanquet's general metaphysics. In this spirit, our concern at present is thus simply whether Bosanquet acknowledged a diversity of individual (personal) natures and, as we have seen, there can be no doubt that he did so.

## C. Higher Natures and Excellences

Up to this point 'individuality' has been used to refer to both the possession of unique natures and the outcome of their development. Although Dewey, for example, sometimes seems to endorse the former usage, holding individuality to be 'potentiality, a capacity for development',[47] there is a good reason for settling on the latter use. A basic theme in a great deal of modern liberal writings is that individuality, to use Bosanquet's words, is a 'determinate achievement or expansion on the part of the self'.[48] Indeed, even Dewey ultimately seemed to think that a distinctive feature of modern liberalism is its understanding of individuality as 'something that is *attained* only by continuous growth'.[49] The remainder of this chapter is thus devoted to examining just how an individual's unique (or at least generally distinctive) nature provides the foundation for the achievement of an individualised personality.

### C.1. Higher and Lower Pleasures

The starting place for any discussion of the cultivation of capacities in modern liberalism is Mill's theory of excellence. One of his major criticisms of Bentham's psychology was that '[m]an is never recognised by him as a being capable of pursuing spiritual perfection as an end; of desiring, for its own sake, the conformity of his own character to his standard of excellence.'[50] In contrast, Mill thought that the pursuit of excellence (as an end) was not only a possibility but, as he indicated in *Utilitarianism*, an innate tendency. Men, he tells us, are born with a capacity to appreciate the 'nobler feelings' or 'higher pleasures'. And if they can be appreciated, they will be preferred to the lower pleasures. 'It may be questioned whether anyone who has remained equally susceptible to both classes of pleasures, ever knowingly and calmly preferred the lower.'[51] Mill, of course, realised that some do prefer the lower pleasures, but, he believed, 'those who undergo this very common change' only do so after they have lost their natural capacity to enjoy the higher pleasures. 'I believe that, before they devote themselves exclusively to the one, they have already become incapable of the other.'[52]

This distinction between higher and lower pleasures has exercised tremendous influence on other modern liberal theorists. Green, Hobhouse, Bosanquet, Dewey and Rawls all take over some such doctrine, most with explicit acknowledgement of Mill's influence.[53] And while, not too surprisingly, they have different understandings of just what the distinction involves, two general themes seem to dominate their interpretations: (i) the cultivation of complex capacities and (ii) the centrality of intellectual (and artistic) pursuits.

## C.2. Complexity

Mill's main concern in *Utilitarianism* (Ch. II, paras. 4-8) is to argue that we naturally prefer the more arduous activity of cultivating our higher faculties to the pursuit of easy pleasures. As such, he seems to assume that the cultivation of higher faculties is obviously a demanding task and so tells us little as to why it is so difficult. Nor is Green of much help here; like Mill he seems mainly concerned with providing philosophic and psychological foundations for 'the conviction that there is a lower and a higher — that there are objects less and more worthy of a man'.[54] Bosanquet, however, is somewhat more explicit as to just why some sorts of cultivation can be so arduous:

> The "arduous" pleasures, or better, satisfactions, have a complex character . . . No one doubts that the satisfaction which they give is fuller and more harmonious than that of bodily pleasures or those which relatively approach the nature of the latter. But every one, except perhaps remarkably gifted natures, experiences a certain resistance in the enjoyment of them. They involve an exertion comparable to that of serious intellectual work, a resolution of discrepancies, and a maintenance of unusual and exhausting moods of feeling.[55]

Although the similarity of Rawls's Aristotelian Principle to Mill's position has been widely noted[56] (including by Rawls himself), it is less often pointed out that it avoids the most problematic part of Mill's doctrine, viz. the existence of 'higher faculties'. Rather than positing the existence of 'higher faculties', the cultivation of which is a difficult but highly satisfying endeavour, Rawls directly postulates as a 'deep psychological fact' that 'other things equal, human beings enjoy the exercise of their realized capacities (their innate or trained abilities), and this enjoyment increases the more the capacity is realized, or the greater its complexity.'[57] Rawls thus streamlines Mill's doctrine by upholding a direct enjoyment of complexity rather than endorsing complexity via the cultivation of higher faculties. However, he allows (with Mill and Green[58]) that this drive to excellence may be defeated or thwarted; the Aristotelian Principle 'formulates a tendency and not an invariable pattern of choice, and like all tendencies, it may be over-

ridden'.[59] We shall see in Chapter IV that this view of natural tendencies is central to the developmental psychologies of modern liberals.

At first glance, Dewey's and Hobhouse's interpretation of Mill's
doctrine seems to run in very nearly the opposite direction from
Rawls's. Whereas Rawls concentrates on the development of particular
capacities in complex and refined ways, Dewey insists that carrying
'special individual abilities to a high pitch' is by no means sufficient to
achieve individuality.[60] In a similar vein, Hobhouse more than once
takes pains to distinguish the cultivation of a particular capacity from
the achievement of an integrated individuality; furthermore, he believed, isolated cultivation of particular capacities actually may be
incompatible with an integrated personality.[61] 'We conclude', wrote
Dewey and Tufts,

> that the truth contained in Mill's statement is not that one "faculty"
> is inherently higher than another, but that a satisfaction which is
> seen, by reflection based on large experience, to unify in a harm-
> onious way his whole system of desires is higher in quality than a
> good which is such only in relation to a particular want in isolation.[62]

It would seem, then, that whereas Rawls focuses on the refinement of
particular capacities, Dewey and Hobhouse stress the overall development of personality. But, as I indicated, this difference is more apparent than real. Hobhouse, for example, can be found distinguishing the
'higher faculties of man' from the 'primitive pleasures' and stressing the
pleasure 'we find in the full development of faculty' while Dewey
praises Plato for advocating the training of each in his special mode of
excellence.[63] Moreover, as we shall see in §D, Rawls and Mill (and
certainly Green and Bosanquet) are very much concerned with organising an individual's capacity repertoire into an integrated personality.
The difference, then, is largely one of emphasis, with Rawls giving
pride of place to particular excellences and Dewey and Hobhouse
stressing the need for overall integration.

## C.3. Intellectual Development

From Mill onwards modern liberal discussions of human excellences
have been premised on the belief that the higher faculties or complex
pleasures are very much intellectual ones while the easy pleasures are
those of the body (as Hobhouse described them, 'the pleasures of eat-
ing, drinking, and sex').[64] Mill himself was fairly explicit in seeing the
doctrine of qualities of pleasure as a 'higher ground' from which to

argue for the 'superiority of mental over bodily pleasures'.[65] Indeed, one recent reader of Mill has gone so far as to conclude that 'the cultivation of individuality is the development of reason'.[66] It would, I think, be equally reasonable to describe any modern liberal conception of individuality in these terms; all their analyses of individuality are informed by the supposition that the development of individuality and the growth of intellect − if not the same − are very closely linked. Even when modern liberals are trying to be most open about possible lines of development, they seem to reveal a bias towards the intellectual. In a short discussion of an eccentric who finds satisfaction in counting blades of grass, for example, Rawls sees fit to assure us that '[h]e is otherwise intelligent and actually possesses unusual skills, since he manages to survive by solving difficult mathematical problems for a fee.'[67]

It is important to realise that in itself the pursuit of individuality does not necessitate a commitment to the centrality of intelligence. We ought to recall that despite his emphasis on individuality, the author of the *First Discourse* was not in the main prone to praise intellectual pursuits.[68] Not even a devotion to individual excellence requires giving such an important place to the intellect. And, indeed, modern liberals sometimes do acknowledge other modes of excellence as, for example, in craft; but even here they are apt to emphasise the 'element of brain-culture' in 'handicraft'.[69] That is, rather than resting their support for crafts (and indeed all sorts of manual work) on their distinctive excellences, they seem to favour assimilating craftsmanship to intellectual pursuits. (Mill's famous support of producer co-operatives is a case in point: the transformation from servants to masters, he strongly stressed, would do much to raise the level of intelligence of the working class and, hence, promote their development.)[70] Although, no doubt, a multitude of plausible explanations could be advanced for preferring 'brain-culture' in this way, I shall content myself with briefly mentioning two.

First, and most obviously, the modern liberal preoccupation with the development of the 'higher faculties' largely arose as a self-conscious alternative to the straightforward hedonism of the early utilitarians. Although Mill believed that an intelligent hedonism could take account of the 'higher faculties',[71] more typical was Green's belief that a consistent and singleminded pursuit of pleasure would lead to the 'embarrassment' of the 'higher impulses'.[72] Once the problem is posed as finding a more adequate conception of the human good than the mere pursuit of pleasure, it does not seem hard to see how the elevation of

intellectual endeavours came about: if the aim is to avoid a pig philosophy, it is natural enough to build one with Socrates in mind. This is
not to say, however, that modern liberals advocate some sort of ascet-
icism. Later on (§ IV.B.2) we shall discover that while they insist that
an adequate life gives pride of place to intellectual development and,
consequently, cannot centre on the pursuit of pleasure, modern liberals
do not wish to entirely divorce pleasure from development. Pleasure,
they will be found to argue, ought not be our goal, but a healthy development nevertheless will lead to a fair measure of pleasure.

Secondly, and more fundamentally, the emphasis on the intellectual
element in all development accords well with what we might call the
liberal conviction of the similitude of men. Although modern liberals
certainly believe that individual natures differ, they also hold the traditional liberal view that all men share a similar nature and, consequently,
their differences — unlike, for instance, those separating Plato's classes
or citizens — do not mark off radically different types or grades of
existences. Whether the claim has been that we are all God's children,
all rational beings or all creatures capable of pleasure and pain (thus,
incidentally, extending similitude to non-human animals), liberals have
insisted that whatever differences individuals manifest, they are essentially the same sort of beings. With regard to individual development,
the corresponding modern liberal claim is that all the differential
individualised developments are manifestations of man's common,
rational nature. This, I would venture, is the feature of Green's theory
that David L. Norton's interpretation seizes upon, though he wrongly
draws the conclusion that it is inconsistent with natural individual
differentiation. Bosanquet expressed the core of Green's thought best,
I think, when saying that '[t]he forwarding of human nature is the
same work in kind whatever may be the particular aspect of the universal in favour of which we have to deny our immediate selves.'[73] This is
not to deny individuality, but to assert the similitude of all development. It is this concern with the similitude of men, I think, that lies
at the heart of the modern liberal emphasis on the intellectual dimension of all individuality.

I hasten to add that similitude does not imply equality.[74] We all
might be capable of reason or intellectual growth, and yet some more
capable than others. Indeed, liberals generally have thought men to be
unequally endowed with such capacities, and modern liberals are not
exceptions. Thus, for example, it will be seen in Chapter VI that Mill
definitely recognises differing degrees of intellectual capacity and,
moreover, maintains that the better endowed — the 'elite' — ought to

have a leading role in politics, being the more competent. But, as we will also see, even here the similitude of men asserts itself. Despite his insistence on intellectual differences, Mill by no means endorses (*à la* Plato) a political caste of those competent to command and rule with other classes destined to simply obey and follow. Some must rely on the judgement of others, but they ought to do so in an intelligent and critical way.[75] Followers, then, are not different sorts of beings, unable to enter into the realm of politics and evaluate their leaders but, rather, they share the same fundamental nature with their governors and, hence, are able to intelligently participate in politics.

## C.4. Art, Emotion and Intellect

The modern liberal conception of individuality is not purely intellectual. But even when they seem inclined to follow Rousseau's emphasis on the emotional life, modern liberals are apt to do it in a markedly intellectual manner. Art, and particularly poetry, occupy a remarkably prominent place in the thinking of Mill, Dewey and Bosanquet. Perhaps it ought to have been expected: reading Wordsworth, after all, brought Mill out of the depression that followed his loss of Benthamite faith. It was during this time, Mill reports, 'that I, for the first time, gave its proper place, among the prime necessities of human well-being, to the internal culture of the individual'.[76] According to J.M. Robson, although Mill believed the appeal of poetry was to the feelings, the great poets must have cultivated intellects.[77] Wrote Mill:

> Where the poetic temperament exists in its greatest degree, while the systematic culture of intellect has been neglected, we may expect to find, what we do find in the best poems of Shelley — vivid representations of states of passive and dreamy emotion, fitted to give extreme pleasure to persons of similar organization to the poet, but not likely to be sympathized in, because not understood, by any other persons; and scarcely conducing at all to the noblest end of poetry as an intellectual pursuit, that of acting upon the desires and characters of mankind through their emotions, to raise them towards the perfection of their nature.[78]

In a similar sort of way, Dewey too stresses that, while the aesthetic is especially concerned with the emotional quality of experience, it also has a meaning, and thus an intellectual element.[79] In Green's early essay on the 'Value and Influence of Works of Fiction' we again meet the idea that while works of imagination 'appeal directly to the emotions', they have an intellectual dimension as well. Green's thesis is that while epic poems, dramas and novels all present emotional appeals, they do so in very different ways. Although he sees some merit in novels — because they concern such a wide range of human character and activity and are 'thus a great expander of the sympathies' — Green ultimately deprecates them as appealing to 'more ordinary minds than the poet'.[80] This contrast between easy and more taxing forms of art becomes a central theme in Bosanquet's aesthetics. Indeed, for Bosanquet, perhaps the most important case of the distinction between easy and difficult pleasures (or satisfactions) concerns the appreciation of what he calls easy and difficult beauty. Appreciation of the latter, he argues, is so arduous as to amount in some persons to repellance: 'in general, one may say that the common mind — and all our minds are common at times — resents any great effort of concentration . . . The kind of effort required is not exactly an intellectual effort; it is something more, it is an imaginative effort.'[81] Yet the necessity of such concentration and effort does not mean that aesthetics is not at bottom concerned with the emotional life: 'Beauty is feeling become plastic.'[82]

While no definitive conclusions can be drawn from such a rapid sketch of the aesthetic theories of modern liberals, it does not seem out of order to put forward one, fairly plausible, thesis. A central aspect of Mill's, Green's, Bosanquet's and Dewey's views on art (and, in particular, poetry) seems to be a concern wtih intellectualising or refining the emotional life. While agreeing that art somehow intrinsically appeals to the emotions, all argue that this emotional dimension does not preclude intellectual elements or complex and arduous cultivation. Again, we need to realise that other options exist, even given an intellectualist understanding of excellence. Like Plato, for example, it might have been maintained that (dramatic) poetry necessarily appeals to, and encourages, the emotions *and not reason* and is on that account suspect. 'It waters the growth of passions which should be allowed to wither away and sets them up in control, although the goodness and happiness of our lives depend on their being held in subjection.'[83] Or, less radically, one could (while still upholding a commitment to cultivation of the intellect) follow Bentham in seeing the 'deeper feelings of human nature' as 'idiosyncrasies of taste' which are of concern neither to the moralist nor to the legislator — nor for that matter to the political philosopher.[84] But Mill, Green, Bosanquet and Dewey neither repress nor ignore the emotional life but instead integrate its development with that of the intellect.[85] As we are about to see, the stress on an inte-

grated development of the diverse aspects of an individual's nature is
fundamental to the modern liberal theory of man.

## D. The Organisation of Individuality

### D.1. Life Plans

Thus far our concern has been with the separate capacities of each
individual. But not only have modern liberals asserted that we have
distinctive capacities, but they have also stressed, as Hobhouse put it,
'the extraordinary range of human potentiality'.[86] Now, as Rawls
argues, the extraordinary range of our potentialities introduces the
problem of organising the capacities into a coherent individuality:

> [O]ne basic characteristic of human beings is that no one person
> can do everything that he might do; nor a fortiori can he do every-
> thing that any other person can do. The potentialities of each
> individual are greater than he can hope to realize; and they fall far
> short of the powers available to men generally. Thus everyone must
> select which of his abilities and possible interests he wishes to en-
> courage; he must plan their training and exercise, and schedule their
> pursuit in an orderly way.[87]

As Rawls takes his conception of a plan of life from Josiah Royce, the
American idealist,[88] it is not perhaps very surprising to find much the
same notion in Bosanquet, who repeatedly talks of 'plans' or 'schemes
of life' according to which 'the contents of the self can be organised'.[89]
But the idea goes back considerably further than Royce and Bosanquet:
indeed, since Mill uses it in the third chapter of *Liberty*,[90] one is
tempted to say that it was present at the birth of the modern liberal
conception of individuality.

Perhaps the most significant feature of emphasising the organising
of one's capacities (and interests and purposes) according to a plan
is the distinction thus introduced between the self (the planner) and
one's capacities (as resources to be utilised and organised).[91] In contrast,
for example, to Hobbes's man – who was essentially a system of passions
– or to James Mill's – who was essentially a bundle of associations –
the modern liberal man is not simply a system or bundle of capacities:
he is rather a selector and organiser of capacities and abilities.[92] Moreover, as Rawls makes clear, the individual cannot be simply identified
with any particular plan: not being detailed blueprints, they are liable

to change and revision throughout our lives. Indeed, in recent restatements of his position, Rawls is particularly concerned with showing that his theory is premised on a conception of persons according to which 'they think of themselves not as inevitably tied to the pursuit of the particular final ends they have at any given time, but rather as capable of revising and changing these ends on reasonable and rational grounds.'[93] Even Bosanquet, who never seems to tire of arguing that the 'I' is not an abstract ego but a system of content, adds that 'this content is not permanent or unchangeable, or essentially attached to the self'.[94]

For the modern liberal, then, a genuine individuality is an ongoing organisation of at least some of one's distinctive capacities into, as Bosanquet put it, 'a unique and creative construction'.[95] It is worth pointing out here that plans can be unique for two reasons. First, as Rawls argues, plans will vary from person to person because endowments and opportunities differ.[96] Even if our endowments were not unique, however, and each shared a roughly similar set of extraordinarily various capabilities, we could still fashion a unique and creative construction. Uniqueness would then turn on the tremendous variety of the ways in which a rich common endowment could be organised instead of deriving from unique natures. Recalling Bosanquet's hesitations about uniqueness of natures, we can now see that he can quite intelligibly talk of unique individualities without adopting a unique natures position. However, a problem persists. In an important sense, this understanding of uniqueness provides a weaker basis for arguments supporting liberty than does a unique natures thesis. One of the main modern liberal arguments for liberty, which we shall uncover in Chapter V, is that which contends that each requires freedom to find or create the life that best suits his nature. Since we all have different complex natures (it is argued), we will be thwarted by any attempt to impose on us pre-existing models of life: we each must discover what our nature permits and requires. On this view human nature is violated not only when adults (who already possess different life plans) are forced to adopt certain models of life, but even when the attempt is made to model children according to some narrow ideal of excellence. Now whatever the merits of this sort of argument, it is clearly weakened if our uniqueness stems not from our unique nature but from the way in which we have organised a common endowment. If the latter is the case, i.e. that we are all 'born the same', individuality is definitely still possible but this 'Millian' argument for liberty loses some of its force. It is thus important to realise that although Bosanquet (and, in general, other modern liberals) rightly insists that unique individualities can arise from the complexity of construction as well as differential natures, he also admits a *diversity* of individual natures (though not a *uniqueness*) and so, to some extent, can apparently avail himself of the 'Millian' argument for liberty.

## D.2. Plans and Coherence

The idea of a plan of life, and in particular its Rawlsian formulation, has been attacked by Robert Paul Wolff as conflicting with 'the organic, developmental character of a healthy human personality'.[97] According to Wolff, Rawls's emphasis on prudential planning and calculation is appropriate to directing a firm, '[b]ut the living of a life is not at all like the managing of a firm. A firm is a legal person, not an organic, natural, living creature.'[98] Wolff is certainly right that calculations and cost-benefit analysis are usually part of planning, and seem to occupy a particularly prominent place in Rawls's discussion.[99] But Wolff's contrast between the notion of a life plan and an 'organic' conception of personality seems puzzling in at least two respects. First, as we have seen, like other modern liberals, Rawls places considerable emphasis on the development of capacities and the evolution of plans: hence his conception seems 'organic' qua development and change. Secondly, Wolff sometimes uses 'organic' in the more-or-less idealist sense as meaning (roughly) interconnections and mutual dependence among members of a whole.[100] Certainly Rawls's plans are organic in this sense too:

> The aim of deliberation is to find that plan which best organizes our activities and influences the formation of our subsequent wants so that our aims and interests can be fruitfully combined into one scheme of conduct. Desires that tend to interfere with other ends, or which undermine the capacity for other activities, are weeded out; whereas those that are enjoyable in themselves and support other aims as well are encouraged. A plan, then, is made up of subplans suitably arranged in a hierarchy, the broad features of the plan allowing for the more permanent aims and interests that complement one another.[101]

As I indicated, this notion of an organisation of capacities and interests into a mutually supporting system is very much a part of idealism, in particular its doctrine of self-realisation. As A.J.M. Milne understands it, the point of the doctrine is that the self is realised through an ongoing development of a way of life that organises one's various native endowments into a coherent whole. Just what activities and capacities form a part of one's plan, and their importance in it, will turn upon the ease or difficulty with which they can be 'incorporated' into 'a coherent way of living'. Certainly this view is characteristic of Green who, as Milne says, always insisted on the self-consistent and coherent development of capacities.[102] Bosanquet is even more emphatic: he postulates an 'irrepressible instinct' to harmony, system, coherence, or order.[103] In our own personality, as in our experience of the world, we are repulsed by contradiction and anarchy and so seek reconciliation, systematisation and unity. The 'best life' for man, then, is one that 'satisfies the fundamental logic of man's capacities' and achieves a systematic whole.[104]

Though not idealists, Hobhouse and Dewey were very much influenced by idealism, and this shows through clearly in their positions on the organisation of personality.[105] Above all, Hobhouse is the exponent of harmony — in the inner life and in the life of society. 'Human nature', he tells us, is only a mass of undeveloped and unorganised hereditary capacities. What can be made of it turns on the way our potentialities are related to one another. 'They may so check and disturb each other that the resulting life is anarchic or mean or concentrated on paltry and limited ends, or they may so harmonise as to constitute a life rich in splendour of achievement.'[106] But it is not merely a matter of choice between different lines of development; adopting an essentially idealist position, Hobhouse conceives 'Practical Reason' as an impulse towards unity and coherence.[107] Dewey has a strikingly similar view. 'Rationality', he writes, 'is not a force to evoke against impulse and habit. It is the attainment of a working harmony among diverse desires.' Given this essentially synthetic conception of reason, it is obvious that a rational plan of life is necessarily one that *does not* ignore the interconnectedness or unity of life (i.e. its 'organic' character). In contrast to the classical liberal, for a modern liberal like Dewey '[t]he office of deliberation is not to supply an inducement to act by figuring out where the most advantage is to be procured. It is to resolve entanglements in existing activity, restore continuity, recover harmony, utilize loose impulse and re-direct habit.'[108]

## D.3. Three Unacceptable Modes of Life

All this talk of harmony, integration and interconnectedness of lives is, however, very abstract. So as to get a clearer idea of just what it involves, it may be helpful to see how it might translate into practice.

Let us approach the question by considering just what sort of 'life styles' are ruled out.

(i)    First, the romantic idea of pure, spontaneous self-expression obviously is at odds with the impulse to coherence and harmony. Not surprisingly, then, Dewey warns of the danger of 'capricious or discontinuous action in the name of spontaneous self-expression'.[109] Although we can find some accolades to spontaneity in modern liberal writings,[110] their assertions of an impulse to coherence and the need to systematise the cultivation of capacities according to a life plan would seem to require that it occupy a subordinate place in any sort of satisfying life. In fact, so far from concentrating on spontaneity and living for the moment, modern liberals have been prone to look to occupations as the key to an integrated life. Again Dewey epitomises the modern liberal view:

> A vocation means nothing but such a direction of life activities as renders them perceptibly significant to a person, because of the consequences they accomplish, and also useful to his associates. The opposite of a career is neither leisure nor culture, but aimlessness, capriciousness, the absence of cumulative achievement in experience.[111]

Whereas Dewey and Rawls stress the importance of occupations for development, the idealists, and particularly Bosanquet, make a great deal of the idea of one's 'station and its duties'. Putting aside for now the element of social service (which we shall see in §III.D also informs the idea of an occupation), Bosanquet's notion of a station − including not only occupation, but family life, etc. − plays very much the same integrating role as Dewey's 'vocation'. 'Our station and its duties', says Bosanquet in a characteristic sentence, 'is the heart and spirit of our own little life.'[112]

At first glance, Mill's individuals may seem a good deal more spontaneous and, so, much less career oriented than, say, either Dewey's or Bosanquet's. After all, in *Liberty* he speaks of 'the element of spontaneity and individuality' and thus at least hints at some necessary connection between the two.[113] And indeed it is probably accurate to say that Mill had more appreciation of the necessity for some spontaneity in life than any other modern liberal. Yet we are not justified in going much further than this. As I said before, the notion of a plan of life plays a prominent role in the argument of *Liberty*. According to Mill, 'he who chooses his plan for himself' utilises all his faculties. 'He must use observation to see, reasoning and judgment to foresee, activity to gather materials for decision, discrimination to decide, and when he has decided, firmness and self-control to hold to his deliberate decision.'[114] Even more to the point, Mill concludes his case for the equality of the sexes by insisting, in *The Subjection of Women* that the 'free direction and disposal' of faculties requires a free choice of occupation. A vocation, he argues, is a focus of 'interests and excitements' that provides 'a worthy outlet of the active faculties'. To be denied a congenial occupation, then, is to be 'fettered and restricted'; to lose one often 'brings ennui, melancholy, and premature death'.[115]

(ii)   Hobhouse — who, as I have said, was if nothing else the theorist of harmony and integration — distinguished what might be called 'weak' and 'strong' conceptions of harmony. At its minimum, Hobhouse says, harmony requires mutual consistency of the development of different aspects of our nature.[116] But in the stronger sense, harmony demands not only consistency but mutual reinforcement as well. 'A perfect organism', says Hobhouse, 'still consists of self-assertive parts, but they are so related that each in the most complete fulfilment of its own tendencies aids in the fulfilment of the remainder. This is the relation of harmony.'[117] What this means, then, is that not only random self-expression but sustained cultivation of isolated interests and capacities also fall short of harmonious integration. One who plays many roles (e.g. a university professor, a mother, a sports fan, and a citizen) but who compartmentalised the performance of each would thus not achieve the 'rational unity' of a 'whole life'.[118] In some — not all that clear — sense, her professorship, say, ought to support her role as a mother, as a citizen, as a sports fan. The attainment of such integration, while in accord with our nature, is of course no easy task, and in any event likely to be incomplete. 'Integration', as Dewey said, 'is something to be achieved. Division of attitudes and responses, compartmentalizing of interests, is easily acquired.'[119] Nevertheless, the modern liberal ideal of self-realisation, especially in the idealists and those they influenced, is to a very great extent premised on the goal of a unified or coherent life (§II.D.2).

(iii)   Critiques of romantic self-expression and compartmentalised roles follow in a fairly straightforward fashion from the modern liberal's emphasis on planning, integration and harmony. Somewhat surprisingly, though, the sort of life which they seem most concerned with criticising is, at least so it seems, consistent with harmony. In his lectures on psychology, Bosanquet seems to say that a self-consistent personality can be achieved by rooting out or repressing any aspects of the self not consistent with some one overriding goal (in his example, private satisfaction). 'It would be an attempt at a kind of system, but narrowed rather than enlarged.'[120] Hobhouse too recognises that an individuality may be dominated by some single overriding object rather than resting on a harmonious adjustment of a wide range of interests informed by 'a rational appreciation of life as a many-sided whole'.[121] Moreover — again, this accords ill with the idea that Bosanquet and Hobhouse were always at odds — both believe that the attempt to achieve harmony by narrowing the contents of the personality is the real root of egoism.[122] It does not appear, then, that it is mere harmony or integration, but a 'fullness of scope for our many-sided nature' that informs a suitable life. And, consequently, not only spontaneous and compartmentalised, but narrow lives as well, are to be criticised.

Like so much of the modern liberal conception of individuality, the ideal of many-sided and full development can be found in the third chapter of *Liberty*. Most explicit, of course, is Mill's quotation from Von Humboldt: ' "The end of man" ', the latter writes in *The Sphere and Duties of Government*, ' "is the highest and most harmonious development of his powers to a *complete and consistent* whole" '.[123] Less explicit but more widespread, though, are Mill's comparisons of human nature to plants, trees, etc., requiring growth and development '*on all sides*, according to the tendency of the inward forces which make it a living thing'.[124] However, as Maurice Mandelbaum has pointed out, despite these straightforward indications of Mill's belief in the desirability and naturalness of a many-sided development, his well-known endorsement of eccentricity strongly suggests that he was not particularly critical of strong, though essentially one-sided, personalities.[125] It does not follow from this, though, that Mill's position is contradictory: he can quite consistently uphold many-sided personality as a higher form of development while simultaneously applauding individualities that, while narrow, manifest more of the trends of the individual's nature than what he saw as the average moulded character of his day.

Still, it is really in the idealists and those most influenced by them that the striving towards a full and rich development assumes a pre-eminent place in liberal theory. Certainly, Green (who very much influenced not only Bosanquet and Hobhouse but Dewey too)[126] conceived of individual development as progressing towards a fuller and richer life. In thinking of ultimate perfection, he says, one 'thinks of it indeed as perfection for himself; as a life in which he shall be fully satisfied through having become all that the spirit within him enables him to become'.[127] The links between this conception of development and idealist positions in logic, epistemology and metaphysics — with their emphasis on coherence, system and completeness — are, however, clearer in Bosanquet:

> Mind and individuality, so far as finite, find their fullest expression as aspects of very complex and precisely determined mechanical systems. This is the law, I believe wholly without exception, for every higher product of the human soul and intelligence and also of cosmic evolution. It follows necessarily from the nature of "being and trueness," as Plato calls them. The greater being must have the more perfect coherence, and the more perfect coherence must have the fuller content.[128]

Interestingly, Bosanquet seems to depart here from his position in *Psychology of the Moral Self*. Whereas in the *Psychology* (as we saw) he seems to allow that coherence can be purchased by narrowing the self, he here maintains that a more perfect coherence requires a fuller content.[129] In seeking narrowness, he says in another place, one tries to repress aspects of his nature, but 'of what is extruded something refuses to be suppressed and forms a nucleus of rebellion'.[130] By maintaining that attempts at suppression and narrowing are only partially successful, then, modern liberals like Bosanquet have tied breadth to harmony, and thus have based their critique of narrow lives directly on the idea of a natural impulse to coherence. Given this — and the elaborate theory of repression and pathology which, we will see in Chapter IV, modern liberals have developed — it is more than a little puzzling that theorists like Hobhouse and Bosanquet are apparently sometimes willing to acknowledge the possibility of a narrow harmony. Presumably, their idea is that the pursuit of harmony can, and sometimes does, lead to eliminating conflict via narrowing although, ultimately, the harmony thus achieved is imperfect since a 'nucleus of rebellion' persists.

I do not wish to suggest by this that the ideal of a harmonious and many-sided personality is in any way dependent upon idealism, but only that the central idealist themes of system and completeness are particularly compatible with it. Hobhouse, and even more Dewey, retains a basically idealist conception of personality while transforming or rejecting the larger idealist philosophy. If anything the conviction that healthy personalities are wide-ranging and balanced, and thus narrowness indicates stunting and distortion, is even more fundamental to the psychology, politics and ethics of these descendants of idealism. It is a commonplace that to Hobhouse 'the Heart of Liberalism [is] a fulfilment or *full development* of personality . . . for all members of the community.'[131] More surprising perhaps is that Dewey adopts practically the same position. The 'moral meaning' of democracy, he says in *Reconstruction in Philosophy*, is 'that the supreme test of all political institutions and industrial arrangements shall be the contribution they make to the *all-around growth* of every member of society.'[132]

## D.4. Specialisation and Discipline

When stressing their core visions, ideals, etc., modern liberals are apt to endorse without qualification 'full development' or simply renounce 'narrow' personalities. But in their more guarded moments, 'development as a whole means development on all sides that can in fact be reconciled', and 'narrowing' is identified with 'over-specialisation'.[133] One of the soundest generalisations that can be made about modern liberals as a group is that while advocating a rich, integrated life, they are quick to add that 'full' development is ultimately impossible for at least two reasons.

(i)   Like modern liberals before him, Rawls believes that institutions ought to encourage individual natures so as to 'achieve the widest regulative excellences of which each is capable'. But, of all our group of theorists, he is perhaps least prone to exaggerating the possibilities of some sort of complete development. Although Rawls admits that it is 'tempting to suppose' that each might develop the full range of his powers and that at least some might become 'complete exemplars of humanity', he thinks such an ideal is illusory. 'It is a feature of human sociability that we are by ourselves but parts of what we might be. We must look to others to attain the excellences that we must leave aside, or lack altogether.'[134] Compare Bosanquet: 'We know that in the development of human nature, which we take to be the ultimate standard of life, no one individual can cover the ground of the whole.' And so, Bosanquet concludes, the development of human nature is best advanced by a differential growth in a 'plurality of centres'.[135] Moreover, as he makes clear, this plurality is not necessary just because we have diverse natures, but because 'whatever abilities lie within one personality, effective work demands the division of labour'. At this point in our argument, what is important is Rawls's and Bosanquet's recognition that not only human nature as a whole but even our own share of it is too great a ground to be covered in our life. (This in no way contradicts the unique natures thesis: each of us may have a special set

of capacities shared by no other person, and yet be unable to cultivate in a single life all the abilities latent in our nature. One who devoted her unique talents to becoming a medical doctor may have also had
the ability of being an artist.)

All this relates to modern liberalism's emphasis on careers or vocations: in pursuit of a career some qualities or capacities are selected and
cultivated with great attention over the greater part of a lifetime.
Now, as Green well recognised, it often 'follows that one who has made
the most of his profession is apt to feel that he has not attained his full
stature as a man; that he has faculties which he can never use, capacities
for admiration and affection which can never meet with an adequate
object.'[136] The modern liberal thus seems caught in a dilemma: concentration and specialisation are necessary if particular faculties are to
be highly developed, yet specialisation seems to lead to feelings of loss
for those possibilities never explored. To escape the dilemma, modern
liberals, though endorsing considerable specialisation, have sought to
show how it can be conjoined with breadth of development. The main
reply, as already indicated in the above quotation from Rawls, relies on
a particular conception of the social nature of man, the subject of the
next chapter. But, secondly, like Mill, most modern liberals have also
argued for a balance of specialisation and general cultivation for each
individual. 'It is not the utmost limit of human acquirement', said Mill
in his 'Inaugural Address' at St. Andrew's University, 'to know only one
thing, but to combine a minute knowledge of one or a few things with
a general knowledge of many things.'[137] Leisure and recreation, especially
in the writings of Dewey and Bosanquet, thus become an integral part
of a suitable life by giving free play to faculties and capacities not
drawn upon in the course of one's occupation.[138] Dewey in particular
assigns to art the role of encouraging well-roundedness in our specialised lives. As he understands it, '[i]t is the office of art in the individual
person, to compose differences, to do away with isolations and conflicts among the elements of our being, to utilize oppositions among
them to build a richer personality.'[139] But the crucial point is not so
much whether a theorist relies on art, liberal education or recreation,
but that, one way or another, modern liberals see specialisation as both
a necessity and a danger,[140] and so seek ways to introduce breadth
into our lives.

(ii) For the reasons that I gave above (§D.3) and which will be
explored in depth in Chapter IV, modern liberals favour a complex
and wide harmony achieved through integration of all aspects of our
nature. Yet even Hobhouse sometimes acknowledges that suppression

of some refractory impulses may be necessary to achieve harmony: 'insistence on harmony, that is the practical reason, aims at extirpating whatever it cannot reconcile with a harmonious order'.[141] One is tempted to say that modern liberal worries about rebellious desires stem from Green; certainly his talk about 'our lower nature' and his approval of efforts to 'suppress the baser elements of man's nature' indicate a deep concern with unruly passions.[142] But though Green's 'evangelical origins' may have made him particularly concerned with 'subordination of fleshy impulses',[143] he certainly cannot be credited (or blamed) with introducing this sort of selective development into modern liberalism. In his essay on *Nature*, Mill argues that men have capacities for evil as well as good; and thus, he concludes, 'the duty of man is the same in respect to his own nature as in respect to the nature of all other things, namely, not to follow but to amend it.'[144] Indeed, Mill sometimes pictures education as aiming precisely at this: i.e. the 'eradicating or weakening' of bad tendencies and the 'exalting' of the good.[145] 'The power of education is almost boundless: there is not one natural inclination which it is not strong enough to coerce, and, if needful, to destroy by disuse.'[146] It is perhaps worth noting that Dewey, whose educational philosophy is premised on the growth of individual natures, agrees with Mill here. After propounding the Rousseauian theory of the unique tendencies of each, he argues in *Democracy and Education* that natural tendencies are not necessarily desirable ones. As he sees it, the task of educators is to provide an environment that encourages the desirable natural tendencies and, furthermore, does so in such a way that the desirable tendencies control the undesirable ones, the ultimate aim being the atrophy of the latter.[147]

I shall argue in Chapter IV that modern liberals' endorsement of suppressing some capacities leads to major difficulties and complications in their general theory of development. At this point, though, we need to deal with the less troublesome, though more often voiced, objection that they have no basis on which to identify capacities as desirable or undesirable.[148] If their goal is the development of human capacities, on what ground can they pick and choose the capacities to be developed?

Pretty obviously, this only presents a difficulty if one holds that human development is the sole end or criterion by which actions (or interests, tastes, etc.) are to be judged. If, on the other hand, plans are to be constrained by principles of right (or value), identifying some capacities as undesirable poses no difficulties. Rawls and Mill (as shown in his essay on 'Nature'), are cases in point. While, as we shall see in

Part Two, they typically premise arguments for liberalism on the obvious desirability of development, they do possess moral principles that can be used to prohibit certain sorts of development.[149] However, two other options exist. (a) First, even if development of human nature is the sole end, it can be held that the development of some capacities in an individual thwart development in a multitude of other people. So, if as Dewey appeared to, we aim at the greatest growth of the greatest number,[150] some capacities may be repressed simply in the interests of development. (b) Secondly, and of much more interest, the modern liberal emphasis on harmony and integration provides some basis on which to condemn certain lines of growth of an individual as narrowing, destabilising or compartmentalising *for that person*. And, once we fill out  the modern liberal theory of man by considering the social side of human nature, we shall see that, according to the modern liberals, each of us has a reason for repressing our 'anti-social' capacities merely on the grounds of promoting our own wider development. (Of course, for such arguments to be effective it must be shown that repression of 'anti-social' capacities is less damaging to breadth and harmony than repression of our social nature.) In fact, one of the things we shall see in Part Two is that all modern liberals — Rawls and Mill included — argue that we ought to accord others equal opportunities for development (and so repress any tendencies we might have that would conflict with doing so) in order to promote *our own* fuller development. That is, restraint of our anti-social impulses, modern liberals will be found to argue, promotes our own growth as well as that of others.

## E.  Perfectionism and Modern Liberal Individuality

Before concluding the exposition of the modern liberal conception of individuality, I would like to briefly consider in just what ways it is and is not a 'perfectionist theory' of man. Without considering all the possible uses of perfectionism (or which are superior) we can distinguish two notions of perfectionism which *do not* apply to the conception of individuality we have been examining: we can call these the 'Aristotelian' and 'external standard' notions.

(i)     According to what Dewey called the 'classical Aristotelian formulation' of development, potentialities are related to predetermined ends, inherent in the individual's nature, which he seeks to realise. Of course the environment plays some role: just as an acorn needs a co-operative environment to realise its potential to become an oak, the development of humans may be supported or thwarted by their surroundings.[151] Obviously, however, when applied to human beings the Aristotelian conception of development must be far more open-ended than when applied to acorns: an acorn can only reach its perfect development by becoming an oak whereas one born with, for example, an artistic nature may find its perfection in a number of different lives. Still, to the extent it can be said that a person's nature indicates a unique line of development, the acorn-oak model of perfection seems applicable.

To the extent the acorn-oak model implies some definite set of capacities of which the individual is largely aware and seeks to realise (as Dewey seemed to think it does), it certainly is not part of modern liberalism. Just what capacities we have, and what sort of individualities may arise out of them, liberals like Dewey have held, is a matter of experimentation and discovery throughout the course of a life.[152] Green was particularly adamant in maintaining that we could not fully know the limits of human capacity since they have not been fully realised 'in any life that can be observed, in any life that has been, or is, or (as would seem) that can be lived by man as we know him'. As Green was quick to point out, this does not mean that we are without any idea of 'the direction which tends to further realise the capabilities of the human spirit', but only that within these bounds a great deal of uncertainty exists.[153]

Of more importance, though, is that the need to select some (proper) subset of our capacities for special attention and cultivation precludes the oak-acorn model. If, from the 'extraordinary range of human potential' we must choose to cultivate some capacities over others, our nature evinces an indeterminancy of possible lines of growth. And, if anything, modern liberals have made too much rather than too little of this range of potentiality. In emphasising the tremendous range of our capacities, they risk a danger of leaving possible lines of development so open-ended that almost any sort of life will be consistent with our capacities: as I have already suggested, should that happen some of their most important arguments for liberty would be weakened (see Ch. V). Modern liberals, then, seek to navigate a course between individual natures that are so determinate that each has a definite destiny and ones that are so diverse as to be in accord with almost any life.

(ii)    What I call the 'external standard' conception of perfectionism has been described by Vinit Haksar as a 'strong sense' of perfectionism. As Haksar depicts it, central to this conception is that some modes of life are intrinsically superior to others, *regardless of human nature, or individual satisfaction, capacities, etc.*[154] It is not hard to see why such perfectionism is typically thought hostile to individuality.[155] If some sorts of life, for instance, those of (to use Rawls's words) 'a certain style or aesthetic grace' or of superior artistic or scientific achievement are elevated as ideals to be either imitated or served, the perfectionist may well be led to advocate suppression (or re-education) of personalities of an inferior sort. But as Haksar argues, he need not make this last move. 'One can quite consistently believe that some forms of human life are inherently superior to other forms of human life, without believing that the person who practices the latter form of life has inferior worth or deserves less (intrinsic) consideration than the former.'[156] Nevertheless, the external standard conception does not put the tendencies of human nature at the very heart of things and, so, is not a part of modern liberal theory. Although modern liberals have indeed identified some lives as inferior to others, the argument always proceeds from human nature.[157] In Haksar's terminology, theirs is a variety of perfectionism in the 'weak' sense. 'Some ends [or forms of life] . . . are more expressive of human nature, of what men really are, than [are] certain other ends [or forms of life].'[158] Even when, say, Green is maintaining the necessity of control of our 'lower nature', the thesis is that such control is necessary for the fuller development (or perfection) of human nature in individuals.

This last phrase is important: the modern liberal commitment to the perfection of human nature translates into a devotion to the development of individual natures. At first glance this may not be as clear in Bosanquet and Green as in the others, for they do sometimes seem to suggest that 'human nature' is some sort of unified whole existing in humanity or 'man' rather than in individuals. But of course they certainly do not deny — indeed, one cannot see how they could — that the only way to develop human nature is to develop it as it exists in persons; i.e. their individual natures. More than that, though, the impulse to self-satisfaction — the realisation of one's own capacities — is held by both to be the driving force working towards the perfection of human nature.[159] For modern liberals, then, the perfection of human nature means the development of individual natures.

## Notes

1.    Zevedei Barbu, *Democracy and Dictatorship: Their Psychology and Patterns of Life* (Grove Press, New York, 1956), pp. 111-13.

2. Mill, *On Liberty* in J.M. Robson (ed.), *The Collected Works of John Stuart Mill* (University of Toronto Press, Toronto, 1963), vol. XVIII, p. 263.

3. Ibid., p. 267.

4. Bosanquet, *The Principle of Individuality and Value* (Macmillan, London, 1912), p. 69.

5. Bosanquet, *The Value and Destiny of the Individual* (Macmillan, London, 1913), p. 36.

6. Bosanquet, *The Philosophical Theory of the State*, 4th edn (Macmillan, London, 1951), pp. 56-58. R.P. Anshutz also criticises Mill for believing 'that a man is only himself when he succeeds in being different from other men'. *The Philosophy of J.S. Mill* (Clarendon Press, Oxford, 1953), p. 27. On Mill and eccentricity, see §I.D.3. On Bosanquet's ascription of a negative conception to Mill, see §II.C.1.

7. Dewey, *Human Nature and Conduct* (Henry Holt, New York, 1922), p. 65; see also his *Individualism: Old and New* (Allen and Unwin, London, 1931), p. 135.

8. Hobhouse, *The Metaphysical Theory of the State* (Allen and Unwin, London, 1926), p. 53.

9. Hobhouse, *Mind in Evolution*, 3rd edn (Macmillan, London, 1926), p. 375.

10. Hobhouse, *Liberalism* (Oxford University Press, Oxford, 1964), p. 60.

11. See Bosanquet, *Social and International Ideals* (Macmillan, London, 1917), pp. 158-59; his *Psychology of the Moral Self* (Macmillan, London, 1904), p. 94; and his *Individuality and Value*, p. 21.

12. Bosanquet, *Value and Destiny*, p. 182. The idea that we do not treasure our 'bare selves' but the values manifested by the growth of capacities is not unique to Bosanquet. See Dewey, *A Common Faith* (Yale University Press, New Haven, 1960), p. 87.

13. Henry Sidgwick, *Lectures on the Ethics of Green, Spencer and Martineau* (Macmillan, London, 1902), pp. 46 ff, 71 ff; W.D. Lamont, *Introduction to Green's Moral Philosophy* (Allen and Unwin, London, 1934), pp. 190-96.

14. H.D. Lewis, *Freedom and History* (Allen and Unwin, London, 1962), Ch. 1. See also John Rodman, 'What is Living and What is Dead in the Political Philosophy of T.H. Green', *Western Political Quarterly*, XXVI (Sept. 1973), p. 577.

15. Green, 'Lectures on the Philosophy of Kant' in R.L. Nettleship (ed.), *Works of T.H. Green*, vol. II (Longman's, Green and Co., London, 1900), p. 154.

16. Green, *Prolegomena to Ethics*, A.C. Bradley (ed.) (Clarendon Press, Oxford, 1890), pp. 266-67.

17. Ann R. Cacoullos, *Thomas Hill Green: Philosopher of Rights* (Twayne, New York, 1974), p. 66. On the importance of intellectual development in modern liberalism, see §C.3.

18. Green, *Prolegomena*, pp. 414, 415.

19. Dewey, *Democracy and Education* (The Free Press, New York, 1916), p. 89.

20. Ibid., p. 90.

21. Dewey, *Democracy and Education*, p. 91. See also his 'Individuality, Equality and Superiority' in Joseph Ratner (ed.), *Characters and Events: Popular Essays in Social and Political Philosophy* (Henry Holt, New York, 1929), p. 489.

22. Dewey, *Democracy and Education*, p. 116.

23. Dewey, 'Time and Individuality' in David Sidorsky (ed.), *John Dewey: The Essential Writings* (Harper and Row, New York, 1977), pp. 134-48.

24. Hobhouse, *Sociology and Philosophy* (G. Bell and Sons, London, 1966), p. 35.

25. Green, 'An Estimate of the Value and Influence of Works of Fiction in Modern Times' in *Works*, vol. III, p. 25.

26. Green, *Prolegomena*, p. 201.

27. David L. Norton, *Personal Destinies: A Philosophy of Ethical Individualism* (Princeton University Press, Princeton, 1976), p. 54. It is true that Green emphasised the 'social element' of individuality, but that does not preclude differences in individual natures. (See §II.C.2.)

28. Ibid., p. 55.

29. Ibid., pp. 54-55; Sidgwick, *Lectures on Green*, p. 63; see also Bosanquet, *Individuality and Value*, pp. 323-24.

30. Cacoullos, *Thomas Hill Green*, pp. 57-58. See note 142 below. I argue further for this interpretation of Green in §IV.C.

31. Green, *Prolegomena*, p. 124. Emphasis added.

32. J.P. Plamenatz, *Consent, Freedom and Obligation*, 2nd edn (Oxford University Press, Oxford, 1968), p. 38.

33. Bosanquet, *Individuality and Value*, p. 37.

34. Bosanquet, *Science and Philosophy* (Allen and Unwin, London, 1927), p. 180. Bosanquet suggests Green might have been afraid of them because they led to differences in treatment *between individuals*.

35. Compare Bosanquet, *Social and International Ideals*, pp. 146-48, and Hobhouse, *Social Development: Its Nature and Conditions* (Allen and Unwin, London, 1924), p. 119. See also Hobhouse's *Social Evolution and Political Theory* (Columbia University Press, New York, 1928), Ch. III.

36. Mill, *On Liberty*, p. 270.

37. Bosanquet, *Science and Philosophy*, p. 234; see also his *Philosophical Theory of the State*, p. 165.

38. Bosanquet, *The Philosophical Theory of the State*, p. 292.

39. Bosanquet, *Science and Philosophy*, p. 249.

40. Bosanquet, *Individuality and Value*, pp. 69, 104-5.

41. Hobhouse, *The Metaphysical Theory of the State*, pp. 61 ff.

42. Hobhouse, *Morals in Evolution* (Chapman and Hall, London, 1951), p. 574. See Peter Weiler, 'The New Liberalism of L.T. Hobhouse', *Victorian Studies*, XVI (Dec. 1972), p. 151.

43. Dewey, in *Essential Writings*, p. 137. However, Dewey's theory also has been charged with having such tendencies. See Horace M. Kallen, 'Individuality, Individualism and John Dewey', *Antioch Review*, XIX (Fall 1959), pp. 299-314.

44. Bosanquet, *Individuality and Value*, p. 68.

45. See John Passmore, *A Hundred Years of Philosophy*, 2nd edn (Penguin, Harmondsworth, 1966), p. 87.

46. See A.J.M. Milne, *The Social Philosophy of English Idealism* (Allen and Unwin, London, 1962), p. 238.

47. Dewey, *Individualism*, p. 156.

48. Bosanquet, *The Philosophical Theory of the State*, p. 117. Bosanquet tended to liken such achievement to self-sacrifice: the self goes outside its former boundaries to include new elements, and in becoming something else, he reasoned, one (in a sense) sacrifices one's former self. See his *Science and Philosophy*, p. 81; *Individuality and Value*, pp. 234, 242; *Philosophical Theory of the State*, p. 145. I consider the problem of self-sacrifice for the community in §III.D.

49. Dewey, *Liberalism and Social Action* (G.P. Putnam's Sons, New York, 1935), p. 39. Emphasis added.

50. Mill, 'Bentham' in *Collected Works*, vol. X, p. 95.

51. Mill, *Utilitarianism* in ibid., vol. X, p. 213.

52. Ibid., pp. 212-13.

53. See Green, *Prolegomena*, pp. 169 ff; Hobhouse, *The Rational Good: A Study in the Logic of Practice* (Watts, London, 1947), pp. 135 ff; Bosanquet,

*Science and Philosophy*, pp. 203 ff; Dewey and James H. Tufts, *Ethics*, rev. edn (Henry Holt, New York, 1932), p. 212; Rawls, *A Theory of Justice* (Harvard University Press, Cambridge, Mass., 1971), p. 426n.

54. Green, *Prolegomena*, p. 285.

55. Bosanquet, *Science and Philosophy*, p. 204.

56. See Brian Barry, *The Liberal Theory of Justice* (Clarendon Press, London, 1973), p. 30.

57. Rawls, *A Theory of Justice*, p. 426.

58. Green, *Prolegomena*, p. 285.

59. Rawls, *A Theory of Justice*, p. 429.

60. Dewey, *Individualism*, pp. 51-52.

61. Hobhouse, *Social Development*, p. 306; and his *Sociology and Philosophy*, p. 44.

62. Dewey and Tufts, *Ethics*, p. 212. Compare Hobhouse, *The Rational Good*, p. 135.

63. Hobhouse, *Mind in Evolution*, pp. 430-33; Dewey, *Democracy and Education*, p. 309.

64. Hobhouse, *Mind in Evolution*, p. 430.

65. Mill, *Utilitarianism*, p. 211.

66. Robert F. Ladenson, 'Mill's Conception of Individuality', *Social Theory and Practice*, IV (Spring 1977), p. 176. Alfonso J. Damico writes of Dewey's theory that '[i]ndividuality is basically the development of one's ability to relate means and ends, to see the interconnections among social forces, and to foresee the consequences of some course of action'. *Individuality and Community: The Social and Political Thought of John Dewey* (University Presses of Florida, Gainesville, 1978), p. 38.

67. Rawls, *A Theory of Justice*, p. 432.

68. J.-J. Rousseau, *Discourse on the Arts and Sciences* in Roger D. and Judith R. Masters (trans.), *The First and Second Discourses* (St. Martin's Press, New York, 1964).

69. Bosanquet, *The Philosophical Theory of the State*, p. x; see also his *Some Suggestions in Ethics* (Macmillan, London, 1919), p. 219. As far as the idealists are concerned, this attitude may derive from Fichte. See Peter Gordon and John White, *Philosophers as Educational Reformers: The Influence of Idealism on British Educational Thought and Practice* (Routledge and Kegan Paul, London, 1979), p. 54.

70. Mill, *Principles of Political Economy* in *Collected Works*, vol. III, pp. 763-94. See §VII.D.

71. Whether or not Mill's theory of qualities of pleasure is consistent with hedonism is a major controversy among interpreters of Mill. Both Bradley and Moore, for example, argued that, if taken seriously, the distinction is incompatible with hedonism while neither Collingwood nor Plamenatz found any real difficulty in the distinction. Others, such as Raphael and Seth, attempt to reduce Mill's qualitative distinctions to quantitative ones. See F.H. Bradley, *Ethical Studies*, 2nd edn (Clarendon Press, Oxford, 1927), pp. 116-20; G.E. Moore, *Principia Ethica* (Cambridge Univeristy Press, Cambridge, 1959), pp. 77-81; R.G. Collingwood, *An Essay on Philosophical Method* (Clarendon Press, Oxford, 1933), pp. 79-80; Rex Martin, 'A Defence of Mill's Qualitative Hedonism', *Philosophy*, XLIX (Apr. 1972), pp. 140-51; John Plamenatz, *The English Utilitarians* (Basil Blackwell, Oxford, 1949), pp. 146-47; D.D. Raphael, 'Fallacies In and About Mill's Utilitarianism', *Philosophy*, XXX (Oct. 1955), pp. 344-51; James Seth, 'The Alleged Fallacies in Mill's Utilitarianism', *Philosophical Review*, XVII (Sept. 1908), pp. 468-88. For a critical discussion of some of these interpretations, see John R. Billings, 'J.S. Mill's Quantity-Quality Distinction', *The Mill News-*

*letter*, VII (Fall 1971), pp. 6-16. For a recent treatment see Rem B. Edwards, *Pleasures and Pains: A Theory of Qualitative Hedonism* (Cornell University Press, Ithaca, 1979).

72. Green, *Prolegomena*, p. 389.

73. Bosanquet, *Science and Philosophy*, p. 180.

74. Many, of course, have tried to derive some sort of equality from the common possession of such traits. For an interesting recent effort, see Amy Gutmann, *Liberal Equality* (Cambridge University Press, Cambridge, 1980), Ch. I. The typical problem with such efforts is that they endeavour to ground equality on traits which obviously seem to be unequally distributed; a pressure is thus usually exerted to convert what would seem to be a continuum into a dichotomy. This is evident in Alan Gewirth, *Reason and Morality* (University of Chicago Press, Chicago, 1978), pp. 119-25. See §V.D.

75. As one reader has rightly pointed out, 'There is no contradiction here with individuality: it is a man's right and duty to develop his powers, to question the views of others and to assert his own; but there comes a point where, if he is honest with himself and the human situation, he must submit to the guidance of those who know better.' F.W. Garforth, *Educative Democracy: John Stuart Mill on Education in Society* (Oxford University Press, Oxford, 1980), p. 72. Chapter 4 of Garforth's book contains one of the best discussions of Mill's 'elitism'.

76. Mill, *Autobiography* (Columbia University Press, New York, 1924), p. 100. See also Thomas Woods, *Poetry and Philosophy: A Study in the Thought of John Stuart Mill* (Hutchinson, London, 1961).

77. John M. Robson, 'J.S. Mill's Theory of Poetry' in J.B. Schneewind (ed.), *Mill: A Collection of Critical Essays* (Macmillan, London, 1968), p. 258.

78. Mill, 'Tennyson's Poems', quoted in ibid., p. 270.

79. Dewey, *Art as Experience* (G.P. Putnam's Sons, New York, 1958), pp. 35-51.

80. Green, 'Value and Influence of Works of Fiction', pp. 20, 39, 40. See Nettleship's 'Memoir' in vol. III of Green's *Works*, pp. xxx-xxxiii.

81. Bosanquet, *Three Lectures in Aesthetic* (Macmillan, London, 1915), pp. 90-91.

82. Ibid., p. 97. See also Bosanquet, *Science and Philosophy*, pp. 392-406.

83. Plato, *The Republic*, Francis MacDonald Cornford (trans.) (Oxford University Press, Oxford, 1941), pp. 338-39 (605c-608b).

84. This is J.S. Mill's statement of Bentham's position in his essay on 'Bentham', p. 96.

85. Hobhouse says precious little about art, but what he does say suggests a similar sort of integration of feeling and intellect. See, for example, *The Rational Good*, pp. 110-12; *Mind in Evolution*, pp. 345-47. Rawls says even less; but as will be argued presently, he too endorses the widest possible harmonious integration of the elements of our nature.

86. Hobhouse, *Social Development*, p. 114.

87. Rawls, *A Theory of Justice*, p. 523.

88. Ibid., p. 408. See Milne, *The Social Philosophy of English Idealism*, pp. 267-88; R. Jackson Wilson, *In Quest of Community: Social Philosophy in the United States, 1860-1920* (Oxford University Press, Oxford, 1968), p. 152.

89. Bosanquet, *Psychology of the Moral Self*, p. 107; see also his *Some Suggestions in Ethics*, pp. 152, 156, and his *Civilization of Christendom* (Swan Sonnenschein, London, 1899), pp. 304-57, 340-41 (see also p. 242).

90. Mill, *On Liberty*, p. 226.

91. It is not clear just how conscious and deliberate this planning need be. Dewey (*Democracy and Education*, p. 103), Rawls (*A Theory of Justice*, pp. 404 ff) and Mill (in *Liberty*) seem to envisage a fairly explicit sort of planning while

both Bosanquet (*Science and Philosophy*, p. 177) and Hobhouse (*Social Development*, pp. 195-96) suggest a less conscious organisation. However, Dewey's emphasis on 'habits' in his later psychology, particularly *Human Nature and Conduct*, indicates that he is also attracted to this less explicit sort of planning. According to Gordon W. Allport, uncertainties as to Dewey's understanding of personality organisation stem from the relatively undeveloped nature of this part of his psychology (as compared with dynamic processes concerned with evolving goals and interests). 'Dewey's Individual and Social Psychology' in Paul Arthur Schlipp (ed.), *The Philosophy of John Dewey* (Tudor, New York, 1951), p. 276. See also Martin Hollis, 'The Self in Action' in R.S. Peters (ed.), *John Dewey Reconsidered* (Routledge and Kegan Paul, London, 1977), pp. 56-77.

92. I consider the extent to which J.S. Mill was an associationist in §IV.A.3.

93. Rawls, 'Kantian Constructivism in Moral Theory', *The Journal of Philosophy*, LXXVII (Sept. 1980), pp. 521-22. See also his *Theory of Justice*, p. 410. In his essay on 'Kantian Constructivism' Rawls seeks to sharply distinguish between the roles played in his theory by a conception of the person – a moral ideal – and a theory of human nature (pp. 534-35, 566). His conception of the person, he maintains, involves 'highest order' interests in realising capacities for an effective sense of justice and to form and revise a conception of the good, as well as a 'higher order' interest in pursuing a particular conception of the good (p. 525). As will become clear as we progress, an essential feature of my interpretation of modern liberal theories – including Rawls's – is that such a radical separation of a theory of human nature and conception of the person does not obtain. Not only does much of what Rawls calls a conception of the person fall under my understanding of human nature (e.g. a capacity to form and revise a conception of the good), but also, as we will see throughout Part Two, the modern liberal theory of human nature functions as a 'moral ideal'.

94. Bosanquet, *Psychology of the Moral Self*, p. 55.

95. Bosanquet, *Some Suggestions in Ethics*, p. 155.

96. Rawls, *A Theory of Justice*, p. 409.

97. Robert Paul Wolff, *Understanding Rawls* (Princeton University Press, Princeton, 1977), p. 137.

98. Ibid., p. 140.

99. Rawls, *A Theory of Justice*, pp. 407-24.

100. For example, Wolff writes that 'Rawls also has an extremely powerful commitment to an Idealist conception of the harmonious and organic society.' *Understanding Rawls*, p. 190.

101. Rawls, *A Theory of Justice*, pp. 410-11. See also 'Kantian Constructivism in Moral Theory', p. 529.

102. Milne, *The Social Philosophy of English Idealism*, pp. 29, 109. See also J.H. Muirhead, *The Service of the State: Four Lectures on the Political Teaching of T.H. Green* (John Murray, London, 1908), pp. 28-29.

103. Bosanquet, *Social and International Ideals*, p. 54; *Value and Destiny*, p. 95; and *Some Suggestions in Ethics*, pp. 42, 129-30. On Green's and Bosanquet's theories of self-realisation see Bertil Pfannenstill, *Bernard Bosanquet's Philosophy of the State* (G.W.K. Gleerup, Lund, 1926), pp. 109-10.

104. Bosanquet, *The Philosophical Theory of the State*, p. 169; *Individuality and Value*, p. 77. Bosanquet connects the idea of a systematic life to his notion of a standing will. 'For such a system of volitions, bound together by organizing principles which, I take it, are considered to be willed more or less explicitly, is *ex hypothesi* comprehensive, and involves the planning of an entire life.' This idea of a standing will is part of Bosanquet's theory of the general will, which will occupy us in Ch. VI. I consider the standing will or real will in Ch. V. See also §II.D.2. Bosanquet, 'The Notion of a General Will', *Mind*, XXIX (1920), p. 78.

105. Dewey's debt to Hegel is a matter of controversy. See, for example, Burleigh Taylor Wilkins, 'James, Dewey, and Hegelian Idealism', *Journal of the History of Ideas*, XVII (June 1956), pp. 332-46; R. Jackson Wilson, 'Dewey's Hegelianism', *History of Education Quarterly*, XV (Spring 1975), pp. 87-92; Morton Levitt, *Freud and Dewey on the Nature of Man* (Philosophical Library, New York, 1960), pp. 15-16. Dewey himself attests that Hegel 'left a permanent deposit' on his thinking. 'From Absolutism to Experimentalism' in Richard J. Bernstein (ed.), *John Dewey: on Experience, Nature, and Freedom* (The Liberal Arts Press, New York, 1960), p. 12.

106. Hobhouse, *Social Development*, p. 115.

107. Hobhouse, *The Rational Good*, p. 83; *Morals in Evolution*, pp. 573-74.

108. Dewey, *Human Nature and Conduct*, pp. 196, 199.

109. Dewey, *Democracy and Education*, p. 102. In his *Elements of Social Justice* [(Allen and Unwin, London, 1922), p. 28] Hobhouse contrasts anarchy and harmony. Although he is explicitly concerned here with social life, the parallel between individual and social organisation is basic to his thought. See §II.B.2.

110. See, for example, Bosanquet, *The Civilization of Christendom*, pp. 361-62.

111. Dewey, *Democracy and Education*, p. 307.

112. Bosanquet, *Essays and Addresses* (Swan Sonnenschein, London, 1891), p. 117; see also his *Some Suggestions in Ethics*, pp. 151-52.

113. Mill, *On Liberty*, p. 264.

114. Ibid., pp. 262-63.

115. Mill, *The Subjection of Women* in Alice S. Rossi (ed.), *Essays on Sex Equality* (University of Chicago Press, Chicago, 1970), p. 239.

116. Hobhouse, *Sociology and Philosophy*, p. 45; see also his *Social Development*, p. 87.

117. Hobhouse, *Sociology and Philosophy*, p. 311.

118. See Hobhouse, *Mind in Evolution*, p. 341, and his *Development and Purpose* (Macmillan, London, 1913), p. 170.

119. Dewey, *The Quest for Certainty* (Allen and Unwin, London, 1930), p. 267.

120. Bosanquet, *Psychology of the Moral Self*, p. 97.

121. Hobhouse, *Social Development*, p. 143.

122. Hobhouse, *The Rational Good*, p. 38; Bosanquet, *Psychology of the Moral Self*, p. 97. See Dewey, *Reconstruction in Philosophy*, enlarged edn (Beacon Press, Boston, 1948), p. 164. However, sometimes Bosanquet was prepared to commend such an overriding of the whole by a single element. See §III.D.

123. Mill, *On Liberty*, p. 261. Emphasis added.

124. Ibid., p. 263. Emphasis added. See also Mill's *Subjection of Women*, pp. 148-49. On the plant analogy in modern liberalism, see §IV.A.3.

125. Maurice Mandelbaum, *History, Man and Reason* (The Johns Hopkins Press, Baltimore, 1971), p. 204.

126. In addition to the references in note 7 of my Introductory, see Dewey's essays on: 'The Philosophy of Thomas Hill Green' and 'Green's Theory of the Moral Motive' in *The Early Works of John Dewey* (Southern Illinois University Press, Carbondale and Edwardsville, 1969), vol. III, pp. 14-35, 155-73; and his 'Self Realization and the Moral Ideal' in ibid., vol. IV, pp. 42-53. See also S. Morris Eames's 'Introduction' to ibid., vol. III, pp. xxvi-xxxi.

127. Green, *Prolegomena*, p. 414.

128. Bosanquet, *Individuality and Value*, p. 146.

129. This seems to be the typical claim of (idealist) coherence theories of truth: comprehensiveness is not treated as a second, independent feature of true theories but as in some sense derivative of coherence. See G.R. Morris, *Idealist Logic* (Macmillan, London, 1933), Ch. X. For Bosanquet's views on truth and coherence, see his *Logic*, vol. II, Ch. IX (Clarendon Press, Oxford, 1911).

130. Bosanquet, *Some Suggestions in Ethics*, p. 107.

131. Hobhouse, *Liberalism*, p. 69. Emphasis added.

132. Dewey, *Reconstruction in Philosophy*, p. 186. Emphasis added. For Dewey's views on self-realisation during his 'idealist period' see his *Psychology*, vol. 2 of *Early Works*, pp. 229-31, 318-19. For an analysis of self-realisation in Dewey's theory, see Robert J. Roth, *John Dewey and Self-Realization* (Prentice-Hall, Englewood Cliffs, N.J., 1962).

133. See Hobhouse, *The Rational Self*, p. 101, and Dewey, *Individualism*, p. 148.

134. Rawls, *A Theory of Justice*, p. 529.

135. Bosanquet, *The Philosophical Theory of the State*, p. 164. Compare Hobhouse, *The Rational Good*, p. 122.

136. Green, 'Value and Influence of Works of Fiction', p. 40.

137. Mill, 'Inaugural Address', in *Dissertations and Discussions*, vol. IV (William V. Spencer, Boston, 1868), p. 343.

138. Dewey, *Human Nature and Conduct*, p. 160; Bosanquet, *The Civilization of Christendom*, pp. 242-58.

139. Dewey, *Art as Experience*, p. 248. See also Bosanquet, *Essays and Addresses*, pp. 71-91.

140. 'Experience proves that there is no one study or pursuit, which practised to the exclusion of all others, does not narrow and pervert the mind.' Mill, 'Inaugural Address', p. 343. And, as Dewey makes perfectly clear, this applies even to art: 'No one is just an artist and nothing else, and in so far as one approximates that condition, he is so much the less developed human being: he is a kind of monstrosity.' *Democracy and Education*, p. 307.

141. Hobhouse, *Development and Purpose*, p. 199; *The Rational Good*, p. 98. See also Morris Ginsberg, 'The Work of L.T. Hobhouse' in J.A. Hobson and Morris Ginsberg (eds.). *L.T. Hobhouse: His Life and His Work* (Allen and Unwin, London, 1931), pp. 180-81; Hugh Carter, *The Social Theories of L.T. Hobhouse* (Kennikat, Port Washington, N.Y., 1927), p. 85.

142. See Green, *Prolegomena*, p. 340; 'Value and Influence of Works of Fiction', p. 27. Opinions differ as to just how central this is to Green's philosophy. In the same sentence in which he refers to repressing the baser elements of our nature, for example, he also mentions the possibility of transforming them, thus suggesting an aversion to mere repression. Ann Cacoullos's position again seems soundest, denying that Green's theory turns on a distinction between higher and lower selves, while still acknowledging that Green was convinced that some capacities ought not to be cultivated. *Thomas Hill Green*, Ch. 3. H.D. Lewis seems to take the opposition of passions and reason as more fundamental; *Freedom and History*, p. 43.

143. See Melvin Richter, *The Politics of Conscience: T.H. Green and his Age* (Weidenfeld and Nicolson, London, 1964), pp. 194-95, but see also pp. 108-14.

144. Mill, 'Nature' in *Collected Works*, vol. X, p. 397. See also Garforth, *Educative Democracy*, pp. 81-82.

145. Mill, *An Examination of Sir William Hamilton's Philosophy* in *Collected Works*, vol. IX, p. 453.

146. Mill, 'Utility of Religion' in *Collected Works*, vol. X, p. 409.

147. Dewey, *Democracy and Education*, pp. 116-17.

148. See Sidgwick, *Lectures on Green*, pp. 47-48. Arthur E. Murphy seems to argue that Dewey has no way to distinguish desirable from undesirable capacities and, in fact, does not even make the attempt. 'John Dewey and American Liberalism', *The Journal of Philosophy*, LVII (1960), pp. 427-28.

149. See Rawls, *A Theory of Justice*, p. 429.

150. See Dewey and Tufts, *Ethics*, pp. 272-77, 331-44. See also Robert L. Holmes, 'John Dewey's Social Ethics', *The Journal of Value Inquiry*, VII (1973), pp. 274-80.

151. Dewey, *Essential Writings*, p. 144. See K.W. Harrington, 'John Dewey's Ethics and the Classical Conception of Man', *DIOTIMA*, I (1973), pp. 125-48. David L. Norton discusses some related issues in Ch. 5 of his *Personal Destinies*.

152. Dewey, *Individualism*, p. 94; Dewey and Tufts, *Ethics*, p. 383.

153. Green, *Prolegomena*, pp. 184, 181.

154. Vinit Haksar, *Equality, Liberty, and Perfectionism* (Oxford University Press, Oxford, 1979), pp. 3-4. Haksar devotes a great deal of attention to Rawls's critique of perfectionism. See also David L. Norton, 'Rawls's Theory of Justice: A "Perfectionist" Rejoinder', *Ethics*, LXXXV (Oct. 1974), pp. 50-57. See Rawls, *A Theory of Justice*, pp. 325-32.

155. Zevedei Barbu, *Problems of Historical Psychology* (Routledge and Kegan Paul, London, 1960), pp. 62 ff.

156. Haksar, *Equality, Liberty, and Perfectionism*, p. 284.

157. I quoted in §C.1 a passage from Mill's essay on Bentham in which Mill advocates a man's pursuing spiritual perfection as an end; of desiring, for its own sake, the conformity of his own character to his standard of excellence' (*Collected Works*, vol. X, p. 95). F.W. Garforth notes that a similar passage occurs in an early edition of Mill's *Logic* (though it is not clear that Mill is actually advocating such a perfectionism there; *Collected Works*, vol. VIII, p. 1155). Alone, these passages might suggest the possibility of some sort of external standard perfectionism in Mill; conjoined with *Liberty* and *The Subjection of Women*, however, they rather suggest the importance of personal ideals in guiding one's own development. See Garforth, *Educative Democracy*, pp. 81-82.

158. Haksar, *Equality, Liberty, and Perfectionism*, p.4.

159. All this is clear in Milne's account of Green and Bosanquet. *The Social Philosophy of English Idealism*, Chs IV, VII.

## II  SOCIABILITY: SOCIAL LIFE

### A.  Individuality, Completion and Social Life

We saw in the previous chapter that, according to modern liberal theory, no individual develops all the potentialities of human nature. As Rawls says, it is a fundamental feature of humans that no one can do everything he is capable of nor is he capable of doing all things that humans can do. 'The potentialities of each individual are greater than those he can hope to realize; and they fall far short of the powers among men generally.'[1] Consequently, modern liberals have held that plans of life must select some capabilities for more intense cultivation, leaving others, to varying extents, underdeveloped. But, as Green realised, even though necessary, such specialisation and concentration tends to give rise to feelings of opportunities lost or developments forgone. To be sure, modern liberal emphasis on a general breadth of development may help alleviate some of these pangs of loss; but clearly, even at best, it is only a palliative. In a sense we remain incomplete: we are but a part of what we might be, and of what human nature has in itself to be. 'We have had to devote ourselves . . . to only a small part of what we might have done.'[2]

To achieve a more adequate completion of our natures liberals like Rawls have looked to social life. Because we develop in diverse directions, he argues, each of us manifests different aspects of human nature. Our developments are thus complementary: we can appreciate those excellences latent or absent in our nature as they are exhibited in the lives of others. 'It is as if others were bringing forth a part of ourselves that we have not been able to cultivate.'[3] To Hobhouse, this effort to achieve completion through others is a main root of all social life:

> In all but the lowest stages, the life of a species depends not only on the efforts of each individual to maintain himself, but on a certain unique relation between different individuals composing the species. At least as soon as distinction of sex appears, the individuals of a species begin to have a need of one another. *They are not complete each in himself, but need a complement, which they find in another individual possessing the same fundamental specific character developed with certain differences.* The most obvious and most per-

manent of this kind is that of sex, but in the highest orders this relationship takes a thousand different shapes.[4]

'The fundamental fact', Hobhouse says in another place, 'is that man needs society for the fulfilment of his own being.'[5] This notion of a drive to completion through social life obviously coheres well with Hobhouse's conception of practical reason as an impulse to harmonise, widen and deepen.[6] The connection between reason and social life is made even more explicit by Bosanquet, to whom 'logic' is 'the impulse towards unity and coherence . . . by which every fragment yearns towards the whole to which it belongs, and every self to its completion in the Absolute, and of which the Absolute itself is at once an incarnation and a satisfaction'.[7] On a more mundane level, this same impulse leads us to seek completion in the social whole which, in a way not so unlike Rawls, Bosanquet conceives as a co-operative endeavour for covering the ground of human nature.[8]

Rawls, Hobhouse and Bosanquet, then, quite clearly maintain that we look to others to complete our nature. (Green's argument that differences in personalities are necessary for the recognition of others as 'alter-egos' also suggests that we view a differently developed person as an 'other-I', and 'I' that I might have been but am not. See §I.B.) This idea of finding completion in others is the crucial conceptual link between the modern liberals' conception of individuality and their avowal of man's natural social interest, i.e. his interest in the lives of others. Because we are incomplete, absorption in our own individuality is not truly satisfying; we are driven outside ourselves, and take an interest and delight in the individuality of our fellows.

## B. Social Interest

In the *Prolegomena* Green argues that a 'distinctive social interest on our part is a primary fact':

> Now the self of which a man thus forecasts the fulfilment, is not an abstract or empty self. It is a self already affected in the most primitive forms of human life by manifold interests, among which are interests in other persons. These are not merely interests dependent on other persons for the means to their gratification, but interests in the good of those other persons, interests which cannot be satisfied without the consciousness that those other persons are satis-

fied. The man cannot contemplate himself as in a better state, or on the way to the best, without contemplating others, not merely as a means to that better state, but as sharing it with him.[9]

Green's notion of a 'social interest' is complex, being composed of at least three claims. According to Green, we are interested in each other as persons because (i) we are aware that, like us, others are capable of pursuing self-satisfaction and (ii) we ourselves find satisfaction 'in procuring . . . the self-satisfaction of the other'.[10] Moreover, (iii) Green maintains that this is, or it leads to, an interest in the good of others. The first claim concerns recognition of others as persons, the second involves an interest in their satisfaction and the third an interest in their good. In the next two subsections I explore what Green and other modern liberals have meant by having an interest in the development or satisfaction of others (claim ii) while §B.3 considers to what extent, if any, this is, or implies, an interest in their good. The first claim, that we recognise others as persons similar to ourselves, is discussed in §B.2.

### B.1. Our Social Nature and Private Society

As Green indicates, the sort of social interest with which he is concerned is distinct from an interest we might have in others merely as a means to our gratification. This is precisely the distinction Solomon E. Asch makes when analysing 'social interest' in his *Social Psychology*.[11] Asch begins his analysis by depicting what he calls 'the "private property" theory of society', according to which individuals enter into social relations only to meet their egoistic needs. Because each possesses different skills and resources, exchanges will be mutually beneficial. We will thus have interest in others, but only as means to the satisfaction of these narrowly self-centred needs. Although Asch acknowledges that this picture captures some important features of social life, he insists that it overlooks the intrinsic interest we have in the lives of others and the need to share experiences with them. Human relations, he thus argues, are directly of intense interest to us, not merely of derivative interest as means to egoistic gratification. Remarkably, Rawls draws very nearly the identical contrast. 'The social nature of mankind', he tells us, 'is best seen by contrast with the conception of private society.'[12] He proceeds to describe a conception of the social order that, for all intents and purposes, is Asch's ' "private property" theory of society'. Again agreeing with Asch, Rawls rejects such a social order as being inadequate to human nature. 'We need one another as partners in ways of

life that are engaged in for their own sake, and the successes and enjoyments of others are necessary for and complimentary [*sic*] to our
own good.'[13]

The market model of society, then, is seen as essentially flawed as
it ignores the intrinsic interest we have in each other's lives. It assumes,
at least as the modern liberal sees it, a conception of human nature
according to which each is absorbed in his own life and unappreciative
of others. (However, see §VII.A.2.) To Bosanquet, such characteristics
are the marks of 'stupidity', being 'irresponsive . . . insensitive, unappreciative, unadaptive'.[14] In *Utilitarianism* Mill took pains to argue that
such a self-centred life was not ultimately satisfying. The 'selfish egotist,
devoid of every feeling or care but those that centre on his own miserable individuality', he maintains, is likely to find life dull and happiness
transitory. 'When people who are tolerably fortunate in their outward
lot do not find in life sufficient enjoyment to make it valuable to them,
the cause generally is, caring for nobody but themselves.'[15] Mill's remedy
for self-absorption is complicated, including private affections and a
concern with the public good, but to a great extent, he recommends a
cultivated intellect capable of taking an interest in things outside oneself, 'in the objects of nature, the achievements of art, the imaginations
of poetry, the incidents of history, the ways of mankind past and present, and their prospects in the future'.[16] While Mill does not clearly
distinguish here a distinctive social interest from a general interest in
the world about one or from communitarian sentiments (see §III.C),
an interest in the lives and accomplishments of others is obviously central to his prescription. And in another place Mill quite clearly identifies
a distinctive social interest, saying that 'a great part of the interest of
human life' derives from the 'multiform development of human nature'
which manifests itself in the unlikenesses of tastes, talents and points of
view.[17] In what almost seems a paraphrase of Mill's argument in *Utilitarianism*, Dewey unambiguously focuses on the central role of social
interest in securing an enduring happiness. 'No amount of outer
obstacles', he writes, 'can destroy the happiness that comes from a
lively and ever-renewed interest in others and in the conditions and
objects which promote their development.' Such interests, Dewey goes
on to say, to some extent flourish in all who have not somehow been
warped, and 'their exercise brings happiness because it fulfils the self'.[18]
Indeed, to Dewey, the mutual enriching of our lives through our differences 'is inherent in the democratic . . . way of life'.[19]

## B.2. Extensions and Complications

At its most basic, then, social interest involves an appreciation of, and a delight in, each other's excellences. It is, however, a notion that lends itself to extensions, has undergone modifications, and rests on important presuppositions. Our account of social interest thus requires elaboration by considering several such complicating points.

(i)    In Asch's description of social interest, it concerns not only an interest in our fellows' lives, but a need or desire to *share* experiences with them. Of course to some extent, sharing is a necessary part of social interest: if I appreciate the development of another it can be said that we are sharing the enjoyment of his capacities. This in fact seems to be the sense behind Bosanquet's (and Green's) notion that human achievements are 'goods which are not diminished by sharing'.[20] One sometimes feels that for Bosanquet we are sharing with others in the full sense of the term when we appreciate a great poem or painting, thereby sharing the values embedded in the creator's achievement. Yet 'sharing' has overtones of a more active sort of coming together. When Dewey, for example, tells us that 'one of the elements of human nature that is often discounted in both idea and practice is the satis-faction derived from a sense of sharing in creative activities',[21] he clearly has in mind a sense of participation in a common endeavour. Rawls's idea that 'we need one another as partners'[22] also suggests, I think, a more active understanding of sharing than is entailed simply by mutual appreciation.

(ii)    Hobhouse's theory of social interest places even more weight upon an active coming together. At the heart of his social psychology is the fundamental need of humans to interact. 'What we imperiously need, like our daily bread, is to be in relation with others.'[23] At the bottom of this need, as he explains it, is our craving for a response from others. 'Without others, nine out of ten of our own activities and emo-tions are incomplete because lacking response . . . Our emotions crave response, and as they crave response, so also on the whole do they respond.'[24] To Hobhouse, this is the root of our social interest. Our craving for response drives us into social relations of various sorts, and regardless of our motives and aims, we retain an intense interest in the interactions, 'and therefore by a logical implication' in those with whom we interact.[25] Thus, Hobhouse concludes, we have a natural interest in social life and the social structure.

In one respect, then, Hobhouse has the most developed theory of social interest of any modern liberal, giving it pride of place in his social psychology. Yet, in another way his account of social interest seems to fall short of that of most other modern liberals. For although he stresses our interest in the lives of others, he does not much emphasise our interest in their development or 'perfection'. As Hobhouse makes very clear, the former sort of social interest implies only that '[t]he solitary life is, for all but the most exceptional of individuals, the least tolerable of all. We choose ... "to dwell in a midst of alarms" rather than to reign in a horrible place of solitude.' Consequently, '[t]hose who we hate are preferable as companions to the desert and the seas.'[26] The obvious difficulty is that such a social interest is satisfied by adversary as well as co-operative, mutually appreciative relations.[27] This is not to say that we cannot find traces of a 'Greenian' conception of social interest in Hobhouse. His understanding of social life as founded upon an urge to complete our nature, his implicit agreement with Mill and Dewey that happiness requires an interest in things beyond oneself, especially in other personalities, and his description of society as a 'social union of personalities' all, I think, suggest a 'traditional' modern liberal conception of social interest.[28] What is puzzling is that Hobhouse is so explicit about our natural interest in others but so sketchy, relatively speaking, about our interest in their development.

The reason for this sketchiness is not hard to find. Although for Hobhouse a craving for response is the most fundamental social feeling, he believes that social interest naturally gives rise to feelings of affection and sympathy.[29] I will argue in the next chapter that 'sympathy' in particular implies a tighter or more intense form of bond between persons than does mere social interest. Whereas social interest leads to a mutually appreciative social life, sympathy suggests communal bonding and fellow feeling. Now like Mill,[30] Hobhouse concentrates on sympathetic social feelings when arguing that satisfaction of our own nature requires the development of our fellows. To see this, consider his notion of our drive to a 'double harmony'.[31] The first harmony at which we aim, as we saw in Chapter I, is a harmonious development of our individual capacities. Hobhouse calls this the principle of 'Personality'. But, he adds, that is not sufficient. Harmony also demands that development of one individual promotes that of the rest. This he calls, revealingly, the principle of 'Love'.[32] Without doubt, Hobhouse believes that both harmonies are required by practical reason: as a drive to integration and coherence, reason impels us not only to harmonise our individual personality but also to seek harmony between ourselves and our fellows. But our desire for this second harmony — the principle of 'Love' — is, Hobhouse clearly thinks, rooted in social psychology and, specifically, in our basic impulse to interact with others, which naturally develops into sympathy. If we have any social feeling in us at all, he says in one place, it will be impossible to develop a harmonious personality if it is in conflict with the development of one's neighbour's personality.[33] The seeds of disharmony will be sown by the failure to satisfy one's sympathetic social feelings in a coherent scheme of living.

In sum, then, although Hobhouse evinces a clear understanding of social interest, he does not for the most part directly draw upon it to show that the development of others is necessary to our growth. Rather, like Mill, he largely relies on a notion of sympathy according to which we desire the good or welfare of our fellows with whom we feel at 'one' and, consequently, a side of us remains unsatisfied if our development and theirs are in conflict. The root of Hobhouse's account is our natural social interest, but he develops and extends it before ultimately supporting Green's conclusion that the satisfaction of our nature requires a consciousness that our fellows are also developing.

(iii)   In his *Discourse on the Origin and Foundations of Inequality Among Men*, Rousseau argues that the appreciation of others leads to a desire that we, in turn, be appreciated by them. According to Rousseau's account, with the rise of social life, '[e]ach one began to look at the others and to want to be looked at himself, and public esteem had a value'.[34] And thus arose the demands for civility and respect: 'As soon as men had begun to appreciate one another, and the idea of consideration was formed in their minds, each one claimed a right to it, and it was no longer possible to be disrespectful toward anyone with impunity.'[35] A similar dynamic is operative in Rawls's theory. As Rawls sees it, a sense of self-esteem depends upon having a satisfying plan of life and 'finding our person and deeds appreciated and confirmed by others who are likewise esteemed and their association enjoyed'.[36] We need, then, to be appreciated by those whom we appreciate: in Rousseau's words, public esteem is valued. Though no other modern liberal comes quite so close as does Rawls to Rousseau's position, Hobhouse's assertion that the 'approbation and respect of our fellows [is] one of the most pervasive of human motives'[37] easily connects with his emphasis on our craving for response from others and the interest we take in their doings. More generally, it would seem that some sort of concern with one's standing in the eyes of one's fellows is a very plausible and natural, though not logical, consequence of a social interest.

(iv)   It might be, of course, that one treats others simply as interesting objects and it never occurs to you that these 'interesting' objects are essentially beings like oneself and, consequently, that they might also appreciate you. If this were the case, 'public esteem' obviously could not be a concern to you. But this is not the modern liberal position: our social interest is an interest in other *persons*. We have already seen that this is an explicit element of Green's formulation. Following Hegel,[38] Green (as well as Bosanquet) emphasises that fundamental to interaction among distinctive individualities is a mutual recognition of each other as personalities, 'of an "I" by a "Thou" and a "Thou" by an "I" ', a mutual recognition upon which self-consciousness is held to rest.[39] Although the Hegelian account of the origin of self-consciousness is not itself an essential part of the modern liberal theory of man, underlying the doctrine of social interest is the supposition that social interest is an interest in personalities recognised as akin to our own. To be sure, individual natures differ, but all are manifestations of a common human nature (§I.C.3). Hence, we do not view our fellows as objects of interest in the way we do waterfalls or mountains, but, in Green's words, as 'alter-egos'.[40]

## B.3. Interest in the Good of Others

Green, it will be recalled, not only asserted an interest in others as a 'primary fact', but he also insisted that we have an interest in the good of others: 'These are not merely interests dependent on other persons for the means to their gratification, but interests in the good of those other persons, interests which cannot be satisfied without the consciousness that those other persons are satisfied.'[41] As Green presents our natural social interest as the foundation of his theory of the common good, it is not surprising that it has been one of the most widely analysed and criticised aspects of his work. Sidgwick, for example, argued that it was the basis of an attempt by Green to show that the good of others is identical with ours, a position that Sidgwick could not see 'justified by anything that we know of the essential sociality of ordinary human beings'.[42] Prichard's criticism was far more radical: because Green thinks we desire the satisfaction of others in precisely the same way as we desire our own satisfaction, he must believe that we treat the satisfactions of others as if they were our own. The upshot of this, says Prichard, is that 'we' become identical with 'them'. Hence 'where a group of, say, five persons are disinterestedly interested in one another, they are not really five persons but one, a state of $A$ being related to a state of another, $B$, just as it is related to another state of $A$ — these states being states of one self'.[43]

The first step in evaluating Green's argument is to distinguish two senses of 'having an interest in something' that he does not seem to always clearly separate.[44] (i) To have an interest in football or poetry may be to find them interesting; when we find something interesting, we generally pay attention to it, enjoy it, appreciate it, etc. Those interesting things that have enduring interest for us, or have a central place in our scheme of life, we often elevate by describing them as 'one of our interests'. We might, for example, find observing passers-by interesting, but normally such observing would not be deemed one of our interests. Although pursuing our interests may not be interesting at every moment (we may have an interest in writing books but be bored by proofreading), our enduring interests are generally interesting. (ii) In contrast, when we say that we have an interest, for example, in lower taxes, higher property values or efficient public transport, we generally mean that they promote our enduring aims or goals, or are means to get what we want, need, etc. In this second sense, we have an interest in everything that furthers our good. Now the basic sense of social interest concerns the *first* sort of interest. To say we have an interest in our fellows' lives means, first and foremost, that we find them interesting, absorbing, etc. When Green, for example, tells us that the self to be fulfilled is not abstract or empty but, rather, enter-tains many interests 'among which are interests in other persons',[45] he seems to be referring to enduring interests in the first sense; interests in the second sense presupposes goals and aims, they do not con-stitute them. However, given this fundamental and enduring interest (in the first sense) in others, it seems we can also say that we have an interest in their development in the second sense too; i.e. their develop-ment is conducive to the satisfaction of our enduring interest in appre-ciating others' excellences.

In what sense (if any), then, do we have an interest in their good? If, like Green, we (i) define a person's good in terms of his self-satisfaction and (ii), hold that self-satisfaction is to be found in the development of one's faculties, then one's good equals the development of one's nature. And, since we have already seen that we have 'an interest in' the devel-opment of others' natures (in both senses), we must also have an in-terest in their good (in both senses). Things change, though, if we take a wider conception of another's good. If instead of equating 'good' with 'development' we expand it to include general welfare, happiness etc.,[46] it may well be that some elements of a person's good (e.g. his robust health) we do not find at all interesting. Nevertheless, if some element of his good which we do not find particularly interesting is a condition for his fuller development, as is plausibly the case with robust health, we could still have an interest in it in the second sense. For it would be something conducive to one of our enduring aims, i.e. his development. So, to the extent that aspects of a person's good contribute to his development, we can be said to have an interest (in the second sense) in them. Thus, only if some elements of his good do not at all further his development could we be said to have no interest (in the second sense) whatsoever in them.

Sidgwick thought that such an argument could go 'a certain way' towards showing that the good of humanity is my good, 'but it has not necessarily any force or tendency to carry me the rest of the way'.[47] Sidgwick believed that our interest in our own perfection was much stronger than the corresponding interest in others, especially those to whom we are not bound by ties of sympathy. Should promoting the two conflict, he clearly thought that the weighing of reasons would favour sacrificing the development of others to promote our own. One is tempted to say that Sidgwick has missed the main point of Green's argument here; our fullest possible development, Green and all our other modern liberals have argued, cannot be achieved without a corresponding growth of others. Not only does satisfaction of our social interest demand developed companions, but we shall see presently (§C.1) that the fullest growth of our own individuality also demands it. Yet, ultimately, Sidgwick is right in concluding that these arguments do not carry us all the way to identifying our own good with that of others. Granted that our fullest development calls for the growth of others too, if nevertheless we are forced to choose between partial developments, it would seem that we would lose less by sacrificing the development of some others to our own (assuming that many remain for us to appreciate) than vice versa. To some extent, communitarian sentiments will add to the reasons supporting 'self-sacrifice' (§III.D), but we still may question whether they will outweigh the more selfish course.

In contrast to Sidgwick's, Prichard's criticism does not seem at all compelling. According to Prichard, Green is caught in a dilemma: either (i) he holds that we are 'disinterestedly' interested in another – i.e. we simply desire his satisfaction the way we do our own – in which case we obliterate the distinction between persons, or (ii) he admits that we are interested in another as a means to the satisfaction of our own nature, in which case our interest is no longer 'disinterested'. Prichard thinks that because Green is committed to the 'disinterestedness' of our interest in others he must opt for (i), thereby denying the distinction between persons.[48] This seems mistaken. Green's reference to 'disinterestedness' is merely another way of pointing out that our interest in others is not instrumental in any meaningful sense: we are not interested in them in order to achieve pleasure, satisfaction or any other end, but simply because we are interested in them. Our satisfaction, to be sure, requires the 'consciousness that those other persons are satisfied' but Green is adamant in maintaining that we are not interested in them *as* a means to our satisfaction; it is because we have an interest in them that we find their satisfaction satisfying. But this certainly does not collapse the distinction between selves: indeed the satisfaction of our social interest requires the consciousness that other selves be satisfied. Our satisfaction thus depends upon the awareness of other persons conjoined with a belief that they are satisfied. Their status as (at least partially) independent centres of satisfaction is essential to our social interest (see §D.2).

## C. Individuality and Social Life

### C.1. *The Mutual Stimulation Argument*

All modern liberals thus proffer some variant of the argument from social interest. The extent to which they develop and rely upon it, however, varies. It is most well developed and important in Green's and Rawls's theories of social life and probably only nascent in Mill's thinking. Some, like Dewey, Hobhouse and Bosanquet, also put forward a different sort of argument that supports the same conclusion: i.e. that our own satisfaction requires that of our fellows. Besides postulating a distinctive social interest, these modern liberals are apt to uphold the importance of social life by pointing to the way in which social life encourages individuality. Wrote Hobhouse:

> The social phenomenon, in short, is not something which occurs in one individual or even in several individuals taken severally. It is essentially an interaction of individuals, and as the capabilities of any given individual are extraordinarily various and are only called out, each by appropriate circumstances, it will be readily seen that the nature of the interaction may itself bring forth new and perhaps unexpected capacities, and elicit from the individual contributing to it forces which, but for this particular opportunity, might possibly remain forever dormant.[49]

Dewey was especially concerned to show that social interaction stimulates our individual development: 'Lack of free and equitable intercourse which springs from a variety of shared interests makes intellectual stimulation unbalanced. Diversity of stimulation means novelty, and novelty means challenge to thought.'[50]   And all that, he adds, means the 'liberation of powers'. Besides stimulation, social intercourse expands our experience and, so, is educational. A participant in genuine intercourse, Dewey and Tufts argue, learns, even if his ideas are largely confirmed, since, to the extent to which genuine give and take occurs, they are 'deepened and extended in meaning'. There is, in short, the 'enlargement of experience' and the 'growth of capacity'.[51]

When Dewey criticised the 'early liberalism' for postulating abstract, ready-made individuals, one of the things he had in mind was its (supposed) abstraction of individuality from social relations. Even in pioneer days, Dewey insists, the growth of individual powers was firmly rooted in, and supported by, neighbourliness and social intercourse.[52] The challenge of the present, as Dewey articulates it in *Individualism – Old and New*, is thus to discover a mode of social life that provides a foundation and orientation for individuality under the condition of twentieth-century urbanisation and industrialisation. Dewey's general criticism of the 'early liberalism' is focused by Bosanquet on Mill. We saw in the last chapter (§ I.A) that Bosanquet ascribes to Mill an essentially 'negative' or 'formal' conception of individuality. An upshot of this conception, Bosanquet believes, is that Mill conceives of individuality as an essentially private affair: it 'is not nourished and evoked by the varied play of relations and obligations in society, but lies in a sort of inner self, to be cherished by enclosing it'.[53] Although one can understand how some parts of *Liberty* might be read to support such a view, it is surely not Mill's. We have already seen (§ II.B.1) that, like all other modern liberals, Mill deplores an absorption in one's own 'miserable individuality', so the tale of the 'inner self, to be cherished by enclosing it' already looks doubtful. But that is just one side of the relation between personality and social life: not only did Mill believe that the properly developed individual took an interest in his fellows, but he also saw that the play of social relations elicited our powers. On a quick reading of Mill, again especially *On Liberty*, this may not seem obvious. For example, Mill's description of 'human nature' as 'a tree, which requires to grow and develope [*sic*] itself on all sides, according to the tendency of the inward forces which make it a living thing', seems to suggest that only 'room to grow', i.e. non-interference, is required to develop individuality.[54] We shall see in Chapter IV (§ A.3), however, that this 'plant theory' of human development (which looms so large in *Liberty*) does not imply that simple non-interference is sufficient to produce healthy growth. Rather, it implies an 'interactionist' view according to which the original nature of the individual requires a supportive environment if a healthy development is to occur. Seen in this light, Mill's concern with reforming industrial conditions is consistent with *Liberty* (at least theoretically, if not always in spirit). His chapter on the 'Probable Futurity of the Labouring Classes' in his *Principles of Political Economy* is informed by the belief that some types of social relations and institutions are more apt to elicit natural individual powers and capacities than others. As Mill saw it, if industrial relations were not based upon dependence and hierarchy but were infused with a spirit of interdependence, equality and co-operative decision making, workers would grow into self-directing, intelligent, developed individuals (§VII.D). And, as we shall see in Chapter VI, similar sorts of arguments are offered by Mill to endorse co-operative, mutually enriching political institutions.

When narrowly interpreted, the 'argument from stimulation' does not necessarily lead to an interest in the fullest possible development of others, but only a concern that they be human enough to engage in intercourse. It is not hard to see, though, how it might be extended to provide for the former sort of interest too. By developing our own nature, as Hobhouse saw, we might 'stimulate and assist the similar development of others'.[55] And, of course, this means that the development of others will have similar effects on our personalities: as Dewey argued, among developed persons relations are mutually enriching. 'Each contributes something distinctive from his own store of knowledge, ability, taste, while receiving at the same time elements of value contributed by others.'[56] On this view, then, mediocrity and lack of genuine individuality in our associates would be numbing to our own development. 'Conformity is a name for the absence of vital interplay; the arrest and benumbing of communication', wrote Dewey.[57]

## C.2. Other Senses of Sociability

In introducing his discussion of our social interest, Rawls cautions us against understanding the 'sociality of human beings . . . in a trivial fashion'. Human sociality, he insists, does not mean simply that humans would perish outside societies or that by living in a society we acquire interests and needs that lead us to co-operate for mutual advantage. 'Nor is it expressed by the truism that social life is a condition for our developing the ability to speak and think, and to take part in the common activities of society and culture.'[58] Rawls is not saying that these are trivial facts, but rather that they provide only a trivial understanding of our social nature. Leaving aside the claim of triviality, however, it is indeed important for us to clearly distinguish assertions of man's social nature premised on such observations from those arising from our social interest and stimulation by the growth of others. For, unlike Rawls, other modern liberals have sometimes made a great deal of our 'social nature' in the former (i.e. Rawls's trivial) sense. Dewey in particular was prone to criticise early liberalism or rugged individualism by insisting '[s]ocial ties and connections are as natural and inevitable as are physical. Even when a person is alone he thinks with language that is derived from association with others, and thinks about questions and issues that have been born in intercourse.'[59] 'Indeed', Hobhouse wrote, as if continuing Dewey's thought, 'the sum-total of all the social relationships in which a man stands must be regarded as so deeply affecting his whole nature that, if we suppose them all cancelled, it may be doubted whether he could still be called human.'[60]

Such arguments, while important in their own right, are not of direct concern here. However, one of Rawls's 'trivial' understandings of sociability requires some attention as it has sometimes been thought to have implications inconsistent with my thesis. According to Green, one of the reasons that personality can only become actualised in a social order is that society provides the individual with the essentials of his self-conception, i.e. it 'supplies all the higher content to this conception, all those objects of a man's personal interest, in living for which he lives for his own satisfaction, except such as are derived from the merely animal nature'.[61] On the face of it this might seem inconsistent with a unique natures conception of individuality:[62] if our interests are supplied by 'society', how can individuality be a development of one's unique nature? On reflection, it seems, pretty easily. To say that we have unique natures, the development of which constitutes individuality, is not to assert that our interests and goals are latent in us at birth. As Rawls notes, 'It has always been recognized that the social system shapes the desires and aspirations of its members; it determines in large part the kind of persons they want to be as well as the kind of persons they are.'[63] This is certainly not to deny, though, that our diverse natures provide the basis of different responses and adjustments to any given social system. Depending upon our nature, some of the options and possible interests will be more appealing than others. And in a very restrictive system, it might be that none of the available options satisfies our nature. In any event, it is important to realise that a unique (or diverse) natures conception of individuality does not commit one to the untenable position that 'one will be what one has it in one to be' regardless of the social environment. (See §IV.A.)

## D. The Organic Conception of Social Life

Conceptualising society as an organism of some sort is a mark of not only Hegelian-idealist theories[64] but of most of the 'new liberals' (e.g. Ritchie, Hobson).[65] With respect to our six modern liberals, Hobhouse and Bosanquet extensively employed the metaphor. It forms the basis of a great deal of Green's writings and, if nothing else, was an important influence on Dewey's thought.[66] Mill and Rawls, coming respectively before and after the long run of organic thinking in liberal political theory, do not, so far as I know, explicitly employ the metaphor, but, as we have seen, it has been said by Wolff and others to be implicit in Rawls[67] and, at least according to Hobhouse, Mill was working towards an organic conception of society.[68] Clearly, then, the organic analogy is an important aspect of the modern liberal theory of social life. It is also, I think, an extremely complex idea, usually involving a psychology, an epistemology, a sociological method, an ontology − indeed what we might call an entire 'social metaphysics'.[69] And as we shall see in the next chapter, it enters into theories of community as well as those concerning social life. My aim here, however, is not to explore the organic metaphor in all its complexity, but to see just how much of it relates to the theory of social life that I have been examining in this chapter.

### D.1. Mutually Dependent Growth

Not surprisingly, liberals (both 'new' and otherwise) who employ the analogy exhibit considerable disagreement as to just what it implies. According to Michael Freeden, Hobhouse, for example, 'restricted himself to the limited idea of organism as denoting interdependence of the people constituting a society'.[70] In support of this interpretation, Freeden directs us to the following passage:

> To speak of society as if it were a physical organism is a piece of mysticism, if indeed it is not quite meaningless. But the life of a society and the life of an individual do resemble one another in certain respects, and the term "organic" is as justly applicable to the one as to the other. For an organism is a whole consisting of interdependent parts. Each part lives and functions and grows by subserving the life of the whole. It sustains the rest and is sustained by them, and through their mutual support comes a common development. And this is how we would conceive the life of man in society in so far as it is harmonious.[71]

Hobhouse thus means to assert more than mere interdependence by using the organic analogy.[72] Indeed, he explicitly contrasts organic and non-organic interdependence, arguing that the latter involves a more intimate sort of relation in which the elements depend on each other for continued growth and activity.[73] In essence, in these (later) elaborations of the organic model Hobhouse does not seem to depart from his earlier, more obviously idealist, view, according to which 'the true conception of an organic society is one in which the best life of each man is and is felt to be bound up with his fellow-citizens'.[74]

A consequence of this sort of organic interdependence is, to use Green's language, that human perfection is non-competitive. In the *Prolegomena*, Green stresses that the interest 'in the perfecting of man or the realisation of the powers of the human soul' is a common interest in the proper sense — 'in the sense, namely, that there can be no competition for its attainment between man and man'.[75] A similar claim lies at the heart of Bosanquet's 'goods which are not diminished by sharing' and informs both Dewey's and Hobhouse's understandings of a common good.[76] It is not hard to see how a belief that development is non-competitive relates to the theories of social interest and mutual stimulation of individualities as well as to Hobhouse's notion of a drive to harmony. A consequence of these doctrines is that the satisfaction of our nature demands that our associates be likewise developed: their growth and satisfaction contributes to ours and vice versa. Hence, Green concluded that an individual's own perfection, i.e. the full satisfaction of his nature, necessarily 'will involve the idea of a perfection of all other beings, so far as he finds the thought of their being perfect necessary to his own satisfaction'.[77]

Green's claim of the non-competitive nature of perfection is obviously problematic. If, like Sidgwick, we focus on the material prerequisites of development, it is not hard to show that a good measure of competition will remain 'so long as the material conditions of human existence remain at all the same as they are now'.[78] But if we refrain from pressing it too hard, it does contain a valuable insight. In the *Second Discourse* Rousseau depicts a sort of social man whose ideal of individual excellence is, first and foremost, competitive. To excel is to outshine one's fellows: all are engaged in a zero-sum game in which winners gain eminence and the losers are eclipsed. And so they are jealous of each other's accomplishments. If we contrast the modern liberal conceptions of individuality and social life to those sorts of men, we can see the point of Green's claim of non-competitive development: other things being equal, the excellence of another does not detract from, but rather adds to, the richness of one's own existence.[79]

However, Sidgwick's resolutely practical line of criticism does alert us to an important bias in the modern liberal model of social life, viz. that it tends to focus on the co-operative and harmonious aspects of society while minimising conflicts of interest and goals that permeate social life.[80] A bias towards harmony and co-operation, in fact, seems intrinsic to the organic metaphor; the very idea of an organism suggests a co-operative and mutually enriching organisation supporting a common life.[81] This is not to say that modern liberals entirely ignore conflict and competition, much less that they positively assert their absence. Hobhouse, Dewey and Rawls, for example, are all certainly cognizant of conflict.[82] And both Mill's and Bosanquet's misgivings about some forms of socialism at least partially stemmed from what they saw as misguided attempts to entirely eradicate competition among individuals.[83] Nevertheless, on the whole the modern liberal outlook stresses harmony and co-operation over conflict and competition.[84] 'To say that all past historic progress has been the result of co-operation and not conflict', Dewey said, 'would be an exaggeration. But exaggeration against exaggeration, it is the more reasonable of the two' (i.e. than the opposite exaggeration).[85]

## D.2. Mutual Completion

'A thing that is dependent upon another', Hobhouse once wrote, 'is, of course, incomplete in itself.'[86] As we saw at the outset of this chapter, it is our incompleteness as solitary individuals that provides the foundation for the modern liberal analysis of social life; it is also a basic premise of the organic analogy. To compare society to an organism is not merely to stress that the parts are dependent on each other for growth, but that the parts are differentiated, their natures and excellences complementing and completing each other. Bosanquet was particularly insistent that a 'true co-operative structure is never characterised by repetition, but always by identity in difference; it is the relation not of a screw to an exactly similar screw, but of the screw to the nut into which it fastens.'[87] Leaving aside the switch from organic to mechanical metaphors (to which Bosanquet was particularly prone), the important point is that the interdependence of social life is characterised by intermeshing differences: hence the point of Bosanquet and Hobhouse's dictum that 'it takes all sorts to make a world'.[88] (The oft-voiced charge that organic theories are hostile to individuality usually overlooks this stress on diversity over uniformity; to the extent that it truly does take all sorts to make a world, there is every reason for organicists like

Bosanquet and Hobhouse to endorse diverse individual development.)[89]

Now if, in a social organism, people complete and supplement each other, the separateness of persons is, in a sense, mitigated. To see the lives of others as exploring latent parts of one's own nature or to see their lives as completing one's own, is to connect individual lives in a way that begins to blur the boundaries between personalities. This, I think, is the valid insight behind Prichard's argument that Green's theory of social interest results in the fusing of many persons into one (§B.3). However, as I argued earlier, Green need not, and does not, go as far along the path to 'fusion' as Prichard would have us believe. Modern liberals, and Green is certainly not an exception, are concerned not with the satisfaction of separate capacities but of individual natures 'as a whole' (§I.D). This being so, the delight we take in the satisfaction of 'others' is not just a delight in the realisation of their separate capacities but in the development of their organised individualities as well. And such delight presupposes the existence of other persons, not just other capacities. Nevertheless, it does seem true that the radical and unqualified separateness of persons is not a bedrock principle of modern liberalism.[90] If anything, I would suspect that most modern liberals would be apt to deny it as resting on an inadequate, i.e. overly individualistic, conception of society.

One may justifiably think, however, that Bosanquet does go too far in this direction and altogether obliterates the distinction between persons. In *The Philosophical Theory of the State*, for example, he asserts that

> there seems little reason to distinguish the correlation of dispositions within the one person from the correlation of the same dispositions if dispersed among different persons. If I am my own gardener, or my own critic, or my own doctor, does the relation of the answering dispositions within my being differ absolutely and altogether from what takes place when gardener and master, critic and author, patient and doctor, are different persons?[91]

And so he concludes that 'we shall find it very hard to establish a difference of principle between the unity of what we call one mind and that of all the "minds" which enter into a single social experience.'[92] One can well understand Hobhouse's reaction to such a theory: 'Common sense confronted by these statements has a feeling of outrage which makes it disinclined to argue.'[93] But given the apparently outrageous nature of the claim, it would do well to pause to ask whether Bosanquet was meaning to say outrageous things.[94] Not surprisingly, his position is less outrageous than it first appears. To begin with, it is clear that he never denies 'the formal distinctness of selves'.[95] '[U]nder normal conditions and *par excellence*', he says, the 'structure and conditions of the unity of a single mind' are straightforward. 'They are nothing mysterious, but just what they are; a continuity of interest and identity of content and quality maintained in ways which are analysed by psychology.' Consequently there is normally no doubt 'as to where one self ends and another begins, and no suggestion that selfhood is a trivial thing.'[96] Indeed, a 'plurality of human beings is necessary to cover the ground . . . which human nature is capable of covering.'[97]

We need to start, then, by realising that Bosanquet does not intend to deny the existence or importance of particular minds. His concern is with providing an account of how selves are organised and related to one another. Although, as we have seen, he often relies on metaphors (e.g. screws and nuts), he also offers a more formal and sophisticated theory premised on the notion of an 'appercipient mass'.[98] In his lectures on psychology Bosanquet tells us that the contents of the mind are organised into various groups which are 'technically known as Appercipient masses or systems . . . Appercipient masses are the ideas which are more or less dominant *pro tem.* and they will vary in prominence according to the interest before the mind, whether this interest be internally or externally originated.'[99] Bosanquet argues that in persons sharing common experiences, i.e. members of a community (see §III.B.1), the leading ideas of one individual's mind will be related to the dominant ideas of his fellows. 'So that the common life shared by the members of a community involves a common element in their ideas, not merely in their notions of things about them, though this is very important, but more especially in the dominant or organizing ideas which rule their minds.'[100] That is, according to Bosanquet, the appercipient systems that form the content of individual minds are themselves knit together in a system and share important common features. It is in this sense that a community has a 'common mind or will', viz. that 'their minds are similarly or correlatively organised'.[101]

This is the psychological basis of Bosanquet's oft-commented-upon idea that a society is a 'macrocosm constituted by microcosms'[102] or a world constituted of worlds. The point of both depictions is that social life is a systematisation of systematised selves. Likewise, this psychological theory is the foundation of Bosanquet's conclusion — with which we began this discussion — that we will find it very hard to establish a difference in principle between personal and social psychic organisation.

Notice that he does not deny the existence of 'individual' minds (given that the macrocosm of social life is based upon microcosms, he cannot) rather, he asserts that the organisation of the 'common mind' is of the same sort. It is absolutely essential to grasp that Bosanquet is concerned with a similarity of principle between individual and social psychic organisation, not with denying the existence of the former.[103] Hence, when he implies that there seems little reason to distinguish the correlation of dispositions when (a) Jones is both an author and critic and when (b) Jones is the author but Smith is the critic, Bosanquet need not be taken as arguing that no significant difference exists between the state of affairs characterised by (a) and (b). To argue that would run directly counter to the modern liberal doctrine that capacities ought not to be cultivated in isolation from one another but, rather, should relate to and colour each other. Jones's plan of life ought to be very different depending on whether or not he is both an author and critic (§I.D.3). But Bosanquet does not take this radical position; he holds only that our response to others' capacities and talents does not 'differ absolutely and altogether' from the way in which we organise our own. Interpersonal, as well as intrapersonal, talents and capacities relate to and colour each other. In sum, then, J.H. Muirhead seems quite right in concluding that Bosanquet's position 'need not be interpreted as by its critics *in sensum deteriorem* of denying the difference of individual personalities'.[104]

To sum up: at the heart of the organic description of society are the claims that (i) the personal developments of members of a society are interdependent and (ii) the differing lives and personalities of members of society complete each other. Both, of course, are central tenets of the modern liberal theory of man, following from the conceptions of unique (or diverse) individual natures, social interest and mutually stimulating development. If this is all that is meant by likening a society to an organism, there is nothing inherently hostile to individuality about the organic theory of society (although the separateness of persons seems qualified). Of course much more is often packed into the organic analogy. It is often thought, for instance, that '[i]f we mean anything by calling Society an organism, we mean that it is the end of the Individuals composing it' (a view which Bosanquet thought was, at best, confused);[105] or, it might be argued that the organic theory requires suppression of individuality to secure the well-being of the organism (a charge that we will consider in the next chapter). In any case, I am certainly not defending here all uses to which the organic analogy has been put nor am I offering an account of its possible variations. My point is

74      *II   Sociability: Social Life*

simply that interdependence of growth and mutual completion of personalities, which seem basal to any organic conception, are essential features of the modern liberal theory of social life. To that extent, all modern liberals are organicists. As we are about to see, modern liberals get into difficulties not because they are organicists in the sense, but because they seek to go 'beyond' organicism to more 'intense' forms of unity.

## Notes

1.    Rawls, *A Theory of Justice* (Belknap Press of Harvard University Press, Cambridge, 1971), p. 523.
2.    Ibid., p. 448.
3.    Ibid.
4.    Hobhouse, *Mind in Evolution*, 3rd edn (Macmillan, London, 1926), p. 375. Emphasis added.
5.    Hobhouse, *Social Development* (Allen and Unwin, London, 1924), p. 63.
6.    See Hobhouse's *Sociology and Philosophy: A Centenary Collection of Essays and Articles* (G. Bell and Sons, London, 1966), p. 41. On Hobhouse's conception of practical reason, see §I.D.2.
7.    Bosanquet, *The Principle of Individuality and Value* (Macmillan, London, 1912), p. 340.
8.    Bosanquet, *The Philosophical Theory of the State*, 4th edn (Macmillan, London, 1951), p. 166.
9.    Green, *Prolegomena to Ethics*, A.C. Bradley (ed.) (Clarendon Press, Oxford, 1890), p. 210. Dewey notes this feature of Green's ethics in his 'Philosophy of Thomas Hill Green' in *The Early Works of John Dewey: 1889-1892*, vol. III (Southern Illinois University Press, Carbondale and Edwardsville, 1969), p. 29. See also Ann R. Cacoullos, *Thomas Hill Green: Philosopher of Rights* (Twayne, New York, 1974), pp. 69-70.
10.    Green, *Prolegomena*, p. 200.
11.    Solomon E. Asch, *Social Psychology* (Prentice-Hall, New York, 1952), pp. 313-16.
12.    Rawls, *A Theory of Justice*, p. 522.
13.    Ibid., pp. 522-23.
14.    Bosanquet, *Some Suggestions in Ethics* (Macmillan, London, 1919), p. 216.
15.    Mill, *Utilitarianism* in J.M. Robson (ed.), *The Collected Works of John Stuart Mill* (University of Toronto Press, Toronto, 1963), vol. X, p. 215.
16.    Ibid., p. 216.
17.    Mill, *Principles of Political Economy* in *Collected Works*, vol. II, p. 209.
18.    John Dewey and James H. Tufts, *Ethics*, rev. edn (Henry Holt and Co., New York, 1932), p. 336. See also Green, *Prolegomena*, p. 264.
19.    Dewey, 'Creative Democracy – The Task Before Us' in *The Philosopher of the Common Man: Essays in Honor of John Dewey* (G.P. Putnam's Sons, New York, 1940), p. 226. See note 56 below.
20.    For further discussion, see A.J.M. Milne, *The Social Philosophy of English Idealism* (Allen and Unwin, London, 1962), p. 110. As Milne notes, Bosanquet's 'goods which are not diminished by sharing' are Green's 'non-competitive' goods. I consider Green's claim of non-competitiveness in §II.D.1.

21. Dewey, *Freedom and Culture* (Allen and Unwin, London, 1940), p. 36.

22. Rawls, *A Theory of Justice*, p. 522.

23. Hobhouse, *Social Development*, p. 156.

24. Ibid.

25. Ibid., p. 157.

26. Hobhouse, *Social Evolution and Political Theory* (Columbia University Press, New York, 1928), p. 127.

27. Hobhouse, *Social Development*, pp. 156-57.

28. Ibid., p. 64. Hobhouse, *The Rational Good: A Study in the Logic of Practice* (Watts, London, 1947), pp. 113, 156. Compare Rawls, *A Theory of Justice*, pp. 520-29; Bosanquet, *The Philosophical Theory of the State*, p. 168.

29. Hobhouse, *Social Development*, pp. 155-59.

30. See Mill, *Utilitarianism*, pp. 231-33. See also § III.C.3.

31. Hobhouse, *The Rational Good*, p. 74. See also his *Development and Purpose* (Macmillan, London, 1913), p. 199.

32. Hobhouse, *The Rational Good*, p. 106. See C.M. Griffin, 'L.T. Hobhouse and the Idea of Harmony', *Journal of the History of Ideas*, XXXV (Oct.-Dec., 1974), pp. 647-61.

33. Hobhouse, *The Elements of Social Justice* (Allen and Unwin, London, 1949), p. 23. This passage relates to Mill's theory of sympathy, see § III.C.3.

34. J.-J. Rousseau, 'Discourse on the Origin and Foundations of Inequality Among Men' in Roger D. Masters (ed.), *The First and Second Discourses*, Roger D. and Judith R. Masters (trans.) (St. Martin's Press, New York, 1969), p. 149.

35. Ibid.

36. Rawls, *A Theory of Justice*, p. 440.

37. Hobhouse, *Social Development*, p. 115.

38. See G.W.F. Hegel, *Phenomenology of the Spirit*, A.V. Miller (trans.) (Clarendon Press, Oxford, 1977), § B.

39. Green, *Prolegomena*, p. 200; Bosanquet, *Psychology of the Moral Self* (Macmillan, London, 1904), pp. 49-51.

40. The relation between respect and personhood is explored by S.I. Benn in 'Freedom, Autonomy and the Concept of a Person' in *Proceedings of the Aristotelian Society*, vol. LXXVI (1976), pp. 117-22.

41. Green, *Prolegomena*, p. 210.

42. Henry Sidgwick, *Lectures on the Ethics of T.H. Green, Mr Herbert Spencer, and J. Martineau* (Macmillan, London, 1902), p. 57.

43. H.A. Prichard, *Moral Obligation and Duty and Interest* (Oxford University Press, Oxford, 1968), p. 73.

44. R.M. MacIver argues that the failure to distinguish these two senses of 'interest' is a source of confusion in Bosanquet's theory of the general will. *Community: A Sociological Study*, 3rd edn (Macmillan, London, 1924), p. 107n. J.H. Muirhead defends Bosanquet against MacIver's charge in 'Recent Criticisms of the Idealist Theory of the General Will (II)', *Mind*, XXXIII (July 1924), pp. 234-36.

45. Green, *Prolegomena*, p. 210.

46. See Georg Henrik von Wright, *The Varieties of Goodness* (Routledge and Kegan Paul, London, 1963), Ch. III; A.I. Melden, *Rights and Persons* (Basil Blackwell, Oxford, 1977), pp. 113, 142-44; Brian Barry, *Political Argument* (Routledge and Kegan Paul, London, 1965), pp. 187-90.

47. Sidgwick, *Lectures on the Ethics of Green*, p. 58.

48. Prichard, *Moral Obligation*, p. 72. See Green, *Prolegomena*, pp. 167-68. See also W.H. Fairbrother, *The Philosophy of Thomas Hill Green* (Methuen, London, 1896), pp. 80-82.

49. Hobhouse, *Political Theory*, p. 30. See also *Social Development*, pp. 176-78.

50.  Dewey, *Democracy and Education* (The Free Press, New York, 1916), pp. 84-85. See also Robert J. Roth, *John Dewey and Self-Realization* (Prentice-Hall, Englewood Cliffs, N.J., 1962), p. 10; Alfonso J. Damico, *Individuality and Community: The Social and Political Thought of John Dewey* (University Presses of Florida, Gainesville, 1978), pp. 114-15.

51.  Dewey and Tufts, *Ethics*, p. 384. See also his essay on 'Individuality and Freedom' in Joseph Ratner (ed.), *Intelligence in the Modern World: John Dewey's Philosophy* (The Modern Library, New York, 1939), p. 620.

52.  Dewey, *Problems of Men* (Philosophical Library, New York, 1946), pp. 374-75.

53.  Bosanquet, *The Philosophical Theory of the State*, p. 57. John Herman Randall Jr notes this criticism of Mill by Bosanquet in his 'Idealistic Social Philosophy and Bernard Bosanquet', *Philosophy and Phenomenological Research*, XXVI (1965-66), p. 495.

54.  Mill, *On Liberty* in *Collected Works*, vol. XVIII, p. 263. I am indebted to John Kleinig for this point.

55.  Hobhouse, *Morals in Evolution* (Chapman and Hall, London, 1951), p. 62. See John E. Owen, *L.T. Hobhouse: Sociologist* (Nelson, London, 1974), pp. 116-17.

56.  Dewey and Tufts, *Ethics*, p. 383. The idea that social relations are mutually enriching can mean either (i) that our lives are enriched and expanded through an interest in the lives of others or (ii) that social relations enrich our lives by stimulating our latent capacities, making for a fuller individuality. Interpretation (i) concerns social interest while interpretation (ii) involves the mutual-stimulation argument. I do not think that this distinction is clear in Dewey's writings and he probably meant both. Thus I have referred to his idea of mutual enrichment in both the discussions of social interest and mutual stimulation.

57.  Dewey, *Individualism – Old and New* (Allen and Unwin, London, 1931), p. 81. However, Bosanquet at one point argues that the 'high' and 'low' nourish each other. Bosanquet, *Some Suggestions in Ethics*, pp. 73 ff.

58.  Rawls, *A Theory of Justice*, p. 522.

59.  Dewey and Tufts, *Ethics*, pp. 247-48.

60.  Hobhouse, *Sociology and Philosophy*, p. 43.

61.  Green, *Prolegomena*, p. 201. Bosanquet describes the individual as 'an expression or reflection of society as a whole from a point of view which is distinctive and unique'. *The Philosophical Theory of the State*, p. 162. I consider this idea more fully in § IV.A.2. Related questions concerning the similarity of members of a society are discussed in §§ II.D.2 and III.B.1.

62.  This seems implied by David L. Norton, *Personal Destinies: A Philosophy of Ethical Individualism* (Princeton University Press, Princeton, 1976), p. 54. See § I.B.

63.  Rawls, 'A Well-Ordered Society' in Peter Laslett and James Fishkin (eds.), *Philosophy, Politics and Society*, 5th series (Basil Blackwell, Oxford, 1979), p. 9. A similar passage occurs in *A Theory of Justice*, p. 259.

64.  See Bosanquet, 'Hegel's Theory of the Political Organism', *Mind*, VII (1898), pp. 1-14.

65.  See, for example, D.G. Ritchie, *Principles of State Interference* (George Allen and Co., London, 1902), pp. 13-22, 72-73; Michael Freeden, *The New Liberalism: An Ideology of Social Reform* (Clarendon Press, Oxford, 1978), pp. 95-116.

66.  According to Damico, during his career Dewey 'modifies considerably his organic conception of society, employing instead the theme of interdependency'. *Individuality and Community*, p. 41. As we shall presently see, however, this does not really make Dewey's position all that much different from 'organ-

icists' like Hobhouse. Dewey's considered position seems to be that the organic analogy was overly abstract and general rather than positively erroneous. See Dewey, *Reconstruction in Philosophy*, enlarged edn (Beacon, Boston, 1948), p. 197, but also his *Philosophy and Civilization* (Minton, Balch and Co., New York, 1931), p. 161. However, he did argue in *Democracy and Education* that it overlimited the place and function of the individual (p. 60). For his early uses of the organic analogy see 'The Ethics of Democracy' in *Early Works*, vol. I, pp. 227-49; and his *Psychology*, in ibid., vol. IV, pp. 286-87.

67. See note 105 of Ch. I.

68. Hobhouse, *Liberalism* (Oxford University Press, Oxford, 1964), p. 67.

69. This term was suggested to me by Stanley I. Benn. He and I explore some other features of the organic model of society in 'The Liberal Conception of the Public and Private' in S.I. Benn and G.F. Gaus (eds.), *Conceptions of the Public and Private in Social Life* (Croom Helm, London, forthcoming).

70. Freeden, *The New Liberalism*, p. 105.

71. Hobhouse, *Political Theory*, p. 87.

72. Hobhouse thought that the 'adjective "organic" ' suggested 'a more fruitful line of investigation' than did the 'substantive organism'. *Social Development*, pp. 64-65.

73. Ibid., p. 65. See also his *Development and Purpose*, pp. 293 ff.,

74. Hobhouse, 'The Ethical Basis of Collectivism', *International Journal of Ethics*, VIII (Jan. 1898), p. 145. The influence of Green's idealism on Hobhouse's conception of an organic society (with special reference to its description in the above essay) is emphasised by Stefan Collini, *Liberalism and Sociology: L.T. Hobhouse and Political Argument in England, 1880-1914* (Cambridge University Press, Cambridge, 1979), p. 174. Collini's interpretation, stressing the influence of Green over that of Darwin, runs counter to Freeden's reading (see note 70). In his 1920 article on 'Sociology', Hobhouse again applied the organic analogy to society, and in doing so indicates a tie between organicism and Green's theory of the common good (in *Sociology and Philosophy*, p. 53). Hobhouse's reference to 'felt' unity in the quoted sentence foreshadows our discussion of 'community' in Ch. III.

75. Green, *Prolegomena*, p. 302.

76. For Bosanquet see: *Some Suggestions in Ethics*, p. 176; *The Philosophical Theory of the State*, p. xlv; and also note 20 above. For Dewey see Dewey and Tufts, *Ethics*, pp. 382 ff. For Hobhouse see *Liberalism*, p. 69; *The Rational Good*, pp. 137 ff.

77. Green, *Prolegomena*, p. 414.

78. Sidgwick, *Lectures on the Ethics of Green*, p. 69. Sidgwick held that Green's claim of non-competitiveness of development applied only to Green's narrow (i.e. moral) conception of capacity. Ibid., p. 71. See §I.A. For an analysis of Sidgwick's criticisms, see Cacoullos, *Thomas Hill Green*, pp. 133 ff.

79. See Green's essay on 'The Influence of Civilisation on Genius' in *Works of Thomas Hill Green*, R.L. Nettleship (ed.) (Longman's, Green and Co., London, 1889), vol. III, p. 18. Of course, even in this limited sense Green's claim is dubious: while we may agree that the development of our associates enriches our life, it is more than a little difficult to see how, as Green thought, this sort of sharing can be extended to all mankind. I consider Hobhouse's similar hope for 'community' of all mankind in §III.B.2.

80. H.D. Lewis criticised Green in this regard. *Freedom and History* (Allen and Unwin, London, 1962), pp. 124-25. See also Peter Weiler, 'The New Liberalism of L.T. Hobhouse', *Victorian Studies*, XVI (Dec. 1972), pp. 141-61.

81. For Hobhouse, 'harmonious' and 'organic' are synonyms. See, e.g., *Sociology and Philosophy*, p. 45.

82. Hobhouse, *Social Development*, pp. 68-69; Dewey and Tufts, *Ethics*,

pp. 357-64; Rawls, *A Theory of Justice*, pp. 126-30, 281.

83.  Both Mill and Bosanquet were critical of extreme competitive individualism yet neither was prepared to entirely do away with the competitive dimension of economic life, at least for the foreseeable future. See Mill, *Chapters on Socialism* in *Collected Works*, vol. V, pp. 713-17, 731 ff., 749; Bosanquet, 'Socialism and Natural Selection' in his *Aspects of the Social Problem* (Macmillan, London, 1895), pp. 291, 306. See § VII.A for modern liberal views on socialism.

84.  Amy Gutmann, I think, underemphasises the importance of harmony as a modern liberal ideal. *Liberal Equality* (Cambridge University Press, Cambridge, 1980), p. 223. See John W. Seaman, 'L.T. Hobhouse and the Theory of "Social Liberalism" ', *Canadian Journal of Political Science*, II (1978), pp. 777-801.

85.  Dewey, *Liberalism and Social Action* (G.P. Putnam's Sons, New York, 1935), pp. 80-81.

86.  Hobhouse, *Social Development*, p. 65. See also his *Sociology and Philosophy*, p. 312.

87.  Bosanquet: *The Philosophical Theory of the State*, pp. 43-44; *Science and Philosophy* (Allen and Unwin, London, 1927), p. 252n; *The Value and Destiny of the Individual* (Macmillan, London, 1913), p. 50.

88.  Bosanquet, *Individuality and Value*, p. 37; Hobhouse, *Social Development*, p. 117.

89.  This is what makes so surprising H.D. Lewis's apparent claim that Green presupposed a homogeneous society. *Freedom and History*, pp. 87-89. See also Cacoullos, *Thomas Hill Green*, pp. 98 ff. There is, however, one plausible argument that organicists are hostile to individuality, viz. it can be argued that while they presuppose diversity, one's distinctive function depends not upon one's individual nature but upon the needs of the social organism. I consider this possibility in § III.D.

90.  Amy Gutmann is noteworthy among contemporary writers as one of the few who accept the idea that a theory can in any way qualify the separateness of persons and still remain liberal. *Liberal Equality*, pp. 156, 226.

91.  Bosanquet, *The Philosophical Theory of the State*, p. 165.

92.  Ibid., p. 166.

93.  Hobhouse, *The Metaphysical Theory of the State* (Allen and Unwin, London, 1926), p. 51.

94.  One reason that we should do so is Bosanquet's insistence that philosophical investigation ought to provide insight into 'obvious, central and sane experiences', although, to be sure, these will not be the same conclusions as a 'first glance' inspection will yield. *Individuality and Value*, Lecture I.

95.  Bosanquet, *Value and Destiny*, p. 47.

96.  Bosanquet, *Individuality and Value*, p. 289.

97.  Bosanquet, *The Philosophical Theory of the State*, p. 165.

98.  In the following I draw heavily upon John W. Chapman's account of Bosanquet's psychology in his *Rousseau – Totalitarian or Liberal?* (Columbia University Press, New York, 1956), pp. 128 ff.

99.  Bosanquet, *Psychology of the Moral Self*, p. 42.

100. Bosanquet, *Science and Philosophy*, p. 260.

101. Bosanquet, *Psychology of the Moral Self*, p. 43. See § III.B.1, and Ch. VI below.

102. Bosanquet, *Individuality and Value*, p. 38. This is the typical and, I think, proper interpretation of Bosanquet's theory of social life. For a somewhat different view, however, see Paul Ramsey, 'The Idealistic View of Moral Evil: Josiah Royce and Bernard Bosanquet', *Philosophy and Phenomenological Research*, VI (June 1946), pp. 554-89. See also G.P. Conger, *Theories of Macrocosms and Microcosms in the History of Philosophy* (Russell and Russell, New York, 1922), pp. 110-18, 128.

103. I am indebted to John Kleinig for much of what follows.

104. Muirhead, 'Recent Criticism of the Idealist Theory of the General Will (II)', p. 238.

105. Bosanquet, 'Hegel's Theory of the Political Organism', p. 1.

# III  SOCIABILITY: COMMUNITY

## A.  Social Life and Community

I have been stressing that the modern liberal view of social life is premised on interdependence and mutual completion. It thus asserts an
organic unity based upon the diversity of individualities. However, this
unity might be largely unrecognised or unfelt by individuals; indeed, it
is often emphasised that Bosanquet regarded most of it to be subcon-
scious.[1] Like parts of an animal organism, each may occupy a place in a
complex network and yet have no cognizance of its unity with the larger
whole. To William McDougall (who dedicated his *Group Mind* to Hobhouse) this was, to be sure, a type of organic unity, but a lower sort. In
higher organisms, McDougall argued, 'over and above' the lower sort of
organic unity, 'a unity of an altogether new and unique kind' develops:
'a unity which consists in the whole (or the self) being present to consciousness, whether clearly or obscurely, during almost every moment
of thought, and pervading and playing some part in the determination
of the course of action and thought'.[2] Although McDougall's contrast is
a stark one between unconscious and conscious unity, it does suggest
one way in which we might distinguish social from community life. The
connections of social life are, of course, not entirely unconscious: we
realise that the development of our associates is complementary to our
own good. But the picture of social life I presented in the last chapter
does not make much of the awareness of one's part in a larger, more
complex network. One can fully participate in social life by appreciating one's fellows without being cognizant that the network of relations between associates forms a systematic whole in which one occu-
pies a particular place. To take a homely example: one might enjoy and
appreciate the relations one has with one's fellow workers without
being aware that they are all part of the complex life of a university, a
life of which one is part by virtue of one's position. However, if one
sees oneself as part of the university community, one does indeed need
to be aware of the larger network. As a social psychologist, Zevedei
Barbu, describes it, one becomes 'aware of himself as a member of an
organised whole'.[3] The difference, then, is between appreciating and
delighting in one's colleagues (social life) and thinking of oneself as a
member of the university and as a participant in its corporate life (community).

A similar sort of distinction is put forward by another psychologist, Solomon E. Asch: 'The need for companionship, for sharing experiences [which we have associated with social interest] , is not identical with attachment of persons and groups or with a sense of unity.'[4] According to Asch these two aspects of our social nature are related but distinct; we may, for example, have a developed social interest without a strong sense of unity. Asch's distinction is thus also one between social life (i.e. social interest) and community (i.e. a sense of unity). But while McDougall is concerned with the consciousness of unity in 'higher' types of organisms – a sort of intellectual awareness – Asch focuses on sentiments and feelings of unity. We might, then, identify intellectual and affective forms of community life. In what follows I will explore both these types of communal awareness, with special attention to how modern liberals have related them to their conceptions of individuality and social life.

## B. Consciousness of Unity

### B.1.  Two Types of Unity

McDougall had Bosanquet in mind when he drew the contrast between 'higher' (conscious) and 'lower' (unconscious) organic unity.

> Bosanquet recognises in national life only the lower kind of unity and not the unity of self-consciousness. He seems to reject the notion of national self-consciousness, on the ground that the life of a nation is so complex that it cannot be fully and adequately reflected in the consciousness of any individual; yet in this respect the difference between the national mind and the individual mind is one of degree only and not kind.[5]

Not too surprisingly, and as others have noted, Bosanquet's position is not quite so simple as McDougall would have us believe.[6] Bosanquet certainly does insist that we are 'unconsiously inspired' by the unity of the whole, and, more particularly, he argued that the full social system of dispositions, ideas, etc. – the common mind (§II.D.2) – is not present in the consciousness of any single person.[7] But (*pace* McDougall) Bosanquet never denies that 'finite individuals' are conscious of their participation in the common mind. Indeed, Bosanquet is very explicit that 'the general will is a process continuously emerging from the rela-

tively unconscious into reflective consciousness'.[8] The notion of the
general will and its relation to consciousness will be more fully explored
in Chapter VI (§B.2); what is important for our present concerns is
that Bosanquet clearly asserts not only the reality of communal consciousness but also its necessity for the existence of a genuine community
possessing a general will. Thus, in arguing against the existence of a
'community of mankind' (see §B.2) Bosanquet implicitly invokes
McDougall's idea of a 'higher' type of organism, holding that 'humanity'
cannot form an organism as no 'consciousness of connection' exists.[9]

McDougall's and Bosanquet's repeated references to 'organisms', as
well as our analysis of the modern liberal theory of social life, naturally
leads one to suppose that the sort of connection of which we are conscious in a community is an *organic* connection of interlocking differences. If this is the case, we might say that the essence of community
is the recognition of the organic nature of social life. While I think it
would be safe to say that to some extent all modern liberals do try to
rest community on such organic connections, one of my main points in
this chapter will be the extent to which modern liberals, for various reasons, have sought to supplement organicism with other understandings
of unity in their theories of community. In particular, using Durkheim's
distinction between 'organic' and 'mechanical' solidarity, I shall try to
show that in their various theories of community, modern liberals rely
a good deal upon Durkheim's 'mechanical' unity, i.e. a unity premised
on commonality and similarity rather than on interlocking differences.[10]
I shall thus argue that whereas the modern liberal theory of social life
is informed by an organic conception of unity, modern liberals' various
conceptions of community are more diverse, combining organicism and
mechanical unity (as well as a wide range of affective bonds).

This is not to say that organic unity is not central to any modern
liberal theory of community. Of all our modern liberals, Green's conception of community is perhaps the most steadfastly organic (although,
as we will see, he too resorts to 'mechanical' unity). This may not be
obvious, however, and at first sight just the opposite may seem more
accurate. It might appear that Green's idea of a community as founded
on a 'capacity for a common idea of permanent good' indicates that he
thinks community is premised on the capacity for (or the recognition
of) commonality:[11] a mark of Durkheim's 'mechanical unity' rather than
the organicist's notion of a system of differences. Apparently, W.D.
Lamont interpreted Green in this way.[12] However, if we turn back and
reflect upon our analysis of social life and social interest, we can see
that Green's 'commonality' is very much premised upon organic rela-

tions. Because we have an interest in each other's differential 'perfection' leading to (or constituting) an interest in their good, we can be said to share a common interest in each other's perfections. Or, as Green wants to argue, we have a common good.[13] Thus to be conscious[14] of a common good is to be aware that we are mutually interested in each other's perfection and that anyone's satisfaction requires the development of his fellows. Simply put, for members of a society to be conscious of a common good is for them to be cognizant of the organic nature of their social life.

The organic basis of Green's understanding of community is better brought out by contrasting it to Bosanquet's, Hobhouse's and Dewey's theories of community, which really do give a prominent place to similarity and commonality. For all his talk of screws and nuts, Bosanquet was convinced that members of a community share a wide store of common ideas, beliefs and values. As we saw in the previous chapter (§II.D.2), his theory of the common mind rests on both the systematisation of differences *and* commonality. 'To say that certain persons have common interests means that in this or that respect their minds are *similarly or correlatively* organised, that they will react in the *same or correlative* ways upon given presentations ... It is', Bosanquet thus concludes, 'this *identity* of mental organisation which is the psychological justification for the doctrine of the General Will.'[15] But this emphasis on commonality is no mere idiosyncrasy of Bosanquet's 'Absolute Idealism'. Despite his diatribes against Bosanquet's 'common self', Hobhouse's own theory of 'the interaction of minds' is much closer to Bosanquet's than he would have us believe.[16] Like Bosanquet, Hobhouse sees the system of minds that form various communities as being composed of both correlated differences *and similarities*. 'Within any group', he says, 'such and such ideas are familiar, such and such methods are in use, a certain habit of mind is prevalent and certain modes of judgement hold the field'. Although (*contra* Bosanquet) Hobhouse is adamant in insisting that this commonality does not constitute a 'social mind', he does call it 'a mental condition widely dominating thought and action'. Indeed, he goes so far as to describe it as a 'social mentality'.[17] However, according to Hobhouse's social psychology, such mental similarity is an aspect of all group life; and while we can discern underlying concern with community and nation in his analysis, he is generally at pains to make it applicable to all sorts of joint enterprises. Dewey, although also very much alive to the diversity of types of joint activities, more often focuses in on the idea of a *community*. And when he does, he very much stresses its foundation in commonality:

There is more than a verbal tie between the words common, community, and communication. Men live in a community in virtue of the things they have in common; and communication is the way in which they come to possess things in common. What they must have in common in order to form a community or society are aims, beliefs, aspirations, knowledge – a common understanding – likemindedness as the sociologists say.[18]

The distinction between a true community, resting on consciousness of commonality, and the impersonal interconnections and dependencies of civil society[19] is at the heart of Dewey's distinction between the 'Great Society' and the 'Great Community'. In *The Public and Its Problems* he argues that we already live in the Great Society; industrial growth has knit together large parts of the world into a complicated network in which actions and decisions in one part have consequences reverberating throughout the structure.[20] But, says Dewey, no matter how much society is an 'organism', mere interdependence does not create a community. For that, a consciousness of shared values and concerns must arise: the parts of the organism must think in terms of 'we' and 'our' as as well as 'I'.[21] And, time and time again, Dewey insists that communication is the key to the development of such consciousness. He sums up the essentials of his argument in *Freedom and Culture:*

There is a difference between a society, in the sense of an association, and a community. Electrons, atoms and molecules are in association with one another. Nothing exists in isolation anywhere throughout nature. Natural associations are conditions for the existence of a community, but a community adds the function of communication in which emotions and ideas are shared as well as joint undertakings engaged in. Economic forces have immensely widened the scope of associational activity. But it [*sic*] has done so largely at the expense of intimacy and directness of communal group interests and activities.[22]

The consciousness of similarity is of the utmost importance here. As illustrated by Mill's proposed science of 'ethology', an unconscious similarity may produce character types but falls short of a communal unity. Mill proposed his science of ethology to explain what he often called 'national character':[23] 'Every form of polity, every condition of society, whatever else it had done, had formed its type of national character.'[24] Thus, Mill tells us, the proposed science's aim is to discover why, for example, 'in a given number of Frenchmen, taken indiscriminately, there will be found more persons of a particular mental tendency, and fewer of the contrary tendency, than among an equal number of Italians or English'.[25] Such similarities are, of course, quite compatible with alienation or atomisation, i.e. a lack of community. Indeed, as Mill notes, the lack of sociability itself may be a national character trait.[26] More importantly, though, no matter what traits are common to a group, if the members fail to perceive the commonality, they would seem to lack a sense of community, no matter how much they may seem 'as one' to an outsider or an 'ethologist'. Character types or common outlooks alone do not make a community, though they may well provide the basis of one.

## B.2. The Scope of Community

Dewey talks not only of a community, but of a 'Great Community'. It is reasonable to ask how great, i.e. extensive, a community can be. As Hobhouse recognised, an 'explicit consciousness of unity' shared by all is 'difficult to attain in a great and complex community'.[27] Consequently, Hobhouse joins Bosanquet in insisting that much of the underlying unity of any community must remain largely unconscious. Nevertheless, Bosanquet and Hobhouse included, all our modern liberals have believed some consciouness of a national unity not only possible but typical. Moreover, it is particularly interesting that, insofar as they do concern themselves with consciousness of a distinctively *national* unity, it is more an awareness of commonality or similarity than of an organic unity. This, or course, is obviously in the spirit of Bosanquet, who, despite his organicism, places a great deal of emphasis on the similarity of the mental organisation of members of a nation. More surprisingly, perhaps, it is true of Green. While, as I have argued, Green's primary understanding of unity is organic, he does think that the life of a nation, being based upon common dwelling places and customs and common ways of 'thinking which a common language and still more a common literature embodies', produces a deep sense of unity.[28] This theme of common languages and traditions giving rise to a sense of nationality — which includes both consciousness of unity and sentiments — is also central to Hobhouse's and Mill's analyses of nationality (§C.6); national unity, as Hobhouse tells us, is 'a composite effect of language, tradition, religion, and manner which makes certain people feel themselves at one with each other and apart from the rest of the world'.[29]

Bosanquet explicitly and Rawls implicitly[30] seem generally content to leave matters thus and not assert any community more extensive than the nation. I say 'generally' as Bosanquet sometimes appears to waiver, but, in the main, he is quite insistent that 'humanity' is not a community, having no consciousness of connection and very little in the way of shared outlooks, beliefs, values, etc.[31] Some day, perhaps, humanity might share a common life, but not yet. Hobhouse takes Bosanquet to task for this limitation of community, apparently agreeing with the 'Comtist' that mankind does indeed possess a spiritual unity above and beyond that of the nation state.[32] Hobhouse in fact is convinced that we can talk of a community of mankind:

> In ethical truth, there is only one ultimate community, which is the human race. This community, alas! has never yet found organized expression. To organize it is now the duty of statesmanship; but in the meantime the principle of community has been represented, with the imperfections and inconsistencies that we are observing, by organized bodies − States, Churches, associations of all kinds.[33]

Sorting out agreements and disagreements between Hobhouse and Bosanquet is seldom an easy task, and this certainly is not an exception. To a large extent, though, their differences seem more apparent than real, for they understand the idea of world community differently. According to Hobhouse, the Comtist conception of humanity is 'true to fact because it recognizes that the higher values, on which Dr Bosanquet insists, are not the achievements of one state or one nation, but of many, that the history of thought, ethics, religion or art, is not a history of separate communities but a world history'.[34] Presumably, then, Hobhouse conceives of the various achievements of different civilisations as interconnected and complementary, each contributing to an integrated human achievement. While it is true that Bosanquet seems considerably more impressed than Hobhouse by the distinctiveness of the lives of different national communities, there is nothing inconsistent with emphasising differences and accepting some sort of organic connection. Quite the contrary, I have stressed repeatedly that organicism presupposes differentiation. Bosanquet's real objections to any claim that a world community exists are (i) that mankind is not *conscious* of any connection and (ii) that, in contrast to national communities, humanity as a whole does not share much in the way of *common* outlooks, beliefs or values.[35] It does not seem that Hobhouse really disagrees with either objection. He appears to explicitly accept the first point, conceding to Bosanquet that mankind does not possess much consciousness of unity.[36] And his discussions of world community make little reference to humanity-wide commonalities, except in so far as he stresses the growing recognition that all people are similar *qua* human.[37] In sum, like Green's, Hobhouse's ultimate ideal seems to be more an extension and intensification of an organic social life to all mankind than the rise of a strong universal commonality. Practical reason, he argues, drives us to extend the principle of harmonious development to all men: 'It is the ideal of Harmony that humanity should become one cooperative whole'.[38] But this apparently does not necessitate that mankind develop a common language, customs, outlooks, etc., which presently mark off national communities, but rather that the co-operative, mutually supporting and mutually completing nature of social life obtain among all men. Only to the extent that Hobhouse emphasises that mankind will develop a *consciousness* of (organic) connection can his ideal be said to go beyond a universal social life to some sort of world-wide community. But even this sort of world community is not the kind that Bosanquet had in mind since it has little or no mechanical unity.[39]

### B.3. Community and Individuality: A First Cut

Following Durkheim, then, we can distinguish two sorts of unity, i.e. 'organic' and 'mechanical', of which we might be aware. Now the latter, a unity based on similarity, which we find prominent in Dewey and Bosanquet, seems perhaps more closely related to our normal understanding of community. Thus, for example, R.M. MacIver began his study of community by telling the reader:

> By a community I mean any area of common life, village, or town, or district, or country, or even wider area. To deserve the name community, the area must be somehow distinguished from further areas, the common life may have some characteristic of its own such that the frontiers of the area have some meaning. All the laws of the cosmos, physical, biological, and psychological, conspire to bring it about that beings who live together shall resemble one another. Wherever men live together they develop in some kind and degree distinctive common characteristics — manners, traditions, modes of speech, and so on.[40]

But if 'mechanical' unity is closer to what we usually mean by 'community', 'organic' unity is still very appealing to the liberal. As Durkheim stressed (and as I suggested in §II.D.2), 'organic' unity, being premised on interlocking differences, is not only consistent with, but requires, individual differentiation. In contrast, 'mechanical' unity, by identifying the communal element with the extent of homogeneity, 'can be strong only if the ideas and tendencies common to all members of the society are greater in number and intensity than those which pertain personally to each member'. 'But', as Durkheim goes on to note, 'what makes our personality is how much of our individual qualities we have, what distinguishes us from others. The [mechanical] solidarity can grow only in inverse ratio to personality'.[41] At least prima facie, then (I return to this question in §§C.6 and E below), the modern liberal seeking to integrate individuality and community is caught in a dilemma: organic unity is appealing as it coheres well with individuality, but, at least alone, is not a sufficiently strong sense of community. On the other hand, mechanical unity, which is very close to our normal notions of community, appears to have serious difficulties accommodating individuality.

But in one sense, both forms of community we have thus far examined seem fairly weak. By considering only consciousness of unity we do not get at the real root of communal bonds, i.e. affective ties. Any such purely 'intellectual' conception of community is bound to leave us unsatisfied: being aware of oneself as included in a larger unity is all well and good, but unless there are some *feelings* of unity it hardly seems as if there is much of a communal bond. Modern liberals, at any rate, have apparently felt so, for without exception they resort to some sort of affective bonding in their theories of community.

## C.  Feelings of Unity

### C.1.  Three Types of Affective Ties

My last sentence was something of an understatement. Not only have modern liberals postulated affective bonds, they have asserted a truly amazing variety of such bonds as well. Patriotism, public spirit, community spirit, feelings of unity, sympathy, fellow feeling, affection, neighbourliness, and family ties all have been pointed to, at one time or another, as bonds uniting members of a community. If we are to make any progress in exploring the nature of affective bonds in modern liberalism we need some scheme, even if only a rough one, according to which we might classify different sorts of communal sentiments. Hobhouse suggests a dichotomy. One's 'relation to the whole', he tells us, 'may be felt directly as in patriotism' or might be experienced in a more indirect way via 'emotions which link one to another who is similarly linked to a third, the chain ultimately connecting all the members of a community'. This second sort of bonding, Hobhouse goes on to say, is 'sometimes described in terms of affection and sometimes in terms of sympathy'. But according to Hobhouse, although 'affection' and 'sympathy' are not usually distinguished they ought to be for 'the two systems of feeling are not the same'.[42] I propose to distinguish them. Sympathy, I hope to show, can be pretty much identified with a form of communal bond intermediate between Hobhouse's direct and indirect ones, a sort of diffuse bond with one's fellows that is both distinct from devotion to the whole and personal affections. This yields a trichotomy in which feelings of communal unity are classified as *patriotic, fraternal* or *neighbourly*. I intend these labels only as general guides to the nature of each sort of social bond; I certainly am not providing full accounts of patriotism, fraternity or neighbourliness. If the reader objects to these, 'direct', 'diffuse' and 'indirect' will suffice. What is important is that the scheme permits us to see that all modern liberals have relied on more than one sort of affective community bonding, sometimes in the hope that the weaknesses of one sort will be compensated for by another. Moreover, as we will see in §C.6, it allows us to say some interesting things about the relation between types of affective bonds and the distinction between mechanical and organic unity.

## C.2. Patriotism

Although, as Bosanquet and Green recognised, neighbourly and fraternal ties enter into what we usually call patriotism,[43] as used here 'patriotism' refers to a devotion to, or feelings of unity with, an 'abstract' whole or collectivity. As we will see in Chapter VI (§B.3), Mill sometimes suggests this sort of bond in his arguments for political participation when he talks of citizens coming to feel themselves to be members of a public sharing a common good. Such bonding is also prominent in Bosanquet's writings (although he certainly would have denied that the whole is abstract). When Bosanquet refers to the desire 'to be at one with a society of good people' or the 'felt unity' we experience with the whole, he does not appear to have in mind fraternal feelings towards one's fellows, much less a deep affection towards them, but rather a sense that one is an element in a more inclusive whole or system.[44] In Green's imagery, one 'feels the pulse of the whole nation beating in his own veins'.[45]

It is significant that Mill refers to the 'public', Bosanquet to a 'society' and Green to a 'nation'. All three referents indicate that 'patriotic' feelings can attach to very large social groupings. Indeed, it would seem that since these sort of communal feelings arise from the experience of participation or membership in a larger whole, they are particularly appropriate to 'great communities'. It is interesting that even Green focuses on the nation as the object of such feelings. This confirms my conclusion in §B.2 that Green, like Hobhouse, really has in mind a universal social life encompassing all mankind, not a universal human community. For if any sort of communal feelings could be shared by mankind, it would be some experience of participating in a common, human, enterprise. But Green apparently does not feel the 'pulse of humanity beating in his veins'. Quite to the contrary, Green was explicit that '[t]he love of mankind, no doubt, needs to be part-icularised in order to have any power over life and action'.[46] Hopes for a world community notwithstanding, modern liberals have apparently seen humanity, at least at present, as too amorphous and diverse a body to elicit anything like the intense feelings of unity that are generated by the nation.[47] However, the prominence of the nation in modern liberal accounts of community only partly arises from its possession of a more distinct corporate unity than mankind at large. Probably more important is the perception of modern liberals that nations are characterised by our second, and perhaps in their eyes most powerful of communal bonds, fraternity.

### C.3. Fraternity

In the third chapter of his *Utilitarianism* Mill writes:

> Not only does all strengthening of social ties, and all healthy growth of society, give to each individual a stronger personal interest in practically consulting the welfare of others; it also leads him to identify his *feelings* more and more with their good, or at least with an ever greater degree of practical consideration for it . . . In an improving state of the human mind, the influences are constantly on the increase, which tend to generate in each individual a feeling of unity with all the rest; which feeling, if perfect, would make him never think of, or desire, any beneficial condition for himself, in the benefits of which they are not included.[48]

Indeed, Mill concludes that '[t]he deeply-rooted conception which every individual even now has of himself as a social being, tends to make him feel it one of his natural wants that there should be harmony between his feelings and aims and those of his fellow creatures'.

Like his doctrine on quality of pleasure, Mill's notion of a natural feeling of unity with one's fellows has exercised tremendous influence on subsequent liberals. Dewey, for example, quotes extensively from these paragraphs in order to demonstrate the advance of Mill's utilitarianism over Bentham's.[49] Rawls paraphrases Mill on this point, holding that we have 'natural sentiments of unity and fellow feeling' and that '[t]he natural end of . . . development is a state of the human mind in which each person has a feeling of unity with others.'[50] And, again like Mill, he proceeds from this to talk of our natural desire for harmony of our feelings with those of our fellows. And harmony, of course, means Hobhouse. As I mentioned in the previous chapter (§II.B.2), in one statement of his theory of harmony, Hobhouse begins by considering the possibility that there might be a radical opposition between one's own satisfaction and that of one's neighbour. But, says Hobhouse, such a 'bald opposition' could only exist if we were thoroughly unsocial beings. 'If there is anything of the nature of Mill's social feeling within me there is a traitor in my camp, and the division between my neighbour and me is reflected in a division of my own feelings.'[51] And, so, again following Mill, we are led by our social feeling to desire harmony with our fellows. Bosanquet is not quite so explicit, but one of the few positive features he seems able to find in Mill is his deep sense of 'social solidarity'.[52]

Prima facie, all this may seem simply another instance of 'patriotism', that is, a devotion to an 'abstract whole'. But although such devotion certainly enters into Mill's analysis, it also contains a crucial dimension absent from our discussion of patriotism: viz. Mill's emphasis on one's *fellows* and the desire to be in harmony with *them*. It is not simply a sense of participation in a larger whole but also one of 'fellow feeling'. Put curtly, it entails a notion of partnership or fraternity rather than simply inclusion or 'feeling a part of'. This fraternal conception of unity seems to underlie modern liberals' many comparisons of societies to families. Rawls, for example, argues that his 'difference principle'[53] corresponds to a 'natural meaning of fraternity'. Just as '[m]embers of a family commonly do not wish to gain unless they can do so in ways that further the interests of the rest', Rawls argues that properly developed citizens do not desire gains except when such gains better the lot of their less fortunate fellows.[54] In this respect, then, it is appropriate to act towards all one's compatriots as if one were bound to them by familial ties. Green is even more explicit: 'patriotism' [*sic*] can only be a passion, he tells us, to the extent an individual feels himself bonded to others 'by ties analogous to those which bind him to his family'.[55]

Dewey congratulated public schools in America 'for what they have done in breaking down class division, creating a feeling of greater humanity and of membership in a single family'.[56] As Rawls's connection between his difference principle and family attitudes also suggests, modern liberals have tended to draw a connection between promotion of fellow feeling, fraternity, civic friendship, etc. and the abolition of class divisions or promoting some sort of equality.[57] Mill was certainly the forerunner here:

> Where the different classes of mankind are divided by impassable barriers, each may have intense sympathies with his own class, more intense than it is almost possible to have with mankind in general; but those who are far below him in condition are so unlike himself, that he hardly considers them as human beings; and if they are refractory and troublesome, will be unable to feel for them even that kindly interest which he experiences for his unresisting domestic cattle.[58]

And should we have any doubts, Mill makes clear in the next sentence that such sympathies are what he means by 'fellow f⌐eling'. That Mill's 'feelings of unity' are fellow feelings (and not what I have called patriotism) and, as such, are premised on sympathy is crucial to the plausibility of his claim that class divisions hinder a sense of unity. Prima facie his claim might seem implausible. Certainly John Grote thought so. 'Little as the experience of the world and of the past may be able to teach us', Grote was sure that it taught us 'that such advance of civilization as consists in breaking down privilege and class interests, and making men in *this* manner equal, has no tendency to produce in them that feeling of unity with others'.[59] But Mill's thesis is not so easily refuted by opposing impressionistic evidence, for it is not only an empirical claim about the correlation of certain feelings with certain social conditions, but a psychological theory about the dynamics of sympathy as well. The best modern liberal exposition of this dynamic is presented by Hobhouse in *Social Development*, his main work on social psychology.

Sympathy, says Hobhouse, is not for the most part feeling something along with another, e.g. feeling hunger along with the hungry, but being able to take up the point of view of others and respond to their situation as if it were our own.[60] It is thus a 'propensity, very general, of various shapes, and of still more various strength, to treat others like ourselves in the sense of doing to them as we would be done by'.[61] This propensity, he goes on to say, is encouraged by three conditions: (i) affection, (ii) comradeship and (iii) mutual understanding and, in particular, like-mindedness. All three help us take up the perspective of others and, by so doing, respond to their needs as if they were our own. Thus, just like Mill, Hobhouse argues that class barriers interfere with this imaginative projection/emotional response, especially by undermining the third condition. We have great difficulty in assuming the perspective of those who appear alien; and if we are unable to take up their point of view, says Hobhouse, we will not be able to have much sympathy with them. So, this sort of Millian sense of community, i.e. fraternal bonds based upon sympathy, seems to require that those so bonded perceive themselves as fundamentally similar.[62]

All this suggests that Mill's hope that fellow feeling might unite 'mankind at large'[63] is even more ambitious than it first appears. Hobhouse, whose philosophy is certainly not short on optimism, sometimes showed signs of more sobriety, acknowledging that '[o]ur relations are best regulated and most humane within the circle which we understand, among our friends, in regard to our own countrymen, and finally our race and colour.' Consequently, 'As we get farther away from intimate acquaintance, the sympathy weakens and gives place to indifference, tempered with suspicion, fear and nascent ill will.'[64] But although Hobhouse seems right in circumscribing the bonds of sympathetic ties in this way, it poses difficulties for his theory. In §B.2 I suggested that, like Green, Hobhouse's universal 'community' seems to be essentially an extension of an organic, co-operative social life to all mankind. Practical reason, he argued, impels us to universalise harmony. However, it will be recalled from the previous chapter (§II.B.2) that underlying this drive to harmony — what he calls the 'principle of Love' — is our social feeling: when our development conflicts with that of our fellows we experience disharmony because we have social feelings that have the good of others for their object. Moreover, as we saw, the social feelings Hobhouse appears to have in mind are sympathetic ones that arise out of our natural social interest. If indeed sympathy does play this role in Hobhouse's drive to social harmony, then his proposal to universalise a harmonious social life is more problematic than we might have initially thought, for it would seem to require a sympathy with all men. And it is just that which Hobhouse's own analysis of sympathy indicates is not likely to be forthcoming. One is tempted to conclude that, as with Mill, Hobhouse's faith in the development of a 'community' of man is very much just that, viz. a faith that remains to a large extent unsupported by his analysis of social sentiments.

## C.4.  Neighbourliness

Avowals of fellow feeling or fraternity occupy an ambiguous place in
modern liberal writings. On the one hand, to varying extents, all appeal
to them at some point and some, like Rawls and Mill, rely on them
extensively. The ideal, in Dewey's words, of a 'fraternally associated
public'[65] obviously has a great deal of attraction for liberals trying to
show that liberalism need not be narrowly individualistic or egoistic.
But it is an ideal beset by problems, many of which modern liberals
have recognised. Most obviously, in very large, complex and inevitably
impersonal societies, it is more than a little difficult to see how the
public can really be 'fraternally associated'. Rawls certainly appears to
have difficulties seeing it at times; at one point, in fact, he seems to re-
tract his allegiance to Mill's vision of fraternal unity by denying that the
citizen body as a whole is 'bound together by fellow feeling between
individuals'.[66] Moreover, as Dewey was prone to emphasise, 'society'
is composed of many societies or associations. The image of a single,
all-inclusive public strongly bound to each other by sympathy seems to
do violence to this multiplicity of ties; given all our overlapping sympathies and ties, those to fellow members of the public in general may
well be relatively weak and minor ones.

These difficulties apparently have not been seen as sufficiently imposing to abandon the ideal of fraternity; indeed, it probably remains
the preeminent conception of communal bonds in modern liberal
theory. But it does provide an impetus to look for some sort of communal ties more obviously consistent with the scale and complexity of
modern societies. The most straightforward response, and one which
arguably has had the most appeal to modern liberals, is to deny that all
communal feelings need be national (or universal), and, consequently,
to give prominence to what Bosanquet called 'neighbourly public
spirit'.[67] Once again, we need go back to Mill. As most students of
Mill's political theory have noted, he looks to participation in government, particularly local affairs, to promote individual development;
what is often overlooked, though, is that he explicitly proffers participation as a solution to the problem of size and community. In his
second review of Tocqueville, Mill accepts that 'the love of country is
not, in large communities, a passion of spontaneous growth' and,
hence,

> it is more and more necessary [under democracy] to nourish patriot-
> ism by artificial means; and of these none are so efficacious as free
> institutions — a large and frequent intervention of the citizens in the

management of public business. Nor does the love of country alone require this encouragement, but every feeling which connnects men either by interest or sympathy with their neighbours and fellow-citizens.[68]

Remarkably, Mill comes very close indeed here to identifying our three forms of communal bonds — patriotism, fraternity, and neighbourliness — and argues that political participation encourages all three (see §VI. B.3).

Mill supports his claims with a long quotation from Tocqueville, in which he had observed that ' "[l]ocal freedom . . . which leads a great number of citizens to value the *affections* of their neighbours, and of those with whom they are in contact, perpetually draws men back to one another" '.[69] Tocqueville's tie between, on the one hand, affection, and on the other, neighbourly and other face-to-face relations, goes to the heart of the matter. Hobhouse, whom we have seen is concerned with distinguishing sympathy from affection, concludes that the latter is distinctive in 'its concentration on particular persons with whom we are in close and happy response'.[70] Unlike sympathy, which Hobhouse thinks can be fairly wide-ranging, ties of real affection are necessarily restricted to those with whom we have direct intercourse. And that is why, for all the comparisions modern liberals have drawn between the bonds uniting citizens and those pertaining among friends or members of a family, the nature of the ties is fundamentally different. A nation, Bosanquet said, can have but 'a tinge of natural affection',[71] whereas in face-to-face relations affections can flourish. Dewey, we might note, resisted the idea that communities, even local ones, were based on affections, preferring instead the notion of 'attachments', believing that, unlike affections, they imply a basis in stable and tranquil relations.[72] Nevertheless, Dewey concurs that face-to-face relations are necessary to community 'in its deepest and richest sense'. 'The Great Community, in the sense of free and full intercommunication, is conceivable. But it can never possess all the qualities which mark a local community . . . Vital and thorough attachments are bred only in the intimacy of an intercourse which is of necessity restricted in range.'[73]

Thus confronted by doubts that large modern communities can be fraternally associated, modern liberals like Dewey have pointed to the variety of neighbourly relations that can flourish in large communities, providing a deeper and richer communal bonding. Like Mill, we might just leave matters there, recognising neighbourly feeling to be a special sort of bond to be placed alongside fraternity and patriotism but having a much more restricted scope. But some, such as Hobhouse (§III.C.1), take a further step, suggesting a network or chain thesis according to which feelings 'link one to another who is similarly linked to a third, the chain ultimately connecting all members of a community'. Dewey too, I think, takes this extra step when speaking of 'that *texture* of friendships and attachments which is the chief bond in any community'.[74] Rawls introduces a variation: instead of arguing that bonds of personal relations ultimately link each to all, he contends that our 'ties of affection and fellow feeling' extend sufficiently wide so that it is well nigh impossible to injure the community at large without also hurting 'our friends and associates along with the rest'.[75] Whereas Hobhouse's web of personal relations thesis suggests, albeit in a fairly loose way, that it is not possible to hurt anyone without also ultimately hurting a friend of a friend, Rawls's formulation implies that one cannot injure the community in general without also injuring a friend, The aim of both versions, however, is to use personal ties of affection as the basis of a wider ranging communal unity.

## C.5.  The Family and Community

For the most part, modern liberals have treated family affections as essentially the same as neighbourliness. This is most obvious in Dewey, who usually does not distinguish between 'family and neighbourhood', treating both as sorts of associations which have sufficiently rich intercourse and strong personal attachments to provide the basis of a real communal life.[76] Moreover, although we find, for example, Dewey, Hobhouse and Bosanquet all worrying that the intense ties within the family can lead to isolation and to hostility towards the outside world,[77] all seem to think that the affections of family life can, in one way or another, connect up with, or spill over into, relations with other members of the larger community, and thus, like neighbourliness, make for a wider unity.[78] Bosanquet is the most interesting on this score, presenting an explicit contagion thesis. According to Bosanquet, family-feeling 'as an element in human nature developed within a given society, is not confined to members of family groups, but becomes a general atmosphere, a feature of the social mind, participated in by those who have of their own no existing family'.[79] Not untypically, it is not easy to see just what Bosanquet means by saying that family spirit is 'contagious' (in one, not very successful, attempt at clarification, he tells us that '[t] he solitary may partake of the family sacrament, so to speak, "by faith" '[80]). Presumably, though, what he has in mind is something like this: families, he says, are premised upon the unification of affection and service;[81] in a social order rooted in family life, an *ethos* is manifest according to which service is linked to affection and, consequently, service out of love will be a moving influence even to those not presently part of a family unit. Nevertheless, as we have seen, Bosanquet thinks a nation can have but a tinge of the family's natural affection.

To a considerable degree, then, modern liberals assign the family and the neighbourhood similar roles in the unification of a community. But some, like Mill, Green, Bosanquet and Rawls, also give the family a more distinctive task: viz. to train or develop that type of communal bond which, to each theorist, is the most important. We have seen, for example, that Mill relies a good deal on sympathy or fellow feeling. In *The Subjection of Women* he argues that a properly constituted family would be 'a school of sympathy in equality, of living together in love, without power on one side or obedience on the other'.[82] Indeed, throughout the *Subjection* Mill either treats family ties as essentially like fellow feeling, being based on sympathy and equality, or as closely connected to 'general social feelings'.[83] By linking family sentiments to wider social feelings in this way, he is able to assign the family a much larger task than merely encouraging personal affections that might spill over into other relations. Rather, having ties that are essentially similar to fraternity, the family becomes the training ground for the wider life of the community. Thus, no doubt, Mill would have enthusiastically concurred with Bosanquet that '[t]he family may be the nursery of manhood (including womanhood) and citizenship, or their grave'.[84]

Green's understanding of the family is particularly interesting in this regard. Although he quite reasonably begins by indicating that the 'sexual impulse' is at the root of family life, he does not proceed to argue that this develops into personal affection or sympathy. Rather, he says, upon the sexual impulse 'there has supervened on the part of the man a permanent interest in a woman as a person with whom his own well-being is united, and a consequent interest in the children born of her'.[85] This is surely an extraordinary account of the family, avoiding as it does all but indirect references to affection and instead concentrating on making another person's good one's own. To explain it, we need to remember that Green's conception of community is very much based on a recognition of our social interest and subsequent organic relations as opposed to, say, recognition of commonality or fraternity. Given the fundamental importance of social interest to both Green's theories of social life *and* community, it is understandable that he tries to show that such an interest arises 'primarily from family ties',[86] thus giving it a grounding in the most basic type of human relations. Unlike Mill and Bosanquet, this is to see the family not so much as a training ground or school for community life but more as the seed or fountainhead of the attitudes upon which social and community life are based.[87] And because Green's primary understanding of communal unity is so devoid of passion, his interest in family relations as the basis of such unity is also remarkably cool.[88] In contrast, Rawls, who also assigns the family this fountainhead function, paints a much warmer picture of family relations, concentrating on how they give rise to the sentiment central to his account of community, fellow feeling.[89]

### C.6. Individuality and Community: A Second Cut

We can thus identify three main types of communal feelings: patriotism (or a devotion to an abstract whole), fraternity (diffuse sympathetic feelings) and neighbourliness (personal affections). Modern liberal treatments of the family, we have just seen, view it either as similar to the neighbourhood or as the source of, or training ground for, other sorts of communal bonds. (Green's account of the family, it ought to be emphasised, focuses more on the role of the family in the development of *social interest* than on its function in the development or training of any of our three *communal* sentiments). At this point it is useful to ask whether Durkheim's two forms of communal unity — the mechanical and the organic — in any way relate to these three varieties of communal sentiments. Now I think our analysis of fraternity, in particular its sympathetic basis, does indeed reveal a significant relation. Hobhouse, it will be recalled, makes much of the importance of like-mindedness in the growth of sympathy; the more we are like others, he theorises, the easier it is to take up their perspective and act accordingly. Thus he argues that men have difficulty sympathising with women, the young with the old and the rich with the poor. And even 'in the most elementary matters many white people seem unable to feel sympathy for the brown or black'.[90] At least according to Hobhouse, then, sympathy thrives on the homogeneity that is the mark of mechanical unity. A similar conclusion is supported by Bosanquet's psychology: one of the essential points of his theory of the 'General Will' is that those united by common experiences share sentiments of unity that help mark them off from other communities.[91]

Hobhouse's sort of analysis has considerable plausibility. When we confront instances of widespread fellow feeling, fraternity or feelings of nationality, we are apt to explain them by pointing to some commonality among those so united. Thus, for example, Mill writes:

> This feeling of nationality [fellow feeling] may have been generated by various causes. Sometimes it is the effect of identity of race and descent. Community of language, and community of religion, greatly contribute to it. Geographical limits are one of its causes. But the strongest of all is the identity of political antecedents: the possession of a national history, and consequent community of recollections; collective pride and humiliation, pleasure and regret, connected with the same incidents in the past.[92]

As I said, this seems a plausible-enough analysis, but it is by no means incontrovertible. Mill saw this. Immediately after explaining that the basis of national fraternal feeling lies in identities of various sorts, he acknowledges that Switzerland, for example, 'has a strong sentiment of nationality, though the cantons are of different races, different languages, and different religions'.[93] More generally, it is not, I think, impossible to imagine participants in an *organic* unity having fraternal feelings towards each other stemming from a recognition that they are partners in a co-operative enterprise. Still, though, without some awareness of commonality — even if only of common aims — it is hard to see strong fellow feeling developing. It is far less difficult to imagine either patriotism or neighbourliness being felt by members of an organic whole. For these two sorts of communal feelings an organic unity seems just as suitable a basis as a mechanical one. Durkheim, in fact, appears to suggest that a network of neighbourliness is especially appropriate to an organic unity. In contrast to a mechanical unity in which the individual is bound directly to the whole without any intermediary, according to Durkheim's understanding of an organic union 'he depends upon society, because he depends on the parts of which it is composed'.[94] When translated, this must mean that in an organic unity each depends on others with whom he is related through his unique functions and, through a Hobhousian chain, to the whole. Hence the presence of intermediaries. The appropriateness of neighbourliness as a bond is manifest, but patriotism also seems in the spirit of such a unity. While, given organicism's emphasis on differentiation it is hard to see how fraternity can get much encouragement, a sense that one is part of a large system or enterprise seems entirely fitting and natural. At one point, for example, Bosanquet describes 'the stages of our "comprehension" of a great city'. At first, he says, the different streets that take us from one place to another are meaningless and insignificant, but, as we become acquainted with the character of the city, we come to know and appreciate the differences of each street and its people. As we do so, Bosanquet thinks, we start to feel the life of the city of which we begin to feel ourselves a part.[95] This seems reasonable enough, and it does not mean that we have any strong sense of commonality or fraternity, or indeed even neighbourliness, with our fellow citizens. Our sense is that of a complex network and of our participation in it.

I hope that the justification of my trichotomous analysis of communal feelings is now apparent. The usefulness of the scheme clearly does not derive from any mutual exclusiveness. Some cases, for example, of what I have called 'fraternity' may well qualify for inclusion under 'patriotism'. Such would seem to be the case when a group shares significant common traits giving rise to both fraternity and a sense that it is a unique collectivity standing apart from others. Being 'an American', for example, may include both a sense of fraternity with other Americans (especially when overseas!) and a sense of belonging to the American nation. However, while some cases may fall under both patriotism and fraternity, we have seen that an important distinction does emerge: patriotism (and neighbourliness) is (are) consistent with organic unity whereas strong fraternity seems to require a mechanical unity. Although these relations are of interest simply in themselves, they do have a wider implication. For if fraternity is especially associated with mechanical unity, and if, as Durkheim suggested (§B.3), mechanical unity is potentially in tension with individuality and the free development of personality, modern liberalism's considerable reliance upon fraternal bonds would apparently undermine its claim to reconcile individuality and community. In contrast, if patriotism and neighbourliness are consistent with organic unity, and if it in turn is consistent with individuality, to the extent modern liberals rely on these two forms of communal feeling, they may well be able to press their claim to have reconciled individuality and community.

But a problem remains. Although diversity of function is essential to an organic understanding of society, it is not quite so clear that the required diversity is inherently consistent with individuality. To take the model of an animal organism: each part has a distinctive function in the operation of the whole, the proper performance is its *raison d'être*. That hardly means, though, that the parts possess anything like what we have been calling individuality. Quite to the contrary, as Hobhouse recognised, the attainment of such a unity may require 'the gradual obliteration of the distinctive characters of the parts, wherein all that is opposed to unity and organisation is worn away'.[96] Leaving the metaphor aside, it would seem that a devotion to the good of the whole may require that we devote ourselves to social service rather than to pursuing our individuality. Brian Barry, for example, has argued that, according to Hobhouse and Green, we cannot be justi- fied in pursuing individual enjoyments that do not contribute to the well-being of others. The implication would appear to be that this conception of the social order, while indeed presupposing differences in functions, is hostile to individuality and, it would seem, essentially illiberal.[97]

Barry's criticism raises a wider point. Irrespective of the distinction between 'organic' and 'mechanical' unity, to what extent does any theory of community that postulates a devotion to social service and the good of the whole conflict with the pursuit of individuality? Com- munal sentiments, and to some respect social interest with its implica- tion that we are concerned with the good of our fellows, indicate that we may naturally desire to serve others and the community in general, but it remains unclear to what extent these natural 'social feelings' conflict with the pursuit of individuality. Just because we might desire to serve the community by no means implies that the development of our individuality may not be sacrificed. To be sure, it will be a self- sacrifice rather than an imposed one, but a sacrifice nonetheless. Before we can make any attempt to finally evaluate the extent to which modern liberals have reconciled individuality and sociability, we need to exam- ine whether social service and the pursuit of individuality can be harm- onised.

## D. Social Service and Individuality

As I mentioned above, Hobhouse was very much aware that an organic unity might be attained by strictly limiting the parts to a function and wearing away all other aspects of their nature. However, this route, he tells us, can only attain a 'lower' or impure type of organic unity since it produces unity by lessening the diversity and complexity of that which it organises. In contrast, '[a] community will be harmonious or organic in the purest sense in proportion as . . . it rests upon and calls forth the personality of its members in all respects in which they are in fact capable of harmonization.'[98] Whatever the merits of this sort of argument — which is very typical of Hobhouse — it is much too abstract to provide us with any clear idea as to how a community can function like an organism and yet not do violence to the individual natures of its parts. Certainly Hobhouse believes that such sacrifice is not necessary, and is even a mark of inferior organisation, but as long as we remain at such heights of generalisation, his oft-repreated proviso that qualities or capacities inconsistent with the working of the whole are to be restrained can take on an ominous tone. To get a clearer idea of how individuality can co-exist with organic membership, or more generally, with social service, we need to turn elsewhere, to Bosanquet and Dewey.

In many respects, of course, Bosanquet talks in far more ominous ways than Hobhouse. It was, after all, not Hobhouse but Bosanquet who was fond of comparing societies to armies.[99] In comparing a society to an army, and in contrasting it with a crowd, Bosanquet was trying to bring to our attention the organised nature of a society; it also serves to suggest, though, that we all have our part to do, our service to perform. According to Bosanquet our social service is typically best rendered through attention to our station and its duties. So far from being demanded, Bosanquet insists that a general do-gooding distracts one from the main tasks of doing 'one's [own] work well and intelligently'.[100] The reference to 'work' here is revealing, for whatever F.H. Bradley may have meant by our 'station', Bosanquet primarily has in mind one's vocation or occupation. Hence, in the normal course of things, our service to the community is rendered through our vocation.[101]

We saw in the first chapter (§D.3) that modern liberals look to vocations, occupations, careers, etc. as a focus for organising capacities into a coherent plan of life. We now see that vocations can be vehicles through which we render our normal service to the common good. The notion of an occupation thus provides a way by which to reconcile or integrate the  demands of individuality and membership in a community. 'An occupation', Dewey said, 'is the only thing which balances the distinctive capacity of the individual with his social service.'[102] The essence of an occupation, at least to liberals like Dewey and Bosanquet, is that one is of service to others while simultaneously developing and organising one's unique capacities. 'The individual has his own nature communicated to him as he is summoned to fit himself for rendering a distinct service to the common good.'[103] While not perhaps as explicit as Dewey and Bosanquet, Green and Hobhouse, for example, evince a similar understanding of one's work as mediating individual ability and social service.[104] More generally, given the importance of occupations and vocations in all our modern liberals' theories of individuality, and given that the very idea of finding a suitable occupation in a free labour market implies some correlation of individual capacity and social service, it seems reasonable to conclude that what is so explicit in Dewey and Bosanquet informs other modern liberal theories as well.

Obviously, if careers are to play this role, the occupational structure in a society must be sufficiently rich and varied to call upon a wide range of human capacities. But even if society is 'a many-sided creature, meeting the varied needs of human nature by functions no less varied',[105] it seems inevitable that some human capacities will either not be called upon at all, or be so lowly rewarded as to discourage their development. 'The basic structure of society', as Rawls says, 'is bound to encourage and support certain kinds of plans more than others by rewarding its members for contributing to the common good'.[106] And so some qualities and capacities will inevitably be neglected and fall into disuse.[107] Does this entail that the 'occupational solution' to the reconciliation of individuality and social service inevitably fails?

Well, given modern liberalism's understanding of unique natures it certainly does not pose as many difficulties as it would if, for example, it operated on what Dewey called the 'Aristotelian theory' (§I.E). The 'Aristotelian' conception of development, it will be recalled, posits unique capacities for each individual which manifest themselves in a unique destiny. But modern liberalism postulates a unique capacity repertoire, all parts of which cannot be fully developed or indeed even known. So the simple fact that not all one's capacities are called upon is not *ipso facto* stifling to individuality, since some selection is necessary in any event. However, if the choice of occupations really available is very restricted so that individuals are required to do something not at all congenial to their nature, then obviously occupations cannot perform the function of harmonising social services and pursuing individuality. The first case we tend to think of here is perhaps the class/occupational structure of Plato's *Republic*,[108] but, as Mill is now famous for pointing out, a more relevant and extreme case has been opportunities for women. Although he is willing to leave it an open question, Mill is more than skeptical of any claim that all women are somehow naturally fitted only for the vocation of wife and mother; if it seems so at present, he says, it is probably only because their individuality has been systematically thwarted and their natures perverted.[109] Freed to find vocations that suit them, many will certainly supplement the traditional feminine roles, while some are very likely to do entirely different things.[110] To force women into the vocation of wife and mother, and only that, is to do violence to their unique individual natures.

This type of drastic limitation of occupational opportunities is not the only way in which an occupational structure might fail to accommodate the individuality of some. We will see in Chapter VII that modern liberals are often critical of the economic order as most of the jobs do not promote the development of individual natures. And, especially in Dewey, we will also find a strong indication that he believed the capitalism of his day slighted many aspects of human nature by its concentration on materialistic gain. Thus, for example, at one point he suggests that, regrettably but understandably, some of those with inclinations leaning, for instance, towards artistic or intellectual life, had fled America, in fact or in imagination, to seek a more congenial environment.[111] Indeed, I will argue later that the ideal of focusing individuality on careers leads to a fundamental critique of the contemporary economic order. (However, grounds also exist for questioning the attainability of this ideal (§ VII.D).)

The problems that we have been considering concern ways in which an occupational structure might restrict the development of some people's individuality, and thus indicate one line of attack on the modern liberal claim that occupations reconcile individuality and social service. The opposite line of criticism is also possible: it can be argued that in some ways occupations do not represent a social service, or at least not always a sufficient one. Leaving aside the point that (arguably), the occupations of bank robber and/or robber baron do not provide a real social service, modern liberals are faced with a more imposing difficulty on this score. Although in the normal course of things one might reasonably be said to best serve the community by diligently performing the duties of one's station − especially one's vocation − in more extraordinary times considerably more may be required (or, we might say, the duties of one's station may expand far beyond one's chosen occupation). Thus, for example, even Hobhouse, who is always concerned with showing that membership in an organic community need not entail a submersion of individuality, is driven to admitting that in an imperfect world the individual may well feel obliged to make extreme sacrifices for the community. 'The service of society may require the entire sacrifice of happiness or life on the part of the individual.'[112] Most obviously, such might be the case in war where the individual's sense of social service may lead him to sacrifice his life. But, less dramatically, in a social order with substantial injustice or poverty, a devotion to the welfare of the community might well require that one work towards alleviating social evils, and thereby forgo an occupation, other activities or income that would better promote the development of one's individual nature. Hence Green tells us that in deciding to cultivate one's taste for music '[t]he question whether it should be sacrificed or culti-vated must depend on the position and general capabilities of the indi-vidual, on the circumstances of his time, on the claims of surrounding society.'[113]

Such statements have led some readers to doubt Green's devotion to individuality, and it must be admitted that his work is rich in praise of those who make self-sacrifices in the performance of duties or services to others.[114] And it is certainly reasonable to conclude that, more than any other modern liberal, Green believes that even in normal times social service often requires some sort of self-sacrifice that de-monstrates highly praiseworthy devotion to the common good.[115] Nevertheless, it would seem that any theory of man that postulates a significant communal devotion would be driven to some such admission that social service may very well call for courses of action inconsistent with the maximisation of one's own individual development. To be sure, like Bosanquet, one may insist that an explicit devotion to social service will often be a better path to developing one's nature than some narrow ideal of self-cultivation.[116] And the 'mutual stimulation' argument pro-vides some grounds for saying that assisting others to develop can help develop one's own individuality (§II.C.1). Still, it appears inevitable that cases will arise in which social service does indeed demand some sacrifice of individuality. It would thus seem that even a thorough-going organic understanding of community, at some point or at some time, is going to be in tension with individuality.

However, Bosanquet's analysis of such self-sacrifice suggests that it is more than a little misleading to simply put the issue in terms of a tension between 'individuality' and 'community'. Although, as I stressed in the first chapter (§I.D.3), Bosanquet, like all modern liberals, thinks the aim of development to be a systematic, inclusive and coherent per-sonality, he is willing to acknowledge that such a multifaceted, harmon-ious development may not always be possible. The development of 'some special and important element', he tells us, might under some conditions, be 'incompatible with the system and balance of the self as a whole'.[117] Now, while we saw in the first chapter that modern liberals generally favour a wider, more inclusive growth, Bosanquet insists that we might properly decide to further this 'all important' element and, consequently, sacrifice the satisfaction of the self as a whole.

This 'all important' element could be any of a number of interests, values or affections, such as truth, justice or beauty: it might also be 'some great work "for others"'.[118] And here lies, I think, the significant point. Not just a devotion to the welfare of the community, but any cherished value could, under certain conditions, be in tension with the cultivation of a multifaceted individuality. Rather than being a case of 'the individual' versus 'the community', the tension is more adequately seen as one between the quest for an integrated, inclusive individuality and the demands made by some 'all important' value, interest or affection which is critically at stake. Whether it be truth, justice or service to others, the cherished element might conflict with the achievement of a well-rounded individuality and, if so, might call for 'self-sacrifice'. Just when we are to sacrifice 'self' and when the cherished value, is, of course, a real moral dilemma on which Bosanquet provides no guidance. The important thing, though, is that the choice between devotion to the community (requiring self-sacrifice) and pursuit of individuality is an instance of a wider class of dilemmas and must be understood in that light.

## E. Individuality, Social Life and Community

It might be helpful here to briefly summarise the main conclusions of these first three chapters. In the first chapter, I examined modern liberalism's conception of individuality. It was, I argued, an essentially positive conception, concentrating on what we have it in us to become rather than on our isolation from others. But it does hold that we are indeed different from others, each having a unique nature upon which his individual development is premised. (We saw that Bosanquet and, perhaps, Green, had a 'diverse' not a 'unique' natures theory.) In the development of these unique natures we prefer the 'higher', i.e. complex intellectual and artistic, lines of development over the 'lower', i.e. bodily, pleasures. Moreover, we aim to fashion our developed capacities into a unique, harmonious and multifaceted individuality.

And there lies the problem which set the stage for the second chapter. For while we are driven towards a wide-ranging personality, some specialisation is necessary if we are to intensely develop some of our gifts and achieve individual excellence. 'We cannot become all we are capable of being' is one of modern liberalism's more important slogans. While leisure activities might help alleviate this conflict, modern liberals suggest a more interesting solution: through social life we can participate in lines of development which we either had to forgo (in order to specialise) or of which we were not capable. Thus the development of others is of interest to us and is, as Green argued, a good. Furthermore, it is typically argued that a social existence with other developed persons spurs the growth of our own individuality.

This, I argued, is the heart of the organic theory of social life. But it seems to fall short of a conception of a community, for it does not strictly entail that members of a social order will recognise that they are related in these ways and thus form a whole. And, in any event, mere recognition of unity without feelings of unity hardly seems to make for a community. However, whereas it makes sense to talk of modern liberalism's theory of individuality and theory of social life, when we come to community we are faced with a greater diversity of views among (and within each of) our modern liberals. So this third chapter engaged in a bit of taxonomising. Following Durkheim, I distinguished recognition of an 'organic unity' – essentially, as in Green, awareness of the interconnections of social life – from a 'mechanical unity' based on commonality and similarity. The latter, I suggested, appears more in tune with our normal understandings of community, but, as Durkheim indicated, it apparently has much greater possibilities for tensions with individuality. We also distinguished three forms of communal feelings – patriotism, fraternity and neighbourliness – and found reason to associate the second, i.e. fraternity, with 'mechanical unity'. The other two, in contrast, seem compatible with either form of unity. And, lastly, we have just been examining the extent to which a devotion to social service, which seems essential to any form of community (including the organic), is consistent with the pursuit of individuality.

As I stated in the Introductory, modern liberals generally have been seen as aiming at some sort of harmonisation of individuality and sociability. This, of course, is a rough and general observation. We can certainly identify among modern liberals some who are more or less ambitious harmonisers. In lieu of a long discussion, I think it is probably safe to say that Green and Bosanquet are the most insistent that, at least in principle, both 'individuality' and our 'social' nature are manifestations of the same principle in human nature – the drive to self-realisation – and, so, are not inherently in conflict.[119] Rawls and Mill are certainly the most cautious. Rawls, for example, is explicit that pursuit of individual plans might conflict with 'social and altruistic motivation'.[120] And in *Liberty* Mill adopts a straightforward *balancing*, as opposed to a *harmonising*, position, describing 'individuality' and 'sociability' as 'opposites' in need of 'reconciling and combining'.[121] And more than once he warned of the danger of so emphasising social unity as to endanger individuality.[122] However, at least with Mill, it is certain that he entertained a more harmonious ideal. Both in his writings on political economy and in his *Autobiography* he testifies that his ideal is an intensification and integration of both individuality and community-mindedness.[123] Our question, then, is to what extent the modern liberal theory of man provides the basis for such a hope.

In some ways, modern liberals have been very effective in undermining the idea that individuality and sociability are 'opposites' in tension. The theories of individuality and social life provide a plausible integration, envisaging social life as the completion, not the opponent, of individuality. To be sure, as Green was apt to emphasise, social life requires some disciplining of individual action but, as we have seen, modern liberals are prone to see a need for discipline in the development of individuality itself. As I have indicated, things become much more complicated when we move to the level of community. It does seem that a 'minimalist' organic conception of community, involving recognition of organic relations, feelings of unity with the whole and a devotion to social service, conjoined with the thesis that occupations reconcile individuality and social service, goes a long way towards harmonising the pursuit of individuality with membership in a community. But, although it seems to carry us part of the way towards harmony, it appears doubtful that it can go all the way. Social service (as well as a whole range of other commitments and values) is likely to conflict with the pursuit of individuality, and when it does, some trade-off will be necessary. (See also §VII.D.)

If matters simply stood thus we could conclude that modern liberalism, if not totally successful in its attempt to harmonise individuality and community, does achieve a good deal along those lines. Yet not even Green, whose conception of community seems to be most thoroughgoingly organic, is content to rest matters there. At some point or other all our modern liberals are driven to a stronger conception of community, premised on shared outlooks, language, history, etc. and giving rise to fraternity/fellow feeling/sympathy. Surely this is a solid sort of community. But, as Durkheim warned, it draws its strength from commonality whereas individuality − and, we might note, the modern liberal conception of social life − is premised on diversity. Now Durkheim, I think, sometimes tends to make too much of this opposition. Considerable commonality of outlook, feeling, etc. is consistent with a great deal of individual diversity. Individuality can exist, indeed thrive, in a community with considerable commonality. As Rawls points out, 'associative ties' may cushion us against self-doubt when mishaps or failures occur.[124] Nevertheless, Durkheim seems right in saying that the dynamics of 'mechanical unity' and individualised personalities are ultimately opposed; at some point the growth of commonality and unity, as Mill warned, will endanger individuality. And, conversely, as Durkheim argued, the growth of individuality breaks down the most intense forms of mechanical solidarity.[125] Thus it would seem that modern liberals are ultimately driven back to the balancing of opposites.[126] Their theory of man goes a long way towards harmony and integration, but it appears that the type of community to which all were ultimately attracted is, in theory, in tension with individual diversity.

Even Bosanquet, probably the most adamant harmoniser of all, seems to recognise this ultimate tension. In his discussion of religious unity, Bosanquet makes much of the total absorption of the self in a larger whole. 'It is the surrender or completion of the finite selfhood in the world of spiritual membership.'[127] Dewey, too, in his early ideal-ist work on psychology, saw the surrendering of the particular self to the whole as the basis of the 'feeling of peace' that accompanies religious belief.[128] What is particularly interesting about both Dewey and Bosan-quet here is that they see such religious feelings as a purer and more complete manifestation of the feelings of unity we experience in society. In social and communal life, as even Bosanquet acknowledges, we are necessarily 'at arm's length' to each other.[129] And while from the perspective of unity this represents a necessary imperfection in social life, it is an imperfection which permits the existence of distinct personalities which, Bosanquet believes, allows each of us to stand for something special and make our own distinctive contribution to human life.[130] Our individualised personality is both valuable to, and a limit on, our emersion into the community.

## Notes

1.    See Ernest Barker, *Political Thought in England: 1848 to 1914*, 2nd edn (Oxford University Press, Oxford, 1959), p. 60; John W. Chapman, *Rousseau – Totalitarian or Liberal?* (Columbia University Press, New York, 1956), pp. 129 ff. Bosanquet's theory is premised on commonality or similarity as well as on a unity based on interlocking differences. As did Bosanquet himself, most accounts fail to distinguish these two aspects of his conception of social unity. See § B.1.
2.    William McDougall, *The Group Mind* (Cambridge University Press, Cambridge, 1920), p. 157.
3.    Zevedei Barbu, *Problems of Historical Psychology* (Routledge and Kegan Paul, London, 1960), p. 112.
4.    Solomon E. Asch, *Social Psychology* (Prentice-Hall, New York, 1952), p. 335.

5. McDougall, *The Group Mind*, pp. 157-58.

6. See Bertil Pfannenstill, *Bernard Bosanquet's Philosophy of the State* (G.W.K. Gleerup, Lund, 1936), pp. 238-39.

7. Bosanquet, *The Value and Destiny of the Individual* (Macmillan, London, 1913), p. 12; see also his *Science and Philosophy* (Allen and Unwin, London, 1927), pp. 264 ff.

8. Bosanquet, *Science and Philosophy*, p. 267.

9. Bosanquet, *Social and International Ideals* (Macmillan, London, 1917), p. 291.

10. Emile Durkheim, *The Division of Labor in Society*, George Simpson (trans.) (Free Press of Glencoe, New York, 1964), Book One.

11. Green, *Prolegomena to Ethics*, A.C. Bradley (ed.) (Clarendon Press, Oxford, 1890), pp. 212, 213-14.

12. W.D. Lamont, *Introduction to Green's Moral Philosophy* (Allen and Unwin, London, 1934), pp. 216-18. See Ann R. Cacoullos, *Thomas Hill Green: Philosopher of Rights* (Twayne, New York, 1974). pp. 131 ff.

13. Green, *Prolegomena*, pp. 250 ff. While this seems the essence of Green's theory of the common good, it is of course expanded in complex ways. I realise that this is not the view of the common good usually attributed to Green; however, Green clearly thought the notion of a social interest fundamental to his theory of the common good; many interpretations (mistakenly, I believe) make little of social interest.

14. Green is clear that consciousness is necessary: 'The foundation of morality, then, in the reason or self-objectifying consciousness of man, is the same thing as its foundation in the institutions of a common life – in these as directed to a common good, and so directed not mechanically but with consciousness of the good on the part of those subject to the institutions' (*Prolegomena*, p. 216). In his *Lectures on the Principles of Political Obligation*, Green admits that the 'ordinary citizen' is not very conscious of the common good, acting instead 'habitually and instinctively' (in R.L. Nettleship (ed.), *Works of Thomas Hill Green* [Longman's, Green, and Co., London, 1900], vol. II, p. 435). However, in noting this Green is critical: such people make loyal subjects but not intelligent patriots – a condition that he thinks democracy might help remedy (see § VI.B.1). In citing this passage from Green's *Political Obligation*, Cacoullos appears to miss its critical tone. *Thomas Hill Green*, pp. 83-84.

15. Bosanquet, *Psychology of the Moral Self* (Macmillan, London, 1904), p. 43. Emphasis added.

16. For Hobhouse's criticisms of Bosanquet, see *The Metaphysical Theory of the State* (Allen and Unwin, London, 1926), Lecture III, 'The Real Will'. For a comparison of Hobhouse's and Bosanquet's views, see Pfannenstill, *Bosanquet's Philosophy of the State*, pp. 250 ff.

17. Hobhouse, *Social Development* (Allen and Unwin, London, 1924), p. 185. McDougall, who generally sides with Hobhouse against Bosanquet, does not seem worried about using the term 'group mind'. See ibid., pp. 181n-182n. All things considered, it would probably be correct to say that Hobhouse's theory of the 'interaction of minds' emphasises differences over similarities whereas Bosanquet's puts considerable stress on similarities.

18. Dewey, *Democracy and Education* (Free Press, New York, 1916), p. 4. See Alfonso J. Damico, *Individuality and Community: The Social and Political Thought of John Dewey* (University Presses of Florida, Gainesville, 1978), pp. 43-44.

19. I use 'civil society' rather than 'social life' since the interconnections and dependencies Dewey has in mind here are not, for the most part, those resting on individuality and social interest but, rather, those stemming from economic

relations. However, this latter sort of interdependencies are very much what Durkheim is thinking of in his description of organic unity. Hobhouse too provides an elaborate account of the distinction between 'society' and 'community' in *Social Development*, Ch. II. 'Civil society' relates to the idea of a 'private society' (§II.B.1). See Rawls, *A Theory of Justice* (The Belknap Press of Harvard University Press, Cambridge, Mass., 1971), p. 521n.

20. Dewey, *The Public and Its Problems* (Swallow Press, Chicago, 1954), pp. 126-28.

21. Ibid., pp. 151-52.

22. Dewey, *Freedom and Culture* (Allen and Unwin, London, 1940), pp. 159-60. See John E. Smith, 'The Value of Community: Dewey and Royce', *Southern Journal of Philosophy*, XII (Winter 1974), p. 471.

23. See L.S. Feuer, 'John Stuart Mill as a Sociologist: The Unwritten Ethology' in J.M. Robson and M. Laine (eds.), *James and John Stuart Mill: Papers of the Centenary Conference* (University of Toronto Press, Toronto, 1976), pp. 86-110; Sir William Ashley's 'Introduction' to J.S. Mill's *Principles of Political Economy* (Augustus M. Kelley, Fairfield, N.J., 1976), pp. xvi-xvii; and Alan Ryan, *J.S. Mill* (Routledge and Kegan Paul, London, 1974), pp. 88-89. See §IV.A.3.

24. Mill, 'Coleridge' in J.M. Robson (ed.), *The Collected Works of John Stuart Mill* (University of Toronto Press, Toronto, 1963), vol. X, p. 141.

25. Mill, *A System of Logic* in *Collected Works*, vol. VIII, p. 866.

26. Mill, 'Bentham' in *Collected Works*, vol. X, p. 105.

27. Hobhouse, *Social Development*, p. 191.

28. Green, *Political Obligation*, pp. 436-37.

29. Hobhouse, *Social Evolution and Political Theory* (Columbia University Press, New York, 1928), p. 146. See also his 'The Past and the Future: The Influence of Nationalism' in J.A. Hobson and Morris Ginsberg (eds.), *L.T. Hobhouse: His Life and Work* (Allen and Unwin, London, 1931), pp. 325-30; and his *Social Development*, Ch. VIII.

30. Rawls, *A Theory of Justice*, pp. 377 ff. See Brian Barry, *The Liberal Theory of Justice: A Critical Examination of the Principal Doctrines in* A Theory of Justice *by John Rawls* (Clarendon Press, Oxford, 1973), Ch. XII.

31. Milne argues that, ultimately, in spite of himself, Bosanquet admits 'that the ultimate moral community is not the state but mankind'. *The Social Philosophy of English Idealism* (Allen and Unwin, London, 1962), p. 259.

32. Hobhouse, *The Metaphysical Theory of the State*, p.115.

33. Hobhouse, *The Elements of Social Justice* (Allen and Unwin, London, 1949) pp. 199-200.

34. Hobhouse, *The Metaphysical Theory of the State*, p. 116.

35. Bosanquet, *Science and Philosophy*, pp. 297, 291. Sometimes Bosanquet goes further and argues that humanity possesses no organic unity at all, being simply an aggregation. On the difference between organic and aggregate unity, see S.I. Benn and G.F. Gaus, 'The Liberal Conception of the Public and Private' in S.I. Benn and G.F. Gaus (eds.), *Conceptions of the Public and Private in Social Life* (Croom Helm, London, forthcoming).

36. Hobhouse, *The Metaphysical Theory of the State*, p. 114.

37. Hobhouse, *The Rational Good: A Study in the Logic of Practice* (Watts, London, 1947), p. 145.

38. Ibid.

39. Dewey's vision of a world 'community' lies in more Bosanquetian directions, resting upon a universal recognition of commonality rather than an organic unity. But Dewey's idea of humanity-wide commonality is a fairly modest one. Because the 'Great Society' is worldwide, he argues, it gives rise to common, cross-

national problems of controlling the consequences of interdependency. In his 1946 'Afterword' to *The Public and Its Problems*, Dewey appears to believe that there is some evidence of the rise of such an international community, seeking common solutions to recognised common problems. Again, though, Dewey does not see any community, including a Great World Community, as resting simply on interdependency, and an awareness of commonality of concerns, outlooks and values is absolutely necessary.

40.   R.M. MacIver, *Community: A Sociological Study*, 4th edn (Frank Cass, London, 1970), pp. 22-23.

41.   Durkheim, *The Division of Labor in Society*, p. 129.

42.   Hobhouse, *Social Development*, p. 152. Durkheim presents a very similar distinction between direct and indirect solidarity. *The Division of Labor in Society*, p. 129.

43.   See Bosanquet, *Social and International Ideals*, p. 3; Green, *Prolegomena*, pp. 436-37.

44.   Bosanquet, *Essays and Addresses* (Swan Sonnenschein, London, 1891), p. 110; and his *Principle of Individuality and Value* (Macmillan, London, 1912), p. 374.

45.   Green, 'The Influence of Civilisation on Genius' in *Works*, vol. III, p. 18.

46.   Green, *Political Obligation*, p. 481. See also Milne, *The Social Philosophy of English Idealism*, p. 163.

47.   This, of course, is not to deny that some day humanity may be capable of exciting real feelings of community. See Peter Gordon and John White, *Philosophers as Educational Reformers: The Influence of Idealism on British Educational Thought and Practice* (Routledge and Kegan Paul, London, 1979), Ch. 3.

48.   Mill, *Utilitarianism* in *Collected Works*, vol. X, pp. 231-32.

49.   John Dewey and James H. Tufts, *Ethics*, rev. edn (Henry Holt, New York, 1932), pp. 266-69.

50.   Rawls, *A Theory of Justice*, p. 502.

51.   Hobhouse, *Social Justice*, p. 23. See also his *Rational Good*, p. 135.

52.   Bosanquet, *The Philosophical Theory of the State*, 4th edn (Macmillan, London, 1951), p. 56.

53.   According to the 'difference principle' 'the higher expectations of those better situated are just if and only if they work as part of a scheme which improves the expectations of the least advantaged members of society. The intuitive idea is that the social order is not to establish and secure the more attractive prospects of those better off unless doing so is to the advantage of those less fortunate.' *A Theory of Justice*, p. 75. See §V.D, Ch. VII.

54.   Ibid., p. 105.

55.   Green, *Political Obligation*, p. 436.

56.   Dewey, *Problems of Men* (Philosophical Library, New York, 1946), p. 43.

57.   According to Piaget, 'the bond between egalitarianism and solidarity is a universal psychological principle'. *The Moral Judgment of the Child*, Marjorie Gabain (trans.) (The Free Press, New York, 1965), p. 320.

58.   Mill, 'De Tocqueville on Democracy in America (II)' in *Collected Works*, vol. XVIII, p. 181.

59.   John Grote in *An Examination of the Utilitarian Philosophy*, Joseph Bickersteth Mayor (ed.) (Deighton, Bell, Cambridge, 1870), p. 337.

60.   'The actual irradiation of feeling, in such wise that the feeling of another becomes mine, is a rarer, a more emotional, and sometimes it would seem a quasi-physical incarnation of the same fundamental impulse, which . . . sometimes works perversely.' Hobhouse, *Social Development*, pp. 152-53. Compare Bosanquet, *Psychology of the Moral Self*, pp. 67-69.

61. Hobhouse, *Social Development*, p. 153.

62. Of all modern liberals Bosanquet is the least worried about classes, seeing them both as vehicles for solidarity and for personality development. But even he worries about their divisive nature: 'I believe that different people will both from taste and from equipment for function always live rather differently. But beyond a certain point externals do separate classes and prevent mutual understanding, and so cause censurable stupidity.' *Some Suggestions in Ethics* (Macmillan, London, 1919), p. 241. For more positive statements about classes, see his *Philosophical Theory of the State*, pp. 291 ff, and his *Ideals*, pp. 193 ff.

63. Mill, *Utilitarianism*, p. 223.

64. Hobhouse, *Social Development*, pp. 154-55.

65. Dewey, *The Public and Its Problems*, p. 109.

66. Rawls, *A Theory of Justice*, p. 474.

67. Bosanquet, *Essays and Addresses*, p. 46; and his *Philosophical Theory of the State*, pp. 282-89.

68. Mill, 'De Tocqueville', pp. 182-83.

69. Tocqueville quoted in ibid., p. 183. Emphasis added.

70. Hobhouse, *Social Development*, p. 158.

71. Bosanquet, *The Philosophical Theory of the State*, p. 251.

72. Dewey, *The Public and Its Problems*, pp. 140-41.

73. Ibid., pp. 211-12.

74. Ibid., p. 26. Emphasis added.

75. Rawls, *A Theory of Justice*, pp. 570, 571.

76. Dewey, *The Public and Its Problems*, pp. 211-19. See Damico, *Individuality and Community*, pp. 43-44.

77. Dewey, *Democracy and Education*, pp. 82-83; Hobhouse, *Social Development*, p. 161; Bosanquet, *Ideals*, pp. 3-4.

78. Dewey, *Democracy and Education*, p. 83; Hobhouse, *Social Development*, pp. 40, 161.

79. Bosanquet, 'Hegel's Theory of the Political Organism', *Mind*, VII (1898), p. 12.

80. Bosanquet, *The Philosophical Theory of the State*, p. 279n.

81. Ibid., p. 279.

82. Mill, *The Subjection of Women* in Alice S. Rossi (ed.), *Essays on Sex Equality* (University of Chicago Press, Chicago, 1970), p. 175.

83. Ibid., p. 163.

84. Bosanquet, *Ideals*, p. 5. Of course Mill and Bosanquet have different reasons for supporting that conclusion: Bosanquet sees family life as a training ground for intelligent devotion to the good of the whole. This understanding of the role of the family seems to have more relevance to children – as opposed to just wives and husbands.

85. Green, *Political Obligation*, p. 540.

86. Ibid., p. 361.

87. Gordon and White emphasise Green's Hegelian roots and, consequently, suggest that, like Hegel, Green sees the family as a training ground for 'community life'. (*Philosophers as Educational Reformers*, pp. 36 ff). While I think they are right that the training ground role is in the main emphasised by idealists, it does seem, as I argue in the text, that Green's theory has a somewhat different emphasis; nevertheless, it is a matter of differing emphases, with both the 'training ground' and 'fountainhead' functions being found in many writers.

88. As we might expect, when Green does want to show that patriotism can be a passion, his depictions of ties to both family and fellow citizens changes, emphasising commonality and strong sentiments. *Political Obligation*, pp. 436-37.

89. See Rawls, *A Theory of Justice*, pp. 462-72, 490.

90. Hobhouse, *Social Development*, p. 154.

91. See Bosanquet, *Ideals*, pp. 292-93.

92. Mill, *Considerations on Representative Government* in *Collected Works*, vol. XIX, p. 546.

93. Ibid.

94. Durkheim, *The Division of Labor in Society*, p. 129.

95. Bosanquet, *Ideals*, pp. 87-88.

96. Hobhouse, *Mind in Evolution*, 3rd edn (Macmillan, London, 1926), p. 414.

97. Brian Barry, *Political Argument* (Routledge and Kegan Paul, London, 1965), pp. 230-32. For a detailed examination of Barry's argument, see Cacoullos, *Thomas Hill Green*, pp. 115 ff.

98. Hobhouse, *Sociology and Philosophy: A Centenary Collection of Essays and Articles* (G. Bell and Sons, London, 1966) p. 45.

99. Bosanquet, *The Philosophical Theory of the State*, pp. 150-51.

100. Bosanquet, *The Civilization of Christendom* (Swan Sonnenschein, London, 1899), p. 182.

101. Bosanquet, *The Philosophical Theory of the State*, pp. 191, 290.

102. Dewey, *Democracy and Education*, p. 308.

103. Bosanquet, *The Philosophical Theory of the State*, p. 290. See §IV.A.2.

104. Green, *Prolegomena*, pp. 201-2; Hobhouse, *Social Justice*, Ch. VII.

105. Bosanquet, *The Philosophical Theory of the State*, p. 283.

106. Rawls, *A Theory of Justice*, p. 425.

107. See Bosanquet's essay on 'Socialism and Natural Selection' in Bernard Bosanquet (ed.), *Aspects of the Social Problem* (Macmillan, London, 1895), pp. 293-94.

108. See Dewey, *Democracy and Education*, p. 90.

109. Mill, *Subjection of Women*, pp. 148-56.

110. Ibid., pp. 239-42. Mill seems to believe, however, that if a woman chooses to be a wife and mother, it is a full-time employment. Only after her children grow up, does he think she should look for other tasks. See Carole Pateman, 'Feminist Critiques of the Public/Private Dichotomy' in Benn and Gaus (eds.), *The Public and Private in Social Life*.

111. Dewey, *Individualism − Old and New* (Allen and Unwin, London, 1931), p. 117.

112. Hobhouse, *The Rational Good*, p. 139.

113. Green, *Prolegomena*, p. 421.

114. See John Luther Hemingway, 'The Emergence of an Ethical Liberalism: A Study of Idealist Philosophy from Thomas Hill Green to the Present', unpublished PhD thesis, University of Iowa, 1979, p. 74. H.D. Lewis also emphasises the underlying need for self-sacrifice in Green's theory. *Freedom and History* (Allen and Unwin, London, 1962), p. 102. See also Melvin Richter, *The Politics of Conscience: T.H. Green and His Age* (Weidenfeld and Nicolson, London, 1964), pp. 129-35. Sidgwick argued that Green's psychology does not permit self-sacrifice, as it is posited on an indefeasible drive to self-realisation. Leaving aside the merits of Sidgwick's argument, it does seem clear that Green could quite intelligibly talk of sacrificing one's individuality (even if not the whole self) for the good of others. *Lectures on the Ethics of T.H. Green, Mr Herbert Spencer and J. Martineau* (Macmillan, London, 1902), pp. 67 ff, 94-95. I consider Bosanquet's account of the 'psychology of self-sacrifice' below.

115. See Gordon and White, *Philosophers as Educational Reformers*, pp. 32-33, 44-45.

116. Bosanquet, *Science and Philosophy*, pp. 174-76. But see also his *Some Suggestions in Ethics*, Ch. 1.

117. Bosanquet, *Psychology of the Moral Self*, p. 97.

118. Ibid.

119. See, for example, Green's essay on 'Popular Philosophy in its Relation to Life' in *Works*, vol. III, esp. pp. 99-103.

120. Rawls, *A Theory of Justice*, p. 281.

121. Mill, *On Liberty* in *Collected Works*, vol. XVIII, pp. 253-54.

122. Mill, *Principles of Political Economy* in *Collected Works*, vol. II, pp. 208-9; see also his *Auguste Comte and Positivism*, pt. II, in *Collected Works*, vol. X. See also Hobhouse, *Sociology and Philosophy*, p. 100.

123. Mill, *Principles of Political Economy*, pp. 210-14; *Chapters on Socialism* in *Collected Works*, vol. V, p. 746; and his *Autobiography* (Columbia University Press, New York, 1924), pp. 162-63.

124. Rawls, *A Theory of Justice*, p. 441. Compare Bosanquet, *Some Suggestions in Ethics*, pp. 96 ff.

125. This was also an important theme of Hobhouse's. See *Social Development*, Ch. 1.

126. See Gerald F. Gaus and John W. Chapman, 'Anarchism and Political Philosophy: An Introduction' in J. Roland Pennock and John W. Chapman (eds.), *NOMOS XIX: Anarchism* (New York University Press, New York, 1978), xvii-xlv. See also S.I. Benn, 'Individuality, Autonomy and Community' in Eugene Kamenka (ed.), *Community* (Edward Arnold, London, forthcoming) in the series *Ideas and Ideologies*.

127. Bosanquet, *Value and Destiny*, p. 226.

128. Dewey, *The Early Works of John Dewey: 1882-98*, vol. 2, *Psychology* (Southern Illinois University Press, Carbondale and Edwardsville, 1967), pp. 291-92.

129. Bosanquet, *Value and Destiny*, p. 133.

130. Ibid., p. 61.

# IV DEVELOPMENTALISM

Throughout the first three chapters my concern has been to examine the modern liberal conceptions of individuality, social life and community. In doing so, I repeatedly had occasion to refer to such notions as 'development of capacities' and 'human growth'. It is now time to turn our attention to this 'dynamic' element and so to look more closely at just what modern liberals have meant by the development of capacities and, more generally, of personality. I begin (§A) by examining the opposing positions of 'nature' and 'nurture' and argue that modern liberals have advocated an *interactionist* and *developmental* approach that seeks to combine the insights of both the 'nature' and 'nurture' positions. I then turn in §B to distinguish *strong* and *weak* variants of developmental theories, maintaining that the modern liberals advocate the former. This leads (§C), as I suggested in the first chapter (§I.D.4), to what I call the 'problem of discipline', i.e. whether modern liberals can consistently advocate both the natural growth of human nature and discipline. I close in §D by briefly considering the relation in modern liberal theory between individual and social development.

## A. Nature and Nurture[1]

### A.1. Instinctivism and Environmentalism

An obvious point of departure for any analysis of how personality traits arise is the longstanding, but by no means exhausted, debate between the proponents of 'nature' and 'nurture'. The radical nature position is typically associated with *instinctivist* theories according to which important personality traits are manifestations of innate dispositions that are not liable to much, if any, change. According to William McDougall, for instance, 'The human mind has certain innate or inherited tendencies which are the essential springs or motive powers of all thought and action.' And, McDougall went on, these innate tendencies 'are the bases from which the character and will of individuals and of nations are gradually developed under the guidance of the intellectual faculties'. Thus, McDougall argues that the characteristics of men from one era to the next are largely invariant since these instincts have a 'stable and unchanging character'.[2] However, the idea of 'instincts' in human beings is a problematic one. As Hobhouse pointed out, instincts are manifested in their clearest and starkest form in lower animals in which they are 'very precise and very insistent'; a particular instinct leads to a particular course of action and is 'difficult or even impossible to throw ... off'.[3] Obviously, when applied to humans and other higher animals the instincts become more generalised: not even the most adamant instinctivist contends that human action is just like the nest-building of wasps.[4] And so, as Lionel Tiger and Robin Fox note, 'old-fashioned' instinctivists relied on tendencies such as ' "maternalism", "self-abasement" and "acquisitiveness" '.[5] To be sure, these theories were apt to postulate an ever-increasing number of such tendencies, each intended to account for a specific department of human behaviour. But still, the instincts remained generalised in the sense that they did not entail a specific pattern of behaviour. Even a classic instinctivist like McDougall acknowledged that an instinct does not always lead to the same sort of behaviour. Even though the instinct itself remains unchanged, McDougall accepted the possibility that learning could help modify the behaviour resulting from instinct.

> An illustration may indicate the main principle involved: One may have learnt to suppress more or less completely the bodily movements in which the excitement of the instinct of pugnacity naturally finds vent; or by a study of pugilism one may have learnt to render these movements more finely adapted to secure the end of the instinct; or one may have learnt to replace them by the habitual use of weapons, so that the hand flies to the sword-hilt or to the hip-pocket, instead of being raised to strike, whenever this instinct is excited.[6]

But still, the main idea is straightforward: men are aggressive because of their pugnacious instinct. In the same vein, McDougall attributes our desire for the company of our fellows to our gregarious impulses.[7]

Although 'old-fashioned' instinctivist theories still have considerable currency (e.g. Lorenz's theory of aggression),[8] most contemporary proponents of the nature position take a somewhat different approach. Rather than offering a catalogue of instincts, people like Tiger and Fox put forward 'an alternative, if more moderate view', that is, 'that the human organism is "wired" in a certain way so that it can process and emit information about certain facts of social life such as language and rules about sex, and that, furthermore, it can process this information only at certain times and only in certain ways'.[9] Edward O.

Wilson seems also to take a 'more moderate' view, emphasising that human genes 'provide a *capacity* to develop a certain array of traits' rather than specifying a single trait. 'In some categories of behavior, the array is limited and the outcome can be altered only by strenuous training — if ever. In others, the array is vast and the outcome easily influenced.'[10] Wilson, like Tiger and Fox, not only shies away from the catalogues of instincts of the earlier instinctivists, but also, again like them, is concerned to draw attention to the role of the environment in stimulating behaviour. We shall see presently (§A.2) that in this respect their positions — as indeed do those of most sophisticated instinctivists — approach interactionist theories.

Traditionally, the main rival to an instinctivist account of personality 'is the view that human properties are predominantly the consequences of learning in response to environmental conditions'.[11] Following Maurice Mandelbaum, we can distinguish two variants of this view: *geneticism* and *organicism*.[12]

(i) As Mandelbaum understands it, 'geneticism' seeks to account for personal characteristics via the particular experiences the individual has undergone. According to the radical geneticist, then, the sole determinants of personality are the experiences that constitute the individual's history. If all had the same experiences, all would be exactly alike; and, presumably, the appropriate manipulation of experiences can produce almost any sort of personality. Personality variations are thus directly and perfectly correlated with variations in individual histories. In the nineteenth century, as Mandelbaum points out, associationists such as James Mill were the leading proponents of geneticism. (I consider James Mill's associationism and his son's modification of it in §A.3.) More recently, behaviourists like John B. Watson offered radical geneticist accounts, holding personality to be 'but the end product of our habit system'.[13] Watson thought that if we could control the experiences of the individual, and thus the habits he forms, we could create any type of person we wish:

> "Give me a dozen healthy infants, well-formed, and my own specified world to bring them up in and I'll guarantee to take any one at random and train him to become any type of specialist I might select — doctor, lawyer, artist, merchant-chief and, yes, even beggar-man and thief, regardless of his talents, penchants, tendencies, abilities, vocations and race of his ancestors."[14]

This, of course, is an extreme position. Even B.F. Skinner admits that '[i]t is no doubt true that early behaviorists were unduly enthusiastic about the learning processes they were discovering and neglected the role of behavioral genetics'.[15] Yet, as Skinner makes very clear in his own *Walden Two*, he also places a good deal of faith in 'behavioral engineering' to produce the desired sorts of people. As his behaviourist hero says: 'We have no truck with philosophies of innate goodness — or evil, either, for that matter. But we do have faith in the power to change human behavior. We can *make* men adequate for group living.'[16]

(ii) As does geneticism, what Mandelbaum calls organicism holds that personality is formed by the environment, but whereas the former looks to the specific experiences of each individual, the organicist bases his explanation on the culture in which the individual is embedded.[17] Clifford Geertz, for example, argues that social and psychological processes are ordered by 'cultural blueprints'. According to Geertz, these cultural patterns are necessary *because* 'human behavior is inherently extremely plastic. Not strictly but only very broadly controlled by genetic programs or models — intrinsic sources of information — such behavior must, if it is to have any effective form, at all, be controlled to a significant extent by extrinsic ones.'[18] Thus, Geertz indicates that one's culture provides the symbols and categories (e.g. kinship roles, social classes, occupations) by which one defines oneself, and thus shapes what we think of as personality. 'And the symbol systems which define these classes are not given in the nature of things — they are historically constructed, socially maintained, and individually applied.'[19]

This idea of cultural blueprints or moulds is the essence of Mandelbaum's conception of organicism. However, he also apparently intends the term to include the notions of interconnection, distinctive collective unity, etc., I discussed in Chapters II and III. Thus, for example, one of his prime exemplars of an organicist is Hegel who, as he reads him, combines a cultural view of human nature with what I have called in earlier chapters an organic understanding of social life and society.[20] However, it does not seem these two uses of 'organicism' are necessarily related. A thoroughgoing cultural analysis of man is entirely consistent with a 'mechanical' view of society (i.e. one based on shared characteristics) while, conversely, social orders can be premised on interconnection and mutual completion without accepting a cultural understanding of man's nature. Any relation between Mandelbaum's 'organicism' and that which has gone by that name in previous chapters thus would seem contingent rather than conceptual. Therefore, in order to avoid misunderstandings, I shall refer to the culture-based account of personality as 'cultural environmentalism', reserving 'organic' for the themes of interdependence, etc. that I examined in previous chapters.

## A.2. Interactionism

The prolonged controversy between proponents of instinctivist and environmentalist ways of thinking has led to an intermediate view that seeks to accommodate the claims of both nature and nurture. According to this third position, often called 'interactionism',[21] personality is the outcome of an interplay of innate tendencies and environmental conditions. It is this view that characterises modern liberal theories. Moreover, they are typically very explicit about it, and none more so than Dewey. After mentioning both the radical nurture and nature understandings of personality, Dewey insists that '[t]here is an alternative to being penned in by these two theories. We can recognize that all conduct is *interaction* between elements of human nature and environment, natural and social.'[22] Although Dewey acknowledged the influence of the natural as well as the social environment, his real concern was the interaction of human nature and culture, which, as he sees it, determines 'what elements of human nature are dominant and their pattern or arrangement in connection with one another'.[23] The environmental element in Dewey's interactionist theory is thus very much a cultural rather than a geneticist one: he is very clear that it was the overall social environment, not the individual's history, that he thought critical in forming character. Nevertheless, while the influence of environment looms large in Dewey's interactionism — certainly much larger than in Freud's[24] — he always insists that humans are not like wax, clay or putty to be moulded, but have a nature which reacts upon, and shapes, the environment.[25]

In all this Dewey is much closer to Bosanquet than we might expect. Or perhaps we ought to expect it, for Dewey's early work in psychology was thoroughgoingly idealist, and although he later abandoned much of Hegel's philosophy, his continuing emphasis on the intimate relation of personality (or mind) and culture is by no means foreign to the idealist outlook. Indeed, as one reader understands it, mind and social environment are in Bosanquet, like all Hegelians, not only intimately related but are inseparable as well, being 'two aspects of the same thing'.[26] However, while pointing to Bosanquet's (and Dewey's) Hegelianism indicates a basic source of their concern with relation of personality and culture, it leaves much unsaid. For as I said above, Mandelbaum points to Hegel as a prime example of a cultural environmentalist (in his terms, 'organicist') because Hegel sees the individual as (simply?) an expression of his society.[27]   Now to be sure even the most casual reading of Bosanquet uncovers a very strong Hegelian influence. It is Bosanquet, after all, who says that 'each individual mind, if we consider it as a whole, is an expression of society as a whole from a point of view which is distinctive and unique' and that '[t]he logic of the self is the nature of the whole working through our given mental formation and our circumstances.'[28] But there is another side to Bosanquet, one which acknowledges that '[w]e are born with many predispositions . . . out of which the mind organizes itself'[29] (hardly an environmentalist sentiment). We need to recognise that Bosanquet was not only a student of Hegel but also a disciple of Green, and to some extent Fichte too. Superimposed on Bosanquet's Hegelian emphasis on the individual as a reflection of his culture is the ideal of self-realisation and the free growth of capacities, central to Fichte's and Green's position.[30] It is in this vein that Bosanquet writes that 'the end is single and clear: to make the most of human nature'. And, following Green, this does not mean merely the moulding of man by culture but the development of human capacities.[31] Ultimately, Bosanquet insists on the 'deep and subtle relation between character and circumstance' and, consequently, rejects any view that sees man as no more than a creation of his environment.[32]

All this is not intended to deny that Bosanquet puts a great deal of weight on the influence of culture in shaping personality. One of the characteristics of the interactionist position is that it lends itself to differing emphases as to the relative importance of nature and nurture in the interaction; and it is probably safe to say that Bosanquet stresses the role of culture a great deal more, say, than Hobhouse (but probably not much more than Green).[33] Indeed, in some ways Hobhouse approaches the other end of the nature/nurture continuum. As I noted in §A.1, Hobhouse believes that in the purest sense instincts are characteristic of lower animals in whom an innate drive produces a definite sort of behaviour, the end or purpose of which is not perceived by the organism. Since such a notion of instincts suggests a rigidity and specificity of response that does not seem to characterise human behaviour, I suggested that the normal response of traditional instinctivists has been to generalise the instinct so that it can be manifested in a wide range of behaviour. Now Hobhouse thinks that we do indeed possess some such instincts, 'like those of sex and maternity, where an innate drive organises behaviour on lines which are in general, though of course not in detail, innately determined'.[34] However, Hobhouse concludes that the persistence of such instincts in the 'higher animals' is the exception; as a rule, the drive remains but its satisfaction now turns on intelligence and experience rather than programmed responses. More than this, he continues, the drives themselves are subordinate in man to 'root interests', of which a group of particular drives are 'offshoots, derivations, limitations'. (In another place Hobhouse describes root interests as clusters of sub-interests which, in turn, initiate impulses.) Thus, for example, Hobhouse considers health to be a root interest to which the drives, impulses and needs relating to hunger, thirst, exercise and sleep are subordinate.[35] More to the point for our purposes, 'social interest' is identified as another such root interest, giving rise to more specific forms such as sympathy and affection.[36]

While much remains unclear in Hobhouse's account, it seems safe to view his theory as a modified instinctivism. Hobhouse recognises the inherent difficulties with a thoroughgoing instinctivist account of personality and so postulates (and, to be sure, tries to empirically demonstrate) a dynamic according to which increasing intelligence is accompanied by disassociating basic drives from programmed behaviour, leading to the subordination of the drives to root interests. The environment, of course, plays a crucial role in determining the conditions under which root interests are pursued and satisfied — indeed we will discover that it determines which impulses and drives are to thrive and which are to be checked — but, in the end, the account remains much closer to the instinctivist position than that of any other modern liberal.

## A.3. Interactionist Developmentalism

Thus far it might seem that in so far as the modern liberal theory of man is interactionist it merely represents a sensible compromise between the equally untenable radical nature and nurture positions. But as with Rousseau, who wrote in the early pages of *Emile* that '[t]he real object of our study is man and his environment',[37] things are more complicated, and interesting, than that. Rousseau was concerned not just with the interaction of human nature and environment, but with man's natural 'impulses', 'tendencies' and 'faculties' (we will see later that the tie among these is of central importance) which the environment can either encourage, leading to their growth, or thwart and stunt. Such an interactionism I will call *developmental*, as it focuses on the interaction of capacity and environment and, more specifically, on whether the environment encourages the growth and *development* of capacities (for individuality, social interest and community) or stifles them.

Rousseau begins *Emile* by likening the child to a sapling. It may, he tells the 'tender, anxious mother', either be bent 'hither and thither' and crushed or deformed, or be watered and bear fruit. This plant analogy, central to Rousseau's conception of development, is a dominating theme of the third chapter of Mill's *Liberty* and his *Subjection of Women*. Most famous, of course, is Mill's assertion that 'Human Nature is not a machine to be built after a model, and set to do exactly the work prescribed for it, but a tree, which requires to grow and develope [*sic*] itself on all sides, according to the tendency of inward forces which make it a living thing.'[38] Bosanquet uses a slightly different analogy in his lectures on psychology when he tells us that the 'soul' is 'not a ready-made machine working on certain material, but a growth of material more like a process of crystallisation, the material moulding itself according to its own affinities and cohesions'.[39] But the Rousseauian-Millian plant analogy is in a sense superior as it more forcefully brings home to us the importance of not only inward forces but environmental conditions as well (which, of course, Bosanquet never would have wished to belittle). One of the main points of the plant analogy is that the characteristics of the mature specimen are a result of the interaction of its innate capacities and environment. The environment may either encourage a healthy, natural growth or produce 'artificial' personalities like trees that are 'clipped into pollards, or cut from the shape of animals'.[40] Mill makes this most clear in the *Subjection*:

What is now called the nature of women is an eminently artificial thing — the result of forced repression in some directions, unnatural stimulation in other . . . [I]n the case of women, a hot-house and stove cultivation has always been carried on of some of the capabilities of their nature, for the benefit and pleasure of their masters. Then, because certain products of the general vital force sprout luxuriantly and reach a great development in this heated atmosphere and under this active nurture and watering, while other shoots from the same root, which are left outside in the wintry air, with ice purposely heaped all around them, have a stunted growth, and some are burnt off with fire and disappear; men, with that inability to recognise their own work which distinguishes the unanalytic mind, indolently believe that the tree grows of itself in the way they have made it grow, and that it would die if one half of it were not kept in a vapour bath and the other half in the snow.[41]

Mill's developmentalism, however, is not to be found only in his uses of the plant analogy. Indeed, it forms the basis of his reformulation of associationist psychology, a reformulation which transforms associationism into a very different theory. As is well known, John Stuart's father, James, was 'the supreme exponent of Associationism', a geneticist theory of mind and personality.[42] Roughly, an associationism such as that of James Mill takes as its starting point the susceptibility of men to sensations. After a sensation ceases, as James Mill said, 'something remains', which we may call a copy or an image of the sensation. 'Another name, by which we denote this trace, this copy, of the sensation, which remains after the sensation ceases, is *IDEA* .'[43] Ideas, then, are things 'similar' (in some sense) to sensations; e.g. the idea of a rose is similar to the sensations produced by roses. Now, and this gets to the centre of the associationist doctrine, ideas can become associated in various ways. James Mill argues for two basic modes of association: synchronous and successive.[44] The former involves sensations that are experienced at the same time; if sensation $X$ is experienced with $Y$, the idea of $X$ becomes associated with that of $Y$. Successive associations, of course, derive from sensations that are experienced one after another; if sensation $Z$ follows $Y$, the idea of $Y$ will 'call up' that of $Z$.[45] (The more that two sensations are experienced either synchronously or successively, or the more 'vivid' the sensations, the stronger will be the association.) Hence James Mill's 'general law of the "Association of Ideas" ': 'Our ideas spring up, or exist, in the order in which the sensations existed, of which they are the copies.'[46]

The analysis of motivation closely follows that of intellect. According to James Mill, sensations can be divided into three classes: the indifferent, the painful and the pleasurable. 'The first is of such a kind, that I care not whether it is long or short; the second is of such a kind that I would put an end to it instantly if I could; the third is of such a kind, that I like it prolonged.'[47] Like all other sensations, those of pleasure and pain leave imprints (ideas):

> My state of consciousness under the sensation I call pain. My state of consciousness under the idea of pain, I call, not a pain, but an aversion. An aversion is the idea of a pain . . . My state of consciousness under the sensation, I call a Pleasure: my state of consciousness under the idea, that is, the idea itself, I call a Desire. The term "Idea of a pleasure", expresses precisely the same thing as the term, Desire.[48]

Motives spring from the fact that we can contemplate the causes of a sensation. For example, say that the idea of $Y$ becomes associated with the idea of pain; we have, then, an aversion to $Y$. But also assume that $Y$ always follows $X$; by the laws of succession, the thought of $X$ will call up that of $Y$. $X$ then will be seen as the cause of pain, and, hence, the thought of $X$ produces an anticipation of pain.

The anticipation of the future from the passed, is so strong an association, that, in interesting cases, it is indissoluble. The thought of the Cause of a passed painful sensation, is the idea of an antecedent and a consequent. The idea of the passed antecedent and consequent is instantly followed by that of a future antecedent and consequent; and thus the feeling partakes of the nature of the anticipation of a future painful sensation.[49]

Now some of the time it is our own actions that are the antecedents associated with pleasurable or painful sensations. It is in those cases that we have a motive for action. That is, we have a motive for doing (or abstaining from) some action if we have associated that act with the production of pleasurable (or painful) experiences.[50]

J.S. Mill is often taken to be, like his father, an associationist, or, in any event, some sort of radical environmentalist. Leslie Stephen, for example, concluded that Mill sought 'to explain differences, even those between the sexes, as due to outward circumstances'. More recently, Alan Ryan has contended that Mill wants to argue that diversity of personalities may well arise from differences in circumstances rather than differential capacities.[51] I do not wish to deny that Mill sometimes sounds very environmentalist indeed (though, of course, as in *Liberty* he sometimes sounds very anti-environmentalist, see §II.C.1). However, it needs to be stressed that the younger Mill adopts many positions (e.g. the distinction between higher and lower pleasures and his qualified acceptance of a self) that, at best, fit uncomfortably into this associationist scheme of things.[52] But for our present purposes his most important innovation was his contrast between 'spontaneous' and 'artificial' associations. He was led to this distinction, he tells us, by his feeling that associations produced merely by conditioning (i.e. artificial associations) were in some sense fragile. Thus he reports that he came to doubt the wisdom of relying too heavily upon 'the old familiar instruments, praise and blame, reward and punishment' to shape character. Not being connected by 'any natural tie' he could not but think 'there must always be something artificial and casual in associations thus produced'.[53] In particular, Mill thought they could be dissolved by intellectual analysis, the aim of which is to 'separate ideas only casually hung together'.[54] In contrast, Mill thinks that some associations do not seem artificial in this way but rather harmonise with, and feel congenial to, our nature. Such, for example, are our moral feelings; they are not, Mill insists, artificial associations simply inculcated by parents and teachers, but outgrowths of the unselfish part of our nature. Indeed, Mill goes on to stress that such associations are capable of arising even in the absence of any 'inculcation from without'.[55] In this same vein we find Mill pointing to our social feelings as capable 'in a certain small degree, of springing up spontaneously; and susceptible of being brought by cultivation to a high degree of development'.[56] Hence, although Mill maintains that fully developed social and moral feelings are not innate, he does see them as natural outgrowths of human capacities, capacities which are capable of some spontaneous development.

Quite obviously, all this is very much in the spirit of interactionist-developmentalism rather than geneticism. According to J.S. Mill, to understand human personality we need to know men's natural capacities, their natural lines of development and the nature of the environment in which capacities grow. I don't think it would be going too far to say that the younger Mill is trying here to integrate the insights of the plant analogy into James Mill's associationism, with the consequence being a transformation of associationism into a developmental psychology premised upon the growth of capacities. In the final analysis, the tension between his father's geneticist psychology and the plant analogy is resolved in favour of the latter.

If we are interested in criticisms of Rousseauian plant analogy developmentalism we would do better to look to Dewey and Green. Dewey was explicitly critical of Rousseau's depiction of development. As we have seen, Dewey embraced a good deal of Rousseau's theory, and in particular its emphasis on the possession by each of differential capacities and their dependency upon the environment for growth. He objected, however, to what he saw as Rousseau's belief that our capacities have natural lines of development which are spontaneously pursued.[57] Although it is certainly arguable that Dewey overestimates the role of 'spontaneous natural development' in Rousseau's psychology, and, consequently, makes too little of Rousseau's thoughts on education and environment, his objection is by no means entirely misguided. Without doubt, Rousseau exhibits a strong devotion to free, *natural* growth, and it is this that Dewey thinks leads to an underemphasising of the training and channelling of capacities into useful directions. Indeed, this belief as to the central importance of giving meaningful, organised expression to basic impulses lies at the heart of his emphasis on the formation of 'habits' in his later writings on psychology.[58] It is important to realise that Dewey does not want to deny that natural capacities give our nature a distinct bent. What he objects to is any idea that capacities have a natural development which they spontaneously pursue apart from use and training; depending upon individual and cultural environmental experiences, the same power (e.g. speech) can, he insists, take many different forms. Now we shall see later (§C.3) that this emphasis on the training and organising of basic capacities and, hence, their different manifestations under different environmental conditions, allows Dewey's theory to surmount most of the difficulties faced by modern liberals regarding the reconciliation of natural growth and the need for discipline. Dewey's psychology builds learning and organisation of capacities into the very idea of development. But he needs to be careful here. If the ways in which our capacities grow and are manifested are entirely dependent upon cultural and individual environment, that is, if, as Dewey sometimes indicates, an impulse can be turned in almost any direction, the distinctive feature of the developmental position (i.e. that we are naturally more inclined towards some sorts of lives than others) is undermined.[59] And Dewey clearly does not want that, for he retains the Millian language of 'forcing' and 'perverting' capacities.[60] So, although Dewey can quite properly insist on the importance of directing, training and organising capacities, he cannot entirely do away with the idea that our capacities have some, albeit perhaps quite broad, natural lines of development, diversion from which would do violence to our nature (see §B.3).

Although he was not entirely immune to the lure of the plant analogy,[61] Dewey's critique of Rousseau indicates that he was not particularly happy with it, suggesting as it does that the *telos* of development lies entirely within the individual's nature. Green too distinguishes human from plant development, and along lines with which Dewey probably would have had considerable sympathy. Unlike plants and animals, Green says, man not only 'undergoes a process of development' but 'presents to himself a certain possible state of himself, which in the gratification of the desire he seeks to reach'. Man 'seeks to, and does, develop himself'.[62] For man, unlike plants, life is thus a conscious quest for development; our capacities do not merely grow along their natural lines but we seek to find ways and means of perfecting our nature. Although Dewey's concern is with education and Green's with volition, both are insisting, as opposed to a strict interpretation of the plant analogy, that development is not simply something that naturally happens (to us) unless blocked, but that it is fundamentally dependent upon human will and direction.

Such worries notwithstanding, Rousseau-inspired developmentalism remains an important position in psychology to this day. It is no less true today than when, in 1899, Bosanquet called educational and childhood psychologists Rousseau's 'spiritual descendants'.[63] This, of course, is an accurate description of Jean Piaget and Lawrence Kohlberg, upon whom, along with Rousseau himself, Rawls draws in his account of moral development.[64] Like them, Rawls presents a stage-developmental account as to how humans develop from a primitive morality based upon authority into autonomous moral agents. According to Rawls, the child progresses from a 'morality of authority' in which moral precepts are accepted because they emanate from the imposing and loved parents to a 'morality of association' which centres on attachments that arise in common enterprises. As one's associates live up to their duties and obligations, 'friendly feelings' develop towards them, and, in turn, these feelings lead one to desire to do one's own part. Finally, when — and if — one progresses to the 'morality of principles', a devotion to just principles arises. Because, moreover, we and those for whom we care benefit from just institutions, we develop a desire to apply and act upon the corresponding principles.[65]

Such stage-developmental accounts, and in particular those of Piaget and Kohlberg, are interactionist-developmental, all looking 'at an interaction between intrinsic (nature) and extrinsic (nurture) variables in accounting for behavioral development'.[66] And it certainly seems, looking at Rawls's theory, that our moral development depends upon our innate capacities for love and fellow feeling and their realisation and transformation in response to various forms of association. Furthermore, this interpretation is supported by Rawls's insistence that his laws of moral development, which specify the conditions under which one progresses from one type of morality to another, 'are not merely principles of association or of reinforcement'.[67] Rather, he says, they are based upon a 'deep psychological fact', viz. the tendencies of our sentiments of love and friendship to be aroused when others, with manifest intention, act for our good.

It would seem, then, that Rawls's theory of moral learning relies on the development of our innate capacities for love, fellow feeling and a sense of justice. However, in his analysis of alternative theories of moral learning Rawls appears to refuse to identify himself with this Rousseauian developmental tradition. According to Rawls, we can identify two main accounts of moral learning. On the one hand is what he calls the 'empiricist tradition' according to which 'the aim of moral training is to supply missing motives: the desire to do what is right for its own sake, and the desire not to do what is wrong'.[68] In contrast, says Rawls, the 'rationalistic' tradition (which I have identified with developmentalism), as exemplified by Rousseau, Piaget 'and sometimes J.S. Mill', holds that

[m]oral learning is not so much a matter of supplying missing motives as one of the free development of our innate intellectual and emotional capacities according to their natural bent ... We have a natural sympathy with other persons and an innate susceptibility to the pleasures of fellow feeling and self-mastery, and these provide the affective basis for the moral sentiments once we have a clear grasp of our relations to our associates from an appropriately general perspective. Thus this tradition regards the moral feelings as a natural outgrowth of a full appreciation of our social nature.[69]

Given Rawls's own moral psychology and these characterisations of the two traditions, it is more than a little surprising to find him saying that he 'shall not try to assess the relative merits of these two conceptions of moral learning'.[70] Certainly it would seem that his account of moral development does indeed view 'the moral feelings as a natural outgrowth of a full appreciation of our social nature'. Rawls appears, however, to refrain from identifying himself with the 'rationalistic' tradition for a least two reasons: (i) his theory stresses the acquisition of new motives (à la the empiricist tradition) and (ii) he does not maintain 'that the stages of development are innate or determined by psychological mechanisms'.[71]

When we look more closely at these reasons, I think we can see that neither really entails departure from the 'rationalist tradition'. Turning first to the acquisition of new motives, the difficulty with Rawls's characterisation here is that both traditions are concerned with such acquisition. Consider Piaget. Small children, he argues, obey rules because they are given by the parents; that is, very young children follow rules because that is what those in authority command. But when a child matures *and* enters into co-operative ventures with others, 'obedience withdraws in favor of the idea of justice and mutual service'.[72] The motive for compliance changes, then, from awe of, and devotion to, authority to concern with participating in an enterprise of equals. The real difference between the empiricist and rationalist accounts in this regard is not whether there is a change in motives — of course there is that — but what is the origin of the change. The empiricist holds that it is simply a matter of learning whereas the rationalist sees such transformations as ultimately founded on the growth of our (social) nature. Of course the rationalist need not claim that it is purely a matter of maturation; Piaget, for example, insists on the importance of co-operative experiences.[73] What seems critical is whether in some sense the transformation is induced by a realisation of our innate capacities. And from our earlier examinations of Rawls's theory of our natural fellow feeling (§III.C.3) and his moral psychology, it appears clear that this is the sort of transformation envisaged by Rawls.

Rawls's second reason for claiming independence from the 'rationalist' tradition does not require much comment. If one recalls his initial characterisation of the tradition, Rawls did not maintain that one of its traits was that 'the stages of development are innate or determined by psychological mechanisms'. Rather, as he put it, its essential feature was that moral development ultimately turns on the development of our nature. Although, perhaps, a rigid devotion to the plant analogy would indicate that the stages of development must be invariable and innate, a more flexible Dewey-like position would have no difficulty in accommodating the idea that our powers may grow in different ways depending upon our experiences and education. Since, then, the 'innateness' of the stages of growth does not seem an inherent feature of a developmental position, its absence in Rawls does not separate him from the tradition.[74] And, all things considered, it does indeed seem correct to say that Rawls's psychology, and in particular his moral psychology, turns on the growth of 'men's natural sentiments of unity and fellow feeling'.[75]

We might observe, finally, that three somewhat different understandings of development seem to inform these modern liberal discussions. (i) The Millian-Rousseauian plant analogy seems premised on a notion of maturation very much on the model of the relation of seed to developed plant: what exists as a potentiality is progressively realised throughout the course of a life. This notion of development[76] relates easily to the modern liberal emphasis on the cultivation of capacities in complex and refined ways (§I.C.1): like a plant, the capacity matures by developing an increasingly complex structure. (ii) When modern liberals talk of the development of 'social capacities' like fellow feeling, however, they seem to have in mind more of an increase in intensity and scope than of complexity in organisation. When Mill, for instance, refers to the development of our social feelings (§III.C.3), he really appears to mean that we will experience social feelings more strongly and in relation to a wider body of people. (iii) Lastly, as with Piaget's stage-developmental account, development implies a transformation of certain sentiments/outlooks into others. In the hands of Rawls (to the extent he actually does follow Piaget), this sort of development is essentially the unfolding of social feelings from more 'primitive' to 'advanced' (and universal in scope) manifestations (thus, it would seem, drawing on (i) and (ii) above).

## B. Strong Developmentalism

### B.1. Strong and Weak Developmentalism

Piaget's account of moral development is concerned with the growth of our innate capacities and the environmental conditions that promote development from a 'heteronomous' to an 'autonomous' morality. Presumably, if the proper sort of parental attitudes and peer group experiences are not forthcoming, development will not proceed to as high a level as it might. But in general such stifled persons are not Piaget's main concern. Apparently they get stuck at a lower level of morality and this is pretty much all there is to be said. In contrast, an interactionist such as Freud concentrates on those who fail to develop.[77] Indeed, the crux of Freudian psychology is that pathologies accompany such arrested development. Not only does Freud acknowledge the possibility that an individual may fail to successfully advance from, for example, the oral through the genital stages, but he also identifies the consequences of such incomplete development.[78] Rousseau in a way does something broadly similar, but rather than concentrate upon the effects of arrested growth, Rousseau's main concern is with deflected, or what Mill would call 'artificial', growth. Pushing individuals into lives that ill suit their natures, Rousseau tells us, produces fragile personalities: 'while the conditions remain the same, habits, even the least natural of them, hold good; but change the conditions, habits vanish, nature reasserts herself'.[79]

This suggests a distinction between what I will call *weak* and *strong* developmentalism. A *weak developmental theory*, let us say, is one which depicts a natural line of development, or asserts that our natures tend to develop in some ways rather than others, and which also acknowledges that, depending on environmental conditions, natural development may or may not occur. It does not, however, tell us whether pathologies or instability will arise as the consequence of unnatural or arrested growth. A *strong developmental theory*, then, takes this extra step: it adds to a theory of 'natural' development an analysis of 'unnatural' development. Although significant in itself, we will see in Part Two that this distinction is important for the attempt to derive political prescriptions from a theory of human nature. A weak developmental theory, to be sure, has some normative force as it depicts a line of growth to which our nature inclines and, so, can make an appeal that such development is man's natural destiny and so should be pursued. Of course, man may have an evil or unruly nature, and our aim (as Mill describes that of a Calvinist) may well be to prevent natural growth.

But it does seem that if we start by presenting a relatively attractive end state (e.g. a personality structure) and then add that this end state is the consequence of our natural line of growth, we have strengthened our original case that this is the end to be pursued. Such appeals to nature, I think, are not without their force. But a strong developmental theory can be much more compelling. Not only can it possess all the normative force of a weak developmental account, but it can point out a wide range of obviously dire consequences stemming from not pursuing that course. Such, at any rate, is the modern liberal strategy. Conjoined to their depiction of natural growth, I will argue, is an analysis of the unnatural, thus making the modern liberal theory of man a strong developmental theory.

## B.2. Happiness, Pleasure and Development

Before turning directly to the more obviously pathological, however, I would like to consider an issue that seems to lie on the border between weak and strong developmentalism: viz. whether a 'natural' development makes one happy (or is pleasurable) and whether unnatural or stunted growth makes one unhappy (or is painful). Mill would seem the most obvious candidate for an intimate link between development and pleasure. At least as Sidgwick understood him, Mill proffers a psychological hedonism, asserting as he does in *Utilitarianism* 'that there is in reality nothing desired except happiness' which, he says, means pleasure or the absence of pain.[80] And on this psychological hedonist reading, it is only *our own* happiness that we ultimately desire. If Mill is a psychological hedonist, and if he maintains − as he certainly does − that we desire our development, development must lead to (or be associated with) pleasure. And Mill does assert such a link. I have already pointed out in the second chapter (§ II.B.1) that he thought the cultivation of social interest essential to happiness; in *Utilitarianism* he also makes it clear that happiness accompanies the development of our higher nature. Although, he says, 'A being of higher faculties requires more to make him happy, is capable probably of more acute suffering, is certainly accessible to it at more points, than one of the inferior type', he is also, ultimately, happier. 'Whoever supposes that this preference [for higher pleasures] takes place at a sacrifice of happiness − that the superior being, in anything like equal circumstances, is not the happier than the inferior − confounds the two very different ideas, of happiness, and content.'[81]

But while Mill clearly thinks the quest for development coincident with the pursuit of happiness, it seems doubtful that he can be adequately described as a psychological hedonist. Even in *Utilitarianism*, probably the work in which Mill is the most hedonistic (both ethically and psychologically), he introduces elements alien to psychological hedonism. For our purposes at the moment, the most important of these is that 'powerful principle of human nature', 'the desire to be in unity with our fellow creatures'.[82] Although, as we have seen, Mill does not want to say that fully developed social and moral feelings are natural, he nevertheless contends that we have a natural inclination towards them. Now if we do indeed have such natural aims and desires, even if they be only embryonic ones, it is hard to see how it can be said that, ultimately, all our desires either are for happiness or stem from the desire for happiness. Admittedly, we may be happy when we have attained such unity, but on Mill's account the natural, ultimate desire is for unity, not happiness. It is important to stress in this regard that Mill does not treat the desire for unity with our fellows, as he does moral virtues, as a desire which is now independent but originally was desired because it was a means to pleasure and, through association, became conjoined with the idea of pleasure. It is a desire that arises directly out of our nature. (Indeed, Mill's account of moral learning seems to depend upon the desire for unity not being one which is merely learned, for it is the natural feeling upon which his account builds.[83]) In any event, in works like *On Liberty* and *The Subjection of Women* Mill adopts a psychological position that has very little to do with hedonism. As we saw earlier, in these works Mill postulates a drive to realise our capacities and, while he is clear that successful cultivation and the happy life are closely bound, the ultimate aim is to grow, not to be happy.

It needs to be emphasised that I am not denying that Mill thinks development and happiness go together — he clearly thinks they do. Rather my point is that he often conceives of development as not just a means to pleasure or happiness but as something desired in itself. If so, this supports what seemed to be Green's belief that Mill was moving away from hedonism towards some form of self-realisation theory.[84] However, Mill is always insistent that even if we do not aim at happiness, the pursuit of development does not require its sacrifice. Now (assuming for the moment that Mill's theory really equates happiness with pleasure and the absence of pain) in a self-realisationist theory such as Green's the relation between development and pleasure is much more complex. In opposition to psychological hedonism, Green insists that our aim is not pleasure but the life in which our capacities will be fully realised. But, he adds, 'because, in such self-conscious beings

as we are, a desire for their realisation goes along with the presence of
the capacities, . . . the form of conscious life in which this desire shall
be satisfied is looked forward to as pleasant'.[85] Hence, according to
Green, 'since there is pleasure in all realisation of capacity, the life in
which human capacities should be fully realised would necessarily be
a pleasant life'.[86] However, and this is the important point, according
to Green, we have no guarantee that some other, less fulfilling life will
not be more pleasurable. While, he says, one who perfects his soul
certainly experiences pleasure, the pleasure he experiences is 'not
necessarily a greater amount than he has to forgo' in order to make his
contribution to human perfection.[87]

Pleasure, then, will accompany the realisation of our capacities,
but the pursuit of pleasure and the perfection of our nature will not
always coincide. Interestingly, at one point Bosanquet suggests that this
lack of coincidence stems from a flaw in nearly all our natures. 'Rare
and gifted minds', he says, may be able to do just what pleases them
and yet be led to the valuable (and, to Bosanquet, 'values are the development of capacities'); 'natural man', in contrast, is certain to go
wrong in doing so.[88] Indeed, all things considered, it would seem that
the tie between pleasures and satisfaction of human nature is even looser
in Bosanquet than in Green. But it certainly does not dissolve: pleasure
continues to be related to the satisfaction and expansion of self while,
conversely, pain — 'a felt contradiction' — results from discord. When
activities are blocked by external impediments — or presumably when
there is inner conflict — pain, i.e. felt contradiction, manifests itself.
Bosanquet thus ascribes pleasure and pain complementary roles in
directing us towards satisfaction of our natures. Pleasure encourages us
to persist in successful, unobstructed activity while pain alerts us to
obstructions and contradictions and, so, in a different way, spurs us to
act. Again, merely because something is pleasurable is not sufficient
reason to conclude that it satisfies our nature; and pain may be necessary to achieve a satisfaction. (What Bosanquet calls an easy pleasure,
for example, is an attempt to avoid contradictions — pains — rather
than resolving them, a path along which satisfaction does not lie.)
Nevertheless, like Green, Bosanquet clearly thinks pleasure and pain to
be rough guideposts to satisfaction of our nature.[89]

If we take Mill at his word, then, and assume that for him happiness
meant pleasure and the absence of pain, we observe a loosening of the
link between pleasure and development as we move from Mill to the
idealists. Apparently, being a psychological hedonist at least some of
the time and a developmentalist at others, Mill wants to argue that the

pursuit of pleasure and development coincide. Our idealists, seeing themselves as anti-hedonists, refuse to accept such ·a coincidence but continue to believe the two connected. However, happiness *is* often distinguished from pleasure, and when it is, it becomes less certain that Mill's and Green's positions even differ this much. In the *Prolegomena* Green distinguishes 'true happiness' from pleasure; true happiness, he tells us, lies not in an unbroken train of pleasures but in the realisation of the object of one's various interests.[90] Hobhouse too makes a distinction between pleasure and happiness, arguing that particular feelings of harmony are pleasurable but an achievement of a deep and wide harmony yields happiness.[91] Although their emphases are different, both Green and Hobhouse are describing happiness in terms of the satisfaction of the organised self, its enduring interests, its capacities, etc., i.e. self-realisation. Rawls, I think, proffers a similar understanding of happiness in terms that seem less foreign to us today when describing a happy man as one whose rational plan of life is being successfully executed.[92] Understanding happiness in these ways, as accompanying self-realisation or the execution of a plan of life, thus seems essentially to perceive happiness as turning on the development of one's nature (see §I.D.1). It seems very likely that this is Mill's position. Although, as I have said, he did assert an equation between pleasure and happiness, his distinction between higher and lower pleasures and his insistence that happiness does not entail contentment but rather is consistent with a struggle for excellence and nobility, strongly suggest, as A.D. Lindsay concluded, that for Mill happiness is not the same as pleasure.[93] Like Green, Hobhouse, Rawls and Dewey[94] it would seem that Mill sees the happy life, more than anything else, as the life of the properly developed person.

## B.3. Pathologies

According to Rawls's Aristotelian Principle, men are naturally inclined to develop their capacities in complex and refined ways (§I.C.2). However, the principle describes 'a tendency and not an invariable pattern of choice, and like all tendencies it may be overridden. Countervailing inclinations can inhibit the development of realized capacity and the preference for more complex activities.'[95] But while acknowledging in true developmentalist fashion that natural inclinations can be defeated, Rawls also indicates that activities failing to satisfy the Aristotelian Principle 'are likely to seem dull and flat, and give us no feeling of competence or a sense that they are worth doing'.[96] Furthermore, Rawls maintains that the development of our capacities in complex and refined ways supports a sense of self-worth or self-respect. Indeed, along with being appreciated by those we esteem and whose association we enjoy (an aspect of social interest, see §II.B.2), Rawls points to satisfaction of the Aristotelian Principle as one of the two main conditions for self-respect. And the consequences of not securing self-respect are indeed dire: 'Without it nothing may seem worth doing, or if some things have value for us, we lack the will to strive for them. All desire and activity becomes empty and vain, and we sink into apathy and cynicism.'[97]

Rawls's account of the dynamics of the Aristotelian Principle, however, is ambiguous as to whether (i) the pathologies result only if we have developed our natural preference for complex and refined activities but have not constructed an adequate plan of life or whether (ii) he who has had his very capacity for the Aristotelian Principle defeated will also experience these dire side-effects. In the first case our nature is asserting itself – we desire the complex and refined activities – but our life plan is not satisfactory; in the second instance our very desire for complexity has been defeated. Both sorts of cases occur in Mill's writings. On the one hand, he is concerned with individuals whose nature is indeed asserting itself but is being blocked or deflected by social pressures, customs, etc. This, for example, is the case with the nature of some women who, according to Mill, are 'schooled' into preventing their capacities and energies from being manifested 'in their most natural and healthy direction, but the internal principle remains, in a different outward form. An active and energetic mind, if denied liberty, will seek for power: refused the command of itself, it will assert its personality by attempting to control others.'[98] But it is clear that Mill also believes that in many, the stifling of their nature has been even more successful. Hence in *Liberty* he writes of those who 'by dint of not following their own nature . . . have no nature to follow: their human capacities are withered and starved'.[99]

We can identify, then, two sorts of pathological conditions: (i) where the person's nature is thoroughly repressed or stifled and (ii) in which the impulse persists but is deflected into pathological directions. When referring to the first case, i.e. those who have 'no nature left to follow', Mill typically maintains that it results in lethargy and apathy: 'They become incapable of any strong wishes and native pleasures.' In a similar vein, Hobhouse contends that '[b]y accommodation to a servile order once firmly established men may lose all moral energy, [and] take things as they find them'.[100] As Hobhouse indicates, underlying this sort of analysis is an energy model of personality and development. According to this model we naturally possess impulses that drive us in certain directions; if these are somehow rooted out, we are left without energy (impulse) and so sink into servility, lethargy, apathy, etc. Now this same model can be used to account for the second sort of pathological condition. Dewey in fact suggests just this when writing of 'cooped-up sentiment which is expanded upon itself . . . Each impulse is a demand for an object which will enable it to function. Denied an object in reality it tends to create one in fancy, as pathology shows.'[101] Dewey concurs with Mill in analysing the 'will to power' as the consequence of a frustrated impulse that 'bursts into flower'. Over-specialisation and monotonous lives also appear to block impulses but in these cases Dewey maintains that the consequence is a pathological pleasure-seeking in an attempt to gain some outlets for impulses and capacities not manifested in ordinary activity.[102]

Unlike Mill's, Dewey's energy model apparently does not admit of a complete rooting out of impulse. 'Suppression', he says, 'is not annihilation. "Psychic" energy is no more capable of being abolished than the forms we recognize as physical.'[103] Hobhouse is more cautious. While generally agreeing that a suppressed impulse persists as a source of inner conflict, he is willing to acknowledge the possibility that 'persistent repression' may perhaps extinguish it, though he quickly adds that 'contemporary psychology sees reason to think that even so it is either apt to emerge again in another form, or to become the centre of a deep-seated division operating below the threshold of our conscious life with ill effect psychological or physical'.[104] The relation of this sort of theory of psychic energy to Freudian psychology is fairly obvious, and was recognised by Hobhouse.[105] The possibility of contrasts and comparisions between Freud's and Dewey's psychologies are particularly rich, but it seems pretty certain that Dewey's 'impulse' is in many ways like Freud's 'drive' (*Trieb*) and that they both maintain that the inhibition of an impulse/drive is the root of pathologies.[106] Moreover, as we will see a little later, Dewey, again like Freud, identifies an alternative to simply expressing or repressing one's impulses, and in doing so offers one of the most sophisticated modern liberal accounts of discipline.

Thus far I have said little about our idealists, Green and Bosanquet, and all things considered it must be acknowledged that they do not say a great deal about specific pathologies, like the love of power or lethargy. However, as we have seen, they did develop an elaborate theory about the relation of pleasure and pain to self-realisation. More importantly, though, what is often overlooked is that at the very heart of their political theory is an analysis of the consequences of checking capacity. Although today we tend to understand the distinction between negative and positive freedom in fairly formal ways, e.g. as the difference between 'freedom from' and 'freedom to', it is important to realise that for Green and Bosanquet it centred on a conception of human nature.[107] Green's ultimate justification for using 'freedom' in what he acknowledged to be a metaphorical sense was that the 'feeling of oppression, which always goes along with the consciousness of unfulfilled possibilities, will always give meaning to the representation of the effort after any kind of self-improvement as a demand for "freedom".'[108] Bosanquet follows Green here, not only quoting this sentence, but adding that the narrow personality, i.e. the man who wills 'narrow and partial desires' (see §I.D.3) 'feels choked and oppressed' even by their fulfilment, 'like one lost in a blind alley which grows narrower and narrower'. Moreover, Bosanquet relates his theory of freedom to Rousseauian developmentalism, telling us that Rousseau's theory of human development is not only central to child psychology but is also 'closely akin to the question of liberty'.[109] It thus seems mistaken to interpret either Green or Bosanquet as simply arguing that (positive) freedom consists in possessing the means to develop, or even that we are free just because we are following our higher or truer or rational self (§V.B.3). Rather, the argument is that in developing one's nature, one is freed from the sense of oppression that accompanies the awareness of unrealised possibilities.

My concern here is not so much whether it is enlightening to describe the demand for self-improvement as a call for freedom, but to emphasise that the entire account is premised on the thesis that we desire the realisation of our capacities and feel oppressed when they are not being developed. However, the association of this oppression with the idea of 'positive freedom', with its suggestion – at least for us today – of the necessity of opportunities (hence the 'positive') as well as the absence of restraints ('negative liberty'), does serve to highlight an important point about pathological development. Impulses can go unsatisfied, and thus pathologies manifest themselves, not only because they are blocked by some impediment but also because the environment does not provide opportunities for their realisation. Dewey in particular made much of this source of pathologies. In *Individualism – Old and New*, for example, he argued that American society, because of its lack of a sense of community, was characterised by an excessive, indeed pathological, habit of joining groups. He also saw excessive 'philanthropy' and 'generosity' as attempts to find expression for aspects of human nature ignored by the existing 'economic regime'.[110] This line of argument has obvious potential as a support for 'new liberal' proposals for economic reorganisation: if healthy growth not only requires the liberty endorsed by Mill in the third chapter of *Liberty*, but also a communitarian, co-operative social order, then it can indeed be plausibly argued that the social and economic policies of the new liberalism are simply the fuller realisation of those ideals upon which the demand for (negative) liberty itself is premised. Nevertheless, the modern liberal needs to be cautious here. One of the features of interactionist theories is that they accord the environment and learning a large role in determining just how capacities are to be manifested. We saw at the outset of the chapter that even an instinctivist like McDougall had to acknowledge a considerable role for learning in this regard. And of course Dewey, who so emphasises this 'absence of outlets' argument, is also the modern liberal who is most insistent that impulses do not have natural manifestations but must be trained (§A.3). If so, it would seem that he — and modern liberals in general — must allow considerable flexibility as to what opportunities are required for the healthy manifestation of impulses. Of course much the same can be said of restraints; but if we have in mind, for instance, marital arrangements in which one 'partner' is a dependent and subject to another, we would seem to have a much clearer case of stifling impulses than Dewey's instance of a social structure that does not elicit social feelings. In the latter instance it is not hard to imagine alternative outlets for the capacity (indeed Dewey does so, but he depicts as pathological such outlets as group joining), whereas, in the case of despotic marital relations, it is much more difficult to see how stifling can be avoided. No doubt these are differences of degree, admitting of all sorts of intermediate cases, but it still seems that as the argument moves from presence of restraints to absence of outlets it becomes increasingly problematic.

## C. The Problem of Discipline

I have provided only a sketch of modern liberal accounts of pathologies; throughout their writings are references to barred activities, repressed impulses, stifled capacities, etc., which, it is said, are the source of a multitude of manifestly undesirable character traits. Rather than attempting to provide a complete account of the entire range of pathologies they discuss — something that itself would require a chapter — I have tried to give some idea of the model of personality underlying these accounts, one based on capacity *qua* impulse that, if blocked, is very likely to turn up elsewhere in some pathological form. This is clearly the model of personality being drawn upon by Mill, Hobhouse and Dewey. However, I will argue below (§C.4) that Rawls just as clearly does not employ such a model; rather than viewing, as Dewey put it, a 'potentiality' as a 'potency' or 'force',[111] we will see that Rawls conceives of them more as opportunities – not demands – for development.

Things are less clear with our two idealists, especially Green. As we just saw, Green talks of our realised and unrealised 'possibilities', suggesting they are (as with Rawls) more opportunities for development than demands of our nature which require satisfaction. Moreover, as Peter Gordon and John White have pointed out, in contrast to later self-realisationists like Edmond Holmes, Green puts great weight on the way that social institutions shape our interests and lines of growth,[112] again perhaps suggesting that we are endowed with a great many possibilities for development that can be shaped by the environment rather than a nature that demands satisfaction of innate impulses and tendencies. While I do not wish to deny that Green, and probably Bosanquet too, is susceptible to differing interpretations on this score (and I certainly to not want to deny that Green places a great deal of weight on social influences) there nevertheless are sound reasons for concluding that Green conceives of our nature as a good deal more assertive than the simple 'possibilities for development' interpretation would suggest. For one thing, it is certain that both Green's and Bosanquet's psychologies rely on an impulse to self-realisation or coherence. So even if they do not see every capacity as an impulse, or as giving rise to a demand for satisfaction, they still adopt the idea that we have an impulse to develop our capacities that presumably can be blocked.[113] Hence the feeling of oppression that is said to accompany awareness of unrealised possibilities. But I think we can even go further than this and say that, like Mill, Hobhouse and Dewey, Bosanquet and Green believe that we possess a multiplicity of impulses, each of which requires some form of satisfaction. Bosanquet, for example, favourably quotes Froebel to just this effect, referring to 'a human education by the appropriate training of the productive or active impulses'.[114] Whether we say that Green adopts a similar position would seem to turn largely on which of two opposing interpretations of his theory of self-realisation we adopt. In the first chapter (§I.B), I distinguished between the view which contends that Green's ideal of self-realisation concerns only the 'higher', rational self, and what I saw as the superior view, that which under-stands his theory to concern the self-as-a-whole. If we follow out this second interpretation, 'instinctive' tendencies, which Green acknow-ledges we possess, must play a part in human development. To be sure, *human* development for Green could not be merely the development of such instinctive tendencies, for that would be a purely 'animal' develop-ment that accords no role for human reason and will – a view that we have already seen that Green rejects (§IV.A.3).[115] But when Green tells us that self-satisfaction is not to be found in following natural im-pulses and desires he does not mean, as he is often taken to mean, that these have no place in self-realisation:

> But though the natural impulses of the will are thus the work of the self-realising principle in us, it is not in their gratification that this principle can find the satisfaction which is only to be found in the consciousness of becoming perfect, of realising what it has it in itself to be. In order to [make] any approach to this satisfaction of itself the self-realising principle must carry its work farther. It must overcome the 'natural impulses', not in the sense of either ex-tinguishing them or denying them an object, but in the sense of fus-ing them with those higher interests, which have human perfection in some of its forms for their object.[116]

Now to the extent modern liberals (again, with the exception of Rawls) employ a model of personality according to which we possess innate impulses or tendencies that require some form of satisfaction – denial of which produces pathologies – they are faced with a funda-mental problem. It will be recalled that in the first chapter (§I.D.4), I argued that our modern liberals appeared caught in a dilemma: they support the widest possible development of the nature of each but also insist on the need for specialisation and discipline. We now see that this dilemma is even more serious than it first seemed. 'One-sided' develop-ment precludes the satisfaction of some aspects of our nature. But, being strong developmentalists, modern liberals do not believe that these unsatisfied capacities merely lie dormant.[117] They are, we are told, deflected into pathological channels or lead to feelings of oppression. Hence Bosanquet's argument (§I.D.3), that the attempt to achieve a coherent personality by narrowing is ultimately damaging: 'of what is extruded something refuses to be suppressed and forms a nucleus of rebellion'.[118] Or at a minimum, those like Mill tell us that if a capacity is really repressed, vital energy is sapped, issuing in other sorts of pathoological characters. Nevertheless, whatever their affinities to some brands of romanticism, modern liberals do not think we can avoid specialisation nor do they believe that men are by nature thoroughly good, thus precluding the presence of bad capacities that need to be controlled. Despite his reference to Froebel, it seems unlikely that Bosanquet would have followed him in asserting that all that is bad in man stems from repression, so that the development of the good man is really a quest to uncover the original, good, side of human nature.[119] As Bosanquet sees it, 'Most people will admit there is a great deal which must be burned out of us'.[120] Again (as we saw in §I.D.4), this is no mere idiosyncracy of idealism. Even Mill in *Liberty*, certainly his strongest ode to human nature, expresses the importance of combining 'Christian self-denial' with a devotion to human development. And in a slight modification of the standard plant analogy, Mill argues in his essay on 'Nature' that 'weeds dispute the ground' with the nobler aspects of human nature, thus requiring (as it were) a gardener to encourage the good and pull up (or at least discourage) the bad.[121]

The dilemma for modern liberals would thus seem to be a real one: they believe that interference with the development of natural impulses/capacities is the root of pathologies, yet they remain sufficiently committed to the Christian concept of man to think that some capacities ought to be prevented from expressing themselves. Having generally sensed this difficulty, they have proposed three main solutions; let us consider each, moving from the least to the most adequate.

### C.1. The First Solution: Self-discipline

It has been said of Green that, in contrast to Freud, he failed to grasp the possibilities of psychological damage of discipline and repression.[122] That seems too far reaching, for as I have said, Green's theory of positive freedom is premised on the sense of oppression that is said to accompany unrealised capacities. However, it does seem true that neither Green nor Bosanquet, for that matter, worries much about the individual who renounces impulses and desires inconsistent with his higher development.[123] Indeed, central to Green's outlook is the belief that self-imposed discipline leads to a moral development which is the heart of a realised personality. Hobhouse, operating within this tradition, is explicit in identifying self-imposed discipline as a solution to the problem of discipline. In his chapter in *Liberalism* on the 'Heart of Liberalism', he tells us that '[t]he foundation of liberty is the idea of growth.' But, he goes on, this brings us 'to the real crux, the question of moral discipline'.

[I]t is of course possible to reduce a man to order and prevent him from being a nuisance to his neighbours by arbitrary control and harsh punishment. This may be to the comfort of the neighbours, as is admitted, but regarded as a moral discipline it is a contradiction in terms. It is doing less than nothing for the character of the man himself. It is merely crushing him, and unless his will is killed the effect will be seen if ever the superincumbent pressure is removed. It is also possible, though it takes a much higher skill, to teach the same man to discipline himself, and this is to foster the development of will, of personality, of self control, or whatever we please to call that central harmonizing power which makes us capable of directing our own lives.[124]

Mill was attracted to a similar sort of analysis. In his *Principles of Political Economy* he argues that being prevented from doing as one is inclined or sees as desirable to do not only is always irksome but tends *pro tanto* to stifle the development of some bodily or mental capacities. But, he adds, it only partakes of the 'degradation of slavery' if the individual conscience does not freely accept it.[125] Since slavery or lack of independence is associated in Mill's other writings with pathologies (e.g. lack of self-respect, lethargy, love of power, envy),[126] he seems to be suggesting here that restraint without pathologies can only be had if the restrained individual freely acknowledges the justice or rightness of the restraint. (A slightly weaker requirement than self-discipline, but I shall not distinguish them.) Hence, Mill argues that although being held to 'rigid rules of justice' helps develop the social sentiments (§V.D), to be restrained simply because another desires it 'developes [*sic*] nothing valuable, except such force of character as may unfold itself in resisting the restraint. If acquiesced in, it dulls and blunts the whole nature.'[127]

As Hobhouse stresses, self-control and self-discipline are fundamental to the liberal vision of free, responsible agents pursuing their ends within the framework of law and morality. But while recognising this, we still need be cognizant of two difficulties with self-control as a way of reconciling discipline with the modern liberals' account of pathological, unnatural development. First, it does not seem to accord well with the energy model which, I argued, underlies the modern liberal theory of pathologies. If capacities are to be viewed as impulses, even self-discipline requires that an impulse (*qua* bad capacity) be blocked or deflected. And if this energy is not allowed to express itself along the natural path(s), it would seem that it must go 'subterranean' and, so, result in pathologies. Or, if self-control somehow could root out impulses, then the problem of lethargy would seem to arise.[128]

Now it might be replied here that the energy model is only a heuristic device, and if at some point it is incompatible with the theory, that only shows the limitations of the device and not difficulties with the theory. Leaving aside, however, the question whether some sort of energy thesis might not be essential to make sense of the theory of pathologies (thus making the energy model far more than a heuristic device), a second problem still remains. If the presence or absence of pathologies turns simply on whether the restrictions are imposed upon, or imposed by (or accepted by), the restrained individuals, it would seem that indoctrination into servile modes of life could produce highly 'artifical' (i.e. dependent, slave-like) but non-pathological individuals. This problem is especially important for Mill as it goes directly to the heart of his analysis of female personalities. According to his account in the *Subjection*, women have been schooled to see themselves as men want them to be, a schooling that generally has been highly successful. To be sure, Mill's remarks on restraints and justice (quoted above) do provide grounds for saying that if a woman acquiesces to the pursuit of the ideal even though she thinks it wrong or improper, it will blunt her nature. But even conceding this, it does not address the case in which a woman is convinced that the ideal is right and proper and, therefore, disciplines herself accordingly. Presumably this is an instance of truly successful indoctrination. If Mill is to avoid the conclusion – as it seems manifestly clear that he wants to – that this sort of self-discipline is psychologically just like moral self-discipline and, therefore, non-pathological, he needs a more elaborate theory of discipline, one that can distinguish between harmful and benign self-discipline.

### C.2. The Second Solution: The Repressible and the Irrepressible

Such a distinction can be found in some of Hobhouse's writings. We saw above in §A.2 that Hobhouse distinguishes impulses from root interests, the latter being some sort of grouping of more specific impulses. Root interests, he argues, 'singly or in combination underlie and direct the course of life, and however frustrated or even ignored belong to and remain in the constitution of the individual'.[129] These clearly cannot be repressed without serious pathologies. Perhaps they cannot really be repressed at all. In contrast, Hobhouse takes a more flexible attitude towards impulses: he is willing to admit that we might have bad impulses that require repression. Although always insisting that the repression of any important impulse would have some pathological consequences, and thus could at best be a necessary evil, Hobhouse nonetheless acknowledges that repression is possible. And both root interests and impulses are to be contrasted with temporary desires, which can be suppressed without doing violence to our basic nature.[130]

The trichotomy of root interest/impulse/temporary desire provides Hobhouse with a basis for arguing that any discipline — imposed from either without or within — that seeks to repress root interests will do great violence to our nature and is thus to be avoided. And this apparently would preclude the self-discipline of women to conform to the traditional ideal of feminine personality, which, presumably, attempts to stifle the root interest of self-regard and the even more fundamental impulse of self-assertiveness, 'the common impulse of mind . . . to assert itself, fulfil its capacities, execute its purposes'.[131] Moreover, and this is an important point, because Hobhouse's psychology postulates only a small number of root interests, it is plausible to argue that to some extent all can be satisfied. And because he also asserts that in themselves no root interests are bad (though they may be developed in certain 'anti-social ways', as with self-interest leading to antipathy), Hobhouse's account of root interests avoids the problem of discipline. As far as root interests are concerned, we can all be truly well-rounded, developing all aspects of our nature. In radical contrast to root interests, temporary desires can be repressed, at least by oneself, with apparently no pathological consequences. On Hobhouse's analysis, then, the problematic case concerns impulses. Their repression does indeed have bad consequences but, at least according to Hobhouse, if an impulse conflicts with the satisfaction of the wider part of our nature, its repression might be necessary. Again, he believes that self-repression is superior to an imposed one as it promotes the development of a conception of the good,[132] but he generally does not try to avoid the conclusion that even this sort of self-repression is indeed an evil, to be justified only if necessary for the wider satisfaction of our nature. This, then, is the point behind Hobhouse's insistence that we should harmonise all that is capable of harmony and that no ineradicable element should be left frustrated, although it might be necessary to suppress refractory impulses.[133]

## C.3. The Third Solution: Sublimation

Hobhouse is thus willing to accept the possibility of an impulse that cannot be integrated into a coherent life, which he associates with bad impulses,[134] and so must be repressed. But he also stresses that this is a very extreme case indeed. 'Instead of achieving unity by the repression of any given capacity', it is much preferable, he says, 'if possible, to take it up, transmute it, and find for it a direction in which it may work with the rest and in so doing . . . [make] for a life which is fuller and more harmonious.'[135] Dewey argues for a similar view. 'In the career of any impulse activity', he tells us, 'there are speaking generally three possibilities.'[136] It may be 'discharged', 'suppressed' or 'sublimated'. In sublimation the impulse is channelled into an intelligent and beneficial course of action, thereby finding a constructive outlet for energy, while directing it away from undesirable directions. Interestingly, some passages in Green point in this direction. When (as in the passage quoted above) Green argues that our natural impulses should be 'fused' with higher interests, he points to those persons in whom the natural passions have been enlisted in the service of the public good or in educating a family. Indeed, it is typical of Green that when he speaks of the need to 'repress' tendencies, he also indicates alternative outlets provided by a co-operative social order.[137]

Hobhouse's and Dewey's accounts of sublimation, however, are separated by an important difference. At least at times, Hobhouse seems to assume that a capacity has a more or less natural manifestation, which, however, might be redirected or 'transmuted'. In contrast, as we saw earlier (§A.3), Dewey is adamant in opposing the idea of a natural *telos* of development. As he depicts it, the simple 'discharge' option (which we might be tempted to equate with a natural outlet) is 'blind' and 'unintelligent' — not at all the sort of thing Mill would have had in mind when talking of the natural expression of impulse and capacity. As Dewey sees it, then, 'sublimation' characterises all intelligent, purposive expression of natural impulse. (To the extent Green could be said to offer a proto-sublimation theory, he would seem to agree with Dewey here.) Now while Dewey's sublimation thesis obviously has no difficulties with the idea of training impulses, it seems to do away with any notion of a natural outlet, bent or direction (either bad or good) of impulse/capacity. All that can be said is that we are endowed with impulses for which some outlet must be found. Consequently, it would appear that pathologies could only be produced if no outlets at all were allowed, as if, for example, it were sought to make people very passive and docile. While it sometimes seems that this sort of repression is all Dewey has in mind,[138] he usually has more definite ideas about suitable environments for man. If, as he surely does, he wants to criticise societies for not providing adequate outlets for men's social natures and their desires to feel a part of a whole

(§B.3), and if he is to insist that each should be free to develop one's unique excellences and to discover those things for which one is best suited (§I.B), he needs to suppose a conception of human capacity that implies some sort of natural development. In this respect, Hobhouse's idea of 'transmuting' an impulse and finding a new direction for it seems more promising. For it suggests a natural direction to impulse that, nevertheless, with considerable effort, may be redirected. In contradistinction to Dewey's account, Hobhouse's indicates that sublimation is not required in all environments for all impulses, but is a special adaptive mechanism to be brought into play when we find the need to restrain some particular impulse. As such, it would seem that it could be employed for adjusting to marginal deviations from the natural line of development but might be overtaxed in environments more radically unsuited to our nature.

The contrast between Dewey's thesis and that which I have attributed to Hobhouse corresponds in a general way to two opposing interpretations of Freud. On the one hand, Freud's theory is very similar to Dewey's. While he insists that repressing instincts is the basis of pathologies, Freud believes that sublimation of instinctual energy is a regular feature of life and the basis of civilisation.[139] If the social environment (i.e. norms, customs, etc.) blocks certain sorts of activities, the healthy response is to find another channel for the energy – i.e. sublimate it. To some this seems essentially conservative because it sees the individual as adjusting to his environment; it is, however, just as easily radical, for it indicates that the individual should be able, in principle, to adjust to a radically different environment. What it does not do is suggest that the environment should be altered to conform to human nature. Yet we can discern another strain in Freud, one that indicates that the demands for control of instinctual energy can go too far. The ego, Freud argues, can only control the energy of the id to a certain limit: if pushed too far, neurosis sets in.[140] Although it would be mistaken to say that even when emphasising this second strain Freud views sublimation merely as a mechanism for marginal adjustments, he certainly believes that the ego can be overtaxed in its effort to control impulse energy and, consequently, that very demanding social orders (i.e. those insisting on a great deal of instinctual control) may make nonpathological development impossible. Hence, the healthy development of personality does, on this interpretation of Freud, make demands as to the nature of the social environment.

It needs to be made clear that the account of sublimation I have attributed to Hobhouse is more implicit than explicit in his writings, and is to be found along with his advocacy of the other two 'solutions' to the modern liberal dilemma that we have discussed. Moreover, he sometimes sounds very much like Dewey, stressing the plasticity of impulses and hence the multiplicity of ways in which they can be adequately expressed. In general, Hobhouse seems to acknowledge a wide range of impulses, ranging from the unchangeable to the plastic and from the specific to the general.[141] Nevertheless, the account I have sketched here does come through in some of his writings; and of all the main modern liberal attempts to reconcile the call for natural development with the recognition of refractory impulses, Hobhouse's sublimation theory seems the most promising.

Almost everything I have said about (self-imposed) discipline would seem to apply in a fairly straightforward way to specialisation. According to the Hobhousian account I have just sketched, by ignoring too much of our nature, overspecialisation could be said to overtax our ability to sublimate, thus requiring repression which, in turn, issues in pathologies. Or, on a Deweyian account, a narrow life would offer no outlets for some impulses, thus again requiring repression. The interesting difference between specialisation and (moral) discipline concerns our social nature and, in particular, our social interest. I argued at length in Chapter II that modern liberals see social life as a solution to the problem of specialisation: through social life we partake of excellences we had to forgo in our individual plans of life. Assimilating this to the energy model, it could be said that our social nature (in this sense) consists of our natural tendency to sublimate unfulfilled capacities/impulses into an interest in the lives of others. That is, social interest could be seen as a sublimation of impulses that cannot achieve direct fulfilment in our individual lives. Now this is what *could* be said; so far as I know, no modern liberal says it. Indeed, they often use a very different argument, postulating a special social impulse, thus understanding social interest as a direct manifestation of natural impulse rather than sublimated energy. Nevertheless, this sublimated energy account is very much in the spirit of the central modern liberal belief that we attempt to find completion of our nature through participation in a mutually appreciative social life (§ II.A).

### C.4. The Rawlsian Solution

None of the difficulties I have been discussing arise for Rawls's theory. Rather than attributing pathologies to the repression of *particular capacities*, Rawls argues that loss of self-respect, which is associated with lack of desire, apathy, etc., stems from failure to pursue an adequate *plan of life*. As we saw in §I.D.1, the idea of a plan of life already assumes selection of some capacities over others for cultivation, so specialisation is assumed right from the start. And in his presentation of the Aristotelian Principle, Rawls is careful to specify that '[a] rational plan — *constrained as always by the principles of right* — allows a person to flourish, so far as circumstances permit, and to exercise his realized abilities as much as he can.'[142] Thus he also stipulates at the outset that a plan of life can fulfil the Aristotelian Principle — hence support self-respect — when limited by principles of right.

Despite, then, some resemblances to the energy model of capacities and pathologies (i.e. the lethargy that results from loss of self-respect), Rawls's theory seems to be of a different sort. It does not appear to see capacities as impulses that either must be manifested, sublimated or repressed. Instead, capacities are what we might call *opportunities for development*. Certainly they are ones we wish to pursue, but they do not each press upon us for satisfaction. Rawls's example of planning a trip is particularly apt here: just as we may wish to visit several cities but can only go to one or two, we may want to develop many of our capacities, but a rational individual can rest content with only taking advantage of some of the opportunities.[143] However, although conceiving capacities in this way allows Rawls to avoid the problem of discipline, it might seem that the way in which he does so entails the abandonment of a central modern liberal conviction. If capacities are simply opportunities, it would appear that someone might be content with taking advantage of just a few, developing a very narrow personality. Prima facie, at any rate, it would seem that a highly specialised life might satisfy Rawls's requirements for self-respect (i.e. successful execution of a plan of life and appreciation by one's fellows) as well as, or better than, a wider ranging one. It might seem, then, that Rawls avoids the difficulties of the question of discipline because he jettisons one of the central modern liberal tenets at the heart of the dilemma: that men desire the fullest possible satisfaction of their nature and any limitation is, *pro tanto*, stunting.

It certainly is true that of all modern liberals Rawls is probably the least worried by specialisation (§I.D.4). Neither does he seem very worried by discipline, talking as he does about desires — and not necessarily 'temporary' ones — being 'weeded out' in ways entirely devoid of any of Hobhouse's agonising.[144] However, Rawls does not abandon the modern liberal endorsement of broad over narrow personalities. According to Rawls, a rational plan of life is characterised by the 'principle of inclusiveness': viz. 'one long-term plan is better than another for any given period (or number of periods) if it allows for the encouragement and satisfaction of all the aims and interests of the other plan and for the encouragement and satisfaction of some further aim or interest in addition'.[145] Rawls contends that this principle is supported by the Aristotelian Principle (which, of course, means that it follows from human nature). Although the Aristotelian Principle indicates a need for specialisation in the pursuit of excellence, Rawls tells us that it also implies that, *ceteris paribus*, we will prefer the life that calls upon the greater number of subtle and refined skills. While this does not mean that we will generally opt for well-roundedness *over* specialisation, it does indicate that a broader cultivation of excellence is more attractive than a narrower one (at the same level of complexity and refinement). It probably even provides some motivation for pursuing breadth even if at some point it conflicts with specialisation.[146]

Rawls's conception of capacities and development, then, allows him to cut through the difficulties that beset the standard capacity/impulse model. By concentrating on adequate plans of life rather than on adequate satisfaction of impulses, he can easily accommodate the selection of some impulses for cultivation over others. However, for this very reason we might wonder whether Rawls's account has as strong libertarian implications as does the impulse/energy model (at least as it is employed by Mill). One of the things Mill wants to argue is that any restraint, *pro tanto*, is a restriction of our nature and thus potentially damaging. We will see in the next chapter (§V.B.4) that this analysis provides a foundation for one of Mill's main arguments for liberty: viz. that any coercive interference with an individual's freedom of action is apt to thwart some aspect of his nature. Now Rawls's theory, because it does not see the active impulses of human nature expanding in this way, also does not appear to have this sort of libertarian implication. Since each impulse does not demand expression, human nature would not seem to have difficulty accommodating itself to a very restrictive social order. Nor would it seem to rebel at coercive measures designed to enforce these restrictions. A great deal can be denied to us, perhaps forced upon us, without putting strains on human nature. This, of course, is not to say that Rawls actually advocates such restrictive principles – he certainly does not – but, rather, that his account of capacity, development and pathology does not in itself seem to provide as strong an argument as does Mill's account against such principles. (We will see in the next chapter that he does have some other arguments against them.) However, a caveat is in order: as we discovered in our examination of Dewey's theory of sublimation, an impulse/

energy model that does away with the idea of natural development and insists on the regular, indeed necessary, role of sublimation would also seem to have considerable capacity to accommodate itself to fairly restrictive social orders. These issues, however, are too complex to be adequately explored here: they provide the focus of the next chapter.

## D. Psychological and Social Development

Before leaving the topic of development, we ought to note the relation between individual psychological development – the concern of the chapter thus far – and the historical development of societies or civilisations. Mill, Green and especially Hobhouse were very much concerned with such social development; indeed, it would be understandable to think that in Hobhouse's work it is a more important sort of development than that of individuals. However, in a fundamental sense all modern liberal theories of social development are subordinate to their conception of individual development, for all perceive the *telos* of social development to be the fuller and wider realisation of individual growth. This is perhaps least obvious in Mill, as he was very impressed by Comte's three-stage account of the historical development of the human mind, an account that has little connection with the conception of individual growth we have examined here.[147] However, Mill also was convinced that personality structures change in the course of history.[148] In several places he asserts that the progress of civilisation tends to tame 'spontaneity and individuality' for the sake of greater development of our social side. Although, as is well known, Mill was worried that this trend was too strong in his own time, he did look forward to a stage in the development of the human race that he hoped would combine a very extensive sociability with a thoroughgoing individuality.[149] Indeed, in his statement in his *Autobiography* of his and Harriet's vision of the 'social problem of the future', the aim is clearly to unite individuality with a co-operative, community-minded social order. And, as if to emphasise that this requires the development of human nature, Mill adds that 'the capacity to do this has always existed in mankind, and is not, nor is ever likely to be, extinct.'[150]

All this becomes much clearer in Green and Hobhouse. 'To speak', wrote Green, 'of any progress or improvement or development of a nation or society or mankind, except as relative to some greater worth of persons, is to use words without meaning.' And, thus, 'There can be no progress of society which is not a development of capacities on the part of persons composing it.'[151] In particular, Green saw historical development as leading towards greater personal development in two ways. First, our conception of proper development and the capacities of men have widened in the modern era. 'Faculties, dispositions, occupations, persons, of which a Greek citizen would have taken no account, or taken account only to despise, are now recognised as having their place in the realisation of the powers of the human soul, in the due evolution of the spiritual from the animal man.'[152] And not only has our conception of development become richer, but our idea of 'human' and the extent of the 'human community' has also broadened. In contrast to the narrow conception of humanity entertained by the Greeks, Green argues that the movement of modern times is towards a recognition of a universal co-operative social life in which each is interested in the good of all.[153]

Hobhouse takes over much of this, but depicts the development of human nature somewhat differently. For Hobhouse (as for Mill) the course of historical development is marked by an increasingly successful synthesis of individuality and sociability. The primitive group, Hobhouse tells us, is characterised by intense solidarity, but 'the group absorbs the individual; its customs dominate him; there is no freedom, no room for initiative, barely the possibility of life apart from it'.[154] With the rise of the great civilisations the solidarity of the primitive community is lost to — or rather, is superimposed upon by — a more universal form of organisation that at least begins to lay the basis for a freedom and individuality founded upon equality of rights. In Hobhouse's story Greece represents a crucial, but ultimately partial and flawed, attempt at combining a common life with free initiative: it was, he says, 'not merely a corporate entity but a partnership of free men'.[155] Like Green, Hobhouse thinks that the Greek ideal was flawed by its limited conception of humanity, a defect which the universalisms of Rome and Christianity were to help make good. The important point for us, though, is not so much the details of Hobhouse's account of historical progress but rather that its aim is towards a humanity-wide social life that combines, on the one hand, individuality, freedom and initiative with, on the other, co-operation, solidarity and mutual service. 'Progress then is an evolution of harmony.'[156]

Mill, Green and Hobhouse thus see the outcome of historical development or progress largely in terms of the fuller realisation of man's nature.[157] Although such modern liberals theorise about the development of societies, what they really would seem to care about is the development of individuals. This relates, I think, to what Larry

Siedentop has called 'The Two Liberal Traditions'. According to Siedentop, the English liberal tradition, as represented, for example, by the social contract theories, is often charged with being premised upon 'an atomised' and 'ahistorical' conception of the individual and being, in general, 'sociologically naive'. In contrast, what Siedentop calls the French tradition in liberal thought is historical and sociological, recognising the social nature of man and the importance of institutions. In particular Siedentop stresses that this brand of liberalism, exemplified by Constant and Tocqueville, developed a theory of social change, specifying that social and economic conditions restricted political options and the range of possible political institutions.[158]

By way of conclusion to Part One, I would like to suggest that our modern liberals remain very much in the English tradition (even if often with a distinct German accent). To be sure, they insist on the social nature of man, the importance of institutions and, at least some, the development of society, but their focus remains primarily on the nature of man rather than on general laws of societies. Siedentop, in fact, suggests something along these lines about Mill, telling us that while he took over a good deal from Tocqueville, he persisted in the traditional English liberal 'mode of argument unaffected by the new sociological mode of argument'.[159] Much the same, I think, can be said of the other modern liberals, even Hobhouse, who has been called a 'founding father' of sociology.[160] I have argued in the last four chapters that the centre of all their theories is a thesis about what we have it in ourselves to be, how this can be brought about and what occurs when it is not. And, as with Hobbes, Locke and James Mill before them, they believe that if we know the nature of man, then we can design suitable political institutions. Having completed our examination of this first part, we can now turn to consider the second part of the hypothetical.

## Notes

1. The analysis of § A owes much to John W. Chapman, 'Toward a General Theory of Human Nature and Dynamics' in J. Roland Pennock and John W. Chapman (eds.), *NOMOS XVII: Human Nature in Politics* (New York University Press, New York, 1977), pp. 292-319, esp. pp. 295-97. See also his 'Political Theory: Logical Structure and Enduring Types' in *L'idée de philosophie politique* (Presses Universitaires de France, Paris, 1965), pp. 57-96.

2. William McDougall, *An Introduction to Social Psychology*, 22nd edn (Methuen, London, 1931), pp. 17-18.

3. Hobhouse, *Social Development* (Allen and Unwin, London, 1924), p. 138.

4.	Which, however, Hobhouse insists is by no means entirely 'mechanical'. *Mind in Evolution*, 3rd edn (Macmillan, London, 1926), pp. 90-94. See Mary Midgley, *Beast and Man: The Roots of Human Nature* (Methuen, London, 1980), pp. 51-57.

5.	Lionel Tiger and Robin Fox, *The Imperial Animal* (Secker and Warburg, London, 1971), p. 16. According to Tiger and Fox, the outcome was a 'theory' that was 'little more than a list of ever-more-specific human attributes' (ibid.).

6.	McDougall, *Social Psychology*, p. 36.

7.	Ibid., pp. 71 ff, Ch. XII.

8.	'The crucial point of Lorenz's view of human nature is the theory that like many other animals we have an innate drive to aggressive behaviour towards our own species.' Leslie Stevenson, *Seven Theories of Human Nature* (Oxford University Press, Oxford, 1974), p. 112. See Konrad Lorenz, *On Aggression*, Marjorie Kerr Wilson (trans.) (Bantam, New York, 1971), Ch. XIII.

9.	Tiger and Fox, *The Imperial Animal*, p. 16.

10.	Edward O. Wilson, *On Human Nature* (Harvard University Press, Cambridge, 1978), pp. 56-57. Wilson discusses Lorenz's views on aggression in Ch. 5.

11.	Solomon E. Asch, *Social Psychology* (Prentice-Hall, New York, 1952), p. 73.

12.	Maurice Mandelbaum, *History, Man, and Reason* (Johns Hopkins Press, Baltimore, 1971), pp. 142-45.

13.	John B. Watson, *Behaviorism*, rev. edn (University of Chicago Press, Chicago, 1930), p. 294.

14.	Ibid., p. 104.

15.	B.F. Skinner, *About Behaviorism* (Jonathan Cape, London, 1974), p. 43.

16.	B.F. Skinner, *Walden Two* (Macmillan, New York, 1962), p. 196. See John Passmore, *The Perfectibility of Man* (Duckworth, London, 1970), pp. 167-70. For an overview of Skinner's view of human nature, see Stevenson, *Seven Theories*, Ch. 8.

17.	Mandelbaum, *History, Man, and Reason*, p. 143. I am disassociating organicism from historicism here.

18.	Clifford Geertz, *The Interpretation of Cultures* (Basic Books, New York, 1973), p. 217. See Chapman, 'Toward a General Theory of Human Nature and Dynamics', for an analysis of Geertz.

19.	Geertz, *The Interpretation of Cultures*, pp. 363-64.

20.	Mandelbaum, *History, Man, and Reason*, pp. 174-86.

21.	See Richard M. Lerner, *Concepts and Theories of Human Development* (Addison-Wesley Publishing Co., Reading, Mass., 1976), Ch. 3.

22.	Dewey, *Human Nature and Conduct* (Henry Holt, New York, 1922), p. 10.

23.	Dewey, *Freedom and Culture* (Allen and Unwin, London, 1940), p. 21. Dewey criticises Mill's 'individualist' psychology on pp. 105-6, ibid.

24.	See Morton Levitt, *Freud and Dewey on the Nature of Man* (Philosophical Library, New York, 1960), p. 162. For other interpretations holding that Dewey emphasised the environmental side of the interaction, see: Alfonso J. Damico, *Individuality and Community: The Social and Political Thought of John Dewey* (University Presses of Florida, Gainesville, 1978), p.85; Katherine Ernst, 'A Comparison of John Dewey's Theory of Valuation and Abraham Maslow's Theory of Value', *Educational Theory*, XXIV (Spring 1974), pp. 139-41. Dorothy June Newbury, however, argues that environment is not dominant in Dewey's theory of education in 'A Search for the Meaning of Discipline in Dewey's Theory of Growth', *Educational Theory*, V (1955), pp. 241-42.

25.	See Dewey, *Democracy and Education* (Free Press, New York, 1916), p. 44; his 'Time and Individuality' in David Sidorsky (ed.), *John Dewey: The*

*Essential Writings* (Harper and Row, New York, 1977), p. 145. The wax analogy is, of course, a longstanding one in environmental thinking. Locke, for example, although he recognised differences in individual natures, was enough of an environmentalist (at least in his educational theory) to consider the child as if he were 'white paper, or wax, to be moulded and fashioned as one pleases'. *Some Thoughts Concerning Education* in Peter Gay (ed.), *John Locke on Education* (Teachers College Press, New York, 1964), p. 176. See also Mandelbaum, *History, Man, and Reason*, pp. 151-52.

26. Stefan Collini, 'Hobhouse, Bosanquet and the State: Philosophical Idealism and Political Argument in England 1880-1918', *Past and Present*, LXXII (Aug. 1976), pp. 96-97.

27. Mandelbaum, *History, Man, and Reason*, p. 182.

28. Bosanquet, *The Philosophical Theory of the State*, 4th edn (Macmillan, London, 1951), p. 162; see also his *Science and Philosophy* (Allen and Unwin, London, 1927), p. 175. Compare Dewey: 'The social environment acts through native impulses and speech and moral habitudes manifest themselves.' *Human Nature and Conduct*, p. 15.

29. Bosanquet, *Science and Philosophy*, pp. 404-5. See also his *Value and Destiny of the Individual* (Macmillan, London, 1913), p. 83.

30. See Mandelbaum, *History, Man, and Reason*, pp. 214-24. Mandelbaum is noteworthy in perceiving these two pulls on Bosanquet. While recognising that there is 'an appreciable distance' between Bosanquet and Green, he also acknowledges that 'there was a much greater similarity between his moral and political thought and that of Green than existed between the thought of Green and the other idealists who have been mentioned [e.g. Hegel, Bradley]'. Ibid., p. 465. See also p. 221. Bosanquet discusses Fichte on patriotism in his *Social and International Ideals* (Macmillan, London, 1917), Chs. I, XIV. For an analysis of Fichte's influence on the educational theories of British idealism, see Peter Gordon and John White, *Philosophers as Educational Reformers: The Influence of Idealism on British Educational Thought and Practice* (Routledge and Kegan Paul, London, 1979), Ch. 5.

31. Bosanquet, *Science and Philosophy*, p. 144. See also his *Philosophical Theory of the State*, p. 164, and *The Value and Destiny of the Individual*, pp. 277 ff.

32. See Bosanquet, *The Civilization of Christendom* (Swan Sonnenschein, London, 1899), pp. 342-43; his 'Preface' to *Aspects of the Social Problem* (Macmillan, London, 1895); his 'Relation of Sociology to Philosophy', *Mind*, VI (1897), pp. 1-8; and his *Philosophical Theory of the State*, Ch. II.

33. See Green's essay on 'The Force of Circumstances' in R.L. Nettleship (ed.), *The Works of Thomas Hill Green* (Longman's, Green, and Co., London, 1900), vol. III, pp. 3-10.

34. Hobhouse, *Mind in Evolution*, pp. 469-70.

35. Ibid., p. 468. See also his *Social Development*, pp. 136-38. See also Morris Ginsberg, 'The Work of L.T. Hobhouse' in J.A. Hobson and Morris Ginsberg (eds.), *L.T. Hobhouse: His Life and Work* (Allen and Unwin, London, 1931), pp. 150 ff.

36. Hobhouse, *Social Development*, p. 155-59. Self-regard is another such interest, pp. 159-62.

37. J.-J. Rousseau, *Emile*, Barbara Foxley (trans.) (Dent, London, 1976), p. 9.

38. Mill, *On Liberty* in J.M. Robson (ed.), *The Collected Works of John Stuart Mill* (University of Toronto Press, Toronto, 1963), vol. XVIII, p. 263.

39. Bosanquet, *Psychology of the Moral Self* (Macmillan, London, 1904), p. 9. Interestingly, Froebel also used the crystalline world as a model of human development. See Irene M. Lilley's 'Introduction' to her *Friedrich Froebel: A Selection from his Writings* (Cambridge University Press, Cambridge, 1967), p. 15.

40. Mill, *On Liberty*, p. 265.

41. Mill, *The Subjection of Women* in Alice S. Rossi (ed.), *Essays on Sex Equality* (University of Chicago Press, Chicago, 1970), pp. 148-49.

42. R.S. Peters (ed. and abridger), *Brett's History of Psychology* (Allen and Unwin, London, 1962), p. 450. See also Mandelbaum, *History, Man, and Reason*, Ch. 9.

43. James Mill, *Analysis of the Phenomena of the Human Mind*, J.S. Mill, ed. (Kelley, New York, 1967), vol. I, p. 52.

44. Ibid., Ch. III. Alexander Bain later posited an additional law of similarity according to which '*present* Actions, Sensations, Thoughts, or Emotions tend to revive the Like among *previous* Impressions or States'. *The Senses and the Intellect*, 3rd edn (D. Appleton, New York, 1885), p. 457. See also J.S. Mill's review of 'Bain's Psychology' in *Dissertations and Discussions*, vol. IV (William V. Spencer, Boston, 1868), pp. 101-56.

45. Hence, associations formed synchronically spring up together whereas successively associated ideas come up in succession. James Mill, *Analysis of the Mind*, vol. I, pp. 78-80.

46. Ibid., p. 78. Also note that '[a]n idea may be excited either by a sensation or an idea.' Ibid., p. 81.

47. Ibid., vol. II, p. 184.

48. Ibid., p. 191.

49. Ibid., p. 202.

50. According to James Mill, whether a motive results in an action depends on the strength of the association between the idea of our doing the act and the 'internal feelings' that produce action. Ibid., p. 254.

51. Sir Leslie Stephen, *The English Utilitarians*, vol. III, *John Stuart Mill* (Augustus M. Kelley, New York, 1968), p. 151; Alan Ryan, *The Philosophy of John Stuart Mill* (Macmillan, London, 1970), pp. 161-62. Mill also has been charged with treating men like clay ('and circumstances are the potter'). James Ward, 'J.S. Mill's Science of Ethology', *International Journal of Ethics*, I (July 1891), p. 452. See also Martin Hollis, 'J.S. Mill's Political Philosophy of Mind', *Philosophy*, XLVII (Oct. 1972), pp. 334-47.

52. Alexander Bain, a later associationist, criticised the younger Mill for thinking some pleasures are psychologically higher than others. *John Stuart Mill* (Kelley, New York, 1969), pp. 113-14. In a note to his father's *Analysis of the Mind*, J.S. Mill attempts to give a not very satisfactory associationist interpretation of his doctrine (vol. II, pp. 253-55). Ultimately J.S. Mill himself seemed uncertain whether associationism could provide an adequate account of higher pleasures; see the 'Inaugural Address', in *Dissertations and Discussions*, vol. IV, p. 379. On the younger Mill's notion of a self and its relation to associationism, see *An Examination of Sir William Hamilton's Philosophy* in *Collected Works*, vol. IX, p. 194, and Alan Ryan, *J.S. Mill* (Routledge and Kegan Paul, London, 1974), pp. 224-26; F.L. van Holthoon, *The Road to Utopia: A Study of John Stuart Mill's Social Thought* (Van Gorcum, Assen, 1971), p. 35.

53. Mill, *Autobiography* (Columbia University Press, New York, 1924), p. 96.

54. Mill, *Utilitarianism* in *Collected Works*, vol. X, p. 230; see also his *Autobiography*, p. 96.

55. Mill, 'Sedgwick's Discourse' in *Collected Works*, vol. X, p. 60.

56. Mill, *Utilitarianism*, p. 230. See Adina Beth Schwartz, 'John Stuart Mill: A Program for Social Philosophy', unpublished PhD thesis, Rockefeller University, 1976, pp. 85-89.

57. Dewey, *Democracy and Education*, pp. 111-15.

58. See Dewey, *Human Nature and Conduct*, pp. 90 ff. See also Gordon W. Allport, 'Dewey's Individual and Social Psychology' in Paul Arthur Schlipp (ed.),

*The Philosophy of John Dewey* (Tudor, New York, 1951), pp. 270-72, 280; Sophie M. Simec, 'Human Nature According to Dewey', *Proceedings of the American Catholic Philosophical Association*, XXIX (1955), pp. 225-34.

59. See Dewey, *Problems of Men* (Philosophical Library, New York, 1946), pp. 180-84. See also Jerome Nathanson, *John Dewey: The Reconstruction of the Democratic Life* (Scribner's, New York, 1951), Ch. 3.

60. Dewey, *Democracy and Education*, p. 114.

61. But it certainly does not play a major role in his thought. See Dewey and Tufts, *Ethics*, rev. edn (Henry Holt, New York, 1932), p. 385; Dewey, *The Public and Its Problems* (Swallow Press, Chicago, 1954), p. 216; and his *Human Nature and Conduct*, p. 296.

62. Green, *Prolegomena to Ethics*, A.C. Bradley (ed.) (Clarendon Press, Oxford, 1890), p. 182.

63. Bosanquet, *The Philosophical Theory of the State*, p. 219.

64. See Stanley Bates, 'The Motivation to be Just', *Ethics*, LXXXV (Oct. 1974), pp. 1-17. Lawrence Kohlberg discusses Rawls's theory in relation to his study of moral development in 'The Claim to Moral Adequacy of a Highest Stage of Moral Judgement', *The Journal of Philosophy*, LXX (Oct. 1973), pp. 630-46. See also John W. Chapman, 'Rawls's Theory of Justice', *The American Political Science Review*, LXIX (June 1975), p. 589.

65. See Rawls, *A Theory of Justice* (The Belknap Press of Harvard University Press, Cambridge, 1971), § § 70-72.

66. Lerner, *Human Development*, p. 140.

67. Rawls, *A Theory of Justice*, p. 494.

68. Ibid., p. 458. 'A second [empiricist] thesis is that the desire to conform to moral standards is normally aroused early in life before we achieve an adequate understanding of the reason for these norms.' (Ibid.) Rawls places Freud in this branch of the empiricist tradition whereas I associate him with an interactionism which has developmental elements. (See § § A.2, B.1, B.3, C.3.)

69. Ibid., pp. 459-60.

70. Ibid., p. 461.

71. Ibid., p. 494.

72. Jean Piaget, *The Moral Judgment of the Child*, Marjorie Gabain (trans.) (Free Press, New York, 1965), p. 404.

73. Ibid., p. 198.

74. In fairness to Rawls, it is not clear from the relevant passage whether he thinks this point separates him from the 'rationalist' tradition, or merely from Piaget and Kohlberg. See Rawls, *A Theory of Justice*, pp. 462n, 495.

75. Ibid., p. 502.

76. Writes Hobhouse: 'As to this particular term, I shall not attempt any new definition. I shall content myself for the present with the familiar conception of maturation of that which previously existed in germ, the active realization of something which is at first a mere potentiality.' Hobhouse, *Social Evolution and Political Theory* (Columbia University Press, New York, 1928), p. 84. According to Mill, development is an 'increase in function, through expansion and differentiation of structure by internal forces'. 'Inaugural Address' in *Dissertations and Discussions*, vol. IV, p. 378.

77. See R.S. Peters, *Psychology and Ethical Development* (Allen and Unwin, 1974), pp. 336-59, 237.

78. See Lerner, *Human Development*, pp. 187-92.

79. Rousseau, *Emile*, pp. 6-7.

80. Mill, *Utilitarianism*, p. 237; see also p. 210. Sidgwick thought Mill an ethical hedonist as well as a psychological one. *The Methods of Ethics*, 7th edn (University of Chicago Press, Chicago, 1907), p. xv.

81. Mill, *Utilitarianism*, p. 212.

82. Ibid., pp. 231 ff.

83. See Maurice Mandelbaum, 'On Interpreting Mill's *Utilitarianism*' in Samuel Gorovitz (ed.), *Mill: Utilitarianism* (Bobbs-Merrill, Indianapolis, 1971), pp. 380-90; and his *History, Man, and Reason*, pp. 194 ff. But see also Joseph Margolis, 'Mill's *Utilitarianism* Again' in Gorovitz, *Mill: Utilitarianism*, pp. 376-79.

84. See Rex Martin, 'A Defence of Mill's Qualitative Hedonism', *Philosophy*, XLVII (Apr. 1972), pp. 141, 149-50. This also serves to undermine one of Mandelbaum's main reasons for putting Mill's and Green's theories of man into different subcategories, although he says both view 'man as a progressive being'. *History, Man, and Reason*, p. 214.

85. Green, *Prolegomena*, p. 408.

86. Ibid., p. 403.

87. Ibid., p. 297.

88. Bosanquet, *Some Suggestions in Ethics* (Macmillan, London, 1919), p. 43; Bosanquet, *Science and Philosophy*, p. 202.

89. Bosanquet, *Science and Philosophy*, pp. 190-94. See also his *Value and Destiny of the Individual*, Lecture VI; and his *Psychology of the Moral Self*, pp. 64-65.

90. Green, *Prolegomena*, p. 253.

91. Hobhouse, *The Rational Good: A Study in the Logic of Practice* (Watts, London, 1947), p. 136.

92. Rawls, *A Theory of Justice*, p. 409.

93. A.D. Lindsay, 'Introduction' to John Stuart Mill, *Utilitarianism, Liberty and Representative Government* (Dent, London, 1910), p. xii. See also Jean Austin, 'Pleasure and Happiness' in J.B. Schneewind (ed.), *Mill: A Collection of Critical Essays* (Macmillan, London, 1968), pp. 234-50.

94. For Dewey see Robert L. Holmes, 'John Dewey's Social Ethics', *Journal of Value Inquiry*, VII (1973), pp. 274-80.

95. Rawls, *A Theory of Justice*, p. 429.

96. Ibid., p. 440.

97. Ibid.

98. Mill, *The Subjection of Women*, p. 238.

99. Mill, *On Liberty*, p. 265.

100. Hobhouse, *Social Development*, p. 86n. Compare Dewey, *Individualism – Old and New* (Allen and Unwin, London, 1931), p. 76.

101. Dewey, *Human Nature and Conduct*, p. 140.

102. Ibid., pp. 141, 158. See also Dewey's *Individualism*, pp. 48-49, 54-55, 122. Compare Hobhouse, *Social Development*, p. 341.

103. Dewey, *Human Nature and Conduct*, pp. 156-57.

104. Hobhouse, *Elements of Social Justice* (Allen and Unwin, London, 1949), p. 25.

105. Hobhouse, *The Rational Good*, pp. 147-48.

106. Morton Levitt, *Freud and Dewey on the Nature of Man*, pp. 155-56. See also Alan Lawson, 'John Dewey and the Hope for Reform', *History of Education Quarterly*, XV (Spring 1975), p. 50.

107. I consider the distinction between positive and negative freedom in §V.A.

108. Green, 'On the Different Senses of "Freedom" as Applied to Will and to the Moral Progress of Man' in *Works*, vol. II, p. 324.

109. Bosanquet, *The Philosophical Theory of the State*, pp. 136, 219.

110. Dewey, *Individualism*, pp. 82-85. See also his *Human Nature and Conduct*, p. 158.

111. Dewey, *Democracy and Education*, p. 41.

112. Gordon and White, *Philosophers and Educational Reformers*, pp. 196-97. See §II.C.2.

113. See Green, 'Fragments of an Address on the Text "The Word is Nigh Thee" ' in *Works*, vol. III, p. 224; see § § I.D, II.A.

114. Froebel quoted in Bosanquet's *Essays and Addresses* (Swan Sonnenschein, London, 1891), p. 71.

115. Green, 'Lectures on the Philosophy of Kant' in *Works*, vol. II, p. 133.

116. Green, 'On the Different Senses of "Freedom" ', p. 327.

117. Not surprisingly, we can find places in which they do indicate that capacities can merely lie dormant. (E.g., Dewey, *Problems of Men*, p. 95.) Nevertheless, as I have argued, their formal analyses suggest otherwise.

118. Bosanquet, *Some Suggestions in Ethics*, pp. 107, 112. See also his *Psychology of the Moral Self*, p. 97.

119. Friedrich Froebel, *The Education of Man*, W.N. Hailman (trans.) (Appleton, New York, 1894), pp. 121-22. Like Rousseau, Froebel argues that the removal of corrupting habits is essential to this quest.

120. Bosanquet, *The Value and Destiny of the Individual*, p. 168n. Ann R. Cacoullos makes clear that Green thought we possessed capacities that ought not to be realised. *Thomas Hill Green: Philosopher of Rights* (Twayne, New York, 1974), pp. 69-70.

121. Mill, *On Liberty*, pp. 265-66; 'Nature' in *Collected Works*, vol. X, pp. 396-97. This side of Mill is often overlooked as, I think, by Maurice Cranston when writing that 'Mill believed in the goodness — still more the potential goodness — of man.' *John Stuart Mill* (Longman's, Green, London, 1958), p. 20. However, in the 'Inaugural Address' Mill himself seems to suggest that man is basically good (p. 388). For a discussion of Mill on discipline, see F.W. Garforth, *Educative Democracy: John Stuart Mill on Education in Society* (Oxford University Press, Oxford, 1980), pp. 104 ff.

122. Melvin Richter, *The Politics of Conscience: T.H. Green and his Age* (Weidenfeld and Nicolson, London, 1964), pp. 256-57.

123. 'Renounces' may not be quite accurate. See § C.3 below.

124. Hobhouse, *Liberalism* (Oxford University Press, Oxford, 1964), p. 66. Compare Hobhouse's thesis about the removal of 'superincumbent pressure' with Rousseau's ideas on unnatural habits (§ B.1).

125. Mill, *Principles of Political Economy* in *Collected Works*, vol. III, p. 938. See also his *Subjection of Women*, p. 242. See Ryan, *J.S. Mill*, pp. 173-74.

126. Mill, *The Subjection of Women*, pp. 227, 238; *On Liberty*, pp. 263-64. In *Representative Government* Mill argues that passive persons are prone to envy (*Collected Works*, vol. XIX, pp. 408-9).

127. Mill, *On Liberty*, p. 266.

128. See Hobhouse, *Morals in Evolution* (Chapman and Hall, London, 1951), p. 600.

129. Hobhouse, *Sociology and Philosophy: A Centenary Collection of Essays and Articles* (G. Bell and Sons, London, 1966), p. 315.

130. See Hobhouse, *Social Justice*, p. 25; and his *Rational Good*, p. 90.

131. Hobhouse, *Social Development*, p. 161.

132. Hobhouse, *Social Justice*, p. 67.

133. Hugh Carter, *The Social Theories of L.T. Hobhouse* (Kennikat, Port Washington, N.Y., 1968), pp. 81-85.

134. As Hobhouse defines the good in terms of harmony, this equation is not as puzzling as it might at first seem. See *The Rational Good*, Chs. IV, V, VI.

135. Hobhouse, *Morals in Evolution*, p. 600.

136. Dewey, *Human Nature and Conduct*, p. 156.

137. Green, 'On the Different Senses of "Freedom" ', p. 327; *Prolegomena*, p. 221.

138. See Dewey, *Democracy and Education*, p. 115.

139. See Sigmund Freud, *Civilization and its Discontents*, James Strachy (trans. and ed.) (W.W. Norton, New York, 1962), Ch. II.

140. See Sigmund Freud, *The Ego and the Id*, Joan Riviere (trans.), James Strachy (ed.) (W.W. Norton, New York, 1962), pp. 20, 35, 44-47; and his *Civilization and its Discontents*, p. 90. See also R.S. Peters, *Psychology and Ethical Development*, pp. 190-91.

141. See Hobhouse, *The Rational Good*, Ch. II. See also § A.2.

142. Rawls, *A Theory of Justice*, p. 429. Emphasis added. See § VI.C.2.

143. Ibid., pp. 412-13.

144. Ibid., p. 411.

145. Ibid., p. 413.

146. Ibid., p. 414.

147. See Mill, *Auguste Comte and Positivism* in *Collected Works*, vol. X, pp. 267 ff. Mill reports in his *Autobiography* that among the ideas he derived from 'Continental' thought was '[t]hat the human mind has a certain order of possible progress, in which some things must precede others, an order to which governments and public instruction can modify to some, but not to an unlimited, extent' (p. 114). See John M. Robson, *The Improvement of Mankind: The Social and Political Thought of John Stuart Mill* (University of Toronto Press, Toronto, 1968), pp. 95-105. See also Hobhouse's *Sociology and Philosophy*, pp. 61-79.

148. See Abram L. Harris, 'John Stuart Mill's Theory of Progress', *Ethics*, LXVI (Apr. 1956), pp. 162 ff.

149. See Mill's *On Liberty*, pp. 264-65; 'Civilisation' in *Collected Works*, vol. XVIII, pp. 122-24; *Principles of Political Economy*, pp. 203-14; *Chapters on Socialism* in *Collected Works*, vol. V, p. 746.

150. Mill, *Autobiography*, p. 163.

151. Green, *Prolegomena*, pp. 193, 295. See Green, 'Lecture on Liberal Legislation and Freedom of Contract' in *Works*, vol. III, p. 371. See also Crane Brinton, *English Political Thought in the Nineteenth Century* (Harper and Bros., New York, 1962), pp. 216-17; H.D. Lewis, *Freedom and History* (Allen and Unwin, London, 1962), pp. 122-23.

152. Green, *Prolegomena*, pp. 280-81.

153. Ibid., pp. 300 ff. See § III.B.2.

154. Hobhouse, *Social Development*, p. 254. On Hobhouse's theory of development see Stefan Collini, *Liberalism and Sociology: L.T. Hobhouse and Political Argument in England 1880-1914* (Cambridge University Press, Cambridge, 1979), Pt. III.

155. Hobhouse, *Social Development*, p. 255.

156. Hobhouse, *Development and Purpose* (Macmillan, London, 1913), p. 287. Formally, Hobhouse argues that social development consists in the increase of: (1) Scale, (2) Efficiency, (3) Freedom and (4) Mutuality (mutual service). *Social Development*, p. 78.

157. Dewey's position is much the same. See Holmes, 'John Dewey's Social Ethics', pp. 278 ff. Bosanquet, though acknowledging that 'man must tend on the whole to add to his moral and social achievements' was wary of theories of progress. *Social and International Ideals* (Macmillan, London, 1917), p. 299. Bosanquet reviewed Hobhouse's *Development and Purpose*, taking exception to its stress on the future. 'Review of *Development and Purpose*', *Mind*, XXII (1913), pp. 383-87.

158. See Larry Siedentop, 'Two Liberal Traditions' in Alan Ryan (ed.), *The Idea of Freedom: Essays in Honour of Isaiah Berlin* (Oxford University Press, Oxford, 1979), pp. 154-56.

159. Ibid., p. 173.

160. Collini, *Liberalism and Sociology*, p. 5. Collini calls Bosanquet's theory unhistorical and ultimately unsociological. 'Hobhouse, Bosanquet and the State', p. 106. See Bosanquet, 'The Relation of Sociology to Philosophy', and his *Philosophical Theory of the State*, Ch. II.

PART TWO
POLITICS

# V  LIBERTY

Having completed the examination of the modern liberal theory of human nature, we can now turn to consider how this theory provides the basis for modern liberal prescriptions. In this chapter I deal with arguments for liberty. Chapter VI then examines the case for democracy and, finally, Chapter VII takes up economic organisation and the 'new liberalism'. Regarding all three, I will argue, the regulative ideal is the promotion of healthy development. However, as I stressed in the Introductory, this is not to say that our six modern liberals always agree on just what institutions and arrangements are required to promote such development. Indeed, in Chapter VI, and especially in Chapter VII, we will discover some significant disagreements. My concern in this part is thus not simply with those matters on which modern liberals agree but also with the areas of, and reasons for, diverging prescriptions.

## A.  Positive and Negative Liberty

My aim in this chapter, then, is to show that modern liberals uphold liberty for all on the grounds of promoting human development. To demonstrate this is essential for my thesis as it connects the modern liberal theory of man to liberty, the fundamental commitment of any liberalism. However, a problem immediately arises. 'Liberty' or 'freedom' (I shall take these as synonyms) would appear to mean different things to different liberals. As we all know, Green proposed a new, 'positive', conception of liberty. There are good reasons, Green argued, for extending the notion of freedom beyond its core meaning — in which it refers to the absence of compulsion in human relations — to a 'metaphorical' sense that concerns 'a positive power or capacity of doing or enjoying something worth doing or enjoying, and that, too, something that we do or enjoy in common with others.'[1] Depending on one's perspective, Green's proposal for extending the notion of freedom in this way has been seen either as a remedy for the unsocial and inadequate 'negative' conception of classical liberal theory[2] or as a repudiation of the 'truer and more humane ideal' of negative liberty for a potentially despotic, illiberal ideal. According to this latter view, stressed by Isaiah Berlin, Green's concern with the power to do what is worth doing can easily lead to the 'enlightened' few coercing those who 'fail' to pursue the 'worthy'; such freedom, Berlin tells us, can turn out to be identical with despotism.[3] Regardless, however, of whether it is thought to be an advance or a betrayal of liberal ideals, it is widely thought that Green's proposal represents a 'restatement of liberal political theory'.[4] Indeed, it would not be going too far to say that for many Green's advocacy of a positive conception of freedom is the watershed in the evolution of liberal theory, dividing the classical and modern versions.

The problem posed by all this for my thesis is fairly obvious. Although Bosanquet, Hobhouse and Dewey can be said to be sympathetic to the positive analysis, Mill is almost always identified with the negative camp.[5] And Rawls (quite understandably) wishes to avoid the whole negative/positive argument.[6] Given this, if the distinction between the two concepts of liberty is really as fundamental as many suppose, my interpretation of the modern liberal tradition, if not instantly undermined, certainly looks problematic.

Recent studies of the development of liberal theory, however, have cast doubt on the importance of the rise of the positive conception of liberty. Michael Freeden, for example, argues that it is but one, and by no means the most important, of a number of changes that occurred in late nineteenth-century liberal theory while Stefan Collini suggests that the traditional account overemphasises the importance of the idea of 'negative liberty' in political argument before Green's time.[7] More radically, following Gerald MacCallum's analysis of liberty, Collini insists that the distinction itself is unsound and, so, is objectionable as a focus for inquiry.[8] Although (at least here) I do not wish to go so far as to deny that the negative and positive are distinct conceptions of liberty, I do want to deny that for our purposes the distinction is necessarily an important one. From the mere fact that one theorist proposes a 'negative' and another a 'positive' conception of liberty, very little follows as to their substantive political positions. Following W.L. Weinstein, I will try to show that positive liberty is not so much a challenge to, or a rejection of, negative liberty, but rather it is a (perhaps misguided) effort to integrate into the very concept of liberty other things such as the value and purpose of (negative) liberty and the circumstances under which it can be effectively and beneficially exercised.[9] And − as I indicated in the previous chapter (§IV.B.3) − it also involves a theory about the effects of thwarting capacities. What this implies, then, is that an advocate of positive liberty like Green can, in principle, agree with Mill (who I will take as a proponent of negative liberty) that negative liberty is valuable, why it is to be valued, its relation to the growth of capacities, and the circumstances under which it can be effectively utilised. All we know for certain before we have examined their cases for negative liberty is that they disagree as to the meaning of 'liberty' or 'freedom'.

In a sense, the whole of this chapter is an attempt to defend this view of positive and negative liberty. I examine in §B modern liberal arguments for negative liberty with the aim of demonstrating that our 'positive' and 'negative' modern liberals actually offer similar arguments. In §§B.1 and B.3, I explicitly deal with Green's and Bosanquet's arguments for positive liberty. Berlin's worry that advocates of positive liberty tend to — or at least in principle can — coerce in the name of freedom ('force to be free') is dealt with in §§B.4 and B.5, which discuss the role of coercion and, in particular, the place of paternalism in modern liberal thinking. From these general arguments for liberty I turn in §C to consider some modern liberal arguments for specific liberties. Liberals, though, do not simply value liberty, but an equality of liberty. I thus close the chapter in §D by examining the grounds on which modern liberals have endorsed *equal* liberty for all. An important topic concerning liberty, however, is not considered in this chapter: I defer until Chapter VII (§B.1) a discussion of the economic preconditions for an effective use of liberty.

## B. Liberty in General

In his analysis of the 'Heart of Liberalism' Hobhouse tells us, 'The foundation of liberty is the idea of growth.'[10] This indeed is the core proposition of the modern liberal defence of liberty. Throughout modern liberal writings we repeatedly encounter arguments contending that freedom is grounded on the quest for self-realisation, self-development or growth. Among these, four broad families of arguments stand out. I shall call these the arguments based on: (i) the quest for self-satisfaction, (ii) the necessity of choice, (iii) the requirements of self-expression and (iv) the dangers of coercion.

### B.1. Self-satisfaction

The most straightforward, and probably the most famous, argument linking liberty and development is presented by Mill in the third chapter of *Liberty*. As we saw in the first chapter (§B), one of Mill's main concerns there is to establish the diversity of human nature; human beings, he tells us, are not sheep, and not even all sheep are alike. The upshot of this diversity, according to Mill, is that no one way of living will promote the development of all. 'The same mode of living is a healthy excitement to one, keeping all his faculties of action and enjoyment in their best order, while to another it is a distracting burthen, which suspends or crushes all internal life.'[11] And, hence, as we all know, Mill argues that each needs to be free to discover what sort of life harmonises with his own circumstances and character. Although Mill sometimes sounds as if the entire problem was discovering a way of living that suits our nature, it would also seem that 'experiments in living' involve an element of *self*-discovery. Dewey, emphasising as always the importance of experience in modifying goals, was insistent on this point. Varied interaction and activities are not only necessary if we are to find out what satisfies us but to discover just what are our possibilities: 'potentialities cannot be *known* till *after* the interactions have occurred. There are at any given time unactualized potentialities in an individual because and in as far as there are in existence other things with which it has not yet interacted.'[12]

   Clearly, though, if these sorts of arguments are to support not only a varied environment but also the liberty of each to decide what is appropriate to him, an additional claim is required: viz. that the individual concerned is generally a good judge of what his capacities are and what is appropriate to his nature. If this claim does not hold true, i.e. if we are each generally bad judges of what is conducive to our development, there seems little point indeed of allowing each the liberty to judge such things for himself. This is an important point: although we will see in §§B.2 and B.3 that modern liberals offer arguments connecting liberty and development that circumvent the need to make this claim, in so far as they argue that each requires liberty to discover his nature and what suits it, the claim is necessary. Modern liberals, in fact, have actually tended to make what would appear to be a stronger claim. *No one*, says Mill, is more interested than the individual concerned or so well acquainted with his situation: 'with respect to his own feelings and circumstances, the most ordinary man or woman has means of knowledge immeasurably surpassing those that can be possessed by any one else'.[13] More surprisingly, perhaps, Bosanquet makes a similar sort of claim. 'Your life', he writes, 'is a construction, and though general elements enter into it, a unique and creative construction. No one but yourself really knows your materials and your situations, and he could not know all of them that there is to be known unless he was absolutely one with yourself.'[14] Both these claims go beyond what is really necessary to provide force to the self-satisfaction argument for liberty. Even if someone else could judge better for one than oneself, there still might be good reasons for providing each with the liberty to decide for himself (e.g. the costs of intervention by others might be high; see §B.4). However, if people were generally bad judges as to what path their development lies along, this argument for liberty would have very little, if any, force.

Mill's and Bosanquet's claims are, however, different in an important sense. Whereas Mill's position is that we each know our own unique natures best, Bosanquet tells us that each knows best his own 'unique and creative construction'. As I indicated in the first chapter (§D.1), Bosanquet's notion of uniqueness seems to provide a weaker defence of liberty than Mill's. According to a liberal such as Karl Popper, for example, the great peril to our liberal civilisation is the attempt to radically and comprehensively remould man and society so as to conform to some aesthetic or perfectionist ideal (see §I.E). In opposition to this totalitarian attitude, Popper demands 'that every man should be given, if he wishes, the right to model his life himself'.[15] Now it is not clear that the 'creative construction' argument can support Popper's claim for individual liberty in the face of such totalitarian ambitions: although it asserts that each knows his own personality best, it does not seem to provide an argument against manufacturing personalities of a certain type. The proposal, for instance, to create a new 'socialist type personality'[16] need not rely on the claim that the makers of the 'new man' know the personality structures of present men as well as, or better than, they (i.e. present men) do themselves. Indeed, the would-be creators may acknowledge that present men are very good judges of the needs and tendencies of their present personalities. They could, then, accept all Bosanquet's claims about 'unique and creative constructions' and yet find no reasons to abandon their project. It would be far more difficult for them to accept Mill's position. According to Mill, we each possess different natures that require outlets and will thus find satisfaction in different endeavours. Any attempt to remake men according to certain ideal models runs the grave risk of doing violence to these unique natures and, consequently, ushering in pathologies. 'Whoever thinks that individuality of desires and impulses should not be encouraged to unfold itself, must maintain that society has no need of strong natures . . . and that a high general average of energy is not desirable.'[17]

Thus, while the 'creative construction' notion of personality differences provides some basis for defending liberty, it seems to be a weaker one than the Millian unique natures position. However, as I argued in the first chapter (§§I.B and I.D.1), it is not Bosanquet's only theory of individual differentiation. He certainly acknowledges a diversity of personal natures. Even in the passage quoted above, in which he emphasises the 'creative construction' notion, he refers to 'your materials' out of which you fashion a personality; in another place he tells us that our course of action ought to depend on our 'own particular powers'.[18] On balance, it seems certain that Bosanquet combines both theories of individual differentiation, understanding individual capacities and powers as elements to be taken up into the system of values, interests, etc. that constitutes the 'unique and creative construction' that is one's personality.

This argument (i.e. that liberty is necessary if we are to satisfy our natures) has provided the basis of a notion of positive liberty. In his lecture 'On the Different Senses of "Freedom" ' Green tells us that the basic, non-metaphorical conception of freedom always concerns 'some exemption from compulsion by others'. Now whatever the popular impression might be, it simply is not the case that Green belittled the importance of such liberty. The claim for negative liberty was, he thought, an expression of the 'self-seeking principle' in man according to which we assert ourselves against others and demand the right to act according to choice or preference.[19] To deny men negative liberty is thus to block their quest for self-satisfaction. However – and this is the move to a positive conception of liberty – Green argues that self-satisfaction is also blocked when the object in which it is sought 'is such as to prevent that self-satisfaction being found'. If because of unruly passions or transitory desires we act in ways inconsistent with self-satisfaction, we remain oppressed, albeit now by parts of our own nature. Indeed, as we saw in §IV.B.3, Green argues that thwarting the quest to self-realisation will produce 'feelings of oppression'. And, he tells us, it is the presence of such feelings that 'will always give meaning to the representation of the effort after any kind of self-improvement as a demand for "freedom" '.[20]

As Weinstein has said of Green, 'the gist of his doctrine is perfectly at home with the language of negative liberty'. Instead of saying that one is more free the more one's moral qualities and other capacities and talents are developed, we can say (i) that one is morally better, or more praiseworthy, the more one has developed one's nature and (ii) that one's negative liberty is more valuable the more one uses it to achieve self-development.[21] And we can add: (iii) that if the development of one's capacities is blocked, either by external restraints or by one's own failures, feelings of oppression will tend to arise. Now it is not at all clear that Mill would disagree with most of this. To be sure, he would object to calling the developed person *morally* better, but that is because he has a complicated theory connecting morality and the liability to sanctions,[22] and, as we will see in §B.4, he has definite reasons for not wanting those who have not properly developed to be liable to sanctions. No doubt, though, he would agree that the developed individual is better or more praiseworthy in some non-moral sense. Moreover, given that he also argues for liberty as a means to achieve self-development, it seems safe to conclude that he too would think liberty employed to promote development is more valuable than that used to promote 'pig pleasures'.

The most interesting point of comparision is whether Mill shares Green's conviction that one's own failures can give rise to some sort of pathological feelings (I have already argued at length that he thinks external restraints do; see §IV.B.3). Admittedly, this type of personal failure, as opposed to external restraints, is not Mill's main concern. Furthermore, because Mill, unlike Green, Bosanquet, Hobhouse and Dewey, does not stress the importance of a systematised personality, we do not find in his writings the condemnation of isolated desires that block a fuller self-realisation (§§I.D., V.B.3). Granted all this, though, it is certain that Mill did think that character flaws could thwart self-development. In *Utilitarianism*, for example, he acknowledges that because of 'infirmity of character' men sometimes prefer bodily to mental pleasures, i.e. act so as not to develop their higher nature.[23] And while Mill does not say they suffer from feelings of oppression, indeed he acknowledges that they might be content,[24] he does argue at length that they lose out on a great deal of happiness and suggests they will have a weakened sense of dignity. Thus, while we certainly would not want to say that Mill and Green are in agreement on all things, it does seem that the extent and nature of their differences cannot be captured by such broad categories as negative/positive or external/internal (restraints). The points of controversy are much finer than that; to a great extent, they centre on fairly detailed differences in their theories of human nature.

## B.2. Choice and Development

The self-satisfaction/self-discovery argument for liberty is important in modern liberal theory. It is also very problematic. As I argued, it seems to require some sort of assumption that each person is likely to be a good judge of the path along which his development lies. If individuals generally judge such things very badly, the argument is undermined.

And although we saw that modern liberals such as Mill and Bosanquet do indeed make an 'each-generally-knows-best' assumption, it is also manifest that they think that, as a matter of fact, people often choose badly. We might misjudge our own powers, cultivate too wide or too narrow an individuality, or prefer some activites that do not do much to spur development. Thus, despite the attractiveness of the self-discovery/self-satisfaction argument, it seems an inadequate foundation for a wide-ranging endorsement of freedom of choice. The problem for the modern liberal is to somehow endorse free choice even when the agent chooses badly.

The solution is to change the focus from what is chosen to the developmental properties of the act of choosing itself. In *Liberty* Mill confronts the suggestion that others may be able to choose well for you and, indeed, guide you along 'some good path'. But if they do so, he responds, you could never develop your distinctly human capacities. 'The human faculties of perception, judgement, discriminative feeling, mental activity, and even moral preference, are exercised only in making a choice.'[25] And, Mill adds, '[h]e who chooses a plan for himself' not only encourages these faculties but cultivates 'firmness and self-control'. Hobhouse and Dewey also put a great deal of weight on these aspects of choice. In arguing that 'liberty is essential to the development of personality', Hobhouse maintains that since personality requires the ability to pursue purposes and projects 'as against the rule of impulse on the one side or external compulsion on the other, it follows that liberty of choice is the condition of its development. The central condition of such development is self-guidance.'[26] One is tempted to say that whereas Hobhouse emphasises the need for choice in developing self-control, Dewey takes a larger view, stressing as does Mill the importance of free choice in all intellectual development. In making choices one evaluates outcomes, examines problems, considers criteria and goals: in short, one learns to think. 'Freedom means essentially that part played by thinking — which is personal — in learning: it means intellectual initiative, independence in observation, judicious intervention, foresight of consequences, and ingenuity of adaptation to them.'[27]

In addition to these straightforwardly developmental claims, 'choosing for oneself' and 'thinking for oneself' relate easily to notions of self-determination and self-mastery. One of the reasons Rawls offers as to why executing a plan of life promotes self-respect (§IV.B.3) is that it arouses in the planner a 'sense of mastery'.[28] In pursuing a plan of life *of one's own devising* one gains a sense of self-mastery and competence. This implies, then, that one may well gain more from executing a plan that one has constructed than from one devised by others that in some objective sense better fitted one's capacities but which, of course, would not induce a sense of mastery. Nevertheless, while the link between self-mastery and self-respect provides a defence of free choice even when it produces sub-optimal results (plans), it does not constitute a defence of very bad choices. Presumably, a really bad plan would be likely to fail, and, consequently, no sense of self-mastery would be elicited.

We might note here that unlike the argument from self-satisfaction, these arguments connecting choice and development (or self-respect) do not necessarily depend upon any claim that individual natures are unique or even diverse. Mill's 'human faculties' of judgement, observation, etc. are those shared by all normal human beings. In fact most of the faculties Mill and Dewey refer to are distinctly intellectual; and, as I argued in §I.C.3, the modern liberal theory of man asserts intellectual development to be a common element of all individual growth. Much the same applies to Hobhouse's 'rational determination' (self-control) and Rawls's self-mastery: at least in principle, they are traits that might characterise all humans and, hence, do not presuppose any theory of differentiation of individual natures. So, although in a sense they concern a sort of individuality since they link development to individual choice, they are not arguments based on individuality in the sense we examined in the first chapter. That is, they focus on the development of the common faculties and traits of men, not on their diverse individualised endowments.

## B.3. Self-expression

Mill directly proceeds from the thesis that we can only develop if we think for ourself — i.e. if 'our understanding is our own' — to the argument 'that our desires and impulses should be our own likewise'.[29] But while this argument also endorses choice even when the decision is a bad one, it is different from what we have been considering since it calls for choice and liberty not so much as a means to develop faculties but as a necessity for self-expression. Mill is concerned in what follows with contrasting two opposing personality types: a person with character 'whose desires and impulses are his own — are the expression of his own nature, as it has been developed and modified by his own culture' and '[o]ne whose desires and impulses are not his own, [who] has no character, no more than a steam-engine has a character.'[30] The second sort of 'character', Mill argues, is the consequence of a social order that induces conformity, a conformity which in modern times is not usually achieved by legal coercion but by a more subtle, but an all-the-more-pervasive and effective, informal social coercion that punishes the non-conformist with ostracism, exclusion from employment and a host of other 'sanctions'. Those who submit to these sanctions act not according to their nature but in accordance with the dictates of custom 'until by dint of not following their own nature, they have no nature to follow'.[31] Free action – action not performed under the threat of coercion – is thus necessary if our desires, opinions and feelings are to be of 'home growth' or properly our 'own'.

Interestingly, this is precisely Bosanquet's line of argument in his defence of positive liberty. Bosanquet acknowledges that '[i]n the straightforward sense of the word . . . I am free when I am not made the instrument of another person's will through physical violence or the threat of it'. At bottom, he suggests, the claim to be free in this sense is grounded on the claim to 'be oneself' (see §I.A): when our actions are determined by the threat of force they are not an expression of our 'self' and we cannot be said to be self-determined.[32] Thus far Bosanquet's argument is much the same as Mill's and is certainly a defence of negative liberty. He tries to move beyond the Millian position, however, by maintaining that it is not only coercion or threats of coercion by others that can prevent one from being oneself. The key here is what is meant by 'oneself' or, more specifically, a 'self'. In a way that is entirely consistent with his account of the organisation of individuality (§§I.D, II.D.2), Bosanquet asserts that a self is not an unorganised collection of volitions, desires or impulses but a system or coherent whole. To be oneself, then, is to act on desires, interests, etc. that cohere with this system. Conversely, to act on a random desire – to give into a temptation to act in a way inconsistent with the organised self – is thus not to be oneself. 'Liberty, then, throughout, is the being ourselves, and the fullest condition of liberty is that in which we are ourselves most completely.'[33]

Certainly by the end of the argument Bosanquet is using 'liberty' in a very different way from that in which Mill (generally) used it. Liberty is no longer a prerequisite for being oneself: it *is* being oneself. Again, however, our concern is not with the use of 'liberty' but with the underlying substantive theory. On the face of it, Mill and Bosanquet agree on a good deal. Both argue that negative liberty is necessary to being oneself and, as we saw in Chapter I, both believe that being oneself involves a personality that organises capacities into a coherent plan of life. But two important differences separate them. For one, since Bosanquet identifies being oneself with a harmonious personality, being oneself is in a sense something that always lies in the future, as very few of us are likely to sustain a perfectly coherent personality. In this sense, then, Bosanquet's argument is as much a self-creation as a self-expression argument. More importantly, because Bosanquet identifies being oneself with acting in accordance with a systematised personality, he rejects the notion that one can be oneself when acting on an isolated desire. Mill would certainly disagree: in his view any manifestations of one's nature, even of isolated desires, are self-expressive.

Thus, as with Green (§B.1), the status of isolated desires (volitions, capacities, etc.) is a major divide between Mill and an idealist like Bosanquet. As C.L. Ten has emphasised, as opposed to Mill, when an idealist philosopher talks of being oneself he does not mean 'the person we meet every day': 'A man's true self is taken to be a rational self.'[34] But we need to be very careful in drawing this sort of contrast. It is certainly true that an idealist such as Bosanquet did think the rational self was somehow more real than the everyday self with its conflicts and tensions, a point on which Hobhouse (quite rightly) took Bosanquet to task.[35] However, we need to always keep in mind that 'rational' here means systematic or harmonious (§I.D.2). So when Bosanquet insists that our real self is our rational self, he is again asserting that we are really ourselves when we act according to the implications of our entire organised personality rather than on volitions or desires inconsistent with it. This is an important point, for many commentators, apparently including Ten,[36] seem to slide from the proposition that 'to the idealist, the real self is the rational self, not the everyday self' to the assertion that 'to the idealist, the rational self can be opposed to all one's actual aims, desires, etc.' But this second proposition is radically at odds with the idealists' conception of a rational self; just because the rational self is a perfectly systematised everyday self, it cannot be opposed *in toto* to the everyday self. To be sure, Bosanquet was apt to stress that the gap could be wide, but he never denies that the rational is grounded on the everyday self.[37]

Mill would certainly disagree with a great deal of this (but see §B.5 below). In particular, he would not discount the present self in a way that Bosanquet often seems willing to. Nevertheless, we ought not to forget that the ideal of a coherent personality is by no means alien to Mill's outlook (§I.D). To a far greater extent than we are perhaps apt to suppose, the sort of differences separating Mill and Bosanquet concern metaphysical questions as to the proper relations among notions such as 'present', 'real' and 'ideal' rather than psychological theories.

## B.4.  Coercive Restraints

Thus far we have seen that modern liberals think that liberty is necessary to express our nature, discover it, satisfy it and, through choice,
develop it. Although it is perhaps to run the risk of being confused with
Greenian talk of positive liberty, it is tempting to call these the positive
arguments for liberty in as much as they provide positive reasons why
liberty is a good thing. But arguments for liberty are often really arguments against coercion. This is particularly true of modern liberals who,
it sometimes seems, are more intent on pointing out the banes of
coercion than the boons of liberty. Mill, it will be recalled, is especially
emphatic about the costs of any coercive interference with the actions
of another. Preventing anyone from doing as he is inclined by threatening him with some evil 'is not only always irksome, but always tends,
*pro tanto*, to starve the development of some portion of the bodily
or mental faculties' and, furthermore, partakes of the 'degradation
of slavery' if the individual's conscience does not freely accept the
interference.[38] And, as we saw in the previous chapter, the condition
of the slave is not an attractive one. Those denied freedom and independence either become lethargic or power-hungry; in either case, they
lose an interest in developing their own character.

Prima facie, it would seem that this libertarian element in Millian
liberalism is rejected by later modern liberals. Hobhouse and Dewey,
for example, make much of the importance of restraints for any system
of equal liberty. Only 'unsocial freedom', said Hobhouse, is freedom to
do what one wills regardless of others; a 'social freedom', in contrast,
depends upon a system of rules which restrains everyone in some respects so that all can enjoy liberty in other ways.[39] Dewey agrees:
*'The system of liberties that exists at any time is always the system of
restraints or controls that exists at that time.'*[40] Thus in apparent
contradistinction to Mill, these later liberals refuse to oppose liberty
and restraint since a system of liberties rests on control or restraint.
'The true opposition', Hobhouse insists, 'is between the control that
cramps the personal life and the spiritual order, and the control that
is aimed at securing the external and material conditions of their free
and unimpeded development.'[41]

Although this would seem to be a direct confrontation and opposition between Mill and the later liberals, they are really arguing about
different things. As indicated by the above quotations, Hobhouse and
Dewey are concerned with endorsing a *system of equal protected liberties*. When we turn to consider specific civil liberties in §C, we will
see that Mill certainly would never deny that the protection of one

person's freedom of conscience, for instance, necessarily involves restraints on others. Nevertheless, he would still insist that in so far as anyone is restrained against his will (we have seen that a freely accepted restraint is very different, §IV.C.1), his development is to some extent hindered. So at this point the issue is not whether a system of protected liberties involves restraints, but rather whether interfering with someone's doing as one wishes is to some extent always damaging to growth. Put in this way, it is certain that most later liberals do not depart from the Millian general libertarian position. Thus, for example, although Dewey acknowledges, as does Mill, that some characters might be challenged and spurred on by restraints they consider oppressive, he also believes that to the extent that anyone yields to restrictions that are seen as 'mere compulsion' or 'arbitrary force' − i.e. that one does not acknowledge to be just or right − there 'develops a slavish weakness.'[42] Even Bosanquet, who is generally regarded as being anything but a libertarian, is explicit that 'violence' is a 'dangerous drug' that runs the risk of producing 'degeneration and senility' by overriding 'intelligent volition'. This is not to say that for Bosanquet, any more than for Mill, coercion is never justified, but only that it always does some harm by 'stimulating lower motives'.[43]

Thus, far from abandoning the Millian libertarian position, the claim that coercion is a dangerous drug is central to nearly all later modern liberal defences of liberty. The wide agreement among modern liberals as to the destructive consequences of coercion is not fortuitous; as Hobhouse made very clear, it relates to the energy/impulse model of personality and the ideal of a harmonious development. Coercion, as Hobhouse sees it, is an attempt to control the 'rebellious individual' by simply repressing him. 'He is coerced but not convinced, his personality is thwarted, and no modified line of development is found to pursue.'[44] And we have already seen in Chapter IV how such repression is inconsistent with development. Either, as Mill was apt to emphasise, it entirely crushes and roots out energy and produces servility (hence the repeated references to the slave), or the energy persists and will either reappear in pathological forms or will push to the surface when the 'superincumbent pressure' is removed. 'Sooner or later', as Bosanquet said, 'the thinking creature will rebel against mere force.'[45] Moreover, as Hobhouse and Bosanquet stressed, to control behaviour in this way is to bypass the individual's reason (*qua* capacity to harmonise and adjust the elements of one's personality), thus to some extent ignoring the very capacity upon which all harmonious growth depends. 'The resort to coercion blocks the more secure road to harmony through the sense of uncompelled allegiance. At the same time it pauperizes the reason itself by requiring it to surrender its work to force.'[46]

Most of this does not apply to Rawls. As I argued in the previous chapter (§C.4), Rawls does not appear to conceive of each capacity as demanding some sort of satisfaction — which, if denied, leads to pathological expression — but instead he seems to view capacities as mere opportunities or possibilities for development. Because of this, it does not seem that Rawls can (or does) think of every coercive interference as a repression of some aspect of a person's personality with all the consequences that implies. Consequently, Rawls cannot say that every coercive interference to some extent hinders development and is *ipso facto* an evil. In this sense his theory of man seems to have weaker libertarian implications than that of other modern liberals. But of course he can argue against coercion in other ways. Most obviously, should one be so coerced that one could not execute a plan of life of one's own devising, self-respect would be undermined and pathologies would arise. More interesting, perhaps, is that Rawls postulates a tendency to reciprocity as a 'deep psychological fact'. Indeed, this tendency forms one of the main foundations of community in Rawls's theory; 'the active sentiments of love and friendship, and even the sense of justice, arise from the manifest intention of other persons to act for our good' (and our tendency to reply in kind).[47] Now, given this, the application of coercive restraints (which are not perceived as just or right) would tend to thwart the rise of communal sentiments and, indeed, they would very likely lead to feelings of hostility. We are not the sort of creatures, Rawls indicates, who respond to force with love and friendship. Thus there seems some foundation for saying that interference with one's action which is seen as *merely* coercive tends to hinder the development of social sentiments and a sense of justice. Rawls, then, might very well agree with Hobhouse's conclusion that 'we have come to look for the effect of liberty in the firmer establishment of social solidarity, as the only foundation on which such solidarity can securely rest'.[48]

## B.5. Paternalism and Development

The strength and limits of these four arguments for liberty are nicely brought out in modern liberal treatments of paternalism. According to Gerald Dworkin's well-known account, paternalism is (roughly) 'the interference with a person's liberty of action justified by reasons referring exclusively to the welfare, good, happiness, needs, interests, or values of the person being coerced.' Jeffrie G. Murphy is even more succinct: 'Paternalism', he writes, 'is the coercing of people primarily for what is believed to be their own good.'[49] Leaving aside the issue of whether or not these are adequate definitions of paternalism,[50] they point to the sort of *coercive paternalism* with which I shall be concerned; more specifically, I want to focus primarily on paternalistic interferences with another's liberty that are justified on the grounds that they promote his development.

The argument from self-satisfaction attacks the presupposition of any paternalistic intervention: viz. that the interferer has a better understanding than the interferee of the latter's good. Mill explicitly used this as an anti-paternalist argument: even when a person is choosing to do something that is likely to lead to considerable harm to himself, Mill argues that he ought to only be *warned* of the danger since 'no one but the person himself can judge of the sufficiency of the motive which may prompt him to incur the risk'.[51] Still, even Mill admitted that the assumption that 'each knows best for himself' does not always hold: 'The uncultivated', he admitted, 'cannot be competent judges of cultivation. Those who most need to be made wiser and better, usually desire it least, and, if they desire it, would be incapable of finding the way to it by their own lights.'[52] The choice and development argument can help block paternalism in such cases: even if one is likely to misunderstand one's interests or what will serve them, the process of deliberation has important positive developmental consequences. The self-expression argument can also be of assistance here to the anti-paternalist, for it suggests that even if the paternalist knows your good better than you do yourself, imposed aims and desires will not be genuine 'home growths'. However, self-expression arguments are two-edged: if it can be argued that one's present actions are inconsistent with one's 'true' or 'real' self, it might be argued that paternalistic measures are required *in order* to achieve self-expression. The most unobjectionable form of this pro-paternalist argument is put forward by Mill in *Liberty* in his famous bad-bridge case:

> If either a public officer or any one else saw a person attempting to cross a bridge which had been ascertained to be unsafe, and there were no time to warn him of his danger, they might seize him and turn him back, without any real infringement of his liberty; for liberty consists in doing what one desires, and he does not desire to fall into the river.[53]

In the hands of Bosanquet, who identifies the real self or will with the systematised one and not the everyday one (§C.3), it would seem that the argument can justify a great deal more. The 'alien and partial will, the tendency to narrower tracks of indulgence' are not expressions of our real self; if they are not controlled but instead dominate, the true self is not expressed but 'feels itself under constraint and a slave'.[54] As Green put it, a person in such a condition 'may be considered in the condition of a bondsman who is carrying out the will of another, not his own'.[55]

On the face of it, then, it would seem that Berlin is justified in think-ing that such 'positive libertarians' are, knowingly or unknowingly, enemies of negative liberty: by conceptualising the 'self' in this way, the aim of self-expression becomes a ground for paternalistic 'inter-ference' which, it is claimed, is not really interfering with the freedom of the true self at all. Indeed, it is said that one is being 'forced to be free'.[56] Now this sort of argument is not without force; it points to an important way in which the idealist conception of the self lends itself to paternalistic projects. However, we cannot simply leave the matter there and conclude that Green and Bosanquet were inclined towards a wide range of paternalist measures. At least two other arguments indicate that paternalistic coercive interference to support the 'real will' over the 'actual will' will be difficult to justify. For one, we have already seen that Bosanquet proffers an 'each knows best for himself' assumption, one implication of which is that (in at least one way) the agent concerned has privileged access to just what his real (i.e. system-atic) self is. Secondly, and far more importantly, Bosanquet and Green can — and do — rely here on the argument against coercion, as did Mill, Dewey and Hobhouse. In this regard it is important to remember that they steadfastly maintained that a man cannot be coerced into being moral.[57] And their conception of moral excellence was a particularly wide one, involving rational self-control and general perfection of one's nature.[58] Their thesis, then, that coercion is inconsistent with moral excellence involves claims that it pauperises reason and self-control and encourages actions based on fear, narrow self-interest, etc. Conjoined with arguments for liberty, this leads Green and Bosanquet to an es-sentially anti-paternalist position. 'No one', Green said, 'can convey a good character to another. Everyone must make his character for himself.'[59]

It is often suggested, however, that Green's proposal for regulating the liquor trade comes close to violating 'his own guiding principle that the state could not enforce virtue'.[60] And indeed Green does advocate coercive measures to encourage development, endorsing laws that require people to 'limit, or even altogether give up, the not very precious liberty of buying and selling alcohol, in order that they may become more free to exercise the faculties and improve the talents which God gave them'.[61] However, if we pay close attention to Green's arguments, I think we can see that, at least as he depicts it, this sort of paternalism is consistent with his theory of development (including its doctrine relating to coercion). More importantly, an examination of this case reveals a general strategy for justifying some cases of paternalism within the constraints imposed by the modern liberal theory of man.

In so far as Green's case for restraining the liquor trade is paternalistic (and it seems fairly clear that this was *not* his main argument),[62] it is premised on the assumption that the perpetual drunkard suffers from impaired judgement. Drink not merely destroys one's health but attacks rational self-control. This is important, for most — if not all — modern liberal arguments for liberty assume that the agent has the capacity to make reasonable decisions and to rationally plan the development of his capacities. The self-satisfaction and choice and development arguments for liberty manifestly depend on this assumption.[63] But so does the argument against coercion: if a person is unable to make informed choices and construct even the most rudimentary plans, there is no ongoing rational organisation of personality for the coercive interference to stifle. Even though the coercion might still lead to some repression, the alternative to such imposed discipline is not self-guidance but aimlessness, which we have already seen is antithetical to the modern liberal understanding of development (§I.D.3). Moreover, Green appears to further undermine the argument against coercion by adding the proviso to his endorsement of restraining laws that no such prohibition should be enacted in 'advance of the social sentiment necessary to give real effect to it'.[64] Although the aim of this proviso can be understood in more than one way, it does have the consequence that Green's position conforms to Mill's dictum that, in order to minimise the repression of personality, a prohibitory regulation ought not to be enacted unless it can be made to 'recommend itself to the general conscience; unless persons of ordinary good intentions either believe already, or can be induced to believe, that the thing being prohibited is a thing which they ought not to wish to do.'[65]

My point, then, is that in his treatment of the drunkard, Green (and Hobhouse in a similar analysis) tries to undermine the arguments for liberty and against coercion by showing that their assumptions are not met in this case; i.e. that the drunkard cannot reap the developmental benefits of liberty, that the alternative to restraint is aimless-

ness and that since the powers of rational self-control are not being
used much anyway, it may well be that the good done by the imposed
discipline will outweigh any damage caused by imposing constraints.
This was essentially Hobhouse's view, who, in likening the drunkard's
condition to that of the 'feebleminded', argued that whether or not
the drunkard was a 'fit object of tutelage' turned in each case on
'whether such capacity of self-control as he retains would be impaired
or repaired by a period of tutelar restraint'.[66] Now whether we find this
a satisfying analysis of the alcoholic's condition, it is the sort of argument that needs to be advanced if paternalism is to be consistent with
the general modern liberal theory of man and the arguments for liberty.
Certainly it provides the most obvious way of justifying modern liberals'
endorsement of custodial care or enforced tutelage for the incompetent.[67] (Whether support will be given to the former or latter would
seem to depend on the possibility of educating the incompetent into
being self-developers.)[68] If this sort of reasoning seems problematic
or troublesome in the case of the alcoholic, it is not because it asserts
that incompetency undermines the case for liberty but for one or
both of two rather more specific reasons.

(i) Most obviously, the alcoholic is not totally incompetent. At
best, he would seem to suffer from a *partial impairment* of reason,
judgement, self-control, etc. If we do accept some such notion of
partial impairment,[69] it obviously becomes an important but terribly
difficult question as to just when the impairment becomes sufficiently
serious to undermine the developmental arguments for liberty. What is
certain is that in the eyes of liberals like Green and Hobhouse, by the
time we reach perpetual drunkards things have got very serious indeed.
Hobhouse's grouping together of 'the idiot, the imbecile, the feebleminded . . . the drunkard'[70] nicely brings home just what they thought
of the drunkard's condition. It is unlikely that this was Mill's view.
Mill explicitly allows for paternalistic coercive interference in some cases
of impaired judgement, i.e. when a person is 'delirious, or in some state
of excitement or absorption incompatible with the *full use* of his
reflecting faculty' and is in danger of harming himself.[71] But Mill never
suggests that the drunkard, though certainly harming himself, suffers
from such impairment of reflective capacity. Indeed (although this is
speculative), one would think that the alcoholic is just the sort of person Mill has in mind when he reminds us that just because we cannot
coercively interfere, it does not follow that a 'benevolent' concern with
others' well-being is out of place. Indeed, Mill stresses that we owe it to
each other 'to help distinguish the better from the worse, and [give]

encouragement to choose the former and avoid the latter ... [C]onsiderations to aid his judgement, exhortations to strengthen his will, may be offered to him, even obtruded on him, by others; but he himself is the final judge.'[72] Mill might well have thought drunkenness was a prime example of choosing the worse over the better that the rational persuasion of friends might reverse.[73] In contrast, Green and Hobhouse certainly thought the drunkard to be so crippled as to be beyond such friendly assistance.

(ii) The other significant difference between Mill, on the one hand, and Hobhouse and Green, on the other, is that whereas Mill permits paternalism only in order to prevent the person from harming himself (what has been called 'negative' paternalism), Green and Hobhouse seem to advocate a 'positive' paternalism aimed at actually promoting development.[74] Considering all that modern liberals say about the dire consequences of coercion on development, it would certainly seem that Mill's position is much easier to justify within the framework of the modern liberal theory of man than any positive interference.

However, it is not really accurate to say that idealists like Green actually sought to induce particular lines of development. Green, in fact, was adamant in maintaining that law could not actually induce growth and '[f]or this reason the effectual action of the state, i.e. the community acting through law, for the promotion of habits of true citizenship, seem necessarily to be confined to the removal of obstacles'.[75] Now, according to Green (and the same holds true for Bosanquet and Hobhouse), strong isolated desires obstruct development by hindering the rational organisation of personality into a coherent system. Hence, as these liberals saw it, to coercively repress a strong isolated impulse is not the same as actively promoting a particular line of development. By removing the obstacle, natural development — along whatever lines one's individuality dictates — is *allowed* to proceed. To be sure, such coercive interference is inferior to a creative solution that sublimates the underlying impulse into a coherent structure, but, in serious cases, it may be necessary (§ IV.C.3).

Although one's first reaction to this argument may well be that it seeks to justify coercing a person to develop in a certain way under the guise of 'removing obstacles', on reflection it does not seem at all distorting to put the case in terms of removing obstacles. For as Green and Hobhouse saw the alcoholic, he was in many ways similar to an obsessive neurotic, i.e. one who feels under the sway of 'impulses which seem alien to him, and he is impelled to perform actions which not only afford him no pleasure but from which he is powerless to desist.'[76]

Now such feelings of compulsion clearly interfere with rational choice and the achievement of autonomy. Those in the grips of obsessions have difficulty adjusting their actions to their settled aims and the very intrusiveness of their obsessions impedes the normal conducting of everyday life.[77] Indeed, as Freud saw it, 'All these things combine to bring about an ever-increasing indecisiveness, loss of energy, and curtailment of freedom.'[78] Viewed this way, it surely makes sense to see the obsession as an obstacle to a healthy, developed personality. And, if so, to 'free' someone from the grip of the obsession is not so much to induce development as to remove a barrier and thus allow it to proceed. I am certainly not arguing here that the state ought to be allowed to coercively interfere with the lives of obsessional neurotics. But it does seem that those who charge that Green's position on drink contradicts his principle that development cannot be induced by coercive measures are far too ready to dismiss the distinction between removing an impediment to the rational organisation of personality and attempting to coercively induce a particular sort of development.

## C. Civil Liberties

The arguments that we have been examining provide reasons why, from the standpoint of development, liberty is good and coercion is bad. However, even a libertarian like Hayek, while insisting that coercion is evil and liberty good, acknowledges that coercion 'cannot be altogether avoided because the only way to prevent it is by the threat of coercion'.[79] Indeed a basic difference between the most libertarian liberal and the libertarian anarchist is that the liberal believes that coercion must be used, in fact institutionalised, despite its evil characteristics.[80] The liberal may well accept that preventing a person from acting in accord with his own intentions always leads to some badness, but he still insists that it may be — indeed it often will be — justified by some overriding consideration such as the protection of another's liberty. It is this sort of reasoning that leads Hobhouse and Dewey (§C.4) to maintain that in practice a devotion to liberty involves constraints: to protect some sorts of liberty requires restraining others from interfering. Indeed, to a liberal like Dewey it is wrong to understand liberalism as committed to any general liberty to do as one likes — even if constrained by some proviso that such liberty be limited by a like liberty for others. What is essential to liberalism, he holds, is a *system of liberties* that allows one to do specific things and restrains

others from interfering. Consequently, Dewey looks to the American
Bill of Rights as a genuine expression of liberal ideals because it guaran-
tees essential liberties.[81] Rawls's position is similar. Although in *A
Theory of Justice* he sometimes seems attracted to a general right to
equal liberty, he has subsequently confirmed H.L.A. Hart's interpretation according to which his equal liberty principle is to be understood
as endorsing a list of basic liberties.[82] And, as Bernard Schwartz has
noted, except for the political rights to vote and hold office, all Rawls's
basic rights are safeguarded by the Bill of Rights.[83] Hobhouse too insists that one's 'liberty' is really a group of specific liberties protected
by rights.[84] Indeed, the general emphasis in idealist writings on the
importance of a system of rights as necessary for the development of
personality indicates that they too are mainly concerned with a system
of specific liberties: 'Our liberty, or to use a good old expression, our
liberties, may be identified with such a system considered as the condition and guarantee of our becoming the best we have it in us to be,
that is, of becoming ourselves.'[85] Of all our modern liberals only Mill
seems to concentrate on a general right to liberty – viz. a right to liberty, the exercise of which does not cause harm to others – but, as we
shall see, he too often focuses on arguments for specific liberties.[86]

Not too surprisingly, modern liberals are by no means unanimous
as to just what liberties are essential. Hobhouse provides an extensive
list in his chapter on 'The Elements of Liberalism', mentioning not only
'civil' and 'personal' liberty but, among others, 'social liberty' (involving liberty of occupation), 'domestic liberty' (equal liberty between
wives and husbands) and 'national' and even 'international' liberty.[87]
Most lists are certainly not this extensive. However, it does seem fairly
certain that our modern liberals all endorse the traditional liberal civil
liberties (e.g. as enunciated in the American Bill of Rights) as an essential minimum. They are obviously encompassed in Hobhouse's analysis
and we have seen that Dewey, and presumably Rawls, has them in mind.
Mill is, perhaps, not as straightforward, but throughout the course of
*Liberty* we find him endorsing freedom of thought, of speech and the
press, of association and religion, and it seems pretty clear that he
assumes those liberties of persons implied by the rule of law.[88] Once
again, the real difficulty is with our two idealists. Green was especially
insistent that the task of the moral philosopher does not include
prescribing particular duties or, it would seem, rights.[89] He does tell us,
though, that certain fundamental rights derive from human nature
itself, including the rights to a free life, to property and certain family
rights. And in his less philosophical writings he specifically points to

the importance of freedom of conscience.[90] Bosanquet is hardly any more explicit, supporting 'civil and moral liberty' and, in an oblique way indeed, indicating as endorsement of freedom of thought, speech and religion.[91] Although there is certainly room for disagreement here, I see no reason to dispute the oft-voiced conclusion — first suggested by Green himself — that Green's (and I would add Bosanquet's) commitment to the traditional liberal civil liberties probably differs little from Mill's.[92]

But not only do our modern liberals seem to concur in endorsing these traditional liberal liberties, but it also appears that most agree with Rawls that not all these liberties are 'on par'. For Rawls, 'The question of equal liberty of conscience is settled. It is one of the fixed points of our considered judgments . . . The reasoning in this case can be generalized to apply to other freedoms, although not always with the same force.'[93] Hobhouse's position is not very different, identifying 'liberty of thought' as a core liberty while Dewey and Tufts write that '[l]iberty to think, inquire, discuss, is central to the whole group of rights secured in theory to individuals in democratic social organization.'[94] Even Bosanquet, who is so often charged with sacrificing the person to the social good, seems to give intellectual freedom pride of place. He thus singles out the 'systematising' of the 'intellectual being' as an endeavour that need not be justified in terms of any social ideal. (Indeed, he asserts that an awakened mind is 'the birthright of a civilized human being.')[95] None of this should be too surprising: the intellect, we have seen, is the heart of all individualised development in modern liberal theory (§I.C.3). Consequently, when Dewey sought to summarise what he understood as the enduring liberal faith, his first tenet was the supreme importance of the intellect as a directing force in life and the second was a devotion to 'freedom of thought and expression as a condition needed to realize this power of direction by thought'.[96]

The strategy, then, is to argue from (i) the central importance of intellect to (ii) freedom of conscience and, as Rawls puts it, 'generalize' the case for (ii) to support (iii), various liberties of action. Assuming that the liberal case for moving from (i) to (ii) is fairly straightforward,[97] it is worthwhile focusing for a moment on the move from (ii) to (iii). Rawls actually seems to have two ways of extending the argument for freedom of conscience to endorse other liberties. The straightforward generalisation argument contends that the reason we require freedom of conscience (i.e. that we form different conceptions of the good, embrace different beliefs, have different interests, etc.) also leads us to value liberties of action (e.g. freedom of association) that are essential to pursuing our plans, interests, beliefs, etc. However, Rawls also 'extends' the argument for liberty of conscience by arguing that certain liberties of action are intrinsically related to it, indeed are included within it. As he sees it, 'liberty of conscience' entails not just freedom to think for oneself, but a liberty of each 'to pursue their moral, philosophical, or religious interests without legal restrictions requiring them to engage or not to engage in any particular form of religious or other practice, and . . . a legal duty [of others] not to interfere'.[98] Since this apparently is not to be viewed as a generalisation of the case for freedom of conscience but as part and parcel of it, the idea here would seem to be that beliefs, convictions, interests — thought itself — generally have practical implications and, consequently, to protect the liberty to form ideas, beliefs, etc. but not to follow them would be to trivialise the liberty. The natural *telos* of thought is action, and so to protect and encourage the former we must protect the liberty to pursue the practical implications of thought. As Hobhouse pointed out, 'liberty of thought is of very little avail without liberty to exchange thoughts — since thought is mainly a social product; and so with liberty of thought goes liberty of speech and liberty of writing, printing, and peaceable discussion'.[99]

Hobhouse's reference to the 'social' nature of thought points to yet another way of extending the case for freedom of thought. Rather than arguing that action is necessary to give effect to thought, it can be maintained (reasonably enough) that action is necessary for the development of thought. Certainly this was Dewey's main theme, insisting as he did that 'there can be no greater fallacy' than divorcing thought and social intercourse. Dewey's constant concern with freedom of communication was a consequence of this insistence, as he held that to repress freedom of speech or writing denies the mind the 'nutriment and sustenance' of varied points of view, thereby engendering mental apathy (§II.C.1).[100] He also thus argues from freedom of intellect to other liberties:

> While the idea is not always, not often enough, expressed in words, the basic freedom is that of *mind* and whatever degree of freedom of action and experience is necessary to produce freedom of intelligence. The modes of freedom guaranteed in the Bill of Rights are all of this nature: Freedom of belief and conscience, of expression of opinion, of assembly for discussion and conference, of the press as an organ of communication. They are guaranteed because without them individuals are not free to develop and society is deprived of what they might contribute.[101]

Although, as always, Dewey focuses here on communication, his argument would seem to extend further. On Dewey's general pragmatic-experimentalist view of knowledge, great stress is laid upon the intimate relation between practical activity — especially observation and experiment — and intellect. And in his educational theory this leads him to insist that freedom of mind cannot be separated from freedom of action.[102] (One is tempted to say that Mill's advocacy of 'experiments of living' is an appropriate extension of Dewey's thesis, being motivated by Dewey-like fears as to the intellectual decay that is brought about by unreflective conformity.) In fact Dewey does seem willing to extend his thesis about the action requirements of intellectual vigour to at least one sort of activity that goes well beyond communication: i.e. occupations. 'A calling', he says, 'is . . . of necessity an organizing principle for information and ideas; for knowledge and intellectual growth.'[103] This, of course, is a special application of the focusing and organising function of vocations in individual development that I considered in Chapter I (§D.3). However, although Dewey's line of argument here implies that intellectual growth requires that one *have* an occupation, it does not seem to entail *a liberty to choose* an occupation. At least to the extent that an occupation is required simply to organise knowledge and information, it would seem that an occupation to which one was assigned might do as well as an occupation chosen by oneself. But the argument from unique natures, combined with this thesis about the more general organising role of careers, indicates that not only a vocation, but a congenial one, is required. 'Nothing', said Dewey drawing on both arguments, 'is more tragic than failure to discover one's true business in life, or to find that one has drifted or been forced by circumstance into an uncongenial calling.'[104] And so, given our unique natures, freedom of occupation is essential (§B.1). Happily, my interpretation of modern liberal theory finds some confirmation here, for not only Dewey but also Mill, Rawls and Hobhouse single out the liberty to choose one's job in life as particularly important, giving freedom of occupation a position co-equal (or nearly) with most of the traditional civil liberties.[105] Characteristically, Green is virtually silent about this particular liberty. Somewhat more troublesome for my thesis, though, is Bosanquet's attitude: 'Provision for adapting vocation to capacity is of course desirable', he acknowledges, 'but in the end, whatever variety may be attainable, capacity must after all in a great degree adapt itself to the vocation.' But Bosanquet immediately proceeds to point out that even where one may not have had a great deal of choice in selecting a vocation, a person nevertheless is able to adapt the 'spirit and temper' of the work to one's character. And, of course, Bosanquet did endorse the principle of careers open to talent.[106] Still, it must be acknowledged that the idea of modifying capacities to suit vocations (rather than the other way around) has the potential to undermine not only the arguments for freedom of occupation, but for many of the traditional civil liberties. As with Dewey's doctrine that the modes of expressing capacities is essentially learned (§IV.A.3), it runs the risk of allowing that nearly any sort of life can suit our nature.[107]

In the main, though, the modern liberal account of civil liberties and freedom of occupation attests to the fundamental place of development, and in particular intellectual development, in the modern liberal scheme of things. To the modern liberal, our liberties are instruments of development, at the heart of which is intellectual growth. Now it is important to realise that this is by no means the only way in which the liberal tradition has conceived of, or argued for, liberty. For example, although Dewey and Rawls seem to maintain that all the liberties protected by the Bill of Rights are either implications or generalisations of the case for freedom of conscience, the American Constitution originally guaranteed freedom of assembly as a distinctively political right related to the right to 'petition the Government for a redress of grievances' (although in the twentieth century the American courts seemed to have moved along Dewey's path of assimilating it into free speech).[108] Indeed, even the freedoms of speech and of the press have been supported as much for their political as for their intellectual benefits.[109] More generally, we need to remind ourselves that liberals have not always conceived of liberties as a means of development. Writing during the French Revolution, Jean-Joseph Mounier extolled the virtues of English liberalism to his countrymen, pointing out that '[t]he English use the words "security", "property" when they wish to define civil or personal liberty. This definition is in fact entirely correct: all the advantages of liberty are expressed in these two words.'[110]

## D. Equal Liberty

### D.1. *Equal Liberty and Proportionate Justice*

Throughout the analysis of civil liberty I have assumed an equality of liberty. But there are good reasons for questioning the desirability of such an equal distribution. If, as do the modern liberals, we argue for liberty on the basis of its development-promoting traits, a good case

can be made out that the distribution of liberty ought to conform to
the distribution of talents, capacities, etc. And since modern liberals
seem generally to believe that 'individuals vary very greatly in their
actual development and even their capacity of development',[111] it
would seem that liberty ought to be unequally distributed. Alan Gewirth
puts this 'Principle of Proportionality' more formally:

> When some quality Q justifies having certain rights R, and the pos-
> session of Q varies in the respect that is relevant to Q's justifying
> the having of R, the degree to which R is had is proportional to or
> varies with the degree to which Q is had.[112]

As Gewirth notes, some such notion seems intrinsic to the Aristotelian
conception of distributive justice; 'the just', says Aristotle, 'is a species
of the proportionate'.[113] If justice does indeed require that equals be
treated equally and unequals unequally, it would seem that 'men being
of unequal capacity for development, their claims will differ.'[114]

In so far as the liberal accepts both the inequality of natural capacities and some notion of proportionate justice, the most typical response
to this case for inequality has been to search for some way in which
men really are equal or alike. According to Amy Gutmann, for example,
classical liberal equality turned on one of two 'equality assumptions';
men were held to have either 'equal passions' or 'equal rationality',
and it was on these sorts of equalities that equal political status was
based.[115] Of our modern liberals, Bosanquet provides a clear instance
of this sort of argument. That '[a]ll men are equal' and so 'by nature',
he tells us, does not mean that all are equally good or equally capable,
but 'that all rational beings' are ' "equal" in having within them a
principle of self-government'.[116]

But this does not really seem to meet the challenge of the 'proportional justice' argument: when pushed, liberals are apt to admit that
men are not strictly equal in their possession of rationality (or passions),
but only roughly equal. But if, as seems likely, the degree of rationality
possessed by men does indeed vary to some extent, then it seems that
proportionate justice – at least in principle – demands an inequality of
rights. More generally, it would seem that any attempt to base equal
rights on the possession of some trait $Q$ is apt to flounder on the existence of some inequality in the distribution of $Q$ among men. Faced
with this sort of problem, some liberals have proffered a more sophisticated argument. According to Gewirth, for example, it is possible to
base a case for equal rights on the possession of some trait $Q$, where it

is a characteristic of $Q$ that although one can approach by degrees the status of possessing $Q$, once one has attained that status, it is not possible to have more or less of $Q$. Gewirth's own argument thus attempts to ground equal rights on our possession of 'purposive agency' which, he insists, does not admit of degrees.[117] Although, he says, one can approach by degrees the status of purposive agency, once one has attained that status, doing things better, or being more intelligent, etc. does not make one more of a purposive agent. Hence those of us who are purposive agents are all equally so.

Though he is less clear about it, Rawls seems to offer a similar account of 'the basis of equality'. According to Rawls's version of the argument, it is not 'prospective purposive agency' but the capacity for moral personality (i.e. to have capabilities of forming conceptions of the good and capabilities for possessing a sense of justice) that provides the foundation of the claim to equal liberty.[118] Although Rawls acknowledges that 'individuals presumably have varying capacities for a sense of justice', he insists that one need only satisfy the minimum conditions to achieve the capacity for moral personality. 'Once a certain minimum is met, a person is entitled to equal liberty on a par with everyone else.'[119] In Gewirth's language, Rawls's argument would seem to be that although the capacities that enter into moral personhood vary, the capacity of moral personality itself does not admit of degrees. If one has it, one has it, and it is impossible to obtain more. And in that sense all who are capable of a moral personality are equal.

Such arguments, then, uphold equal liberty by trying to demonstrate an underlying equality among men. As such, they implicitly accept the Aristotelian conception of justice as the basis for distributing rights: to establish that people ought to be accorded equal rights, it is maintained that people are really equal in the relevant respect. While these are important arguments, what seems particularly interesting about modern liberal theory is the extent to which such arguments are *not* drawn upon to endorse equal liberty. Modern liberals, I want to suggest, often – if not typically – argue for an equality of liberty not on grounds of justice but on the basis of instrumental/consequentialist considerations. *Equal liberty, they hold, promotes the development of everyone – those with the greater liberty as well as those with the lesser – better than an inegalitarian distribution, even one that might seem to be in accordance with Aristotelian distributive justice.* And it is held to do so because of man's social nature. More specifically, equal liberty finds support in the modern liberal theories of (i) social life and (ii) community.

## D.2.  Arguments from Social Life

It will be recalled (Ch. II) that the basic tenet of the modern liberal
theory of social life, as articulated by the doctrines of *social interest*
and the *mutual stimulation of individualities*, is that the development
of others is necessary to our own satisfaction. As Hobhouse reminds us,
there is one important difference between human and plant development: 'the flower may become perfect at the expense of its neighbours,
while for the man, this method of attaining perfection destroys it.
The perfection of the human soul is a function of the perfection of
others.'[120] Pretty obviously, this provides a foundation for arguments
against inegalitarian distributions of liberty that sacrifice the development of some for the supposed greater development of others. Because
the growth of others is a good to us, and necessary to our own satisfaction (§II.B), to thwart the development of one's fellows is *ipso
facto* to hinder the satisfaction of one's own nature. Moreover, because
(according to the mutual stimulation argument) we require developed
associates to spur our own individuality, each of us has a strong interest
in encouraging the growth of our fellows.[121] As Bosanquet would say,
acknowledging the claims of others does not constitute a 'diminution
of the self' or a 'curtailment'; rather, each 'so far from surrendering
some of his capacity for life through his fellowship with others [and
admitting their rights], acquires and extends that capacity wholly in
and through such fellowship.'[122]

This line of reasoning underlies Green's well-known thesis that a
right – including that to life and liberty – 'is a power claimed and recognised as contributory to a common good.'[123] According to Green,
for one person to acknowledge the claim of another as a genuine right
and appropriately respond, the two need to share and recognise a common good:

> There can be no right without a consciousness of a common interest
> on the part of members of a society. Without this there might be
> certain powers on the part of individuals, but no recognition of these
> powers by others as powers of which they allow the exercise, nor
> any claim to such recognition; and without this recognition or claim
> to recognition there can be no right.[124]

As we saw in an earlier chapter, according to Green's doctrine of social
interest, we are aware that each other's development is mutually
satisfying; consequently, I am aware that your development is a good to
me as well as to you. In this sense, then, my acknowledgement of your

claim to develop your nature does indeed rest on my recognition of a common good between us. But although strictly speaking all Green needs here is the theory of social interest, he actually goes further to call on (at least) the 'weak' notion of community *qua* consciousness of the organic unity of social life (§III.B.1). Green is not simply concerned with a common good between any two individuals but a shared good of the right claimant and a *society*. As Green depicts it, for the practice of rights to exist, a group of people must be cognizant of a group-wide common good; being aware of the common good, the group — i.e. the community — secures to each those powers necessary for the individual to contribute.[125] In this sense, then, Green's theory of rights presupposes not only that men share a social life but also that they be alive to the community-wide scope of these organic relations.

Green appears to have thought that such 'fellowship' (which admittedly has overtones of affective ties too) required that persons recognise each other as 'equal and alike' (§II.B.2). Indeed, he believed that all rights are necessarily equal rights.[126] However, it is not at all clear that the theory of social interest — even if combined with the weak sense of community — really provides a basis for a strict equality of liberty. If each is accorded liberty proportionate with his or her capacities for development, each will be able to make a contribution to social life proportionate with those abilities. Hence, he or she will still enrich others and they in turn will contribute to his or her development. In order, then, to establish that liberty should be not only widely distributed but also equally distributed, something else seems to be needed. It is here that Rawls's extension of social interest (§II.B.2) comes into play. In Rawls's view, not only do we have an intrinsic interest in the lives of our associates but we also require that they confirm the worth of our plans and projects. Now Rawls believes that in a system of unequal liberty those with the lesser liberty are apt to lose self-respect; their 'subordinate ranking in the public forum expressed in the attempt to take part in political and economic life, and felt in dealing with those who have greater liberty, would indeed be humiliating and destructive of self-esteem'.[127] Moreover, this loss of self-respect would produce, as it were, a ripple effect throughout society: those who do not respect themselves, we are told, are grudging in their affirmation of others' worth which, in turn, damages the basis of others' self-respect. In sum, Rawls contends that an inequality of basic liberties would make a mutually appreciative and mutually enriching social life 'difficult if not impossible to achieve'.[128]

### D.3. Arguments from Community

Green and Rawls thus centre their main arguments from human nature
for equal liberty on the theory of social life. To be sure, Green's goes
somewhat beyond, to a weak theory of community, but it does not
seem to call on communitarian sentiments. Mill's argument does. In
the third chapter of *Liberty*, Mill squarely faces the problem of the
great man: viz. might not an insistence upon the (equal) rights of all
lead to a 'compression' of 'the stronger specimens of human nature'?
Mill's answer is a 'yes, but', adding quickly that the strong man so contained receives

> a full equivalent in the better development of the social part of his
> nature, rendered possible by the restraint put upon the selfish part.
> To be held to rigid rules of justice for the sake of others, develops
> the feelings and capacities which have the good of others for their
> object.[129]

This ought not to be viewed as an isolated remark. In *The Subjection
of Women* Mill identifies justice with a morality premised on *equality*,
as opposed, for instance, to moralities based on chivalry or generosity.
And we have already seen that Mill's psychology connects sympathetic
feelings and equality (§III.C.3); consequently, Mill tells us that human
relations are properly grounded upon equality infused with 'sympathetic
association'.[130]

The basic argument, then, is (to use Green's language) that even if
the strong man's 'special qualities of command' are less developed in an
egalitarian order, 'the capabilities implied in social adjustment become
what they could not be before'.[131] An order premised on equal rights
to liberty is held to give rise to a civic community resting on loyalty
and public feelings, or, to use a word often employed by Dewey,
fraternity.[132] In this respect, then, modern liberals hold that the French
Revolution's triumvirate of values — Liberty, Equality and Fraternity
— are not only interrelated but, at least potentially, are mutually supporting. However, although on this analysis fraternity seems to have
significant egalitarian implications, it certainly is consistent with some
sorts of inequalities and, at least in Rawls's eyes, this includes some
instances of unequal liberty. Although Rawls seems to share Mill's
conviction that unequal liberty normally interferes with the unfolding
of communitarian sentiments,[133] as is well known, he allows that under
some conditions an unequal distribution of liberty might be justified.

If, say, economic conditions are so dire that some persons (*P*) are unable to really exercise a basic liberty, Rawls maintains that it may be permissible to pursue policies that infringe this liberty of *P* if the policies are instrumental in bringing about conditions in which the liberty can be effectively exercised by *P*. Now in these special conditions Rawls holds that this unequal distribution of liberties is an expression of fraternity. Comparing the community to a family (§III.C.3), Rawls writes that '[t]hose better circumstanced are *willing* to have their greater advantages *only* under a scheme in which this works out for the benefit of the less fortunate'.[134]

In some respects Bosanquet's position is similar. As Bosanquet sees it, individuals possess 'prima facie' equal claims (rights), and differences in treatment not only have to be justified but generally must be done in a way that will satisfy the person being denied 'equal justice'. 'He knows that different people need different things; but he does not think he has justice unless he approves the reason for the difference.' And if reasons are not forthcoming, Bosanquet believes that unless he is 'domesticated' and slavish, a person will in the end rebel. For Bosanquet, though, it would seem to be appeals to the 'public good' that are 'satisfying' and thus allow for the infringement of individual rights without hostility. If citizens are devoted to the common good, then the 'violation' of individual claims to justice can be consistent with social solidarity. However, we should not conclude from this that Bosanquet thought individual rights unimportant or that the individual should generally be forced to sacrifice for the common good; it was self-surrender of rights, not an imposed surrender, that Bosanquet had in mind. 'It is true in the most literal sense that justice comes before generosity, though not above it. A man can only surrender what is recognised as his.'[135]

It is doubtful that Mill would be as prepared as either Bosanquet or Rawls to allow that social solidarity can be had in the presence of inequalities of basic liberties. For in addition to his general account of sympathy, Mill advances a specific thesis as to the corrupting consequences of 'privilege'. In *The Subjection of Women* Mill is explicit in maintaining that the inequality of status between men and women not only has distorted and cramped the development of females but also has corrupted males. 'There is nothing which men so easily learn as . . . self-worship: all privileged persons, and all privileged classes, have had it.' Those who occupy such 'privileged' positions are thus said to be 'arrogant' and 'overbearing' and lack respect for their inferiors. Indeed, Mill depicts them as perverted 'both as . . . individual[s] and as . . . social being[s]'.[136] Dewey and Tufts agree that all are perverted as social beings by such inequalities:

> A very considerable portion of what is regarded as the inherent self-ishness of mankind is the product of an inequitable distribution of power – inequitable because it shuts out some from the conditions which evoke and direct their capacities, while it produces a one-sided growth in those who have privilege.[137]

On this view an inegalitarian distribution of liberties is a danger to human development even if (as Rawls asserts) it works out for the benefit of those with the lesser liberty, for it would still presumably tend to corrupt the apparently privileged. Mill and Dewey thus seem to postulate a tighter link between equality and fraternity than, say, either Rawls or Bosanquet.

By linking equal liberty and fraternity in this way modern liberals seem to again be asserting that individuality and community can be reconciled, indeed harmonised (§III.E). Community can only exist, they tell us, if all are assured equal rights to plan their own lives. But while this does indeed imply that a good deal of community is consistent with individuality, it does not seem that the argument does away with the tension. For essential to the modern liberal position here are claims that those denied equal liberty will be alienated and hostile or that those with greater liberty will be arrogant, self-glorifying etc. But for these reactions to occur, it must be true that people are not fully immersed in the community. If, as Bosanquet suggests, each were entirely and without reservation devoted to communal well-being (or as Hume would say, we all were to 'kindle in the common blaze'), it would seem that those with the lesser liberty would not be alienated nor would those with the greater be corrupted. All would be emersed in the commonweal with no thought of self. The modern liberal link between community and equal liberty thus assumes individualised personalities sufficiently concerned with self to be alienated or corrupted, and so it would seem, a condition far short of 'total community'.

To conclude: my concern in this section has been to show that modern liberals have upheld an equality of liberty on the grounds that it promotes the development of all. The arguments supporting this claim have been various indeed, pointing to some extent to the benefits of equality for individuality but, primarily, emphasising the way in which equal (or at least widely distributed) liberty encourages social interest and fraternity (community). It is important to attend to these arguments. The consequence of not doing so is, I think, to entertain a distorted view of the status of equal liberty in modern liberal theory. Perhaps the most striking instance of such distortion is Rawls's own analysis of Mill, in which he clearly lays out Mill's argument linking individuality and liberty but then concludes:

> But Mill's contentions, as cogent as they are, will not, it seems, justify an equal liberty for all . . . One must suppose a certain similarity among individuals, say their equal capacity for the activities and interests of men as progressive beings, and in addition a principle of the diminishing marginal value of basic rights when assigned to individuals. In the absence of these presumptions the advancement of human ends may be compatible with some persons' being oppressed, or at least granted but a restricted liberty.[138]

All this would be true enough if the only arguments for liberty from human nature were those based on the promotion of individuality. But if nothing else is clear by now, it should be manifest that neither the modern liberal theory nor arguments from it to liberty are exhausted by individuality. Because the modern liberal man — with whom both Mill and Rawls are concerned — is a social being, and because modern liberals posit an intimate tie between sociability (especially community) and equality, a commitment to equal liberty goes far deeper in Mill's theory of man than Rawls suggests.

## Notes

1. Green, 'Lecture on Liberal Legislation and Freedom of Contract' in *Works of Thomas Hill Green*, R.L. Nettleship (ed.) (Longman's, Green, and Co., London, 1889), vol. III, p. 371. See also Green's essay 'On the Different Senses of "Freedom" as Applied to Will and to the Moral Progress of Man' in *Works*, vol. II, pp. 307-33.

2. See D.G. Ritchie, *Principles of State Interference* (Allen and Unwin, London, 1902), pp. 145-51; Hobhouse, *Liberalism* (Oxford University Press, Oxford, 1964), pp. 70 ff; Dewey, *Liberalism and Social Action* (G.P. Putnam's Sons, New York, 1935), pp. 24-34; Dewey, 'Philosophies of Freedom' in Richard J. Bernstein (ed.), *On Experience, Nature and Freedom* (Liberal Arts Press, New York, 1960), pp. 261-87; Bosanquet, *The Philosophical Theory of the State*, 4th edn (Macmillan, London, 1951), Ch. VI; Bosanquet, *The Civilization of Christendom* (Swan Sonnenschein, London, 1899), pp. 358-83.

3. Isaiah Berlin, 'Two Concepts of Liberty' in his *Four Essays on Liberty* (Oxford University Press, Oxford, 1969), pp. 153-54. See also Berlin's introductory essay. For an analysis and defence of Berlin's views on liberty, see Robert A. Kocis, 'Reason, Development and the Conflict of Human Ends: Sir Isaiah Berlin's

Vision of Politics', *American Political Science Review*, LXXIV (Mar. 1980), pp. 38-52. See also note 8 below.

4. George H. Sabine, *A History of Political Theory* (Harrap, London, 1937), pp. 673 ff. See also Guido de Ruggiero, *The History of European Liberalism*, R.G. Collingwood (trans.) (Oxford University Press, London, 1927), pp. 350-57.

5. See W.L. Weinstein, 'The Concept of Liberty in Nineteenth Century English Political Thought', *Political Studies*, XIII (1965) p. 145; Berlin, 'Two Concepts of Liberty'. However, Kenneth R. Hoover maintains that Mill anticipated the idea of positive liberty. 'Liberalism and the Idealist Philosophy of Thomas Hill Green', *Western Political Quarterly*, XXVI (Sept. 1973), p. 560n.

6. Rawls, *A Theory of Justice* (The Belknap Press of Harvard University Press, Cambridge, Mass., 1971), p. 201.

7. Michael Freeden, *The New Liberalism: An Ideology of Social Reform* (Clarendon Press, Oxford, 1978), pp. 6, 53-55. Stefan Collini, *Liberalism and Sociology: L.T. Hobhouse and Political Argument in England, 1880-1914* (Cambridge University Press, Cambridge, 1979), pp. 46-47.

8. Ibid. On MacCallum's analysis, both 'negative' and 'positive' liberty have the same logical form, i.e. an agent $X$ is free from a constraint $Y$ to perform (or to be, etc.) $Z$. 'Negative and Positive Freedom' in Peter Laslett, W.G. Runciman and Quentin Skinner (eds.), *Philosophy, Politics and Society*, 4th series (Basil Blackwell, Oxford, 1972), pp. 174-93. It is because Rawls accepts MacCallum's analysis that he avoids the negative/positive issue (see text at note 6 above). For a critique of MacCallum's analysis, see Kocis, 'Reason, Development and the Conflict of Human Ends', pp. 42-44.

9. Weinstein, 'The Concept of Liberty', p. 146.

10. Hobhouse, *Liberalism*, p. 66.

11. Mill, *On Liberty* in J.M. Robson (ed.), *The Collected Works of John Stuart Mill* (University of Toronto Press, Toronto, 1963), vol. XVIII, p. 270. See also C.L. Ten, *Mill on Liberty* (Oxford University Press, Oxford, 1980), p. 71, and Rawls, *A Theory of Justice*, pp. 209 ff.

12. Dewey, 'Time and Individuality' in David Sidorsky (ed.), *John Dewey: The Essential Writings* (Harper and Row, New York, 1977), p. 144. See Jerome Nathanson, *John Dewey* (Scribner's, New York, 1951), p. 75.

13. Mill, *On Liberty*, p. 277. See also Alan Ryan, *The Philosophy of John Stuart Mill* (Macmillan, London, 1970), pp. 253-54; H.J. McCloskey, 'Mill's Liberalism', *Philosophical Quarterly*, XIII (1963), pp. 148 ff.

14. Bosanquet, *Some Suggestions in Ethics* (Macmillan, London, 1919), pp. 154-55.

15. K.R. Popper, *The Open Society and Its Enemies*, vol. I: *The Spell of Plato* (Routledge and Kegan Paul, London, 1966), p. 165.

16. See Georgi Smirnoff, *Soviet Man: The Making of a Socialist Type Personality* (Progress Publishers, Moscow, 1973).

17. Mill, *On Liberty*, p. 264. On energy and pathologies see § IV.B.3.

18. Bosanquet, *Psychology of the Moral Self* (Macmillan, London, 1904), p. 80.

19. Green, 'The Different Senses of "Freedom" ', pp. 309, 323.

20. Ibid., pp. 308, 324.

21. Weinstein, 'The Concept of Liberty', p. 153.

22. For Mill's account of moral evaluation, see Alan Ryan, *J.S. Mill* (Routledge and Kegan Paul, London, 1974), pp. 104-6, 147-50; David Lyons, 'Mill's Theory of Morality', *Nous*, X (1976), pp. 101-20. I consider Lyon's interpretation in my article, 'Mill's Theory of Moral Rules', *The Australasian Journal of Philosophy*, LVIII (Sept. 1980), pp. 265-79.

23. Mill, *Utilitarianism* in *Collected Works*, vol. X, pp. 212-13. Mill is quick to add that the social system, especially as it concerns occupations, tends to produce such characters.

24. Mill can claim that such thwarting might be consistent with contentment since his model of capacities allows for their complete uprooting as well as blockage. In this particular argument he refers to capacities being 'killed'. Ibid., p. 213. See §IV.B.3.

25. Mill, *On Liberty*, p. 262. On the importance of choice in Mill's theory, see Ten, *Mill on Liberty*, pp. 68-70; Isaiah Berlin, 'John Stuart Mill and the Ends of Life' in his *Four Essays on Liberty*, pp. 173-206. Robert Ladenson discusses Berlin's interpretation of Mill in his 'Mill's Conception of Individuality', *Social Theory and Practice*, IV (Spring 1977), pp. 167-82. For a critical discussion of the relation of this choice argument to the self-satisfaction argument for liberty, see Richard Lichtman, 'The Surface and Substance of Mill's Defense of Freedom', *Social Research*, XXX (1963), pp. 487 ff.

26. Hobhouse, *Social Evolution and Political Theory* (Columbia University Press, New York, 1928), p. 199.

27. Dewey, *Democracy and Education* (Free Press, New York, 1916), p. 302. See also *Intelligence in the Modern World: John Dewey's Philosophy*, Joseph Ratner (ed.) (Modern Library, New York, 1939), pp. 619-27. See also Alfonso J. Damico, *Individuality and Community: The Social and Political Thought of John Dewey* (University Presses of Florida, Gainesville, 1978), p. 87.

28. Rawls, *A Theory of Justice*, p. 441. See David A.J. Richards, 'Free Speech and Obscenity Law: Toward a Moral Theory of the First Amendment', *University of Pennsylvania Law Review*, CXXIII (Nov. 1974), pp. 62-63, 80.

29. Mill, *On Liberty*, p. 263.

30. Ibid., p. 264. See Adina Beth Schwartz, 'John Stuart Mill: A Program for Social Philosophy', unpublished PhD thesis, Rockefeller University, New York, 1976, pp. 76 ff.

31. Mill, *On Liberty*, p. 265. On not having a nature to follow, see §IV.B.3.

32. Bosanquet, *The Philosophical Theory of the State*, pp. 129-34. Compare this with F.A. Hayek, *The Constitution of Liberty* (Routledge and Kegan Paul, London, 1960), pp. 20-21.

33. Bosanquet, *The Philosophical Theory of the State*, p. 136.

34. Ten, *Mill on Liberty*, p. 72.

35. Hobhouse, *The Metaphysical Theory of the State* (Allen and Unwin, London, 1926), pp. 45-46. Although Hobhouse agreed with Bosanquet that a harmonious personality is our proper goal, he insisted that most selves were not harmonious and it was simply misleading to call this unfulfilled ideal more real than existing selves.

36. Ten does not explicitly attribute this view to the 'British idealists', but his argument implies it. *Mill on Liberty*, p. 73.

37. See Bosanquet, *The Philosophical Theory of the State*, p. 111. See also §VI.C.1.

38. Mill, *Principles of Political Economy* in *Collected Works*, vol. III, p. 938. In *The Subjection of Women*, Mill writes: 'Every restraint on the freedom of conduct of any of their human fellow creatures (otherwise than by making them responsible for any evil actually caused by it), dries up *pro tanto* the principal fountain of human happiness, and leaves the species less rich, to an inappreciable degree, in all that makes life valuable to the individual human being' (in Alice S. Rossi (ed.), *Essays on Sex Equality* [University of Chicago Press, Chicago, 1970], p. 242). Again: 'Whenever the sphere of action of human beings is artificially circumscribed, their sentiments are narrowed and dwarfed in the same proportion.' *Considerations on Representative Government* in *Collected Works*, vol. XIX, pp. 400-1.

39. Hobhouse, *Liberalism*, p. 50.

40. Dewey, *Problems of Men* (Philosophical Library, New York, 1946), p. 113.

41. Hobhouse, *Liberalism*, p. 78.

42. Dewey and Tufts, *Ethics*, rev. edn (Henry Holt, New York, 1932), p. 236. See also Dewey, *The Public and Its Problems* (Swallow Press, Chicago, 1954), p. 168. Compare Mill, *On Liberty*, p. 266.

43. Bosanquet, *The Philosophical Theory of the State*, pp. 169-80.

44. Hobhouse, *The Elements of Social Justice* (Allen and Unwin, London, 1949), p. 70.

45. Bosanquet, *Social and International Ideals* (Macmillan, London, 1917), p. 199. Bosanquet thought only the slavish would accept force and not rebel. See also Hobhouse, *Liberalism*, p. 66; Dewey, *Freedom and Culture* (Allen and Unwin, London, 1940), p. 129.

46. Hobhouse, *Social Justice*, p. 71. Compare Dewey, *Democracy and Education*, pp. 83-84.

47. Rawls, *A Theory of Justice*, p. 494. John Chapman stresses this aspect of Rawls's theory in his 'Rawls's Theory of Justice', *American Political Science Review*, LXIX (June 1975), pp. 588-93. See also Jesse Landrum Kelly, Jr., 'Justice and Utility: The Role of Moral Desert in the Political Writings of John Rawls', unpublished PhD thesis, University of Florida, 1978.

48. Hobhouse, *Liberalism*, p. 67. See also Green, *Lectures on the Principles of Political Obligation* in *Works*, vol. II, p. 514.

49. Gerald Dworkin, 'Paternalism' in Peter Laslett and James Fishkin (eds.), *Philosophy, Politics and Society*, 5th series (Blackwell, Oxford, 1979), p. 78; Jeffrie G. Murphy, 'Incompetence and Paternalism' in his *Retribution, Justice, and Therapy* (Reidel, Boston, 1979), p. 165.

50. It has been argued that paternalism need not involve coercion or interference with liberty. See John Kleinig, 'Paternalism: What is at Stake?' unpublished paper, Philosophy Department, Research School of Social Sciences, The Australian National University, 1981; Bernard Gert and Charles Culver, 'Paternalistic Behavior', *Philosophy and Public Affairs*, VI (Fall 1976), pp. 45-57.

51. Mill, *On Liberty*, p. 294.

52. Mill, *Principles of Political Economy*, p. 947.

53. Mill, *On Liberty*, p. 294; see J.P. Day, 'On Liberty and the Real Will', *Philosophy*, XLV (July 1970), pp. 177-92.

54. Bosanquet, *The Philosophical Theory of the State*, pp. 132-33. I have benefitted greatly here from John Kleinig's work.

55. Green, 'On the Different Senses of "Freedom" ', p. 308.

56. According to Melvin Richter, this is the central argument of *The Philosophical Theory of the State* (*The Politics of Conscience: T.H. Green and His Age* [Weidenfeld and Nicolson, London, 1964], p. 202). What is usually not noted is that Bosanquet no sooner uses the phrase than he points to his discussion of its limitations, which, we shall see, are not inconsiderable. See *The Philosophical Theory*, pp. 118-19, and A.J.M. Milne, *The Social Philosophy of English Idealism* (Allen and Unwin, London, 1962), pp. 250-52. As we will see in Chapter VI, the doctrine really relates to politics and the 'general will' rather than to paternalism.

57. H.J. McCloskey, writing of Hobhouse, calls this 'the traditional but fallacious liberal contention that real moral excellence is incompatible with the use of coercion'. 'The Problem of Liberalism', *Review of Metaphysics*, XIX (1965-66), p. 267. See also D.J. Manning, *Liberalism* (Dent, London, 1976), p. 134. For Green see his *Political Obligation*, p. 340; for Bosanquet see *The Philosophical Theory of the State*, pp. 175 ff.

58. See Ann R. Cacoullos, *Thomas Hill Green: Philosopher of Rights* (Twayne, New York, 1974), Ch. 3.

59. Green, *Prolegomena to Ethics*, A.C. Bradley (ed.) (Clarendon Press, Oxford, 1890), p. 365. See also Crane Brinton, *English Political Thought in the 19th Cen-*

*tury* (Harper and Bros., New York, 1962), pp. 219-20. In a similar vein, Bosanquet tells us that 'the individual to-day has to shape his own life'. *The Civilization of Christendom*, p. 289.

60. John Rodman, 'Introduction' to his edited collection, *The Political Theory of T.H. Green* (Appleton-Century-Crofts, New York, 1964), p. 29.

61. Green, 'Liberal Legislation', p. 386.

62. Green tells us that he justifies restraining laws 'on the simple ground of the recognised right on the part of society to prevent men from doing as they like, if, in the exercise of their peculiar tastes in doing as they like, they create a social nuisance'. He takes pains to point out how 'the excessive drinking of one man means an injury to others in health, purse, and capability, to which no limits can be placed'. Ibid., pp. 383, 384.

63. In so far as the self is understood as an organised system, the self-expression argument would also seem to depend on this assumption. But if we view self-expression as including the expression of isolated capacities, then it does not seem to demand much rational self-control, planning etc.

64. Green, 'Liberal Legislation', p. 384. Richter notes but seems to dismiss this proviso. *The Politics of Conscience*, pp. 258-59.

65. Mill, *Principles of Political Economy*, p. 938. See also §IV.C.1.

66. Hobhouse, *Liberalism*, pp. 80-81. See also his *Political Theory*, p. 202.

67. See Hobhouse, *Social Justice*, p. 85; Bosanquet, 'Socialism and Natural Selection' in his edited collection, *Aspects of the Social Problem* (Macmillan, London, 1895), pp. 302-3; Mill, *Principles of Political Economy*, pp. 951-52, and *On Liberty*, p. 224; Dewey, *The Public and Its Problems*, p. 62; Rawls, *A Theory of Justice*, pp. 248 ff. Green's discussion in *Political Obligation* (p. 464) is particularly interesting; he insists that 'even hopeless idiots and lunatics' have a right to life but seems unsure why.

68. The status in modern liberal theory of those unable to develop and, hence, contribute to the common good is problematic. For a Millian-inspired account distinguishing paternalism for those who can and cannot develop, see F. D'Agostino, 'Mill, Paternalism and Psychiatry', *The Australasian Journal of Philosophy* (forthcoming).

69. For an analysis supporting a dichotomous rather than a continuous conception of competency, see Daniel Wikler, 'Paternalism and the Mildly Retarded', *Philosophy and Public Affairs*, VIII (1979), pp. 377-92.

70. Hobhouse, *Liberalism*, p. 80.

71. Mill, *On Liberty*, p. 294. Emphasis added. This sort of paternalism is what is called 'weak' as opposed to 'strong'. See Ten, *Mill on Liberty*, Ch. 7. See also Margaret Spahr, 'Mill on Paternalism in its Place' in Carl J. Friedrich (ed.), *NOMOS IV: Liberty* (Atherton Press, New York, 1962), pp. 162-75; Richard J. Arneson, 'Mill Versus Paternalism', *Ethics*, XC (July 1980), pp. 470-89.

72. Mill, *On Liberty*, p. 277.

73. The importance of such friendly advice (and hence Mill's theories of social interest and fellow feeling) is overlooked by critics such as Anschutz and Hamburger who charge that Mill's conceptions of liberty and individuality are somehow atomistic. A.D. Lindsay put it well in likening Mill's vision to a 'society of friends'. See R.P. Anschutz, *The Philosophy of J.S. Mill* (Clarendon Press, Oxford, 1953); Joseph Hamburger, 'Mill and Tocqueville on Liberty' in John M. Robson and Michael Laine (eds.), *James and J.S. Mill: Papers of the Centenary Conference* (University of Toronto Press, Toronto, 1976), pp. 116-19; and A.D. Lindsay, 'Introduction' to *Utilitarianism, Liberty, and Representative Government* (Dent, London, 1910), p. xviii.

74. See Michael Bayles, 'Criminal Paternalism' in J. Roland Pennock and John W. Chapman (eds.) *NOMOS XV: The Limits of Law* (Lieber-Atherton, New York, 1974), p. 176.

75. Green, *Political Obligation*, pp. 514-15. See also Bosanquet, *The Philosophical Theory of the State*, pp. 178 ff; Hobhouse, *Liberalism*, pp. 78 ff.

76. Sigmund Freud, *A General Introduction to Psychoanalysis*, Joan Riviere (trans.) (Liveright, New York, 1935), p. 229.

77. See R.S. Peters, *Psychology and Ethical Development* (Allen and Unwin, London, 1974), pp. 340 ff; S.I. Benn, 'Freedom, Autonomy and the Concept of a Person', in *Proceedings of the Aristotelian Society*, LXXVI (1976), pp. 124 ff.

78. Freud, *Psychoanalysis*, p. 230.

79. Hayek, *The Constitution of Liberty*, p. 21.

80. See James M. Buchanan, 'A Contractarian Perspective on Anarchy' in J. Roland Pennock and John W. Chapman (eds.), *NOMOS XIX: Anarchism* (New York University Press, New York, 1978), pp. 29-42; Robert Nozick, *Anarchy, State and Utopia* (Basic Books, New York, 1974). Pt. I.

81. Dewey, *Intelligence in the Modern World*, p. 404. See also his *Problems of Men*, pp. 111-25. Dewey conceives of liberties as 'powers', thus often infusing a notion of effective liberty into his analysis. See §VII.B.1 on effective liberty.

82. H.L.A. Hart, 'Rawls on Liberty and its Priority' in Norman Daniels (ed.), *Reading Rawls: Critical Studies of A Theory of Justice* (Basic Books, New York, 1974), pp. 236-37. Rawls explicitly accepts Hart's interpretation in 'A Well-Ordered Society' in Laslett and Fishkin (eds.), *Philosophy, Politics and Society*, p. 12n.

83. Bernard Schwartz, *The Great Rights of Mankind* (Oxford University Press, New York, 1971), p. 201. On the political rights, see Ch. VI below.

84. Hobhouse, *Social Justice*, Ch. IV. As one of Hobhouse's contemporaries understood his view, 'Liberty proper is thus a group of liberties.' Lewis Rockow, *Contemporary Political Thought in England* (Leonard Press, London, 1925), p. 205.

85. Bosanquet, *The Philosophical Theory of the State*, p. 119; see also p. 189.

86. On the distinction between a general right to liberty and an enumeration of specific liberties, see Hayek, *The Constitution of Liberty*, p. 19; Ronald Dworkin, *Taking Rights Seriously* (Harvard University Press, Cambridge, Mass., 1978), pp. 266-72. On Mill's general right to liberty, see Ten, *Mill on Liberty*.

87. Hobhouse, *Liberalism*, Ch. II. As Collini has said, Hobhouse 'spoke with the authentic voice of traditional Liberalism' on issues concerning civil liberty. *Liberalism and Sociology*, p. 141.

88. Mill stresses the importance of rules and regular procedures. See 'Dr Whewell on Moral Philosophy' in *Collected Works*, vol. X, pp. 181-92; *Utilitarianism*, pp. 255 ff.

89. See Cacoullos, *Thomas Hill Green*, p. 134; Green, *Prolegomena*, pp. 335 ff.

90. Green, *Political Obligation*, pp. 463-65. See Cacoullos, *Thomas Hill Green*, p. 142. Green points to the importance of freedom of conscience in his 'Four Lectures on the English Commonwealth' in *Works*, vol. III, e.g. pp. 296-97. See §VII.A.1 for Green's notion of property rights.

91. Bosanquet, *The Philosophical Theory of the State*, pp. xiv, 134. Interestingly, on the liberty to marry as one chooses, Bosanquet may be more libertarian than Mill. Compare pp. 62-64 of *The Philosophical Theory* with p. 304 of *Liberty*. But see also Bosanquet's *Ideals*, p. 156.

92. See Green, *Prolegomena*, p. 398; J.H. Muirhead, *The Service of the State: Four Lectures on the Political Teaching of T.H. Green* (John Murray, London, 1908), pp. 85-86; Richter, *The Politics of Conscience*, p. 263.

93. Rawls, *A Theory of Justice*, p. 206.

94. Hobhouse, *Liberalism*, p. 19; Dewey and Tufts, *Ethics*, p. 398. Mill too gives freedom of thought a preeminent place; see *Liberty*, pp. 225-26.

95. Bosanquet, *Psychology of the Moral Self*, p. 95-96; *Essays and Addresses* (Swan Sonnenschein, London, 1891), pp. 76-79. In the latter Bosanquet is

concerned with the appreciation of beauty, but of course in his view that is very similar to an intellectual endeavour. See §I.C.4.

96. Dewey, *Characters and Events: Popular Essays in Social and Political Philosophy*, Joseph Ratner (ed.) (Henry Holt, New York, 1929), vol. I, p. 100. Dewey adds a third tenet: 'The experimental character of life and thought'. Ibid.

97. See Mill, *On Liberty*, Ch. II; Ten, *Mill on Liberty*, Ch. 8; Ryan, *J.S. Mill*, pp. 125-39. For a different sort of argument, see Dewey, 'Time and Individuality', p. 147.

98. Rawls, *A Theory of Justice*, pp. 202-3.

99. Hobhouse, *Liberalism*, p. 19.

100. Dewey and Tufts, *Ethics*, pp. 402-3. Dewey also proffers the 'natural *telos* of thought' argument, stressing that if denied expression, ideas 'are likely to die from inanition'. Ibid.

101. Dewey, *Intelligence in the Modern World*, p. 404.

102. Dewey, *Democracy and Education*, p. 302. See also his *Experience and Nature* (Dover, New York, 1958).

103. Dewey, *Democracy and Education*, p. 309.

104. Ibid., p. 308.

105. Mill, *The Subjection of Women*, p. 144, Ch. 3; Hobhouse, *Liberalism*, p. 21; Rawls, *A Theory of Justice*, pp. 274, 310. Although Rawls does not include liberty of occupation in his list of basic liberties, he does call it an 'important liberty': it is sufficiently important that Rawls deems unacceptable any economic system that infringes it. (See §VII.A.2.) Rawls also indicates that the principle of open positions is largely premised on developmental considerations. Ibid., p. 84.

106. See Bosanquet, *Science and Philosophy* (Allen and Unwin, London, 1927), p. 282. See also *Some Suggestions in Ethics*, pp. 150-51; *The Philosophical Theory of the State*, p. 255. Bosanquet also agrees, however, that if most people are denied choice, 'our system is so far a failure'. *The Civilization of Christendom*, p. 363. Green does mention a 'free career in life', but his point is to endorse the providing of the conditions for a developed life rather than specifically freedom of occupation. 'Liberal Legislation', p. 374. See also §VII.A.

107. Dewey, in fact, also argues that capacities must accommodate themselves to occupations (as well as vice versa). See *Intelligence in the Modern World*, pp. 428-29. See also *Individualism – Old and New* (Allen and Unwin, London, 1931). p. 154.

108. See Robert F. Cushman, *Cases in Civil Liberties* (Appleton-Century-Crofts, New York, 1968), p. 400.

109. Such arguments, of course, are not entirely absent from modern liberal writings. See, for example, Bosanquet, *Ideals*, p. 125.

110. In Walter Simon (ed.), *French Liberalism: 1789-1848* (Wiley, London, 1972), p. 15.

111. Hobhouse, *Social Justice*, p. 112. The existence of such inequality is a pervasive theme in modern liberal writings. To be sure, we find differences in emphasis; it is probably least prominent in Green while it is a dominating concern of Rawls. But even Green talks of great men of genius. See his essay on 'The Influence of Civilisation on Genius' in *Works*, vol. III, pp. 11-12. Dewey, at least at times, takes a somewhat different view, arguing that because individualities are unique, the natural differences among men cannot yield rankings of 'inferior' and 'superior'. Individualities, he argues, are incommensurable and, because of this, give rise to claims to equal treatment. If we accept this argument, Dewey's position is not subject to the argument for proportional justice that I examine in this subsection. See his *Characters and Events*, vol. II, pp. 854-55.

112. Alan Gewirth, *Reason and Morality* (University of Chicago Press, Chicago, 1978), p. 121.

113. Aristotle, *The Nicomachean Ethics*, Sir David Ross (trans.) (Oxford University Press, London, 1954), p. 113; 1131(a)27-1131(b)14. Bosanquet's notion of justice is particularly Aristotelian. See his *Ideals*, pp. 195-211.

114. This is Morris Ginsberg's account of Hobhouse's position. 'The Work of L.T. Hobhouse' in J.A. Hobson and Morris Ginsberg (eds.), *L.T. Hobhouse: His Life and Work* (Allen and Unwin, London, 1931), p. 200. Hobhouse, of course, endorsed equal basic liberties. See his *Democracy and Reaction* (T. Fisher Unwin, London, 1904), p. 91.

115. Amy Gutmann, *Liberal Equality* (Cambridge University Press, Cambridge, 1980), Ch. 1. See my review of Gutmann in the *Australasian Journal of Philosophy* (forthcoming).

116. Bosanquet, *Ideals*, p. 199.

117. Gewirth, *Reason and Morality*, p. 122.

118. Rawls, *A Theory of Justice*, p. 505. Rawls characterises moral personality as a potentiality, but he also speaks of the 'capacity for moral personality'. For a somewhat different formulation of the idea of moral personhood, see Rawls's 'Kantian Constructivism in Moral Theory', *Journal of Philosophy*, LXXVII (Sept. 1980), pp. 524 ff.

119. Rawls, *A Theory of Justice*, p. 506.

120. Hobhouse, *Mind in Evolution*, 3rd edn (Macmillan, London, 1926), p. 388.

121. See Dewey and Tufts, *Ethics*, p. 386. See §II.C.1.

122. Bosanquet, *The Philosophical Theory of the State*, p. 55.

123. Green, *Political Obligation*, pp. 416, 460 ff. In what follows I draw heavily upon Ann R. Cacoullos's analysis. See *Thomas Hill Green*, Ch. 5. For a more traditional treatment of Green's views on rights and recognition, see John Plamenatz, *Consent, Freedom and Political Obligation*, 2nd edn (Oxford University Press, London, 1968), pp. 90 ff.

124. Green, *Political Obligation*, p. 354. Bosanquet's position seems very similar: 'the recognition of a common good by members of society, as realised in each others' lives . . . is the foundation of all rights'. 'The Principle of Private Property' in Bernard Bosanquet (ed.), *Aspects of the Social Problem* (Macmillan, London, 1895), p. 308. Cacoullos, however, argues that Bosanquet and Green had different understandings of 'recognition'. *Thomas Hill Green*, pp. 94-95.

125. Again, it is worth emphasising that the development of one's nature is itself a contribution to the common good or, as Green put it, a 'general service' (Green, *Prolegomena*, p. 305). However, as we saw in §III.D, Green insists that in some circumstances one may better contribute to the common good through activities that call for some form of self-sacrifice. In such circumstances, those who still pursue the development of their individuality (i.e. refuse to make the sacrifice) are certainly open to moral criticism. But Green rejects the suggestion that they ought generally to be coerced into performing these praiseworthy actions. And, again, the argument relates to his theory of development. In a way reminiscent of Mill, Green argues that to attempt to coerce the performance of acts 'which ought to flow from social interests' interferes 'with the spontaneous action of those interests, and consequently checks the growth of a capacity which is the condition of the beneficial exercise of rights'. (Green, *Political Obligation*, pp. 514-15. Compare Mill, *Auguste Comte and Positivism in Collected Works*, vol. X, pp. 336-39.) The argument here is that since coercion is liable to stifle the growth of human nature (including our social nature), it ought not to be used to compel all praiseworthy acts. As coercion is such a generous drug, liberals like Green and Bosanquet insisted that it be used sparingly, to overcome a definite impediment to growth, 'the removal of which is a small matter compared to the capacities to be set free' (Bosanquet, *The Philosophical Theory of the State*, p. 179).

126. See Cacoullos, *Thomas Hill Green*, pp. 98-99. See also Green, *Political Obligation*, pp. 461-62. To the extent 'fellowship' is intended to imply some sort of affective bonding, Green's argument is similar to that which I consider in §D.3. below.

127. Rawls, *A Theory of Justice*, pp. 544-45.

128. See ibid., pp. 546, 534 ff. Brian Barry criticises this argument, objecting that even if we accept the basic dynamics, it does not require 'the absence of society-wide status inequality': a society segmented into groups of differing status in which the 'significant others' were one's own group would suffice. *The Liberal Theory of Justice: A Critical Examination of the Principal Doctrines in* A Theory of Justice *by John Rawls* (Clarendon Press, Oxford, 1973), pp. 48-49. On Rawls's connection between self-respect and liberty, see Henry Shue, 'Liberty and Self-Respect', *Ethics*, LXXXV (Apr. 1975), pp. 195-203; Daniels, 'Equal Liberty and Unequal Worth of Liberty' in his *Reading Rawls*, pp. 273 ff.

129. Mill, *On Liberty*, p. 266. Rawls refers favourably to this passage in *A Theory of Justice*, p. 490n.

130. Mill, *The Subjection of Women*, pp. 173-74. See also *Utilitarianism*, pp. 231 ff.

131. Green, *Prolegomena*, p. 221. Green also argues that equal liberty will spur the intellectual development of the gifted. Ibid., p. 278.

132. See Hobhouse, *Morals in Evolution* (Chapman and Hall, London, 1951), pp. 62 ff, 354 ff; Dewey, *The Public and Its Problems*, pp. 149 ff. See also J. Roland Pennock, *Liberal Democracy: Its Merits and Prospects* (Rinehart and Co., New York, 1950), pp. 94-96.

133. See, for example, 'Constitutional Liberty and the Concept of Justice' in Carl J. Friedrich and John W. Chapman (eds.), *NOMOS VI: Justice* (Leiber-Atherton, New York, 1963), pp. 110-18. See also the account of Rawls's moral psychology in §IV.A.3.

134. Rawls, *A Theory of Justice*, p. 105. Although Rawls is referring here specifically to the 'difference principle', he explicitly relates the difference principle to the 'general conception of justice' which justifies an inequality of liberty — or any other social value — when this works out to everyone's benefit. Ibid., pp. 83, 62-63, 247. See §VII.B.1.

135. See Bosanquet: *Ideals*, pp. 193-99, 211; *Some Suggestions in Ethics*, p. 27; *Civilization of Christendom*, p. 363; *The Value and Destiny of the Individual* (Macmillan, London, 1913), pp. 135, 143 ff.

136. Mill, *The Subjection of Women*, pp. 172-73, 218-20. See also *Liberty*, pp. 269, 218; and Ryan, *J.S. Mill*, p. 156.

137. Dewey and Tufts, *Ethics*, pp. 386, 236. See also Dewey, *Democracy and Education*, pp. 86 ff.

138. Rawls, *A Theory of Justice*, pp. 210-11. Rawls's point in this argument is that any theory concerned with maximising value is liable to have significant inegalitarian implications and, thus, he asserts the importance of principles of justice. As should be clear by now, my interpretation of Rawls implies that his own theory seeks to 'maximise development' far more than he seems to think.

## VI  DEMOCRACY

### A.  Protective and Developmental Democracy

After explaining the English notion of 'civil or personal liberty' to his
compatriots (§V.C), Jean-Joseph Mounier went on to note:

> There is another kind of liberty, called political liberty, without
> which the first [civil or personal] cannot endure. Montesquieu
> says that it consists in the conviction of being secure. It would
> perhaps be even better to say that political liberty is the collection
> of means sufficient to guarantee and maintain personal liberty,
> to shelter it as much as possible from the errors and passions of
> those who exercise sovereign power.[1]

In so far as classical liberals are democrats at all, this would seem to be
their main case for democracy. Theirs is what C.B. Macpherson has
called 'protective democracy';[2] political liberty − most importantly
the right to vote − is held to be essential to protect the liberties and
interests of the governed from potentially tyrannical and oppressive
governors. Such a conception of democracy remains dominant to this
day in those usually classified as classical liberals; F.A. Hayek, for
example, reminds us that democracy 'is an ideal worth fighting for
to the utmost, because it is our only protection . . . against tyranny.
Though democracy itself is not freedom . . . it is one of the most important safeguards of freedom.'[3] As the classical liberal sees it, then,
the value of political liberty largely stems from its importance in protecting the all-important civil (or personal) liberties.[4]

To some extent, this 'protective function' of political liberty persists
in modern liberalism. Indeed, Mill's first argument supporting democracy
as 'the ideally best form of government' is that 'the rights and interests
of every or any person are only secure from being disregarded, when
the person interested is himself able, and habitually disposed, to stand
up for them'.[5] Pretty obviously, underlying this defence of suffrage is
some assumption that each is the best judge and guardian of his own
rights and interests or, in Dewey's homely phrase, each knows better
than anyone else 'where the shoe pinches'.[6] Now the importance of this
argument in liberal theory ought not to be underestimated: it again

points to the fundamentally anti-paternalistic perspective of liberals, insisting as they do that normal adult citizens are not dependents or wards of the state (or of anyone else for that matter), and are thus responsible for looking after their own interests.[7] Nevertheless, important as this argument is, it is not the case for democracy dear to the hearts of our modern liberals. As commentators such as Macpherson and Carole Pateman have quite rightly argued, the emphasis of liberals like James Mill on 'protective democracy' gives way in J.S. Mill and those who follow him to advocacy of a 'developmental democracy'. To the modern liberal, the superiority of democracy over other forms of government chiefly rests on its superior ability to encourage the 'self-development of all the members of the society.'[8]

I begin this chapter, then, by examining in just what ways modern liberals have thought democracy, or more particularly, democratic participation, encourages the development of human nature (§B). However, I show in §C that these developmental arguments are not the only way in which the modern liberal theory of human nature enters into their analysis of democracy: in order to have a non-despotic democracy, liberals like Mill, Hobhouse and Bosanquet have insisted on the necessity of a 'spirit of community'. I also take up in §C other issues relating to despotic regimes, including their possible justification (§C.3). Finally, I close in §D by briefly suggesting that Mill (as well as many contemporary writers) generally overestimates the importance of democratic participation in promoting the development of human nature.

## B. The Developmental Case for Democracy

### B.1. Intellectual Development

In what might reasonably be regarded as the canonical modern liberal text on developmental democracy, *Representative Government,* Mill stresses the intellectual benefits of participating in public affairs:

> Notwithstanding the defects of the social system and moral ideas of antiquity, the practice of the dicastery and the ecclesia raised the intellectual standard of an average Athenian citizen far beyond anything of which there is yet an example in any other mass of men, ancient or modern . . . A benefit of the same kind, though far less in degree, is produced on Englishmen of the lower middle class by their liability to be placed on juries and to serve parish offices;

which, though it does not occur to so many, nor is so continuous, nor introduces them to so great a variety of elevated considerations, as to admit of comparison with the public education which every citizen of Athens obtained from her democratic institutions, must make them nevertheless very different beings, in range of ideas and development of faculties, from those who have done nothing in their lives but drive a quill, or sell goods over a counter.[9]

The idea that participation in political affairs is educative or spurs intellectual growth is a pervasive one in modern liberal writings. Green, for instance, claims that only if one has either a direct or indirect role in government — 'by himself acting as a member or by voting for the members of a supreme or provincial assemblies' — can he be an 'intelligent' patriot rather than simply a loyal subject.[10] Hobhouse is more straightforward, telling us that 'the exercise of popular government is itself an education.'[11] And, of course, Dewey was particularly insistent on the educational benefits of democracy; the 'full education' of 'personality', he writes, 'comes only when there is a responsible share on the part of each person, in proportion to capacity, in shaping the aims and policies of the social groups to which he belongs.' And this 'fact', Dewey concludes, 'fixes the significance of democracy'.[12]

We saw in §V.B.2 that all deliberative choice promotes development, so to some extent the argument for political participation is simply an extension of the developmental case of liberty in general. But modern liberals see the educative/developmental case for political participation as more than simply a special case of the argument for free choice. It educates, they suggest, in a way that goes beyond that depicted by the choice and development argument. Thus, for instance, Mill argued that involvement in political affairs was especially stimulating and educative as it 'elevates the mind to large interests and contemplations; the first step out of the narrow bounds of individual and family selfishness, the first opening in the contracted round of daily occupations'.[13] *Political* deliberation thus promotes intellectual development not only because it requires the exercise of the reasoning faculties in making a choice (as does all practical deliberation), but also because it encourages citizens to dwell on subjects that transcend their everyday experience and, so, stretches their intellectual horizon.

Such expansion can occur in two distinct ways. First, merely by entering the political realm the citizen is introduced to a range of ideas and issues which are not encountered in his everyday life. As Mill says in our canonical text, one who participates in politics is introduced to a far wider 'range of ideas' than those 'who have done nothing in their lives but drive a quill, or sell goods over a counter'. This sort of expansion apparently can take place even if one's aim when participating in politics is to advance self-interest. By taking the pursuit of self-interest into the political realm the citizen will face new problems and gain a wider perspective of his own welfare than if, say, he restricts himself to commercial activities. However, Mill suggests a way in which even greater expansion might occur. In the sentence following the passage I quoted, Mill turns to the 'moral part of the instruction afforded by the participation of the private citizen, if even rarely, in public functions'. If, Mill goes on to say, one engages in public affairs with the aim of promoting the common good rather than private interest, one comes to see problems in a new light since one is then 'to be guided, in cases of conflicting claims, by another rule than his own partialities'. Rawls, paraphrasing Mill, maintains that such deliberation 'leads to a larger conception of society and to the development of his intellectual and moral faculties'.[14] When participating in politics in this way, not only does one confront a different range of issues than encountered in everyday life, but one undergoes an expansion in aims and thus gains a new perspective on problems and, in general, the nature of the social order (see §B.2).

Dewey's argument is a bit different. To Dewey, 'democracy' does not simply denote a form of government characterised by the selection of governors through frequent elections in which all, or at least the great majority, of adult citizens have the right to vote. As Dewey understands it, these traditional forms of political democracy are 'expedients' for realising a broader, more democratic way of life and are thus 'not a final end and a final value'.[15] In its wider sense, 'democracy' means for Dewey a type of society characterised by a free exchange of ideas, varied intercourse, and an 'intelligent' attitude towards and within social institutions. The democratic community, in short, is one in which the ideals of intellectual growth and the liberation of individual powers inform all social life and institutions.[16] It is not hard to see, then, how Dewey's democracy is educative (indeed, the claim comes close to being analytic). More difficult, though, is to make out how this provides a special case for the political forms normally associated with democracy. Is there anything *especially* educative about political participation, or is it simply one sort of educative experience, to be placed alongside schools, 'cultural appreciation', work experience, etc.? (See §D.)

Although at times it might seem that Dewey does not think democratic political forms to be especially important or educative, he engages in at least one line of reasoning that does uphold their somewhat special educative status. As we saw at the beginning of this section, Dewey argues that the full education of personality requires that each have a 'responsible share' in 'shaping the aims and policies of the social groups to which he belongs'. In Dewey's eyes, participation in group decision-making both (i) leads one to learn from the perspectives and experiences of others and (ii) to the extent one is willing to take responsibility for the outcomes, the intellect is developed as one comes to forecast outcomes, consider alternatives, etc. '[R]esponsibility as an element in intellectual attitude is . . . the disposition to consider in advance the probable consequences of any projected step and deliberately to accept them: to accept them in the sense of taking them into account, acknowledging them in action, not yielding a mere verbal assent.'[17] Apparently it is the conjunction of these two features — an enrichment induced by the differences of others and an encouragement of responsible attitudes — that leads Dewey to stress the intellectual benefits of collective decision-making. While, as Dewey emphasises, it is not only governmental decision-making that expands and educates in this way, political participation is certainly an instance of a common deliberation that yields a collective decision and is thus a particularly educative experience.

Dewey's focus on responsibility and collective decision-making is important as it provides a way to connect the modern liberal thesis about the developmental benefits of *participation* with *suffrage* (or in some way actually having a voice in the decision-making process). It is imperative for modern liberals to make some such connection, for although most of their arguments are about the happy developmental consequences of participating in political affairs, they want to use such arguments to support a universal adult suffrage (or something very close to it). Consequently, they must somehow argue against the possibility that one might gain the educative benefits of participation (through following political events, forming an opinion about them, etc.) without actually having a voice in how political issues are to be decided. Dewey's 'responsibility argument' suggests one way of doing it: viz. that only by having a 'responsible share' in shaping the group's policies and aims will one reap the full educative benefits of participation. Mill proffers a different argument:

> A person must have a very unusual taste for intellectual exercise in and for itself, who will put himself to the trouble of thought when it is to have no outward effect, or qualify himself for functions

which he has no chance of being allowed to exercise. The only sufficient incitement to mental exertion, in any but a few minds in a generation, is the prospect of some practical use to be made of its results.[18]

It needs to be emphasised that neither Mill nor Dewey argues that the act of voting once every few years is especially educative.[19] The thesis is that voting is a necessary condition for any real interest in politics (Mill) or to gain the full benefits of participation (Dewey). *Participation* and *deliberation*, then, are the prime educative experiences, voting being subsidiary though necessary.

## B.2. Consciousness of Community

Dewey's arguments for the educative benefits of democracy typically make two distinct claims. According to the one that we have been examining, democratic participation promotes the development, particularly the intellectual development, of individuals. But, secondly, and perhaps even more importantly in Dewey's eyes, the exchange of views and communication inherent in democractic participation widens the area of shared interests and values. 'In order to have a large number of values in common', Dewey writes, 'all the members of the group must have an equable opportunity to receive and to take from others. There must be a large variety of shared undertakings and experiences.'[20] In the absence of common undertakings and shared experiences, society tends to split into mutually suspicious classes unable to understand each other's life experiences. As Dewey sees it, then, democratic deliberation increases the *scope and awareness* of commonality; translated into the terms of our analysis in Chapter III, it encourages a conscious like-mindedness, which, we saw, is fundamental to his understanding of community (§III.B.1). This, then, is the basis of Dewey's claim that democracy 'is the idea of community life itself.'[21]

Green proffered a similar sort of argument although, consistent with his focus on organic unity (§III.B.1), he stressed how democratic participation educates the citizen 'to regard the work of the state as a whole, and to transfer to the whole the interest which otherwise his particular experience would lead him to feel only in that part of its work that goes to the maintenance of his own and his neighbour's rights'.[22] Democratic participation thus expands one's intellectual horizon by promoting an awareness of the way in which the state advances the good of all rather than seeing it simply as a device to protect one's private rights and interests. As Green puts it, the active citizen comes to appreciate 'the good which in common with others he derives from the state'.[23] This, of course, is simply another aspect of the Millian educative argument that we explored in the previous section. In so far as the citizen engages in politics with the aim of promoting the common good, not only is his intellectual horizon expanded, but it expands in such a way that he comes to appreciate the unity (be it 'organic' or 'mechanical') of the state and thus becomes cognizant of his status as a member of a larger community.

It has been said that Bosanquet's conception of democracy differs significantly from Green's and, indeed, all other modern liberals.[24] Unlike Green, and even more Mill and Dewey, it might seem that Bosanquet does not endorse a deliberative democracy giving rise to a consciousness of communal unity. If we recall Bosanquet's theory of the 'common mind or will' (§II.D.2), we remember that he believes that those who share a common will have many leading ideas in common and, indeed, '[t]heir minds are similarly or correlatively organized'. This common mental organisation of members of a community is the psychological basis of Bosanquet's theory of the 'general will'. The 'general will' of a community is its 'system of dominant ideas' implied by its collective life. As such, the 'general will' cannot be identified with any single vote or expression of public opinion at any particular time. And Bosanquet is also very clear that no individual, 'not the greatest statesman or historical philosopher, has in his mind, even in theory, much less as a practical object, the real development in which his community is moving'. The concrete manifestation of the general will thus is not to be found in the consciousness of either the masses or of great men, but in the laws and institutions which inform the life of a particular community.[25]

All this supports the claim that Bosanquet's theory places a great deal of weight on unconscious unity and, consequently, puts less stress than, say, Dewey's, on deliberative democracy as a way to promote consciousness of unity. More than that, though, because settled institutions rather than expressions of popular opinion are more apt to be bona fide manifestations of the general will, Bosanquet adamantly opposes any move towards plebiscitary democracy. Such democracy, he argues, attempts to move away from 'the organised life, institutions, and selected capacity of a nation to that nation regarded as an aggregate of isolated individuals'.[26] Having said that much, however, it needs to be emphasised that Bosanquet's theory does ascribe significant roles to both consciousness or unity and political deliberation.

To begin with, we need to realise that Bosanquet's thesis is that a great deal of the basis of social unity is unconscious, *not* that members of a community are unaware of the fact that they are unified and share a common good. Indeed, Bosanquet asserts that a 'consciousness of connection' is necessary to the formation of a general will. Moreover, following Green, Bosanquet insists that 'either [taking] part in the work of the State, or at least be[ing] familiar with such work, through interest in his fellows' share of it' is necessary if one is to go beyond simple inclusion in the social mind and 'be in some degree aware of the connection between its place and the whole – of the appercipient structure to which it belongs.'[27] But, as I said in the third chapter, Bosanquet not only asserts that members of a community are conscious of their unity, but that 'the general will is a process continuously emerging from the relatively unconscious into reflective consciousness' (§III.B.1). As Bosanquet depicts it, the dominant system of social ideas – the general will – 'is never quite harmonious' and so stands in need of constant rationalisation, i.e. harmonisation (see §I.D.2). Now while this too is accomplished to some extent unconsciously via the clash of interests and viewpoints within the community, it also occurs through 'reflective discussion'. Discussion and deliberation thus serve an important function in interpreting just what the general will is and, through criticism, producing a more coherent system of social ideas. What Bosanquet really wants to stress in regard to deliberation and criticism is that they should be an ongoing process in one's life and not 'a single casual reflective judgement', i.e. an occasional act of voting. Consequently, Bosanquet insists that it is regarding matters with which we are most intimately acquainted and in our own locality that the process of criticism and reformulation will be most effective, and it is in this way that the general will emerges into consciousness.[28]

This emphasis on the developmental consequences of participation in local affairs is, of course, a central theme in a great deal of modern liberal-democratic writings, particularly Mill's. Indeed, because it affords a greater opportunity for continuous involvement by a large number of people in public affairs, Mill maintained that 'local administrative institutions are the chief instrument' for the 'nourishment of public spirit and the development of intelligence' of citizens.[29] We saw in Chapter III (§C.4) how local public spirit might spill over into or connect up with a more extensive national public spirit. However, it is less clear how local participation would contribute to consciousness of one's unity with the larger community. If anything, it would seem to have considerable potential for inducing a narrow, provincial outlook. Of course this is not a damning objection to such participation; it may merely provide a good reason for using Green's life as our model and participating in national as well as local affairs so as to counteract any narrowing effects of the latter.[30]   However, organicists such as Hobhouse and Bosanquet apparently resist this idea; properly understood, involvement in 'local' affairs should, they believe, lead to a consciousness of a wider communal unity. 'The modern State', Hobhouse points out, 'is a vast and complex organism.' If the citizen begins with those issues that affect him directly, 'the affairs of his trade union or, again, of his chapel', he 'comes into touch with wider questions — with a Factory Bill or an Education Bill'.[31] And in dealing with these issues, Hobhouse goes on to say, the citizen is not acting as a lone individual but as a member of an 'intermediate organization' which provides a focus for his involvement as well as a sense of efficacy. Now while this is not, strictly speaking, an instance of involvement in 'local affairs', the same principle would seem to apply. If the affairs of a community really do form a complex network, it is plausible to argue that intelligent involvement at one level provides a perspective for insight into the organic unity of the nation's life. Ideally, at any rate, concern with affairs that most directly affect one's life leads to increasingly remote issues, demonstrating the interconnection and complexity of the community's affairs.

### B.3. Communal Sentiments

As I said in the third chapter, modern liberals have not been satisfied with conceptions of community premised simply on cognizance of communal unity. Again and again they are drawn to some notion of affective ties among members of a community. This attraction is especially manifest in their developmental arguments for democracy. If we return once again to our canonical text, we will see that Mill immediately follows his educative arguments for political participation with a thesis about the growth of social sentiments. Not only does one who engages in politics with a view towards promoting the commonweal gain in 'understanding' but he also 'is made to feel himself one of the public'. Such participation is thus said to be a 'school of public spirit' giving rise to an 'unselfish . . . identification with the public'.[32] While no doubt these comments are open to differing interpretations, it would appear that Mill has in mind here the sort of affective communal bonding that I have called 'patriotism', i.e. feelings of unity with an abstract whole (§III.C.2). And this would seem a reasonable enough extension of the consciousness of the unity/common good argument: as one becomes aware of oneself as a member of a more inclusive public united by a common good, one may well develop feelings of loyalty and devotion to the whole. Now what is especially interesting here is that, despite both the obviousness and plausibility of this sort of argument, it is not that upon which our modern liberals (including perhaps Mill himself) mainly rely. As I suggested in the third chapter, modern liberals seek a fairly intense form of community and thus are driven from patriotism to sympathy/fraternity (§III.C.3). Green is very clear about this. After advancing the claim that democratic participation induces an awareness of connection and a common good, he immediately adds that this is not sufficient to render patriotism a 'passion'. For really strong sentiments of unity to arise, Green believes that one must feel bound to one's compatriots 'by ties analogous to those which bind him to his family, ties derived from a common-dwelling place with its associations, from common memories, traditions and customs, and from common ways of feeling and thinking which a common language and still more a common literature embodies'.[33]

It is not Green, however, but Hobhouse (and, oddly enough, Mill) who is most explicit in tying the rise of this type of social feeling to democratic government. According to Hobhouse's *Democracy and Reaction*, democratic self-government 'is the natural instrument of a growing sense of social solidarity and the appropriate organ of a stirring national life'.[34] As Hobhouse understands it, the distinction between democratic and undemocratic governments is that between governments that represent the whole community and those in which one part of the community directs a government that is apt to be seen as alien and hostile by the rest.[35] Mill — whose writings on democracy rely on both 'patriotism' and 'fraternity' — saw undemocratic governments in a similar light, telling us that those who are denied a voice in government are prone to be either 'malcontents' or absorbed in private affairs.[36] In neither case are they likely to develop that public spirit/sympathy with their fellows which, Mill was convinced, is nurtured by participation in public affairs. In contradistinction, democratic government endeavours to break down the aristocratic distinction between rulers and ruled and so, as Hobhouse says, generates 'mutual confidence' and 'charity', or as Mill would say, '*fellow*-feeling', among citizens.[37] All this, of course, is in the spirit of Hobhouse's and Mill's analyses of sympathy, according to which class divisions inhibit the perception of commonality upon which sympathetic sentiments are held to rest (see §III.C.3). Democratic government is thus said to promote fellow feeling as all citizens share a common, and presumably equal, political status. (But things are a bit more complicated; see §C.3 below.)

## C. Community, Democracy and Despotism

### C.1. The Communal Foundations of Democracy

Although Hobhouse maintains that democratic institutions and practices encourage the growth of solidaric sentiments, he does not believe that they are likely to create a community where none exists. A properly functioning democracy, he tells us, presupposes a principle of 'community'. 'A spirit rather than a formula, it means that all differences within the body which it animates are differences within and subordinate to a deeper and more comprehensive agreement, and that within this agreement no section is left out.'[38] In the absence of this spirit of solidarity and unity (as Green put it, 'that impalpable congeries of the hopes and fears of a people, bound together by common interests and sympathy'),[39] Hobhouse concludes that the minority are apt to look upon the majority as an alien, oppressive power, even in a democratic regime. If the state is split 'into two (or more) portions by race, religion, colour, nationality, or whatever it may be', and if one is a standing majority and the other a perpetual minority, the consequence is the same as a constitutionally oligarchic regime. 'We do not govern ourselves', Hobhouse has the minority saying, 'because we are not one with you.'[40]

Hobhouse's principle or spirit of community shares some important similarities with Bosanquet's theory of the general will, a doctrine of which Hobhouse is the leading critic. According to Bosanquet, because we share a common life with others in our community, in order to arrive at our 'real' or 'rational' will (§V.B.3) not only must 'what we want at any moment . . . be corrected and amended by what we want at all other moments', but it also must be corrected so 'as to harmonise it with what others want, which involves an application of the same process to them'. Now just why this should be so is not clear; if the minds of members of the same community are *similarly* organised, it would seem that the consequence ought to be that the process of rationalisation in each will yield similar sorts of 'real wills', not that (as Bosanquet maintains), everyone's rationalisation depends on the rationalisation of everyone else. (The claim of *correlative* organisation may help here: if the ideas of each are closely correlated with all one's fellows, then a change in one should produce changes throughout the system.) Leaving aside these not inconsiderable difficulties, however, the upshot of Bosanquet's doctrine is that 'when any considerable degree of such correction and amendment had been gone through, our own will would return to us in a shape in which we should not know it again'. And this despite the fact that 'every detail would be a necessary inference from the whole of wishes and resolutions which we actually cherish'.[41]

This doctrine has often been deemed totalitarian, and not without some reason. As John Plamenatz notes, it implies 'that the individual, when he appears to be forced to obey the law against his apparent wish, is really being forced to do what he wishes, and is thus a consenting party to all enforcements of the law'.[42] Hobhouse is quite right to insist against 'Dr Bosanquet' that while it may well be one's duty to obey the law even when opposed to it, that does not mean one is not really opposed to it.[43] Acknowledging all that, however, if we take a sympathetic look at Bosanquet's underlying concerns, we will see that his theory of the general will is by no means as totalitarian as it seems.

Bosanquet's point of departure is an insistence that even in democratic regimes the individual *can be* oppressed. However much 'self-government' has replaced 'despotism', Bosanquet insists that 'it is flying in the face of experience to suggest that the average individual self, as he exists in you and me, is *ipso facto* satisfied, and at home, in all the acts of public power which is supposed to represent him'.[44] But although the individual is capable of rebelling against the government, and the majority capable of tyrannising over the minority, healthy polities are not characterised by rebellion and repression. And, ultimately, the reason they are not is that in a healthy political community the laws and institutions are expressions of the values, ideals, aims, etc. which inform the life of the community and the persons in it. Because in such communities law is ultimately an expression of things 'actually cherished' by the individual — and this includes the good of his fellows to whom he is bound by social sentiments — he can recognise the law as 'his own' even when as a member of the minority he opposed it. Viewed in this way (which admittedly bypasses its more extreme claims), one aim of Bosanquet's theory of the general will is much the same as Hobhouse's principle of community: viz. to explain why, in a healthy polity, minorities do not perceive themselves as oppressed by alien powers.

The upshot of both Hobhouse's and Bosanquet's analyses is that democratic institutions are not sufficient to avoid oligarchy, or even despotism. In the absence of communal bonds arising out of a common life, government is apt to be simply the vehicle of one group's will ruling over that of another. This sort of analysis provides an insight into Mill's fear of the tyranny of the majority, a fear which in the main our other modern liberals do not share.[45] It is at least plausible to suggest that Mill alone was so concerned about the possibility of tyrannical class legislation because, in contrast to our other modern liberals, he perceived little 'spirit of community' informing the society in which he lived. Thus, for example, in his essay on the 'Claims of Labour' he points to 'that *sourde* animosity which is universal in this country towards the whole class of employers, in the whole class of the employed'. And, on the other side, he indicates a general lack of 'sociability' and understanding of the ways and feelings of workers by others. Mill thus recognises 'the need of greater fellow-feeling and community of interest' between the employed and employers, so that they 'have the feelings of friendly allies, not of hostile rivals whose gain is each other's loss'.[46] And, indeed, his essay on Tocqueville evinces a real faith that democratic institutions will help overcome these class barriers and so spur 'sentiments of philanthropy and compassion'.[47] But he certainly thought that such developments lie in the future, and in the meantime a democratic England was in danger of class legislation. It was, I think, to a great extent for this reason that Mill was so enthusiastic about Hare's scheme for proportional representation as it at least guaranteed minority representation in the legislature.[48]

However, although Mill acknowledged that the legislative despotism of the majority was a genuine danger, he insists that the really formidable danger of modern civilisation is a 'tyranny over the mind'.[49] Any reader of *Liberty* will recognise this theme, stressing as it does what Mill saw as an increasing conformity and mediocrity threatening individuality in modern societies. In *Democracy in America* Tocqueville held that this trend towards homogeneity was a consequence of democratic equality but, as Alan Ryan points out, Mill thought Tocqueville mistaken. 'The evil is not in the preponderance of a democratic class, but of any class.' As Mill saw it, 'whenever any variety of human nature becomes preponderant in a community, it imposes upon the rest of society its own type; forcing all, either to submit to it, or to imitate it.'[50] Thus Mill argues that in a commercial country like England, which is dominated by the middle class, the agricultural and learned classes play an important role in counteracting the influence of the dominant class.

On the face of it, Mill thus seems caught in a dilemma: the rise of fraternal feelings among citizens (which seems important in avoiding tyranny) requires that class divisions be broken down, but this very trend towards similarity poses the threat of a conformist society and so he seems to need a multiplicity of classes to protect diversity. The roots of Mill's apparent dilemma extend to the heart of the modern liberal theory of man, viz. the unresolved tension between the dynamics of fraternal community and individuality (§III.E). As I argued in the third chapter, modern liberals ultimately seem to rely on a mix or balance of individuality and fraternity, and this certainly seems to be the case here with Mill. While he opposes extreme 'impassable' class barriers which render impossible any sympathy between classes, we have also seen that he does not favour total abolition of class distinctions, at least in so far as they are premised on different modes of life.[51] Mill's way out of the apparent dilemma, then, is to advocate a measure of fraternity (and similarity), but one that stops well short of a homogeneous society. And there is no reason to think that this is not a perfectly adequate response to the dual threat of tyranny. In order to avoid a fragmented polity liable to the legislative despotism of one portion over the other, Mill's (or Hobhouse's) theory requires only sufficient commonality and fraternity so that all citizens perceive themselves as 'friends' or 'fellow countrymen' and thus are not divided by 'jealousy' and 'mutual antipathies'.[52] It is by no means obvious that this extent of commonality is inconsistent with a great deal of individual and local diversity, thus avoiding mass society's 'tyranny of mind'.

Rawls appears to believe that even less 'spirit of community' is required. In his recent essay on 'Social Unity and Primary Goods', he seems to accept the possibility of a just − non-despotic − 'society divided into two parts, the members of which affirm different and opposing ways of life'. Rawls in fact goes so far as to 'assume that those in one group appear to regard the way of life of the other with distaste and aversion, if not contempt. These conceptions of the good are incommensurable because their final ends and aspirations are so diverse, their specific content so different, that no common basis for judgement can be found.' In such a society, Rawls concludes, 'social unity is secured by an allegiance to certain public principles of justice, *if indeed it can be secured at all*'. Rawls's main point here is that social unity does not require agreement on a particular conception of the good and, so, he believes, is consistent with individuality. But surely, given his own moral psychology − and in particular the place of fellow feeling in giving rise to a devotion to just principles (§IV.A.3) − Rawls is more than justified in wondering whether such a society will even attain the extent of unity implied simply by 'allegiance to certain public principles of justice'. Without a sense of partnership and fellow feeling, it is not clear that such allegiance could arise. Some 'spirit of community' seems essential.[53]

## C.2. Despotic and Democratic Restraint

I have focused here on 'democratic despotism' so as to bring out the

dual relation in modern liberal theory between community and democracy. Democratic institutions (and particularly political participation)
are held to induce a perception of community and communal sentiments, but some degree of community seems required to avoid a despotic democracy, i.e. a democratic regime in which one class or group
exercises the power of government and rules over others in a way that
promotes the dominant group's interest. By this point it should come as
no surprise that according to modern liberalism all forms of despotism
— democratic or undemocratic — stunt development. Even 'benevolent
despotisms', i.e. non-representative governments in which the rulers
stand in a tutelary relation to the people,[54] are typically held to thwart
growth (but see §C.3). The arguments here are essentially extensions of
those for equal liberty which we have already examined (§§V.D.2, 3),
so I will not repeat them. Suffice it to say that once again liberals like
Mill, Green, Hobhouse and Dewey argue that *everyone's* development is
thwarted in a despotic regime. Those *ruled over*, says Mill, are apt to
develop lethargic-apathetic personalities. In a similar vein, Dewey indicates that submission to 'despotic power' produces 'slavishness',
and Hobhouse maintains that such 'subordination' saps 'vitality' and
'energy' (§IV.B.3).[55] On the other side, Mill insists that having *power
over others* is corrupting, leading to egoism, self-glory, etc. As Dewey
put it, 'The final obstacle in the way of any aristocratic rule is that in
the absence of an articulate voice on the part of the masses, the best
do not and cannot remain the best, the wise cease to be wise.'[56]

However, in one important respect the case for democratic over
despotic government differs from the argument for equal liberty. For
one of the features of democratic government is that, like all government, the citizen's actions are often restrained by the decisions of
others. If subjection to the rule of others produces 'slavishness' in non-
democratic governments, why does it fail to produce it when one has
voted against the government imposing the restrictions? Now as Mill
sees it, what is unique about democratic government is that the citizen
'feels himself under no other external restraint than the necessities of
nature, or *mandates of society which he has his share in imposing*' and
which, if he thinks them wrong, may publicly dissent and endeavour to
alter.[57] Mill is concerned here with democratic institutions, but the
argument goes to the heart of his theory of human nature. According
to the self-discipline solution to the problem of discipline, constraints
on the development of capacities that are self-imposed or are perceived
as just or right are not pathology-producing (§IV.C.1). Mill's thesis
about democratic institutions, then, is that they can impose constraints

without pathologies because the constrained person believes he has had a 'share' in imposing them (and if he disagrees with them he is at liberty to work to have them altered). It is in this sense that citizens in a democracy can, at least ideally, be said to be self-governing. But clearly alone this will not do, for an individual may feel oppressed even in a democratic regime. And this again points to the fundamental importance of a 'spirit of community' or a 'general will' as a foundation of democracy.[58] As Dewey argued, a person is not apt to perceive constraints as oppressive and arbitrary if they are in some way understood 'as expressions of a whole to which he himself belongs'.[59] It is thus not democracy alone, but a democracy founded upon community that allows the imposition of restraints without pathologies.

As I argued in Chapter IV (§C.4), constraints on development do not pose the same difficulty for Rawls as for our other modern liberals since he sees pathologies arising from inadequate *lives* rather than from inadequate expression of *capacities*. However, it nevertheless is the case that if some restraint seriously affects one's life prospects, it may prevent one from forming an adequate life plan and, thus, endanger self-respect. Moreover, Rawls acknowledges that all governments do indeed 'affect permanently men's prospects in life' and so, it would seem, might harm self-respect in doing so. However, Rawls indicates that a constitutional democratic regime will not undermine self-respect because such a regime is *just* and will be perceived to be so. Like Mill (§IV.C.1), Rawls believes that constraints understood to be just do not pose a threat to healthy development; indeed, quite to the contrary, his moral psychology postulates that institutions and principles perceived as just will become the objects of feelings of devotion.[60] Now, it is enlightening to pause here and consider just why Rawls thinks democratic institutions are just, for I think we can see that to a very large extent indeed, his theory of justice is premised on his theory of human nature. Let me explain.

Rawls's well-known argument supporting his two principles of justice takes the form of a social contract: purely self-interested persons, meeting behind a 'veil of ignorance' (according to which they know no specific facts about themselves or their society), agree to Rawls's two principles of justice over several alternative moral theories. (Most relevant for our present purposes is his first principle of justice, according to which all are to have equal basic liberties, including the rights to vote and run for office.) Prima facie it would seem that the parties to Rawls's 'original position' are rational egoists: they are concerned only with reaching an agreement that best advances their good (as far as they know it) with no direct interest in the good of the other parties.[61] However, one of the things we have discovered about modern liberalism is that one's good is intimately bound to the development of human nature in one's self and one's fellows, and this is certainly so in Rawls. According to Rawls, one of the main aims of the parties in the original position is to secure their own self-respect. As he puts it, they 'would wish to avoid at almost any cost the social conditions that would undermine self-respect'. Now, knowing the Aristotelian Principle (§I.C.2) and other facts of moral psychology, the parties realise that their self-respect will suffer if they do not form a plan that refines their unique natures. And so they will seek to ensure that they are able to pursue such a plan, i.e. they will insist on liberty to develop their individuality. Moreover — and this is essential for our present concern — Rawls insists that an inequality of either civil or political rights will be 'humiliating and destructive of self-esteem' of those with the lesser liberty. Knowing this, all parties have a strong reason to insist that they be granted at least as much civil and political liberty as others. However, Rawls also says that the parties to the original position know that their self-respect depends upon their plans being encouraged by others. And as we have already seen (§V.D.2), that means that they know they must secure the self-respect of their fellows, for those who are not confident of their own worth are grudging in their affirmation of that of others. So not only does each party have a reason to want equal political rights for himself, but he has reason to want the same for others.[62]

My point here, then, is that because Rawls's theory of human nature is so important in the derivation of his principles of justice, the claim that democratic institutions are just implies that they are consistent with the demands of human nature, at least to the extent that they encourage self-respect in everyone. The relation between self-respect and justice in Rawls's theory is thus twofold: (i) Rawls's principles of justice are explicitly designed to promote self-respect and, as a more general principle, (ii) Rawls seems to argue that constraints imposed by institutions recognised as just do not damage the self-respect of those so constrained. It would seem, however, that (ii) is only plausible given something like (i), for if the principles of justice thwarted self-respect, their perception as just would not alter their damaging nature. All we might reasonably say is that even in the absence of (i), the perception that principles are just might act to minimise the harm done to self-respect.

### C.3. Two Limitations on the Case for Democracy

Before turning a more critical eye to the modern liberal case for democracy, we ought to be cognizant of two potential limitations on the modern liberal commitment to democracy: (i) the possibility of a legitimate 'benevolent despotism' for 'uncivilised' peoples and (ii) the (sometimes) competing claim of competency.

(i)   As Ryan (and many others) has noted of Mill, he straightforwardly asserted that '[d]espotism is a legitimate mode of government in dealing with barbarians'.[63] But this is not a Millian idiosyncrasy. Hobhouse acknowledges that 'a semi-despotic system like that of our Crown colonies' may be best for some peoples, and Bosanquet asserts that parliamentary government is not likely to be superseded 'for civilised peoples'.[64] Indeed even Dewey, who is certainly the most adamant democrat of all modern liberals here studied, seems to approve of a 'paternal' government towards 'our alien visitors' (i.e. immigrants).[65] Dewey's use of 'paternal' here is suggestive, for it points to a structural parallel between the main modern liberal argument for 'benevolent despotism' and the case for paternalism that we considered earlier (§V.B.5). Again, Mill, who devoted so much attention to the problems of democracy and representative government, is clearest. According to him, 'a people in a state of savage independence, in which every one lives for himself, exempt, unless by fits, from any external control, is practically incapable of making any progress in civilization, until it [i.e. the people] has learnt to obey'. And to do that, 'the constitution of the government must be nearly, or quite, despotic'.[66] As Maurice Cranston notes, 'Mill nowhere offers a precise criterion for determining when a country is "ripe for democratic government" ', but the whole direction of his political theory indicates that a significant number in the community must have come 'to appreciate the value of reason, liberty and toleration' and 'have accustomed itself to the rule of law'.[67] In short, Mill sees a non-representative, tutelary government as legitimate if (a) the population does not generally possess the character and intellectual traits that are necessary to obtain the developmental benefits of democratic government and (b) the despotic government can help provide these conditions. Given all Mill says about the typical pathological consequences of non-democratic government, we might be a little surprised that Mill believes that (b) holds in a good number of cases. Presumably, as in the case for paternalism, the claim is that (non-democratic) coercive restraints are not as damaging to those who have little in the way of rational self-control or, even if such constraints do some damage, it is outweighed by the developmental benefits.

On the face of it, Hobhouse seems to reject the idea that there are substantial psychological prerequisites for the proper functioning of democratic government. Those who insist that the people are too lazy or ignorant for democracy, he tells us, forget that '[t]he exercise of popular government is itself an education'. In order to justify a non-democratic government, '[t]here must be a well-grounded view that political incapacity is so deep-rooted that the extension of political rights would tend only to facilitate undue influence by the less scrupulous sections of the more capable part of the people.' Hobhouse's main concern here is with the self-protective, not the developmental, case for democracy (§A): if as a matter of fact the extension of political rights tends only to increase oppression and exploitation, the self-protection case is obviously undermined. Yet Hobhouse is explicit that self-protection is only one side of democracy; the other side of the democratic principle assumes an ability of citizens to enter into a common life and take an interest in the common good. '*Where and in so far as this assumption definitely fails, there is no case for democracy.*' Like Mill, Hobhouse believes that a people for whom this assumption does not hold can still progress 'but it must depend on the number of those who . . . advance knowledge or "civilize life through the discoveries of art" or form a narrow but effective public opinion in support of liberty and order'. And, Hobhouse is clear, this may well be accomplished in a non-democratic government.[68]

None of this implies that modern liberals are all committed to 'benevolent despotisms' for the 'uncivilised'. It does imply, though, that in so far as (a) their case for democracy rests on its developmental benefits and (b) they postulate intellectual, character or social preconditions for these benefits to accrue[69], their case will not apply to societies — or perhaps groups within a society — which do not meet the preconditions. Again: in so far as modern liberals hold that a certain degree of communal awareness is necessary for a really healthy democracy, the case for democracy in societies lacking this awareness will be much weaker. It does not necessarily follow, however, that modern liberals advocate some form of paternalistic government for these societies. As Hobhouse suggests, the justification of non-democratic government may require undermining the self-protection argument as well as the developmental one; or it might be contended that in the absence of a communal foundation, a constitutional regime with an extensively circumscribed majoritarian rule might suffice. In any event, if it is denied — as Dewey very often seems to — that a 'despotic' rule can really promote development, the developmental case for a benevolent despotism cannot, as it were, get off the ground. The important point, though, is that advocating a paternalistic non-democratic government under some conditions is not at all inconsistent with the developmental case for democracy; indeed, given the presuppositions of the case, it is not surprising that some modern liberals have advocated it.

(ii) In my discussion of democratic and despotic constraints, I indicated that the main argument in favour of democracy was essentially an extension of the case for equal liberty. Democracy is seen as a form of equality. As such, it is reasonable to assume that the modern liberal case for democracy endorses an equality of political rights. But as we all know, Mill advocated a system of 'plural' votes; indeed, as Macpherson quite rightly points out, Mill thought it a positive good, not just a necessary evil, that the 'mentally superior' be awarded extra votes.[70] Certainly this is an exception to his general democratic egalitarianism. However, what is often overlooked is that Mill renders this exception consistent with his developmental arguments for liberty by making a corresponding exception to his psychological theory. Whereas, for example, Rawls assumes that an inequality of political liberty generally has the same destructive consequences for the development of social interest and civic friendship as does unequal civil liberty, Mill disagrees.[71] In Mill's view, what is crucial is having a voice in the management of common affairs, but it need not be an equal voice:

> Entire exclusion from a voice in the common concerns, is one thing: the concession to others of a more potential voice, *on the ground of greater capacity for the management of the joint interests*, is another. The two things are not merely different, they are incommensurable. Every one has a right to feel insulted by being made a nobody, and stamped as of no account at all. No one but a fool, and only a fool of a peculiar description, feels offended by the acknowledgment that there are others whose opinion, and even whose wish, is entitled to greater consideration than his.[72]

Regardless of what one thinks of Mill's psychological insight, the important point is that he explicitly argues that the psychodynamics that render unequal civil liberty so pernicious do not apply to political rights. By postulating an exception to his general psychological principles, Mill clears the way for an inequality of votes.

But that does not explain why Mill was attracted to plural voting in the first place. It is clear that Mill thought plural voting to have a number of benefits, including the promotion of excellence through institutional recognition of the importance of education and helping to prevent 'class legislation of the uneducated'.[73] However, as indicated in the above quotation, Mill's main justification of unequal votes was that some possess 'greater capacity for the management of joint interests'. Since Mill conceives the polity as a sort of joint enterprise association aiming at a common good – he compares it to a business partnership – he insists that it is no affront to justice to give a greater voice to those more adept at managing common affairs.[74] Interestingly, Rawls also seems somewhat attracted to this view.[75] Accepting – as do all our modern liberals – that political activity ought in the main to be directed at securing the common good, he also appears open to the possibility that some may be more competent in attaining this good. And so he admits that, in principle, a case for plural voting can be made out. Given all this, it seems plausible to conclude that Rawls's ultimate insistence on an equality of political rights stems from his conviction that the psychodynamics that render unequal civil rights so harmful to development apply here as well.

In so far, then, as Mill's commitment to political competence results in his espousal of plural votes, that commitment would seem to result in his theory's being less than fully democratic. Now the most obvious way for a liberal-democrat to avoid Mill's position is to deny, as Dennis Thompson says Dewey and Hobhouse do, that some are especially competent in general political affairs. Such 'citizenship theorists', Thompson says, 'do not assert that there can be no experts in public administration. They mean that on questions of the broad direction politics should take, such as those decisions presented to voters, all men should be treated equally able (or unable) to judge.'[76] However, it does not seem that the democrat need really reject the idea that some are more politically (as opposed to administratively) competent than others. Indeed, as Montesquieu understood it, 'The principle of democracy is corrupted not only when the spirit of equality is extinct, but likewise when they [the citizens] fall into a spirit of extreme equality, and when each citizen would fain be upon a level with those whom he has chosen to command him.'[77] Less radically, some democratic theorists have acknowledged that while *domination* has no place in a democratic order, political *leadership* does. Whereas one who dominates others, either through threats of force or more subtle sorts of conditioning, suppresses the autonomy and critical faculties of his followers, '[t]he followers of a leader accept his leadership willingly, not against their will and not automatically (i.e. as automatons)'.[78] More than that, although the political leader formulates policies, devises political strategies, etc., the followers do not abandon their critical faculties; while they may give special weight to the judgement and exhortations of their leaders, they do so with 'their eyes open' and subject to the proviso that the leader's authoritative position depends on their continuing evaluation of his performance.

Mill looks (as I think do Hobhouse and Green) to this sort of leadership to secure political competence moreso than to plural voting. Thus he tells us that the 'honour and glory of the average man' is to follow the lead of the wise or defer to their judgement.[79] However, when arguing that the average citizen should follow the lead of an intellectual elite, Mill never indicates that the masses are 'mindless' and so ought to abandon their own judgement in favour of that of the elite.[80] Quite to the contrary, Mill's proposal is *not* for 'the blind submission of dunces to men of knowledge, but the intelligent deference of those who know much, to those who know more'.[81] And as David Spitz rightly notes, 'There is never the suggestion in Mill that if the average man does not voluntarily follow the initiative of intellectually eminent men, he must be compelled to do so'.[82] Mill thus only endorses the average man's following the wiser when he does so voluntarily and 'with his eyes open'. Indeed, not only are these the necessary conditions for intelligent and non-pathological followers, but as Hobhouse argues, 'The perfection of leadership itself lies in securing the willing, convinced, open-eyed support of the mass'.[83]

## D. Development, Politics and Education

I have tried to stress in this chapter that development through political participation is only one of the ways in which modern liberals' account of human nature enters into their theory of democracy. As I have argued, the modern liberal thesis concerning the preconditions for non-despotic democracy draws heavily on the notion of community, especially in so far as community derives from perceived commonalities. Nevertheless, as I indicated at the outset, it has been the developmental case for participation in politics which has attracted the most attention. Indeed, I do not think it would be going too far to say modern liberals' developmental theory of human nature is typically associated as much, or more, with their case for democracy than with that for liberty. However, there are at least two grounds for concluding that political participation is not as critical for promoting development as all this suggests.

(i) First, even if we accept its main claims, the developmental case for democracy establishes the importance of participating in *public* affairs, not necessarily *political* ones. Bosanquet — often accused of being something of a state worshipper — recognised that political action was but a subset of public activity. 'Public', as he uses it, denotes 'those functions and interests that are more than private, and demand in some way the best attention of the community.' Within that class, he goes on to tell us, we can distinguish 'the functions which are strictly political from those which might rather be described as social or public without being political'.[84] In a similar vein, Mill argues that in 'an advanced stage of civilisation' many services 'necessary or important to society' can be performed 'by voluntary associations, or by the public indiscriminately'.[85] But if this is so, participation in political affairs is just one way in which the citizen can transcend his daily experiences and take up the perspective of the common good. Involvement in non-political communal affairs would thus seem able to provide that sense of membership in a larger public and feelings of unity that liberals such as Mill attribute to political participation. Indeed, membership in a voluntary organisation may well be more apt to draw on any special expertise of the citizen than would the normal course of political debate, thus engendering a more intelligent and enthusiastic participation. In any event, the modern liberal developmental case for democracy does tend to slide rather too quickly from the benefits of participation in communal affairs to political action.

But Bosanquet goes on to argue that not even 'direct public action' is necessary to be a good citizen. More than his fellow modern liberals, Bosanquet has a deep appreciation of the complexity of the life of a modern community — and the corresponding diversity of individualised development. Thus, in contrast to Rawls (whose theory has been said to be impregnated by an ideal of a 'public-spirited citizen who prizes political activity and service to others as among the chief goods of life'),[86] Bosanquet insists that 'the duties of citizenship will not necessarily drag us out of private life into politics, administration, or philanthropy'. Indeed, Bosanquet believes that 'to expand direct public or political action over our whole lives' would narrow rather than widen them. But that does not mean that Bosanquet thinks communal consciousness unimportant. Rather, given his perception of the community as a co-operative enterprise in which each has functions (one's station and its duties), Bosanquet maintains that in modern communities such consciousness stems from understanding 'our whole lives in the light of citizen ideas, in the light of the common good'. Although direct public action is not to be disparaged — indeed 'it may well be that everyone ought at least to be prepared to participate in such functions if the occasion should arise' — it need not be a central concern of most citizens in a healthy modern community.[87]

(ii) Although Bosanquet's distinction between public and political affairs seems sound, it is reasonable to doubt his thesis that consciousness of unity will arise in the absence of participation in overtly public affairs. Of all the modern liberal claims linking participation and development, that connecting participation in public (of course, they usually say 'political') affairs with perception of community seems most compelling. Much less persuasive is what appears to be the central Millian claim: viz. that political participation is a major force behind intellectual growth. Thompson, I think, is quite right in objecting that 'Mill offers little reason to believe that for most citizens this general intellectual education is a likely result of political participation.'[88] To the extent that the aim is to spur intellectual growth, schemes for improved public education are apt to be far more useful. (Moreover, as Green argued, not only can education induce a more intelligent understanding of the public interest, but a common education tends to mitigate class differences and so induce sentiments of unity.)[89] In this light, the emphasis of Green and his followers on educational reform (and their relative lack of attention to the problems of democracy) is not only understandable but also reasonable: if the object is to develop the intelligence of the 'masses', the provision of education — both for children and adults — would seem a much more efficacious strategy than encouraging political participation.[90] Dewey can be understood in a similar way. While, to be sure, he was an insistent proponent of democracy, we have already seen that 'political forms' did not loom large in his understanding of it. More than anything else, Dewey's democracy focused on education and to a large extent formal education. Indeed, it is no accident that he is remembered today more as an educational than a political theorist.

Let me emphasise that I am not denying that the modern liberal theory of human nature provides a developmental case for democracy. Rather, my point is that contemporary writers on 'developmental democracy' and political participation — drawing especially on Mill — give inordinate weight to the role of political democracy in promoting development, particularly intellectual development. To some extent this overemphasis stems from our modern liberals: although Mill certainly did not ignore educational reforms, his writings stress political participation. And Hobhouse says very little about education.[91] Not only, though, are political affairs not the whole of public affairs, but it seems doubtful that the modern liberal theory of man warrants the weight given by Mill and Hobhouse to participation in public affairs. Formal education — and as we shall see in the next chapter, perhaps 'industrial democracy' — would seem far more effective in bringing about the sort of development modern liberals envisage. Again, this is not to say that democratic participation has no place at all in promoting development, but it seems hard to sustain the central role which is often ascribed to it.

## Notes

1. Jean-Joseph Mounier quoted in Walter Simon (ed.), *French Liberalism, 1789-1848* (Wiley, New York, 1972), p. 15.

2. C.B. Macpherson, *The Life and Times of Liberal Democracy* (Oxford University Press, Oxford, 1977), Ch. II.

3. F.A. Hayek, *Law, Legislation and Liberty*, vol. 3: *The Political Order of a Free People* (Routledge and Kegan Paul, London, 1979), p. 5.

4. Rawls, *A Theory of Justice* (The Belknap Press of Harvard University Press, Cambridge, Mass., 1971), pp. 229 ff.

5. Mill, *Considerations on Representative Government* in J.M. Robson (ed.), *The Collected Works of John Stuart Mill* (University of Toronto Press, Toronto, 1963), vol. XIX, p. 404. See also Bosanquet, *The Philosophical Theory of the State*, 4th edn (Macmillan, London, 1951), pp. 127-28; Hobhouse, *Liberalism* (Oxford University Press, Oxford, 1964), pp. 27-29.

6. *Intelligence in the Modern World: John Dewey's Philosophy*, Joseph Ratner (ed.) (Modern Library, New York, 1939), p. 402. See Dennis F. Thompson, *The Democratic Citizen: Social Science and Democratic Theory in the Twentieth Century* (Cambridge University Press, Cambridge, 1970), Ch. 1. In another place, however, Thompson argues that a weaker assumption may be sufficient. *John Stuart Mill and Representative Government* (Princeton University Press, Princeton, 1976), p. 19. As John Plamenatz notes, J.S. Mill was more willing to acknowledge exceptions to this maxim than was Bentham. *Democracy and Illusion* (Longman Group, London, 1973), pp. 98-99. See §§V.B.1, V.B.5.

7. The importance of this 'each knows best for himself' assumption to liberal anti-paternalism is brought out nicely in James Mill's argument excluding women from the suffrage. See his *Essay on Government* (Cambridge University Press, Cambridge, 1937), pp. 45 ff.

8. Macpherson, *Life and Times*, p. 47. Macpherson distinguishes J.S. Mill's argument from that of Hobhouse and Dewey. See also Carole Pateman, *Participation and Democratic Theory* (Cambridge University Press, Cambridge, 1970), pp. 28 ff; Thompson, *Mill and Representative Government*, Ch.1; Alan Ryan, 'Two Concepts of Politics and Democracy' in Martin Fleisher (ed.), *Machiavelli and the Nature of Political Thought* (Atheneum, New York, 1972), pp. 76-113.

9. Mill, *Representative Government*, pp. 411-12.

10. Green, *Lectures on the Principles of Political Obligation* in R.L. Nettleship (ed.), *Works of Thomas Hill Green*, vol. II (Longman's, Green, and Co. London, 1900), p. 436. See Melvin Richter, *The Politics of Conscience: T.H. Green and His Age* (Weidenfeld and Nicolson, London, 1964), p. 347.

11. Hobhouse, *Liberalism*, p. 119, and see pp. 117 ff; and his *The Elements of Social Justice* (Allen and Unwin, London, 1949), p. 89. See also Philip D.

Poirier, 'Introduction' to Hobhouse, *The Labour Movement*, 3rd edn (Harvester Press, Brighton, 1974), p. xxi.

12. Dewey, *Reconstruction in Philosophy*, enlarged edn (Beacon Press, Boston, 1948), p. 209. For a comparison of Mill's and Dewey's educative arguments for democracy, see Alfonso J. Damico, *Individuality and Community: The Social and Political Thought of John Dewey* (University Presses of Florida, Gainesville, 1978), pp. 102 ff. See also Thompson, *The Democratic Citizen*, p. 21. On the problem of participation 'in proportion to capacity', see §C.3.

13. Mill, 'Thoughts on Parliamentary Reform' in *Collected Works*, vol. XIX, p. 322. Mill was apparently led to this conclusion by Tocqueville's estimate of the average American's intelligence and 'how close the connection is between these qualities and their democratic institutions'. *Representative Government*, p. 468. See also Mill's second review of Tocqueville: 'DeTocqueville on Democracy in America (II)' in *Collected Works*, vol. XVIII, p. 170. See §D.

14. Rawls, *A Theory of Justice*, p. 234; see also p. 358.

15. Dewey, *The Problems of Men* (Philosophical Library, New York, 1946), pp. 57-58. On the meaning of 'democracy', see J. Roland Pennock, *Democratic Political Theory* (Princeton University Press, Princeton, 1979), Ch. 1.

16. See Dewey, *Democracy and Education* (The Free Press, New York, 1916), Chs. 1, 2 and 7; see also his 'Creative Democracy – The Task Before Us' in *The Philosopher of the Common Man: Essays in Honor of John Dewey* (G.P. Putnam's Sons, New York, 1940), pp. 220-28. See also Damico, *Individuality and Community*, pp. 118 ff. This notion of 'democracy' as an educative way of life can also be found in Mill's thought. See F.W. Garforth, *Educative Democracy: John Stuart Mill on Education in Society* (Oxford University Press, Oxford, 1980), Ch. 3.

17. See Dewey, *Democracy and Education*, p. 178, and also Chs. 1, 2, 7. See Dewey's *Reconstruction in Philosophy*, pp. 205 ff, and his 'Creative Democracy – The Task Before Us', p. 226. This educative argument is typically conjoined in Dewey's writings with the argument premised on the growth of shared outlooks (§B.2). Rawls also argues that the 'Powers and prerogatives of offices of responsibility are needed to give scope to various self-governing and social capacities of the self'. 'Social Unity and Primary Goods' in A.K. Sen and Bernard Williams (eds.), *Utilitarianism and Beyond* (Cambridge University Press, Cambridge, 1982), p. 166.

18. Mill, *Representative Government*, p. 400.

19. Indeed Mill denies it was sufficient; see 'Tocqueville (II)', pp. 167-68. Richter makes the same point about Green. *The Politics of Conscience*, p. 366.

20. Dewey, *Democracy and Education*, p. 84.

21. Dewey, *The Public and Its Problems* (Swallow Press, Chicago, 1954), p. 148.

22. Green, *Political Obligation*, p. 436.

23. Ibid.

24. See John W. Chapman, *Rousseau – Totalitarian or Liberal?* (Columbia University Press, New York, 1956), pp. 128 ff.

25. See Bosanquet, *The Philosophical Theory of the State*, pp. xxx-xxxi, 102; *Science and Philosophy* (Allen and Unwin, London, 1927), pp. 261-65; *The Psychology of the Moral Self* (Macmillan, London, 1904), p. 43.

26. Bosanquet, *The Philosophical Theory of the State*, p. 109.

27. Bosanquet, *The Philosophic Theory of the State*, p. 272; and his *Social and International Ideals* (Macmillan, London, 1917), p. 291.

28. Bosanquet, *Science and Philosophy*, pp. 265-67, pp. 285 ff.

29. Mill, *Representative Government*, p. 535. See also Mill's essay on 'Centralisation' in *Collected Works*, vol. XIX, pp. 579-613.

30. In short, Green's patriot is someone whose life pivots about the well-being of the state, promoting it not only by some kind of internal or external social service but also by participating in democratic government at different levels. Few could have better exemplified his ideal than Green himself, with his work in education and temperance reform on the one hand and his activities as Oxford City councillor and Liberal Party propagandist on the other. Peter Gordon and John White, *Philosophers as Educational Reformers: The Influence of Idealism on British Educational Thought and Practice* (Routledge and Kegan Paul, London, 1979), p. 45. See also Green, *Political Obligation*, p. 432.

31. Hobhouse, *Liberalism*, p. 118.

32. Mill, *Representative Government*, p. 412. See also p. 469, where Mill talks about both consciousness and feelings of unity in the same sentence.

33. Green, *Political Obligation*, pp. 436-37. This, of course, is paradoxical since Mill typically stresses the sort of communal sentiments Green is describing, which are not in the main those that Green relies upon. See §§III.C.2, C.3.

34. Hobhouse, *Democracy and Reaction* (T. Fisher Unwin, London, 1904), p. 186. Commenting upon this passage, J.H. Muirhead reports: 'This I believe to be the gospel-truth, but it is truth which the writer owes, I venture to think, to Green, and not to Mill.' *The Service of the State: Four Lectures on the Political Teaching of T.H. Green* (John Murray, London, 1908), p. 87.

35. See Hobhouse, *Sociology and Philosophy* (G. Bell and Sons, London, 1966), pp. 40-41.

36. Mill, *Representative Government*, p. 469. Mill is talking here specifically of those who are denied the vote 'in an otherwise popular government'.

37. Hobhouse, *Social Justice*, p. 186. See also his essay on 'Aristocracy' in *Sociology and Philosophy*, pp. 191-206. For Mill, see his review 'Tocqueville (II)', p. 181.

38. Hobhouse, *Social Justice*, p. 192.

39. Green, *Political Obligation*, p. 404. This, of course, is Green's description of the 'general will'.

40. Hobhouse, *Social Justice*, pp. 191-92.

41. Bosanquet, *The Philosophical Theory of the State*, p. 111.

42. J.P. Plamenatz, *Consent, Freedom and Political Obligation*, 2nd edn (Oxford University Press, Oxford, 1968), p. 39. See also H.D. Lewis, *Freedom and History* (Allen and Unwin, London, 1962), pp. 105 ff.

43. Hobhouse, *The Metaphysical Theory of the State* (Allen and Unwin, London, 1926), p. 59.

44. Bosanquet, *The Philosophical Theory of the State*, p. 70.

45. John MacCunn, e.g., points out that Green did not share Mill's fear of the masses. *Six Radical Thinkers: Bentham, J.S. Mill, Cobden, Carlyle, Mazzini, T.H. Green* (Edward Arnold, London, 1907), p. 262. Harvey Mansfield makes a similar point about Rawls, albeit in a more critical vein. *The Spirit of Liberalism* (Harvard University Press, Cambridge, Mass., 1978), pp. 90, 104.

46. Mill, 'The Claims of Labour' in *Collected Works*, vol. V, pp. 363-89. Mill is arguing here that in modern times such friendly feelings cannot be based on a 'feudal' paternalistic basis, although he does talk of fellow feeling between 'the mass of the people and those who are by courtesy considered to guide and govern them'. See §C.2. See also Geraint L. Williams, 'Introduction' to his edited selections, *John Stuart Mill on Politics and Society* (Fontana/Collins, Glasgow, 1976), pp. 43 ff.

47. Mill, 'Tocqueville (II)', p. 181.

48. See Mill, *Representative Government*, Ch. VII; and his 'Recent Writers on Reform' in *Collected Works*, vol. XIX, pp. 341-70. Hobhouse also endorses proportional representation, especially for heterogeneous populations. *Social*

*Justice*, p. 191. Bosanquet objected to Hare's scheme, arguing that rather than bringing home to the voters his responsibility to choose the best candidate, it suggests that he should group together with others sharing 'some special bias of his own' with the aim of returning 'a member like-minded with them'. It also, he argued, disregards neighbourhoods. *The Philosophical Theory of the State*, pp. 287-88n.

49. Mill, 'Tocqueville ((II)', p. 178.

50. Ibid., p. 196. See also Alan Ryan, *J.S. Mill* (Routledge and Kegan Paul, London, 1974), p. 47, but also p. 161; J.H. Burns, 'J.S. Mill and Democracy, 1829-61', *Political Studies*, vol. V (1957), p. 168.

51. Mill, 'Tocqueville (II)', pp. 181, 198.

52. In Ch. XVI of *Representative Government*, Mill provides a wide range of arguments as to why '[f]ree institutions are next to impossible in a country made up of different nationalities', i.e. '[a]mong a people without fellow-feeling' (p. 547). The question Mill does not directly face here is whether a nation divided by class conflicts possesses, as Ryan puts it, 'a basic consensus, on the basis of which political institutions could be worked, and within which conflicts could be argued out'. *J.S. Mill*, p. 214. See also R.J. Halliday, *John Stuart Mill* (Allen and Unwin, London, 1976), p. 38.

53. This paragraph is drawn from Rawls, 'Social Unity and Primary Goods', pp. 179 ff. Emphasis added. My analysis here also suggests that traditional constitutional devices designed to prevent majoritarian tyranny may require a foundation in a 'spirit of community'. See Rawls, *A Theory of Justice*, pp. 228-29. On the relation of constitutionalism, democracy and liberalism, see J. Roland Pennock and John W. Chapman (eds.), *NOMOS XX: Constitutionalism* (New York University Press, New York, 1979), esp. the essays by Schochet, Sigmund and Miller.

54. See Ryan, *J.S. Mill*, p. 193. Ryan talks of 'democratic despotism' on p. 134.

55. See Mill, *Representative Government*, pp. 406 ff; Jack Lively, *Democracy* (Basil Blackwell, Oxford, 1975) pp. 138-39; Dewey and Tufts, *Ethics*, rev. edn (Henry Holt, New York, 1932), pp. 236-37; Dewey, 'Philosophies of Freedom' in Richard J. Bernstein (ed.), *On Experience, Nature and Freedom* (The Liberal Arts Press, New York, 1960), pp. 279 ff; Dewey, *Democracy and Education*, pp. 83 ff; Hobhouse, *Social Development* (Allen and Unwin, London, 1924), pp. 70 ff; MacCunn, *Six Radical Thinkers*, p. 252.

56. Dewey, *The Public and Its Problems*, p. 206.

57. Mill, *Representative Government*, p. 411. Emphasis added.

58. H.D. Lewis has doubted whether democracy is necessary to the theory of the general will. (*Freedom and History*, p. 115). Leaving aside this wider point, it is manifest that both Green and Bosanquet were democrats. Bosanquet, in fact, was more insistent than Dewey that '[p]arliamentary government, in one shape or another, seems hardly likely to be superseded as the normal form for civilised peoples' (see §C.3). He did, however, emphasise that, as demonstrated by the role of the judiciary, the expression of the general will was not confined to elective bodies. *The Philosophical Theory of the State*, pp. xxx-xxxi. See also his *Ideals*, pp. 124 ff, p. 278n. For Green see MacCunn, *Six Radical Thinkers*, pp. 239, 246; Crane Brinton, *English Political Thought in the Nineteenth Century* (Harper and Brothers, New York, 1962), p. 221; Ernest Barker, *Political Thought in England, 1848 to 1914*, 2nd edn (Oxford University Press, Oxford, 1959), pp. 30-31.

59. Dewey and Tufts, *Ethics*, p. 236. Dewey's particular concern here is the child *vis à vis* the family, but the analysis is intended to be of wider application. Compare Dewey's analysis to Rawls's in *A Theory of Justice*, §71. (See §IV.A.3.)

60.  Rawls, *A Theory of Justice*, § § 36, 72, and p. 243.
61.  See ibid., § 3. Because of this it is often thought that such an 'egoistic' argument is inconsistent with Rawls's theory of man. My point here, of course, is that it is consistent. See Milton Fisk, 'History and Reason in Rawls' Moral Theory' in Norman Daniels (ed.), *Reading Rawls: Critical Studies of* A Theory of Justice (Basic Books, New York, 1974), p. 65; Benjamin R. Barber, 'Justifying Justice' in ibid., pp. 316-18.
62.  The material in this paragraph is drawn from Rawls, *A Theory of Justice*, pp. 440, 544-45, 178-79.
63.  Mill quoted in Ryan, *J.S. Mill*, p. 128. Garforth also quotes this sentence in *Educative Democracy*, p. 16. The original occurs in *On Liberty* in *Collected Works*, vol. XVIII, p. 224.
64.  Hobhouse, *Liberalism*, p. 120. For Bosanquet, see note 58 above.
65.  Dewey, *Characters and Events: Popular Essays in Social and Political Philosophy*, Joseph Ratner (ed.) (Henry Holt, New York, 1929), vol. II, p. 468. Dewey's attitude toward immigrants has been a matter of dispute. See Clarence J. Karier, 'John Dewey and the New Liberalism: Reflections and Responses', *History of Education Quarterly*, XV (Winter 1975), pp. 417-43.
66.  Mill, *Representative Government*, p. 394; see also p. 435.
67.  Maurice Cranston, *John Stuart Mill* (Longman's, Green, London, 1958), p. 26. See Garforth, *Educative Democracy*, p. 16.
68.  Hobhouse, *Liberalism*, pp. 116-20. Emphasis added.
69.  Rawls focuses on social rather than psychological preconditions for democratic government. See *A Theory of Justice*, pp. 229 ff. See § V.D.3.
70.  Macpherson, *Life and Times*, p. 59. In his early work, 'Thoughts on Parliamentary Reform', Mill actually provides a scale: 1 (vote) – unskilled labourers; 2 – skilled labourers; 3 – foremen; 3 or 4 – farmers, manufacturers and traders; 5 or 6 – professionals; at least 5 or 6 – university graduates (pp. 324-25). However, we ought not to make too much of this scale as Mill omits it from his later and more important *Representative Government* (see p. 475). For an examination of the evolution of Mill's views on democracy see Burns, 'J.S. Mill and Democracy', pp. 281-94.
71.  See David Miller, 'Democracy and Social Justice' in Pierre Bernbaum, Jack Lively and Geraint Perry (eds.), *Democracy, Consensus and Social Contract* (Sage, Beverly Hills, 1978), pp. 96-97.
72.  Mill, *Representative Government*, p. 474. Emphasis added.
73.  See ibid., pp. 474-79. See also Thompson, *Mill and Representative Government*, pp. 100-1.
74.  See Mill, *Representative Government*, p. 473. See also Thompson, *Mill and Representative Government*, pp. 95-100. For a critique of this conception of political association see Michael Oakeshott, *On Human Conduct* (Clarendon Press, Oxford, 1975), Essay III, esp. pp. 203 ff.
75.  Rawls, *A Theory of Justice*, p. 233. See Brian Barry, *The Liberal Theory of Justice: A Critical Examination of the Principal Doctrines in* A Theory of Justice *by John Rawls* (Clarendon Press, Oxford, 1973), pp. 144 ff.
76.  Thompson, *The Democratic Citizen*, p. 151. 'The thinker represents, indeed, individual intelligence, but the masses represent the enduring and pervasive intelligence of the race, more deeply seated in the past, more patiently and courageously engendering the future.' Dewey, *Character and Events*, vol. I, p. 42. Nevertheless, Dewey argues that '[p] ersons of a liberal outlook, captured by fear of dictatorship, join with persons whose special and anti-social interests are unfavorably affected . . . [and who fail] to see that new administrative bodies are so imperatively needed that the real problem is building up an intelligent and capable civil-service under conditions that will operate against formation of rigid bureau-

cracies.' *Freedom and Culture* (Allen and Unwin, London, 1940), p. 65. See Damico, *Individuality and Community*, p. 64, and also Ch. 6.

77. Montesquieu, *The Spirit of the Laws*, Thomas Nugent (trans.) (Collier Macmillan, London, 1940), p. 109. This passage is referred to by Giovanni Sartori in his *Democratic Theory* (Wayne State University Press, Detroit, 1962), p. 117. The following discussion draws on pp. 115-20 of Sartori.

78. J. Roland Pennock, *Democratic Political Theory*, p. 472. Thompson also allows that 'citizenship theories' can accommodate leadership. *The Democratic Citizen*, pp. 26-27.

79. Mill, *On Liberty*, p. 269; see also the references in note 81.

80. See Pennock, *Democratic Political Theory*, pp. 478-79; Shirley Robin Letwin, *The Pursuit of Certainty* (Cambridge University Press, Cambridge, 1965), pp. 306-8.

81. Mill, *Auguste Comte and Positivism* in *Collected Works*, vol. X, p. 314. See also *Representative Government*, p. 512; his 'Spirit of the Age' in Geraint L. Williams (ed.), *John Stuart Mill on Politics and Society*, p. 175; and his 'Inaugural Address' in *Dissertations and Discussions* (William V. Spencer, Boston, 1868), vol. IV, p. 344. See Garforth, *Educative Democracy*, pp. 58 ff.

82. David Spitz, 'Freedom and Individuality: Mill's *Liberty* in Retrospect' in Carl J. Friedrich (ed.), *NOMOS IV: Liberty* (Atherton, New York, 1962), p. 185. See Richard B. Friedman, 'An Introduction to Mill's Theory of Authority' in J.B. Schneewind (ed.), *Mill: A Collection of Critical Essays* (Macmillan, London, 1968), pp. 379-425.

83. For Mill, see *On Liberty*, p. 269; for Hobhouse, see *Liberalism*, p. 118. For a somewhat different interpretation of Hobhouse's views on leadership, see Kenneth R. Hoover, who compares Hobhouse and Green in his 'Liberalism and the Idealist Philosophy of Thomas Hill Green', *Western Political Quarterly*, XXVI (Sept. 1973), pp. 550-65.

84. Bosanquet, *Ideals*, p. 123. Stanley Benn and I discuss the relation of 'political' and 'public' in liberal theory in our 'Liberal Conception of the Public and Private' in S.I. Benn and G.F. Gaus (eds.), *Conceptions of the Public and Private in Social Life* (Croom Helm, London, forthcoming).

85. Mill, 'Centralisation' in *Collected Works*, vol. XIX, pp. 603-4. The advocacy of voluntary associations to meet community needs can be found in both 'classical' and 'welfare state' liberals. See F.A. Hayek, *Law, Legislation and Liberty*, vol. 2: *The Mirage of Social Justice* (University of Chicago Press, Chicago, 1976), p. 151; Lord Beveridge, *Voluntary Action: A Report on Methods of Social Advance* (Allen and Unwin, London, 1948). See also J. Roland Pennock and John W. Chapman (eds.), *NOMOS XI: Voluntary Associations* (Atherton, New York, 1969).

86. H.L.A. Hart, 'Rawls on Liberty and its Priority' in Daniels (ed.), *Reading Rawls*, p. 252.

87. The material on Bosanquet in this paragraph is drawn from his *Science and Philosophy*, pp. 276-79. Bosanquet also argues that 'a healthy political interest is one mark of a good citizen'. Ibid., p. 276.

88. Thompson, *Mill and Representative Government*, p. 49.

89. Green, 'Lecture on the Work to be Done by the New Oxford High School for Boys', *Works*, vol. III, pp. 456-57, 460, 474-76. See I.M. Greengarten, *Thomas Hill Green and the Development of Liberal-Democratic Thought* (University of Toronto Press, Toronto, 1981), pp. 92-94; Gordon and White, *Philosophers as Educational Reformers*, pp. 70 ff.

90. See Gordon and White, *Philosophers as Educational Reformers*, pp. 70 ff.

91. For Mill, see Garforth, *Educative Democracy*, and for Bosanquet see his comments in *The Philosophical Theory of the State*, p. 63. As one of Hobhouse's contemporaries pointed out, because '[t]he problem of education is obviously

vital . . . it is curious that nowhere does Professor Hobhouse refer to this question at any length.' Lewis Rockow, *Contemporary Political Thought in England* (Leonard Press, London, 1925), p. 214.

# VII  ECONOMIC ORGANISATION

In this final chapter I turn to some issues concerning economic organisation and 'the new liberalism' with which we began in the Introductory.
I consider here modern liberal positions on private property and the
market (§A), economic equality (§§B and C) and industrial life (§D).
The new liberal position, as it emerges in Hobhouse, Dewey and Rawls
is (in the main) characterised by a somewhat unenthusiastic endorsement of private property and a critical acceptance of the market, strong
support for some form of state provision of a social minimum and endorsement of some redistribution of income and, especially, wealth.
Although not prominent in Rawls, various forms of factory legislation
concerning safety and hours of work have also been traditional elements
of the new liberal programme. We shall see that Green and Mill agree
with some of the new liberal positions and Bosanquet with very few.
One of the main aims of this chapter is to show that Bosanquet's more
traditional 'radicalism', as well as Hobhouse's new liberalism, can be,
and has been, justified on developmental grounds. As I indicated in
the Introductory, by positing additional psychological dynamics or by
re-conceptualising notions like private property to give them an important developmental dimension, Bosanquet can quite consistently
embrace the modern liberal theory of man while rejecting the new
liberal conclusions Hobhouse seeks to draw.

## A. Private Property and the Market

### A.1. Private Property

No one can study classical liberal theory without being struck by the
absolutely fundamental place of private property, or perhaps more
accurately, the right to private property. Without making any claims to
exhaustiveness, the essential classical liberal case for property seems to
have two dimensions, one concentrating on the public interest and the
other on liberty.

  (i) The first dimension, prominent in the classical political economists, centres on the claim that a market economy premised on private
property and the pursuit of private interest promotes the commonweal
by increasing the aggregate wealth of society. This claim is the upshot

235

of Adam Smith's insight that, if properly structured by a framework of rules and institutions, the 'private interests and passions' of individuals would lead each to employ his capital and industry where it will produce the greatest value. And since, according to Smith, the aggregate revenue of a society is equal to the exchangeable value of the produce of its industry, his conclusion was that each unknowingly worked to maximise the aggregate revenue of society. It was in this sense that Smith thought that the pursuit by each of his private interest promotes 'the publick interest'.[1]

(ii) Classical liberty-claims focusing on private property are various, but two stand out. (a) From Smith to Lord Robbins classical liberals have insisted that a private property market economy is uniquely consistent with individual liberty, allowing each to live his life – including employing his capital and labour – as he sees fit.[2] The market, it is said, is the institutional *embodiment* of natural liberty. (b) It is also argued by classical liberals that a 'competitive economy based on private property is the institutional *guarantee* of freedom.'[3] Here the idea is that the dispersion of power that results from a private property market economy protects civil and political liberty against encroachment by government. As Hayek argues, 'There can be no freedom of the press if the instruments of printing are under the control of government, no freedom of assembly if the needed rooms are so controlled, no freedom of movement if the means of transport are a government monopoly, etc.'[4] Moreover, it has been widely held that the independence engendered by property-holding allows the man of property to serve as a guardian of liberty, being in a position to effectively oppose 'capricious and absolute government'.[5]

Taken together, these indicate the central position of private property in classical liberal theory. Indeed, to a large extent classical liberalism can be understood as a theory about the benefits of private property and the political conditions for its maintenance. Now, as Brian Barry has noted, one of the outstanding features of Rawls's liberalism is the extent to which it abandons this classical devotion to property, making 'private property in the means of production, distribution and exchange a contingent matter rather than an essential part of the doctrine.'[6] Not only does Rawls explicitly omit a right to such property from his list of basic liberties, but he also acknowledges that a market socialist economy, as well as a capitalist one, is compatible with his liberalism.[7] And he certainly is not alone here. Indeed, Dewey is probably much more socialistic than Rawls, apparently endorsing (at least sometimes) some sort of democratic socialism that seems fairly hostile to private property in the means of production.[8] Mill too called himself a 'socialist'. Whether or not we accept that self-designation, it certainly is true that he was open to the possibility of a liberal-socialism (and could be very critical indeed of the Victorian economic system).[9] Hobhouse, while rejecting a 'State Socialism' aiming at direct 'public management' of all industry, did endorse a 'Social Liberalism' or a 'semi-Socialism' aiming at public control. And, he added, 'We must not assume any of the rights of property as axiomatic.'[10] In contrast to our other modern liberals, Green and Bosanquet are strong defenders of private property (we will see why presently), though even they seem willing to contemplate the possibility of socialism with a calmness not characteristic of most classical liberal discussions.[11]

Most modern liberals are willing to seriously consider the possibility of socialist economic systems because, for various reasons, they do not perceive much persuasiveness or force in the main classical liberal arguments for private property. A central factor behind this move away from private property was certainly an increasing doubt among many liberals that a market premised on the pursuit of private interest functions as smoothly and efficiently as classical liberal economists maintained. Dewey and Hobhouse were especially critical of the claims of classical economics, insisting that instead of a spontaneous order of private interests promoting the common good, the reality is a ruthless competition engendering chaos and waste. As Hobhouse saw it, 'Competition has failed and we live among its debris with no established freedom of social co-operation to take its place, but with the struggles of organized capital and labour confronting us.'[12] It certainly is no accident that, of all our modern liberals, Bosanquet and Green are not only the strongest defenders of a private property economy, but (with the possible exception of J.S. Mill) are the least critical of classical economic analysis.[13]

But a change in the analysis of the way in which a market economy functions is not by any means the whole story behind the general de-emphasis on property in most modern liberal theories. For our purposes more relevant are transformations in the perception of government, society and man. As has been widely noted, in lieu of the classical liberal's distrust of government as a potential instrument for tyranny and despoliation of the people [see argument (ii)(b) above], a new liberal like Hobhouse sees in 'the central authority a machine which he may hope to control in the interest of the public'. And so, Hobhouse concluded, 'for the democrat the old *laissez faire* position is no longer logically tenable'.[14] But while new liberals like Hobhouse emphasised the democratic character of the contemporary state as underlying this new perception of it as a friend of the people and instrument of the public welfare, it is certain that more is involved. For although a classical liberal may well be a democrat, he is not apt to abandon his suspicion that power is a threat to liberty. Conjoined with the democratic character of the modern liberal state is a generally very optimistic and co-operative view of men and institutions. This is most manifest in Rawlsian social psychology, which holds that 'social institutions generate an effective supporting sense of justice. Regarding society as a going concern, its members acquire as they grow up an allegiance to the public conception [of justice] and this allegiance usually overcomes the temptations and strains of social life.'[15] If citizens – including public officials – develop out of their natural fellow feelings (§ IV.A.3) an allegiance to the principles and institutions of a liberal society, they would not seem particularly apt to use positions of power and influence to unjustly restrict the liberty of others.

More fundamentally, however, the modern liberal is likely to be indifferent to private property because, unlike the classical liberal, his ideal of personality assigns economic pursuits a subordinate position. C.B. Macpherson's work has been especially important in bringing to our attention this fundamental difference between pre- and post-Millian liberalism. On Macpherson's interpretation, liberal theory from Hobbes to Bentham conceived of man 'as essentially a consumer of utilities, an infinite desirer and infinite appropriator'.[16] Such a man, Macpherson submits, is a market man whose vocations are consumption and appropriation. As Macpherson observes, starting with J.S. Mill and Green, a very different understanding of human nature is introduced into liberalism, one which depicts man as a self-developer and maximiser of human powers. Now without accepting Macpherson's entire thesis (see § A.2), he is quite right to insist that the modern liberal theory of man is not in essence a theory about economic man. As I argued in Chapter IV (§ B.2), modern liberals reject the model of human nature based simply on the pursuit of pleasure and the avoidance of pain, instead seeing men as aiming at a coherent development of their natures. But more than that, modern liberals often indicate straightforwardly that economic activities do not have an exalted place in their scheme of things. From Mill onwards we find modern liberals engaging in diatribes against what they see as an overly pecuniary and overly materialistic culture. For example, according to Dewey and Tufts:

> If the economic dominates life -- and if the economic order relies chiefly upon the profit motive as distinguished from the motive of

professional excellence, i.e., craftsmanship, and from the function-
al motive of giving a fair return for what is received — there is danger that a part of life, which should be subordinate or at most co-
ordinate with other interests and values, may become supreme. It is
as true now as when the words were uttered that life is more than
meat. And when wealth is made a chief if not the sole interest, some
of the precious and finer things in life — love, justice, knowledge,
beauty — are liable to be displaced.[17]

When economic activities are depreciated in this way, while aesthetic, craft, scientific and social service orientations are praised, it is
not at all difficult to understand how the classical concentration on
private property can give way to the relative indifference of Rawls
and Dewey, and perhaps even Mill. It indicates, most obviously, how
economic liberty comes to be seen as a less essential liberty [see (ii)(a)
above], one that can be infringed without really interfering with a
person's good. Consequently, to the extent that modern liberals continue to insist upon traditional liberal 'economic' rights, they do so
largely by casting them in non-economic terms. We have already seen,
for example, that liberty of occupation is supported on the basis of its
importance in organising individual development and co-ordinating it
with social service (§§IV.C,V.C). Even in their endorsement of equality
of opportunity, they are apt to stress its developmental benefits at least
as much as its traditional role of simply allowing all to compete for (unequal) economic and social resources. Thus, for instance, Hobhouse
holds that 'free scope for the development of personality in each member of the community' is the foundation not only of 'equal rights before
the law' but also of 'what is called equality of opportunity'.[18]

The depreciation of economic activities also provides a foundation
for attacking the classical case for property from the public interest
[(i) above]. Besides challenging the classical economic analysis underlying the case, it also can be argued that classical economists like Smith
operated with an impoverished conception of the public interest — one
based on the maximisation of wealth — because they had an impoverished conception of human nature and the human good. Thus even if
the market functions as classical economists maintained, their theory
remains open to the criticism that it assumes a faulty notion of the public good. Thus, for example, although J.S. Mill accepted the central
tenets of classical economics, he nevertheless hoped that the existing
type of social life, consumed with the pursuit of riches, was only a
temporary and passing phase. 'In the meantime, those who do not ac-

cept the present very early stage of human improvement as its ultimate type, may be excused for being comparatively indifferent to the kind of economical progress which excites the congratulations of ordinary politicians; the mere increase of production and accumulation.'[19]

Other things being equal, then, these sorts of attacks on the classical liberal case for private property and the market tend to relegate private property in the means of production to a fairly peripheral commitment of modern liberal theories. However, it is possible to develop a modern liberal case for private property — just as for liberty of occupation and equality of opportunity — by conceptualising it in a new way so as to relate it to developmental concerns. And this is precisely what Green and Bosanquet do. Although Green's theory of property has some Lockian elements, the essence of his account is Hegelian. 'Appropriation', he writes, 'is an expression of will; of the individual's effort to give reality to a conception of his own good; of his consciousness of a possible self-satisfaction as an object to be attained.'[20] As Bosanquet maintained, action in the external world through 'dealing with things' in the form of property is necessary for one to possess a conception of oneself as persisting through time with an enduring good. To be denied property — the power to intervene in the world on a stable and continuing basis — is to be relegated to the life of a child, unable to 'organise its future, and restricted to receiving what is deemed necessary from day to day'.[21] Thus, Green concludes, 'human personality' cannot develop 'without a recognised power of appropriating material things.'[22]

As Hobhouse and Dewey apparently perceived, even if one accepts this sort of general developmental argument in favour of property, it does not justify the complex of property rights existing in a particular society at a particular time. It is one thing to acknowledge, say, that the execution of a life plan requires an ongoing and stable access to resources and quite another to justify property as it existed in nineteenth- or early-twentieth-century capitalist societies.[23] For example: it may be argued that an independent and responsible life requires an assured income (see §B.1) and personal property, but not necessarily private property in the means of production.[24] Interestingly, Bosanquet takes this sort of new liberal socialism to task, indicating that property that can only be used for consumption undercuts the developmental benefits of proprietorship by engendering egoism. Because such possession is divorced from any possibility of increasing the 'general output', he argues, it becomes simply a device for satisfaction of self-centred aims and enjoyments.[25]

My concern here, however, is not to evaluate (much less endorse) these idealist arguments for private property, but to emphasise that they present just the sort of case that is required if private property is to be a core element of the modern liberal programme. Because Green and Bosanquet insist that private property is essential for development, they avoid the relative indifference of Rawls and Dewey. But their case for property is very much a modern liberal one, offering a conceptualisation of property that significantly departs from (at any rate, from English) classical liberal theory. All this indicates, I think, that modern liberal positions on private property provide a clear example of the 'looseness' of political argument to which I pointed in the Introductory. By proffering an additional thesis as to the developmental benefits of property-holding, Bosanquet and Green can fairly easily turn the modern liberal theory of man, which at one level seems indifferent to private property, into the foundation of a strong defence of proprietorship.

## A.2. The Market and Human Nature

As I said above, most modern liberals are willing to allow the legitimacy of some forms of socialism (though certainly not what they consider the more extreme forms).[26] Nevertheless, it would seem that ultimately all our modern liberals endorse, or at least assume, some sort of regulated private property economy.[27] It will be recalled, though, that the modern liberal doctrines of social interest and a co-operative, mutually appreciative social life stand in stark contrast to 'the private property theory of society' (§II.B.1). The question thus arises whether it is consistent with the modern liberal theory of human nature to allow, much less endorse, the legitimacy of a private property market order as it seems premised on egoism and competition, and so is apparently fundamentally at odds with the social nature of man.

To begin with, strictly speaking no inconsistency presents itself here. If we recall Solomon Asch's discussion of the private property theory of society, his point was not that market relations are damaging or corrupting, but that they are inadequate and partial. Bosanquet seems to recognise this most clearly. Following Hegel (and it is worth noting that following Hegel does not always cause difficulties for a liberal), Bosanquet accepts civil society, with its 'cash nexus' as 'representing human nature' in a 'special, though necessary, aspect'.[28] But, consistent with the modern liberal view, he also believes that it concerns a subordinate sort of activity, providing the material foundations for a social life in which each other's developments can be appreciated and shared.[29]

However, at least as read by some, Green's theory does not permit such accommodation to a competitive market order. According to I.M.

Greengarten, 'Green apparently found *all* competition morally unjusti-
fiable. Green's notion of a non-competitive good [see §II.D.1] and his
defence of the market system allows no compromise.'[30] By insisting
that the good of man is strictly non-competitive, it would seem that
Green leaves no room for a market economy. But consider what Green
actually argues:

> Civil society may be, *and is*, founded on the idea of there being a
> common good, but that idea *in relation to the less favoured members
> of society is in effect unrealised*, and it is unrealised because the
> good is being sought in objects which admit of being competed for.
> They are of such a kind that they cannot be equally attained by all.
> The success of some in obtaining them is incompatible with the suc-
> cess of others.[31]

Market relations as such thus do not imply a competition of human
goods. For all but the least favoured, civil society '*is*' a co-operative
effort to achieve a common good. For the less favoured, then, economic
life is not this sort of co-operative enterprise. In this same paragraph
Green tells us that they are left 'to sink or swim in the stream of un-
relenting competition, in which we admit that the weaker has not a
chance'. Consequently, those at the bottom of the economic order are
not provided 'much real opportunity of self-development'. In sum, it
would seem that, at best, the less favoured do not gain the fruits of
economic co-operation and, at worst, they are exploited. Instead of
civil society being structured so as to promote the good of all, the poor
are losing so that others may gain. It is in this sense that the success of
one is incompatible with that of others.

On Green's view, then, market relations and civil society do not necessarily involve the *competition of the goods of the participants* (or
seeking their *good* in objects which admit of competition). The reason
that Green singles out 'relentless' competition (Dewey and Tufts use
'ruthless'[32]) is that it points to a sort of competition in which the life
and well-being of the competitors itself is at stake. Ann R. Cacoullos
thus seems quite right that Green's theory only precludes some forms
of competition, i.e. those that result in a 'bestial scramble'.[33] But, as
Hobhouse realised, a competition premised on the pursuit of a common
good is quite another thing. As he points out, '[T]here is rivalry and rivalry. There is the rivalry of the keenly contested game, subject to the
rules of honourable sportsmanship in which the underlying impulse is
one of co-operation in getting the best out of effort; and there is the

rivalry that is reckless of means and ready to destroy.'[34] The modern liberal aim is thus, as Mill put it, to effect 'the transformation of human life, from a conflict of classes struggling for opposite interests, to a friendly rivalry in the pursuit of a good common to all'.[35]

## B. Economic Equality: A Minimum

### B.1. *Cases for a Social Minimum*

This analysis of the market, so central to Green, thus conceives of the market order as a co-operative effort rather than a struggle among egoists. Besides this *conceptual reform*, Green also proposes a *moral reform*, calling on men to recognise the co-operative nature of social and economic life and (for one thing) thus institute the appropriate *social and economic reforms* so that none are omitted from the fruits of co-operation. As Adam Ulam has noted, his ultimate proposals — revising the system of land tenure, public education, factory acts and temperance legislation — 'strike us today as being incongruously mild when set against Green's original thesis'.[36] Although Green's analysis is often regarded as laying the philosophic foundations of the welfare state,[37] it is Hobhouse who actually argues for new liberal 'conclusions'. In accordance with the Greenian co-operative understanding of civil society, Hobhouse maintains that 'every citizen should have full means of earning by socially useful labour so much material support as experience proves to be the necessary basis of a healthy, civilized existence'. He goes beyond this statement of principle, though, to propose that 'if in the actual working of the industrial system the means are not in actual fact sufficiently available he [the citizen] is held to have a claim not as of charity but as of right on the national resources to make good the deficiency'.[38] Hobhouse thus endorses a 'civic minimum', which is the minimum reward due to all citizens contributing to the common good. This minimum, he tells us, is to be set at a level designed not only to maintain the worker's health but also to put him 'in a position *to develop and exercise his faculties*, to enter upon marriage and parenthood, and meet whatever costs of a normal family are not undertaken by the community'.[39]

At least in the hands of Hobhouse, this argument is very much about securing a minimum to all *contributors* to the common good. It explicitly leaves out of account those who are not active participants in economic life, for, at least in this narrow sense, they are not engaged in the co-operative economic effort. To be sure, Hobhouse argued that 'the general economy should be directed to meeting the needs of all members of the community in proportion to their urgency', but he insisted that, in contrast to contributors to the collective effort, the young and the handicapped (for example) are 'dependents'.[40] Hobhouse also insisted that 'the lot of the independent labourer be more eligible than that of the pauper'. And he was prepared to be especially hard on the 'determined idler' who was not contributing to the collective economic enterprise out of choice (rather than by force of circumstance). Hobhouse thus seems at least attracted to the idea that for 'him a labor colony must be provided, where he must learn to work and gain his discharge as soon as he can prove himself efficient enough in mind and body to stand the stress of industrial competition.'[41]

The modern liberal theory of man, however, provides the basis for two other, rather less tough-minded, arguments for a social minimum, ones that do not require distinguishing producers from non-producers.

(i) The first, and surely the most powerful, is the argument from effective liberty. I argued at length in Chapter V why modern liberals care so deeply about liberty. Each of us not only requires liberty to develop his individuality, but the satisfaction of social interest and the growth of communitarian sentiments necessitate that others be likewise free to cultivate their natures. Now Green's notion of positive liberty (§V.A) implies that guaranteeing others equal negative liberty is not sufficient to promote their development; and more to the point at present, it indicates that certain material conditions are necessary for development to proceed. And, as Green saw, this opens up the possibility of state action with 'a view to securing such freedom among its members'.[42] Again, though, Green drew modest prescriptions from his analysis (in this case compulsory schooling), but in the hands of a (radical) new liberal like Dewey it has considerably wider application. Distinguishing between 'purely formal or legal liberty' and 'effective liberty', Dewey holds that the latter requires 'material security'. In Dewey's eyes one of the most objectionable features of the economic system was that it had 'consistently and persistently denied effective freedom to the economically underpowered and underprivileged'.[43] However, although Dewey seems to endorse unemployment insurance and a Hobhousian sort of civic minimum, he employed his effective liberty argument to insist on the necessity for wide-scale reorganisation and public supervision of the economy so that citizens would be provided with the material prerequisites for such growth in the normal course of things. The aim was thus 'a society in which daily occupations and relationships will give independence and substantial living to all normal individuals who share in its ongoings, reserving relief for extraordinary emergencies'.[44]

One may well be suspicious of casting these material prerequisites for development in terms of 'positive' or 'effective' liberty. After all, the issue is what a person needs to develop, not what he needs in order to have (negative) liberty. It might thus seem to be merely confused — or, worse, positively misleading — to collapse both issues into liberty issues. But within modern liberal theory, there are good reasons for linking these material pre-conditions for development to questions of liberty. For, as we have already seen, the modern liberal case for (negative) liberty rests on the developmental benefits of liberty; if, then, conditions are such that even with liberty development cannot proceed, the developmental case for liberty will be without much force. In so far, then, as the force of the argument for liberty requires assumptions about the material conditions for development, it seems justified to use the notion of an *effective liberty* to indicate the complex of conditions consisting of negative liberty and the material foundations required for its exercise to yield developmental benefits. Moreover, linking liberty and the conditions for its beneficial exercise in this way serves to stress that proposals designed to secure these conditions derive from the central commitments of the theory — indeed are part and parcel of the endorsement of liberty itself.

It is important, however, to distinguish three notions: formal liberty, effective liberty and the worth of liberty. The distinction between formal and effective liberty is that emphasised by Dewey and is that with which we have been concerned: whereas formal liberty is simply the legal guarantee of certain rights and liberties, effective liberty requires that one have sufficient resources to take advantage of these legal assurances. Rawls's argument for his general conception of justice is based precisely on this distinction. As Rawls argues, conditions might be such that the equal basic liberties assigned to all by the first principle of justice cannot be 'effectively exercised'. The general conception specifies that in such circumstances an unequal distribution of liberties is just if it works out to the long-term benefit of the least favoured, the ultimate aim being the creation of conditions that allow for an effective equal liberty for all.[45] But this idea of an effective liberty is to be distinguished from what Rawls calls the 'worth of liberty' which, he tells us, is proportional to a person's capacity to advance his ends.[46] The sorts of talents one possesses, one's authority and one's wealth will all affect the worth of particular liberties. Now to say all should be guaranteed an effective liberty is not necessarily to claim that the worth of liberty should be the same for all. The former only requires that each have sufficient resources so that the exercise of liberty yields significant developmental benefits whereas the latter points to something like equal developmental benefits. This latter notion is problematic; natural differentiation coupled with individual choice would seem to inevitably entail differential worth of specific liberties. Indeed, differences in natural talents may well result in inevitable variance in the worth of the entire system of liberties. However, I do not wish to deny that modern liberal arguments for equality of liberty (§V.D) provide a basis for endorsing some notion of equal worth of liberty. To the extent that they do, it may well be that modern liberal theory contains the germs of a much more egalitarian theory of income distribution than we normally assume (see §C).[47]

(ii) The argument from positive (or effective) liberty has been described as a case for social reform which nevertheless remains 'definitely non-Socialist'.[48] (We might also note that a similar sort of argument for a social minimum can be based on the notion of a fair or effective equality of opportunity — i.e. one in which 'positions are not ... only open in a formal sense', but in which all 'have a fair chance to attain them'.[49] By basing the case for economic intervention on an understanding of the requirements of individual liberty (or equality of opportunity), it can be argued that liberals avoid the typical socialist appeals to community, solidarity and mutual aid.[50] But while this may be a plausible interpretation of the argument from effective liberty, it remains true that an important strain in new liberal economic proposals focuses on precisely the 'socialistic' themes of mutual aid and fellowship. Hobhouse, who surely emphasises such arguments more than any other of our modern liberals, centres his whole theory of social development (§IV.D) on the rise of such feelings. In radical contrast to those social Darwinists who uphold the continuing evolutionary gains produced by individual struggle, Hobhouse insisted that intellectual, moral and social evolution was characterised by 'the continual restriction of the sphere of the struggle for existence upon which natural selection depends'. For 'with the expansion of mental life come affections and sympathies, and later on religious and ethical sentiments inculcating mutual aid, discouraging the struggle of each for himself and enjoining the preservation of many who but for such assistance would go under in the life storm'.[51] Thus, as Hobhouse understood it, a 'public-spirited liberalism' integrated the traditional liberal devotion to individual liberty with socialistic 'solidarity', a solidarity which expressed itself in provision for the least favoured members of society.[52] This concern with social solidarity — which of course goes straight to the heart of the modern liberal theory of community — outlived the biological and evolutionary themes that loom so large in Hobhouse's writings. As we have already seen (§ III.C.3), Rawls points out that his 'difference principle' corresponds 'to a natural meaning of fraternity: namely, to the idea of not wanting to have greater advantages unless this is to the benefit of others who are less well off'.[53] 'Presumably', Rawls tells us, one of the practical implications of this solidaristic difference principle is a guaranteed social minimum to all.[54] Fraternity, as Dewey suggested, is thus expressed in the refusal to abandon those who, because of inferior capacities or opportunities, are left behind in a world with an inevitable competitive dimension.[55] In this respect, the modern liberal theory of community is an important counterweight to the competitiveness of the market, insisting as it does that the growth of true community is inconsistent with entirely leaving the life chances of any of one's fellows to the contingencies of the market.

## B.2. The Rejection of New Liberal Welfarism

The strong commitment of modern liberals to community makes it hard to see how any of them could be entirely indifferent to the fate of the less fortunate in the market. It does not necessarily follow that modern liberals are committed to new liberal welfare measures. Mill, for instance, is second to none in his stress on the importance of fraternal relations, and his sympathetic discussion of socialism in his *Principles* makes very clear that he thinks fellow feeling can play a large part in the economic sphere. Yet, like Bosanquet, Mill supported the principles of the Poor Law of 1834, which provided for compulsory labour in the workhouse for those on relief. This poor law, 'hated and dreaded by the working class', was the target of attack by new liberals like Hobhouse.[56] But Mill had at least two reasons for opposing poor relief given on anything but the harshest terms.

For one, Mill was a fairly straightforward Malthusian on population.[57] Following Malthus, Mill argued that population increased geometrically, whereas 'the produce of the land increases, *ceteribus paribus* in a diminishing ratio to the increase in the labour employed'. That is, once a society is fairly well developed (settled), the $n + 1$ unit of labour yields less of an increase in food production than did the $n$th unit. As a result, Mill held that population pressures are always threatening to reduce the standard of living: 'The new mouths require as much food as the old ones, and the hands do not produce as much.' Although Mill thought that technological improvements could win a

respite from this dynamic, he did not believe they could achieve a permanent victory. The key, then, to prosperity thus lay in controlling the
population. But the problem, as Mill saw it, was that such restraint is
not usually forthcoming. 'It has been the practice of a great majority of
the middle and poorer classes', he observed, 'whenever free from external control, to marry as early, and in most countries to have as
many children, as was consistent with maintaining themselves in the
condition of life which they were born to, or were accustomed to consider as theirs.' This last phrase is crucial, for if a couple were accustomed to living at $x$ level of comfort, and their income was increased to
$x + y$, Mill argued that they would continue to have children until the
family's well-being sunk back to $x$.[58] Such a response to an increased
income, Mill argued, was not absolutely necessary: if the workers grew
accustomed to their new level, they would not increase their families
until they sunk back to the old level. More importantly, he stressed
that with the development of practical intelligence, the lower class
could come to develop the prudence necessary to restrict their numbers
for their own good.

We can now understand Mill's rejection of a new liberal social minimum (or state-imposed minimum wage): it would induce an increase
in population and thus would serve to impoverish the society.

> Leave the people in a situation in which their condition manifestly
> depends upon their numbers, and the greatest permanent benefit
> may be derived from any sacrifice made to improve the physical
> well-being of the present generation, and raise, by that means,
> the habits of their children. But remove the regulation of their wages
> from their own control; guarantee to them a certain payment,
> either by law, or by the feeling of the community; and no amount
> of comfort that you can give to them will make either them or
> their descendants look to their own self-restraint as the proper
> means of preserving them in that state. You will only make them
> indignantly claim the continuance of your guarantee to themselves
> and their full complement of possible posterity.[59]

Interestingly, Mill is very clear that the difficulties posed by this sort of
analysis override a legitimate argument for assistance to the labouring
class:

> The higher and middle classes might and ought to be willing to sub-
> mit to a very considerable sacrifice of their own means, for improv-

ing the condition of the existing generation of labourers, if by this they could hope to provide similar advantages for the generation to come. But why should they be called upon to make these sacrifices, merely that the country may contain a greater number of people, in as great poverty and as great liability to destitution as now?[60]

But although, in lieu of the problems posed by the growth of population, Mill may have more strongly favoured a transfer of income from the upper and middle classes to the workers, he still would have opposed a social minimum divorced from the necessity to work. For, like Bosanquet after him, Mill was very much worried that such assistance might sap 'energy and self-dependence'. 'There are', he said, 'few things for which it is more mischievous that people should rely on the habitual aid of others, than for means of subsistence, and unhappily there is no lesson which they more easily learn.'[61] Neither Mill nor Bosanquet took this as precluding all assistance; rather, given the potentially destructive consequences of such aid, it becomes imperative to distinguish cases in which aid will harm from those in which it will lead to self-help and independence. This was precisely the aim of the Charity Organisation Society to which Bosanquet was committed (and which was a favourite target of new liberal attacks). According to Bosanquet, providing help without creating dependency was an art that required both extensive training on the part of the helper and an intimate knowledge of the client's circumstances. And, although it is quite wrong to say that Bosanquet denied the importance of changes in the material and environmental conditions of the poor, he did insist that the relation between character and conditions was extremely complex, and, therefore, reform of conditions *alone* could not reform the character of the poor. The upshot of all this was an emphasis on social work and a deep suspicion of statutory provisions based upon general (i.e. class) descriptions. 'We have found that charity cannot be in "ironclad" form, as the Americans say; it cannot be purely statutory, though it may co-operate with a statutory committee.'[62]

Now if one is convinced that provision of a minimum income to all will only spur a population growth which will eventually impoverish society or is apt to encourage continuing dependency, the new liberal espousal of state provision of welfare as a matter of right to all the needy begins to look very problematic indeed. (New liberals recognised this and so attacked the dependence thesis.[63]) Bosanquet, however, posed a more fundamental challenge to the new liberal programme. In a paper read to the Fabian Society, Bosanquet charged that the attempt by

'Economic Socialism' to create a co-operative social order by legislation was inherently faulty. 'We want a general good life', Bosanquet has
socialists saying, 'let us make a law that there shall be a general good
life.'[64] Bosanquet's argument here is often slighted but is not without
force. In so far as the new liberals' arguments depend on the thesis
that men are naturally co-operative and possess natural capacities for
mutual aid, it would seem an equally plausible conclusion that because
they are capable of such a co-operative existence, new liberalism – not
to say state socialism – is less necessary than it would be if men didn't
have these natural capacities. The attempt to 'mechanically create' a
'good life' may be as easily taken as lack of faith in the capacities of
human nature as an institutional manifestation of it.[65]

However, again it is not my intention to evaluate the cogency of
either the new liberal arguments or the counter-arguments of those like
Mill and Bosanquet. Rather, for the thesis of this book, what is significant is that both the new liberal proposals and their rejection by Mill
and Bosanquet are consistent with the modern liberal theory of man. It
is by no means inconsistent with the theory of human nature we examined in Part One to maintain, as do Mill and Bosanquet, that income
divorced from work can lead to pathological personalities devoid of
energy and independence. We may, *perhaps*, be justified in saying that,
given their theory of human nature, i.e. one centred on the drive to
development and excellence, the dependency dynamic is a bit surprising and does not strike one as a 'natural' extension of the theory. But
that is about as far as we can go: there is no question of logical inconsistency. (And not even this much can be said of Bosanquet's argument
that 'Economic Socialism' attempts to artificially create a true co-
operative order.) In sum, the modern liberal theory of human nature,
which generally remains at a fairly abstract level of analysis, is consistent with both the new liberal welfare measures and 'old-fashioned'
nineteenth-century radicalism. Again, though, it needs to be stressed
that rejection of new liberal welfarism does not constitute an indifference to the plight of the poor. The Poor Law, Charity Organisation
Society work, support of trade unionism, factory legislation and
land reform to encourage widespread proprietorship have all been
offered by various modern liberals as reforms aimed at improving
the condition of the working class and the poor, though ones that
do not entail new liberal welfare measures. Whether they are acceptable or adequate responses is, of course, the crux of the debate between
traditional liberal 'radicals' and the new liberals.[66]

## C. Economic Equality: A Maximum

Marc F. Plattner has recently argued in favour of a sharp theoretical distinction between 'the welfare state' and 'the redistributive state'. Writing in reference to the American experience, Plattner insists that 'social-insurance programs were meant to provide a cushion against particular contingencies, and welfare and other anti-poverty measures were intended to relieve those who were unable to provide for their own needs in a minimally acceptable fashion'. This concern with meeting the needs of the least well off, Plattner indicates, is the regulative aim of the welfare state. 'But', he continues, 'one can easily accept the principle of public insurance on the one hand and public charity or relief on the other without acknowledging the propriety of governmental efforts to promote the goal of greater equality of incomes.' It is this goal of equalisation of incomes which Plattner thinks is characteristic of the redistributive state. And as he sees it, 'There is an immense gulf in principle between the welfare state and the redistributive state, which can only be crossed at the gravest peril to a liberal political order.'[67]

Plattner's thesis is not without merit. A genuine theoretical distinction can be made between provision of a minimum and pursuit of economic equality. And, historically, it is true that new liberals like Hobhouse did believe that 'the minimum is more important than the maximum'.[68] However, contrary to what Plattner leads us to expect, an examination of the modern liberal theory from Mill onwards does not uncover an 'immense gulf' between the welfare and redistributive states. Quite the opposite, important arguments for economic equality − or, what is related, limiting inequality − are extensions of the sorts of considerations that underlie the new liberal case for the welfare state. To see this, let us briefly examine several modern liberal arguments for limiting economic inequality.

(i) Most important in this regard is the argument from the co-operative nature of the economic order. We have already seen how this provides the basis of a concern for the lot of the less well off which, in the hands of a new liberal like Hobhouse, can lead to a case for a 'civic minimum'. As Hobhouse also makes clear, though, it provides the foundation for a proposal for a maximum level of income. Writing in 1911, Hobhouse concluded 'that when we come to an income of some £5,000 a year, we approach the limit of the industrial value of the individual' and, hence, a 'super-tax' on higher incomes was justified.[69] That is, in Hobhouse's view, no one's contribution to the collective economic effort was worth more than £5,000 a year, so those with incomes above that were certainly gaining more than their contribution to the common good warranted. Although Hobhouse's analysis is informed by a strong notion of just deserts that is absent from Rawls's theory, his argument for a maximum nevertheless shares important similarities with Rawls's difference principle. One of the upshots of the difference principle is that larger incomes for some are only to be permitted if they serve to increase the life prospects of the least advantaged; i.e. if incomes were more equal, the prospects of the least fortunate would be even lower than they are. Recalling Green's analysis of civil society and the common good, we can see that Rawls's principle articulates Green's ideal, i.e. that economic life should be a co-operative effort to advance the good of all. As long as the difference principle is satisfied, the good of the least favoured is being maximised, and thus civil society is essentially co-operative rather than competitive. This is not to say that Rawls's theory is necessarily egalitarian. Depending on the incentives required to induce the more gifted to perform important functions,[70] and the relation between the personal accumulation and economic growth etc., improving the lot of the least well off may require more or less inequality. Consequently, depending on the assumptions one makes about these issues, Rawls's theory has been variously described as 'radically egalitarian',[71] and clearly inegalitarian (but see (iii) below).[72]

The most obvious target for the 'incomes only as a reward for contributing to the common good' argument, though, is inherited wealth. It may well be an open question as to whether very high earnings can be regarded as appropriate rewards for contributions to the common good; it seems fairly certain that inherited fortunes cannot be so regarded.[73] Inheritance has thus been a subject of criticism of modern liberals since Mill, who was prepared to limit the amount any person could inherit to that sufficient to afford a 'comfortable' or 'moderate' independence.[74] Hobhouse was willing to go a good deal further, maintaining that 'property in general should pass to the community at death'.[75] Mill stopped short of Hobhouse's proposal for several reasons, including his conviction that parents owed it to their children to give them a fair start in life and his (fairly conservative) belief that society is better off for having both an affluent body of labourers and a 'much larger body of persons than at present, not only exempt from the coarser toils, but with sufficient leisure, both physical and mental, from mechanical details, to cultivate freely the graces of life, and afford examples of them to the classes less favourably circumstanced for their growth'.[76]

Hobhouse was certainly less enticed by this vision of a leisured class and, so, was prepared to do away with inheritance. However, like Mill, he was less critical of outright gifts. Both theorists indicate that fundamental attacks on the right to give away one's property may well be inconsistent with an advocacy of private property. As Mill put it:

> Nothing is implied in property but the right of each to his (or her) own faculties, to what he can produce by them, and to whatever he can get for them in a fair market; together with his right to give this to any other person if he chooses, and the right of that other to receive and enjoy it.
>
> It follows, therefore, that although the right of bequest, or gift after death, forms part of the idea of private property, the right of inheritance, as distinguished from bequest, does not.[77]

Hobhouse disagreed: the principle of private property, he argued, required the right of gift while one was living but not after one had died.[78] What is significant, though, is that this line of reasoning — based upon what is implied by the notion of private property — serves to blunt the force of the critique of unearned income which seems implied by the common good-based interpretation of the market.[79] If (a) private property is justified, and if (b) it requires the right to alienate one's accumulated wealth, and if (c) the right to alienate property implies the liberty of others to accept it, then a strong case exists for the legitimacy of some sorts of unearned incomes.[80] And that, in turn, weakens the anti-inheritance redistributive implications that we have been considering.

(ii) We saw in Chapter V (§D.3) that modern liberals have postulated a link between equality and the growth of fraternity, a link that has deep foundations in the analysis of sympathy. Some readers, noting the commitment to fraternity in liberals like Rawls have thus held that any inequality in wealth or income may tend to inhibit 'the development of a sense of community among the members of a society'.[81] Just as a fraternal society requires civil equality, it is argued that fraternity can only thrive in a regime of economic equality. Rawls has resisted this conclusion. While he acknowledges that community is destroyed when those who are less well off doubt their own worth and harbour feelings of resentment towards the more favoured members of society, Rawls denies that the sorts of inequalities permitted by his difference principle would induce such rancorous feelings. Rather, he argues, because a properly structured economic order is a co-operative endeavour promoting the welfare of all rather than a zero-sum game (i.e. a game in which there are losses corresponding to all gains), those who are less well off do not experience the better fortune of others as costs to themselves. Indeed, the higher gains of some benefit all. Moreover, Rawls reminds us that these economic inequalities occur against a background of full civil and political equality, thus supporting the self-respect of poorer individuals.[82]

However, Rawls does seem to acknowledge that sufficiently great economic inequalities may engender an (excusable) envy destructive of fraternal feelings. More generally, the modern liberal analysis of sympathy would seem to imply that economic inequalities ought not to be so great as to interfere with the necessary imaginative projection/ response. As Hobhouse reminds us, the rich have difficulty sympathising with the poor or, as Green put it, 'The master cannot enter into the feelings of the servant, nor the servant into those of his master.'[83] As I stressed in the third chapter, the modern liberal account of fraternity does not cohere well with a class-stratified society: the differences in ways of living, plans, values etc. that mark off classes would seem to hinder the growth of fellow feeling between members of different classes. On the face of it, then, it seems surprising that modern liberals have been so uncritical of economic orders characterised by fairly stark class (or occupational) division. Green, for example, calmly notes that '[i]n every nation, perhaps, there must be a certain separation between those who live solely by the labour of their heads or by the profit of capital, between members of the learned profession and those engaged constantly in buying and selling, between those who are earning their money and those who are living on the income of large accumulated capital.'[84] And should we be tempted to attribute this to Victorian complacency or Green's reluctance to follow out the implications of his theory, we would do well to remember that Rawls too supposes that society is legitimately broken up into classes of property owners and unskilled labourers (with differing prospects in life).[85]

No single factor accounts for this modern liberal willingness to accept an economically class-stratified society, even at the apparent cost of harming the growth of fellow feeling (see §VI.C.1). No doubt, as is manifest in Rawls, it partly derives from a conviction that the less well off are better off in such a society than in a more egalitarian one. Moreover, the liberal insistence on equality of opportunity means that while society is stratified, the strata do not constitute castes; the possibility of upward (and downward) social mobility should serve to lessen the insulation of classes.[86] But perhaps most fundamentallay, modern liberals are not apt to posit a strong *necessary* connection between social class and a distinctive 'consciousness' or outlook. This is nicely brought out in Greengarten's treatment of Green. As he shows, although Green both accepts class divisions and acknowledges that they can in practice divide society, he holds that particularistic class perspectives can be overcome. Again, as we saw in the last chapter, for Green the main vehicle for the rise of such a common outlook was a common education, the 'true social leveller'.[87] As long as classes are not too isolated from, and alien to, each other, modern liberals seem to believe that a common public outlook can be shared, providing the foundation for some degree of a community-wide sense of fraternity.

(iii) Again, then, the upshot seems to be that the extent of inequality ought not to be so great that those at the bottom and those at the top of the economic order lead lives that are so different that they encounter each other as aliens, unable to appreciate each other's lives. But Rawls's main argument for limiting inequality is neither that premised on the co-operative nature of economic life (as articulated by the difference principle) nor that of securing civic friendship, but rather it is aimed at ensuring what he calls the 'fair value' of the equal liberties. In particular, Rawls focuses on the political liberties which, he holds, 'lose much of their value whenever those who have greater private means are permitted to use their advantages to control the course of public debate'.[88] At some point, Rawls argues, inequalities can be so great that those at the top of the economic order possess an inordinate ability to influence government, hence undermining the effective political liberties of others. Accordingly, one of the compensating steps to be taken is to 'impose a number of inheritance and gift taxes' and set 'restrictions on the rights of bequest'. Rawls is explicit that the aim of these taxes is not to raise revenue for government expenditure but 'gradually and continually to correct the distribution of wealth and to prevent concentrations of power detrimental to the fair value of political liberty and fair equality of opportunity'.[89] Hence, 'There is a maximum gain permitted to the most favored on the assumption that, even if the difference principle would allow it, there would be unjust effects on the political system and the like.'[90]

(iv) At one point in his *Lectures on Political Obligation*, Green explicitly asks whether the 'rationale of property' is consistent with substantial inequalities. He begins by acknowledging that *if* an 'inequality of fortunes' were the cause of a propertyless 'proletariate', i.e. if large fortunes for some precluded proprietorship for others, then the principle of property would be inconsistent with unchecked freedom of appropriation. In examining this possibility Green insists 'that the increased wealth of one man does not naturally mean the diminished wealth of another', again alluding to the co-operative ('positive-sum') nature of economic life.[91] But he also indicates that unchecked freedom of appropriation is implied by the argument for property. 'If', he tells us, 'we leave a man free to realise the conception of a possible well-being, it is impossible to limit the effect upon him of his desire to provide for his future well-being, as including that of the persons in whom he is interested, or the success with which at the prompting of that desire he turns resources of nature to account.'[92] Bosanquet, so often accused of giving a reactionary interpretation of Green's 'progressive' doctrines, denied that the principle of property requires unlimited acquisition, although he did hold that '[m]an never has enough so long as his capacity for foresight and management, for treating life as a unity with a past and a future, is not taxed to the full.'[93] This is surely an important point of disagreement between, on the one hand, Green and Bosanquet and, on the other, liberals like Mill, Hobhouse, Dewey and Rawls, who really do think that too much property is bad for the soul.[94] As Rawls puts it, 'beyond some point it [wealth] is . . . likely to be a positive hindrance, a meaningless distraction at best if not a temptation to indulgence and emptiness'.[95] This attitude towards wealth clearly accords with the general depreciation of economic pursuits and 'materialism'. While, to be sure, personal development requires a material foundation, a satisfying life does not concentrate on material gains; consequently, as Rawls says, great wealth may be a meaningless distraction or even corrupting. It is also worth noting here that this sort of argument is characteristic of modern liberalism: by maintaining that great wealth harms the development of the wealthy, egalitarian measures which obviously benefit the less privileged can also be said to be in the ultimate interests of those who prima facie lose out.

All this has been regrettably summary. Nevertheless it does seem clear that Plattner's wide gulf between the advocacy of a welfare state and of a redistributive state does not seem present in modern liberal theory. Many of the same ideas that underlie proposals for a social minimum — a co-operative economic order, civic friendship and effective liberty — also serve as foundations for redistributive proposals. As I have stressed, the spirit of these proposals is not radically egalitarian — to slightly alter Mill, they aim at a state where none are poor but none are too rich.[96] Again, though, although redistributive proposals have deep roots in the modern liberal theory of human nature, modern liberals like Green can avoid them by stressing the boons of unfettered accumulation, both to the less well off and the rich. Just as Green shares the new liberal conviction that none ought to be poor, it would seem he would concur that a more egalitarian distribution of wealth and income is better than a very unequal one, *other things being equal*. But it by no means follows that he must endorse either the welfare or redistributive state.

## D. Industrial Life

As I indicated in the analysis of arguments for a social minimum, the real sympathy of a new liberal like Hobhouse was with the workers rather than the poor in general. Hobhouse, we saw, was prepared to be very hard on some categories of non-working poor, and all non-working poor receiving assistance (excluding pensioners and some categories of the unemployed) were regarded as 'dependents'. I think it is fairly safe to say that (at least until we come to Rawls) the main thrust of modern liberal economic reforms has been to improve the condition of the working class rather than the poor in general. This is manifestly the aim of the central new liberal proposals for factory legislation (regulating working conditions and hours) and for old age pensions. It is perhaps less obvious that the new liberal's concern with unemployment focuses on the workers (the unemployed, after all, are not working). The notion, however, that the liability to unemployment is a particular curse of the working class is never far below the surface; as Hobhouse reminds us in one of his discussions, 'Large numbers of respectable and hard-working men are thrown out of work through no fault of their own.'[97] But the new liberals were not the only ones concerned about the workers. Bosanquet, though as always worried about inducing dependency and, so, wary of state provision, nevertheless was explicit about the importance of an 'effective income' and shorter working hours.[98] I will not repeat here the familiar account as to how notions of self-development enter into liberal arguments on these matters. Suffice it to say, following Hobhouse, that the regulative aim was to produce conditions 'upon which mind and character may develop themselves' and which allow all to participate in the common life.[99]

What I wish to consider in this concluding section is Dewey's insistence that this new liberal programme of social, and particularly industrial, legislation is insufficient to achieve the ideal of free development for all. Mere 'changes in wage, hours of work and sanitary conditions', he argued, are not sufficient to give the worker a 'sense of freedom and personal interest in the operations of production'. For that, some 'kind of participation [by] the worker . . . in the production and social disposition of the wares he produces' is necessary.[100] And Dewey is by no means alone in considering such 'a radical social alteration'; Mill, Bosanquet, Hobhouse and Rawls all note the possibility of worker participation in industrial decisions, the former two with enthusiasm.[101] Now unless modern liberalism is to be simply bourgeois (in the sense that it applies only to the career-orientated middle class), it seems hard to avoid the conclusion that some sort of worker participation in industrial management is essential.[102] Some must operate the machines upon which industrial society is built, to abandon them to a monotonous, soul-destroying division of labour[103] would be nothing less than an acknowledgement that the modern liberal ideal of a personality organised around a career cannot be universalised in a modern industrial society. For modern liberalism to truly apply to manual workers in advanced industries (rather than simply in traditional crafts work), they must reap significant developmental gains from their employment. And for that to occur, not only must each be confronted with a variety of tasks, but, as Dewey makes clear, workers must not be treated simply as 'hands': each must be accorded opportunity for significant exercise of judgement.[104] We must remember that our modern liberals insist that the intellect is the key to all development. Accordingly, if an occupation is to spur the worker's development, it must provide some intellectual challenge. To be sure, not every aspect of a job must be (or can be) interesting and challenging — even the most interesting vocations include dull tasks — but if the modern liberal ideal is to be universalisable within advanced industrial societies, no one's life work can be restricted to a deadening tedium.

All this points to the desirability of some sort of worker participation in management decisions. As Amy Gutmann has pointed out, however, workers need not have total control. Workers, she suggests, can 'have complete autonomy to decide issues related to job structure and shop-floor activity' while owners retain significant decision-making powers over matters like investment.[105] However, in some ways the modern liberal theory of development inclines towards a more extensive worker control. If we recall the arguments of Chapter VI concerning the developmental benefits of participation, one of the main themes was how political participation expands the intellectual horizon of the citizen beyond his everyday affairs so as to place those affairs in a wider context. The same reasoning provides an argument for some worker participation in higher level management decisions. This does not entail the abolition of managers (just as the case for political democracy does not require the abolition of leaders). It does, though, seem to call for some active involvement of workers in management decisions, or at least in choosing managers.

Mill believed that in a free market, worker-managed industries would displace traditional enterprises. As the workers became educated, he argued, the co-operative firms 'would tend more and more to absorb all work-people, except those who have too little understanding, or too little virtue, to be capable of learning to act on any other system than that of narrow selfishness'.[106] Thus far Mill's predictions have not been borne out. The British producer co-operative movement, in which he placed so much hope, died just a few years after he did.[107] Although in principle 'large-scale capitalist enterprises and small-scale labour-managed co-operatives' can 'exist and compete side by side',[108] in practice the labour-managed enterprises were driven out of the market. According to P.J.D. Wiles, they were beset by a multitude of problems, including a lack of labour discipline, lack of initial capital, refusal to plow back earnings and inability to attract the best managers. As Wiles has put it, they seem unable to survive in a 'neutral and unsympathetic market'.[109] Given tax advantages and other state assistance, however, they have shown themselves to be viable. Nevertheless, as demonstrated by the Yugoslav experience, they still manifest serious inefficiences and discriminate against some categories of workers (i.e. the young and technically well educated).[110]

These are serious difficulties. Efficiency is a cardinal virtue of economic systems, and one to which both classical and new liberals have been committed.[111] Nevertheless, the ideal of healthy development is so fundamental to modern liberalism that, unless these problems are so serious as to undermine the viability of the economy, efficiency considerations alone would seem insufficient to induce the abandonment of a reform as crucial to development as worker participation would seem to be. From the perspective of modern liberalism, much more troublesome is John Plamenatz's contention that the benefits attributed to worker self-management may be largely unattainable in advanced industrial societies.[112] According to Plamenatz, 'All or most of the workers in an organization can take a creative part in managing it, only if two conditions hold: if the organization is small and they all take part in making the major decisions.' In the sorts of enterprises that characterise advanced industrial societies neither condition obtains: corporations will necessarily be bureaucratic and, even if 'democratically run ... the sense of distance between managers and managed, between "them" and "us" is not wholly removed'. Plamenatz acknowledges that ordinary workers would still have an important role as electors (though not as 'creative managers'), but he clearly questions just how much that will change the life of the typical worker. In contrast, Plamenatz does seem to see somewhat more potential in organising work so that 'a great part of it is done by teams of workers who are left to themselves to get on with the jobs allocated to them'. But he is clearly sceptical whether this sort of reform requires any significant worker participation in most management decisions. 'Already', he notes, 'there is a good deal of it in some industries.'

Ultimately, however, Plamenatz has very grave doubts that the majority of tasks in an industrial society can be made challenging. 'That the work that most people in an industrial society do to earn their livings is dull is a fact that just has to be accepted, as Marx himself recognized in his later years.' Plamenatz thus poses a fundamental challenge to the modern liberal thesis that careers must be the focus of a suitable life. Instead of concentrating on employment, he maintains, we might look at the whole of a life. Just as the dull parts of an interesting and creative career are made less boring by the recognition that they contribute to the creative and interesting task, '[s]o, too, the "uncreative" worker may find his work the less dull for recognizing that it is the price he pays for the opportunity to do other things, which have more that is creative and satisfying about them.' As Plamenatz makes clear, the upshot of this analysis is that if workers are to lead 'creative' lives, they would 'be well advised to care more about being paid well for the work they do, having a shorter working day and better conditions at work than about workers' management in industry'.[113] (And, of course, equality of opportunity will be of central importance in securing to all the chance to attain the more attractive positions.)

Just as modern liberals divided over the desirability of new liberal welfare measures, so too can they disagree over worker management. However, perhaps unlike the previous divide, this disagreement has repercussions throughout the modern liberal theory of man itself. Dewey's position, insisting on the inadequacy of new liberal industrial reform, remains faithful to the important modern liberal tenet that the centre of a plan of life is a career. If that tenet stands, it seems impossible to avoid some thoroughgoing industrial reform advocating much more extensive worker participation in industrial decisions. If, however, Plamenatz is right, the modern liberal theory of man has been intrinsically bourgeois, incapable of extension to most industrial workers. Plamenatz's suggested reorientation, away from careers and towards lives as a whole, calls for significant changes in the modern liberal theory of man, especially its doctrine of individuality. I suspect that industrial life can and ought to be made less tedious by forms of worker participation which do indeed contribute to a more challenging life for workers. But, while Plamenatz has overstated his case, he is no doubt right that most workers in an industrial society cannot have creative and challenging careers in the sense that artists, craftsmen or academics do. Consequently, if modern liberals are to be at peace with industrial society, it would seem that they need to rethink their idea of a healthy and rewarding life, lessening the centrality of careers while still doing the utmost to improve the quality of industrial life.

## Notes

1.  Adam Smith, *An Inquiry into the Nature and Causes of The Wealth of Nations*, W.B. Todd (ed.) (Clarendon Press, Oxford, 1976), pp. 456, 630. See my 'Public and Private Interests in Liberal Political Economy, Old and New' in S.I. Benn and G.F. Gaus (eds.), *Conceptions of the Public and Private in Social Life* (Croom Helm, London, forthcoming).

2.  See Lord Robbins, *The Theory of Economic Policy in English Classical Political Economy* (Macmillan, London, 1961), p. 104, and his *Political Economy: Past and Present* (Macmillan, London, 1977), p. 124. J.R. McCulloch disagreed that liberty is most important: 'Freedom', he wrote, 'is not, as some appear to think, the end of government; the advancement of the public prosperity and happiness is.' *Principles of Political Economy* (Adam and Charles Black, Edinburgh, 1864), pp. 186-87.

3.  This is John W. Chapman's description of Hayek's view. 'Justice, Freedom and Property' in J. Roland Pennock and John W. Chapman (eds.), *NOMOS XXII: Property* (New York University Press, New York, 1980), p. 293. Emphasis added.

4.  F.A. Hayek, 'Liberalism' in his *New Studies in Philosophy, Politics, Economics and the History of Ideas* (Routledge and Kegan Paul, London, 1978), p. 149.

5.  Kenneth R. Minogue, 'The Concept of Property and its Contemporary Significance' in Pennock and Chapman (eds.), *NOMOS XXII: Property*, pp. 7-8. For an analysis of the relation of political and economic freedom, see P.J.D. Wiles, *Economic Institutions Compared* (Wiley, New York, 1977), Ch. 17.

6.  Brian Barry, *The Liberal Theory of Justice* (Clarendon Press, Oxford, 1973), p. 166.

7.  See Rawls, 'Reply to Alexander and Musgrave', *Quarterly Journal of Economics*, LXXXVIII (Nov. 1974), p. 640; and his *Theory of Justice* (The Belknap Press of Harvard University Press, Cambridge, Mass., 1971), pp. 273-74. Chapman writes of Rawls that '[h]e is even willing to consider market socialism, revealing an indifference to private property quite anathema to Hayek.' 'Review — *Law, Legislation and Liberty*', *Journal of Economic Literature*, XVI (March 1978), p. 97.

8.  Dewey is reputed to have said: 'I think that on the basis of *Liberalism and Social Action*, and to some extent *Individualism — Old and New*, I can be

classed as a democratic socialist. If I were permitted to define "socialism" and "socialist" I would so classify myself.' Jim Cork, 'John Dewey and Karl Marx' in Sidney Hook (ed.), *John Dewey: Philosopher of Science and Freedom* (Dial Press, New York, 1950), p. 349. George R. Geiger writes that Cork's chapter, 'along with some of the early work of Hook, is perhaps the chief effort to ally Dewey not merely with socialism, but with the Marxist philosophy itself'. *John Dewey in Perspective* (Oxford University Press, New York, 1958), p. 179n. For a Marxist critique of Dewey, see George Novack, *Pragmatism versus Marxism* (Pathfinder Press, New York, 1975).

9.    The central discussions here are Mill's *Chapters on Socialism* in J.M. Robson (ed.), *The Collected Works of John Stuart Mill* (University of Toronto Press, Toronto, 1963), vol. V, pp. 703-53; his *Principles of Political Economy* in *Collected Works*, vol. II, pp. 199 ff; and his *Autobiography* (Columbia University Press, New York, 1924), pp. 161 ff. See also Donald L. Losman, 'J.S. Mill on Alternative Economic Systems', *American Journal of Economics and Sociology*, XXX (Jan. 1971), pp. 85-104; L.E. Fredman and B.L.J. Gordon, 'John Stuart Mill and Socialism', *The Mill Newsletter*, III (Fall 1967), pp. 3-11; Pedro Schwartz, *The New Political Economy of J.S. Mill* (Weidenfeld and Nicolson, London, 1972), Ch. 7.

10.    Hobhouse: *The Elements of Social Justice* (Allen and Unwin, London, 1949), p. 172; *Liberalism* (Oxford University Press, Oxford, 1964), pp. 54, 86-87, Ch. VIII. As Michael Freeden makes very clear, Hobhouse wished to reform rather than abolish private property. *The New Liberalism: An Ideology of Social Reform* (Clarendon Press, Oxford, 1978), p. 46. See also Peter Weiler, 'The New Liberalism of L.T. Hobhouse', *Victorian Studies*, XVI (Dec. 1972), pp. 154-55.

11.    Based upon Green's notes on Plato's *Republic* (among his unpublished papers in Balliol College Library at Oxford), John Morrow has argued that Green saw possible merits in communal property. 'Idealism and Socialism in Britain, 1880-1920', unpublished PhD thesis, York University, 1980. See, however, Green's *Lectures on the Principles of Political Obligation* in R.L. Nettleship (ed.), *Works of Thomas Hill Green* (Longman's, Green, and Co., 1889), vol. II, pp. 523 ff. Although, as Collini notes, Bosanquet was anti-socialist, it is also true that his sympathies seemed to be with labour after World War I. See Stefan Collini, 'Hobhouse, Bosanquet, and the State: Philosophical Idealism and Political Argument in England, 1880-1918', *Past and Present*, LXXII (Aug. 1976), p. 87; J.H. Muirhead (ed.), *Bernard Bosanquet and his Friends* (Allen and Unwin, London, 1935), p. 217. Adam Ulam argues 'that there are no implications in [Bosanquet's] . . . *theory as a whole* that the state should be socialist or non-socialist in its character'. *Philosophical Foundations of English Socialism* (Harvard University Press, Cambridge, Mass., 1951), p. 60. See Bosanquet's *Civilization of Christendom* (Swan Sonnenschein, London, 1899), pp. 304-57, and his 'Socialism and Natural Selection' in his edited collection, *Aspects of the Social Problem* (Macmillan, London, 1895), pp. 289-307.

12.    Hobhouse, *Sociology and Philosophy: Centenary Collection of Essays and Articles* (G. Bell and Sons, London, 1966), p. 216. See my 'Liberal Political Economy' for a more detailed examination of this critique.

13.    In an early essay on 'The Force of Circumstances', Green asserts precisely the notion that is anathema to new liberals like Dewey or Keynes, viz. that '[t]he recognition of the laws of political economy is in itself an admission that men have no control over the results of their own combined energies, which operate in a system as independent of human will as that which regulates the motion of heavenly bodies.' *Works*, vol. III, p. 9. Compare J.M. Keynes, 'Am I a Liberal?' in his *Essays in Persuasion* (Macmillan, London, 1972), p. 305. Bosan-

quet stresses the merits of an 'automatic' system over one based on 'discretionary intervention'. *Social and International Ideals* (Macmillan, London, 1917), p. 220.

14. Hobhouse, 'The Ethical Basis of Collectivism', *International Journal of Ethics*, VIII (Jan. 1898), p. 143. I consider the change in perception of the state from classical to new liberal political economy in more detail in my 'Liberal Political Economy'.

15. Rawls, 'A Well-Ordered Society' in Peter Laslett and James Fishkin (eds.), *Philosophy, Politics and Society*, 5th series (Basil Blackwell, Oxford, 1979), pp. 7-8.

16. C.B. Macpherson, *Democratic Theory: Essays in Retrieval* (Clarendon Press, Oxford, 1973), p. 24. See essays I, II, III and IX. Macpherson presents a somewhat different thesis in his essay on 'Liberal-Democracy and Property' in his edited collection, *Property: Mainstream and Critical Positions* (University of Toronto Press, Toronto, 1978), pp. 199-207. See also his 'Rawls' Models of Man and Society', *Philosophy of Social Sciences*, III (1973), pp. 341-47.

17. Dewey and Tufts, *Ethics*, rev. edn (Henry Holt, New York, 1932), pp. 487-88. See also Mill, *Principles of Political Economy*, pp. 754-60; Rawls, *A Theory of Justice*, p. 290.

18. Hobhouse, *Liberalism*, p. 70. Rawls, too, sometimes associates equality of opportunity with equal rights, contending that both uphold the basic equality of all citizens (see §V.D). Rawls also explicitly ties the principle of open positions to 'the realization of the self'. See *A Theory of Justice*, pp. 84, 106. For Dewey see *Problems of Men* (Philosophical Library, New York, 1946), pp. 53, 60. In the main, the developmental arguments for equal opportunity are much the same as for equal liberty.

19. Mill, *Principles of Political Economy*, pp. 754-55.

20. Green, *Political Obligation*, pp. 518-19. See Melvin Richter, *The Politics of Conscience: T.H. Green and His Age* (Weidenfeld and Nicolson, London, 1964), pp. 276 ff. On the Hegelian theory of property, see Peter G. Stillman, 'Property, Freedom and Individuality in Hegel's and Marx's Political Thought' and Christopher J. Berry, 'Property and Possession: Two Replies to Locke – Hume and Hegel', both of which are to be found in Pennock and Chapman (eds.), *NOMOS XXII: Property*, pp. 130-67, and 89-100.

21. Bosanquet, 'The Principle of Private Property' in *Aspects of the Social Problem*, 310-15. See also his *Philosophical Theory of the State*, 4th edn (Macmillan, London, 1951), pp. 281 ff.

22. Green, *Prolegomena to Ethics*, A.C. Bradley (ed.) (Clarendon Press, Oxford, 1890), p. 201.

23. See Dewey, *Human Nature and Conduct* (Henry Holt, New York, 1922), p. 117; Hobhouse, *Sociology and Philosophy*, pp. 83-106. Bosanquet, however, also opposed a rigid conception of property. *Essays and Addresses* (Swan Sonnenschein, London, 1891), pp. 43-44.

24. See Hobhouse, *Social Justice*, pp. 158-59; and his *Sociology and Philosophy*, pp. 85 ff. See also Peter Clarke, *Liberals and Social Democrats* (Cambridge University Press, Cambridge, 1978), p. 153.

25. Bosanquet, *Ideals*, pp. 223-24. See also his 'Private Property', p. 314.

26. Rawls, for example, precludes a command socialist economy (i.e. one that entirely replaces markets with the authoritative allocation of resources and income) since it is apt to infringe liberties, including 'the important liberty of free choice of occupation'. *A Theory of Justice*, pp. 272-74. See §V.C. Mill too has worries that some forms of socialism, viz. those that insist on absolute equality, might endanger individuality. *Principles of Political Economy*, p. 209. See Richard J. Arneson, 'Mill's Doubts About Freedom Under Socialism', *Canadian Journal of Philosophy*, supp. vol. V (1979), pp. 470-89.

27. Although Mill endorsed the principle of *laissez faire*, he introduced a wide range of qualifications, so much so in fact that Robert Paul Wolff depicts his analysis as laying the foundation for 'Welfare State Liberalism'. *The Poverty of Liberalism* (Beacon Press, Boston, 1968), pp. 20 ff. Of all our modern liberals, the only doubtful case here is Dewey. Some, at least, have held that he too ultimately supported a new liberal 'state capitalism'. See Edgar B. Gumbert, 'John Dewey and the New Liberalism: Reactions to the U.S.S.R.', *Educational Theory*, XXII (Summer 1972), p. 347. See also Daniel Bell, 'The Background and Development of Marxian Socialism in the United States' in Donald Drew Egbert and Stow Persons (eds.), *Socialism and American Life* (Princeton University Press, Princeton, 1952), vol. I, pp. 369 ff. But see in addition David F. Bowers, 'American Socialism and the Socialist Philosophy of History' in ibid., pp. 423 ff.

28. Bosanquet, *The Philosophical Theory of the State*, p. 256.

29. Bosanquet, *Some Suggestions in Ethics* (Macmillan, London, 1919), pp. 43-44, 176-78. See also Dewey, *Liberalism and Social Action* (G.P. Putnam's Sons, New York, 1935), p. 88.

30. I.M. Greengarten, *Thomas Hill Green and the Development of Liberal-Democratic Thought* (University of Toronto Press, Toronto, 1981), p. 103. See also John W. Seaman, 'L.T. Hobhouse and the Theory of "Social Liberalism" ', *Canadian Journal of Political Science*, XI (1978), pp. 777-801.

31. Green, *Prolegomena*, p. 263. Emphasis added.

32. See Dewey and Tufts, *Ethics*, p. 286. For other modern liberal comments critical of extreme competition, see Dewey, *Characters and Events: Popular Essays in Social and Political Philosophy*, Joseph Ratner (ed.) (Henry Holt, New York, 1929), vol. II, p. 491; Mill, *Principles of Political Economy*, p. 754; Hobhouse, 'Collectivism', pp. 150 ff. Bosanquet seems to be the only modern liberal who was not at all put off by the competitive dimension of life, going so far as to applaud at one point the 'personal struggle for existence'. Even he, though, seemed to object only to the attempt at *total* suppression of the struggle rather than efforts to mitigate it. See 'Socialism and Natural Selection', pp. 291, 306. On Bosanquet and the struggle for survival, see Rodney Barker, *Political Ideas in Modern Britain* (Methuen, London, 1978), pp. 60-62.

33. Ann R. Cacoullos, *Thomas Hill Green: Philosopher of Rights* (Twayne, New York, 1974), pp. 137-38. Greengarten criticises Cacoullos on pp. 102-3 of his *Green and Liberal-Democratic Thought*.

34. Hobhouse, *Social Development* (Allen and Unwin, London, 1924), p. 331. Compare Dewey, *The Public and Its Problems* (Swallow Press, Chicago, 1954), p. 217.

35. Mill, *Principles of Political Economy*, p. 792.

36. Ulam, *English Socialism*, p. 40.

37. See Barker, *Political Ideas*, pp. 14 ff; Helen Merrell Lynd, *England in the Eighteen-Eighties* (Oxford University Press, London, 1945), pp. 176 ff; John Rodman, 'Introduction' to his edited collection, *The Political Theory of T.H. Green* (Appleton-Century-Crofts, New York, 1964), p. 1. According to Thomas P. Neill, 'Green is important in the history of Liberalism not so much for what he said as for the conclusions which were to be drawn logically from his stress on the common good and the individual's participation in it.' *The Rise and Decline of Liberalism* (Bruce Publishing Co., Milwaukee, 1953), p. 257.

38. Hobhouse, *Liberalism*, pp. 96-97.

39. Hobhouse, *Social Justice*, p. 134. Emphasis added.

40. Ibid., pp. 132, 138.

41. Hobhouse, *Liberalism*, p. 96; and his *Social Evolution and Political Theory* (Columbia University Press, New York, 1928), p. 179, but see also pp. 171 ff.

42. Green, 'Lecture on Liberal Legislation and Freedom of Contract' in *Works*, vol. III, p. 374. See Barker, *Political Ideas*, p. 14.

43. Dewey, *Liberalism and Social Action*, pp. 34, 56-57; and his *Intelligence in the Modern World: John Dewey's Philosophy*, Joseph Ratner (ed.) (Modern Library, New York, 1939), pp. 351-52; and his *Human Nature and Conduct*, pp. 306 ff.

44. Dewey, *Individualism – Old and New* (Allen and Unwin, London, 1931), pp. 84-85. See also Dewey and Tufts, *Ethics*, pp. 457, 483. Compare, however, Hobhouse, *Political Theory*, pp. 172-73.

45. Rawls, *A Theory of Justice*, pp. 151-52.

46. Ibid., p. 204.

47. See Norman Daniels, 'Equal Liberty and Unequal Worth of Liberty' in his edited collection, *Reading Rawls: Critical Studies of* A Theory of Justice (Basic Books, New York, 1974), pp. 253-81; Virginia McDonald, 'Rawlsian Contractarianism: Liberal Equality or Inequality?', *Canadian Journal of Philosophy*, supp. vol. III (1977), pp. 71-94; John J. Flynn and Piero Ruffinergo, 'Distributive Justice: Some Institutional Implications of Rawls' *A Theory of Justice*', *Utah Law Review* (1975), p. 139.

48. D.A. Hamer, *Liberal Politics in the Age of Gladstone and Rosebury* (Clarendon Press, Oxford, 1972), pp. 234-35.

49. Rawls, *A Theory of Justice*, p. 73. Rawls argues that a society which is characterised simply by careers open to talents rather than a fair equality of opportunity may endanger the self-respect of the poor (ibid., pp. 106-7). Rawls, however, does not explicitly base his argument for a social minimum on fair equality of opportunity, though he does point to the provision of educational opportunities as well as to 'political and legal institutions which regulate . . . the overall trends of economic events' (ibid., p. 73). See also Hobhouse, *Political Theory*, p. 75.

50. See David Miller, *Social Justice* (Clarendon Press, Oxford, 1976), Ch. VII; Amy Gutmann, *Liberal Equality* (Cambridge University Press, Cambridge, 1980), pp. 78-86.

51. The first quotation is from Hobhouse's *Social Development*, p. 107; the second is from his *Development and Purpose: An Essay Towards a Philosophy of Evolution* (Macmillan, London, 1913), p. 9. The new liberals' use of biological argument is the focus of Freeden's study, *The New Liberalism*, see esp. Ch. III. As I observed in note 32 above, Bosanquet was somewhat inclined *towards* 'individual struggle'.

52. Hobhouse, *Democracy and Reaction* (T. Fisher Unwin, London, 1904), pp. 226, 237-43. As Freeden notes, new liberals saw old-age pensions as an expression of social solidarity (*The New Liberalism*, p. 203). It has been argued, however, that notions of community do not provide an adequate foundation for welfare rights. See Raymond Plant, Harry Lesser and Peter Taylor-Gooby, *Political Philosophy and Social Welfare* (Routledge and Kegan Paul, London, 1980), Pt. III.

53. Rawls, *A Theory of Justice*, p. 105.

54. Ibid., p. 277. The relation between the difference principle and the social minimum is not entirely clear (thus Rawls's use of 'presumably'). For example, is it the difference principle alone that accounts for the social minimum or, as Michelman argues, is it also tied to other parts of Rawls's theory (e.g. fair equality of opportunity)? However, I shall leave this, and related, questions aside, assuming that the difference principle does require a social minimum. For discussions of some of these difficulties see: Frank I. Michelman, 'Constitutional Welfare Rights and *A Theory of Justice*' in Daniels (ed.), *Reading Rawls*, pp. 319-47; J.E.J. Altham, 'Rawls's Difference Principle', *Philosophy*, XLVIII (Jan. 1973), pp. 75-78; Brian Barry, *The Liberal Theory of Justice*, pp. 104-5; David Copp, 'Justice and the Difference Principle', *Canadian Journal of Philosophy*, IV (Dec. 1974), pp. 229-40.

55. Dewey and Tufts, *Ethics*, p. 388.

56. William A. Robson, *Welfare State and Welfare Society: Illusion and Reality* (Allen and Unwin, London, 1976), p. 20. For Mill's early views on the poor law, see Schwartz, *The New Political Economy*, pp. 46-47. See also John M. Robson, *The Improvement of Mankind: The Social and Political Thought of John Stuart Mill* (University of Toronto Press, Toronto, 1968), p. 216. A crucial divide between traditional and new liberals occurred in the Royal Commission on the Poor Law set up in 1905. The division in the Commission is often characterised as that between the majority (of which Helen and Bernard Bosanquet were prominent) which endorsed a relief-as-charity concept and the minority (led by Beatrice Webb) which focused on preventing destitution by structural reforms. Hobhouse, who apparently worked on the Webb committee, also opposed the poor law, insisting that relief should be a right rather than charity. See Clarke, *Liberals and Social Democrats*, pp. 118-27; Weiler, 'The New Liberalism', pp. 144-45; Bosanquet, *Civilization of Christendom*, pp. 339 ff. The debate between 'charity' and a 'right' to assistance continues to this day. See Plant, Lesser and Taylor-Gooby, *Political Philosophy and Social Welfare*, Chs 2, 4.

57. The material in this paragraph is drawn from Mill's *Principles of Political Economy*, Bk. I, Chs X, XII and XIII, and his 'Claims of Labour' in *Collected Works*, vol. V.

58. Wrote David Ricardo: '[S]o great are the delights of domestic society, that in practice it is invariably found that an increase of population follows the amended condition of the labourer.' *On the Principles of Political Economy and Taxation*, Piero Straffa (ed.) (Cambridge University Press, Cambridge, 1951), p. 407. Writing of Mill, F.L. van Holthoon has called this 'the automatism of the proletarian response'. *The Road to Utopia: A Study of John Stuart Mill's Social Thought* (Van Gorcum, Assen, 1971), p. 140.

59. Mill, *Principles of Political Economy*, pp. 358-59.

60. Mill 'The Claims of Labour', p. 375.

61. Mill, *Principles of Political Economy*, p. 961. Mill added: 'Energy and self-dependence are, however, liable to be impaired by the absence of help, as well as its excess.'

62. Bosanquet, *Ideals*, p. 113; see also p. 131. See his 'Character and its Bearing on Social Causation' in his edited collection *Aspects of the Social Problem*, pp. 103-17, as well as his 'Preface'. See §IV.A.2.

63. A typical line of attack was that if unearned income were demoralising, the wealthy ought to be demoralised too. (See Clarke, *Liberals and Social Democrats*, p. 53.) Bosanquet, in fact, did not hold that unearned income itself was necessarily harmful and even argued that '[a] large pension or gift of property to a man not yet demoralised will probably do no harm.' *Civilization of Christendom*, p. 344. See also Dewey, *Liberalism and Social Action*, p. 38.

64. See Bosanquet's *Civilization of Christendom*, p. 330. Bosanquet's argument is more complex than I have presented here.

65. S.I. Benn has argued that welfare organisations are not properly seen as instances of community. See his 'Individuality, Autonomy and Community' in Eugene Kamenka (ed.), *Community* (Edward Arnold, London, forthcoming, in the series *Ideas and Ideologies*).

66. Peter Clarke's distinction between 'moral reformists' and 'moral regenerationists' is relevant here. According to Clarke, a moral regenerationist like Bosanquet 'acknowledges that society is imperfect; he puts this down essentially to defects in individual conduct and character; the remedy is the remoralisation of character'. In contrast, the moral reformist (e.g. Hobhouse) 'believes that social defects are systemic; the remedy therefore is to reform the system'. Though Clarke tends to greatly over-emphasise the differences between Bosanquet and

Hobhouse, his distinction does point to a general difference in emphasis. *Liberals and Social Democrats*, pp. 14-15, 65.

67. Marc F. Plattner, 'The Welfare State vs. the Redistributive State', *The Public Interest*, LV (Spring 1979), pp. 29, 48.

68. This remark occurs in the context of fair wages. See Hobhouse, *The Labour Movement*, 3rd edn (Harvester, Brighton, 1974), p. 35.

69. Hobhouse, *Liberalism*, p. 104. See also his *Labour Movement*, pp. 123n-124n; and his *Social Justice*, p. 146.

70. On this question see Wiles, *Economic Institutions Compered*, Ch. 2; Lester C. Thurow, *Generating Inequality: Mechanisms of Distribution in the U.S. Economy* (Basic Books, New York, 1975). Rawls tells us that 'the need for incentives' is but one reason for inequalities. 'The Basic Structure as Subject' in Alvin I. Goldman and Jaegwon Kim (eds.), *Values and Morals* (D. Reidel, Dordrecht, 1978), p. 56.

71. Alan H. Goldman, 'Rawls's Original Position and the Difference Principle', *Journal of Philosophy*, LXXIII (Dec. 1976), p. 845. Goldman accepts that Rawls's own application of the principle may not be radically egalitarian. See also Flynn and Ruffinergo, 'Distributive Justice', p. 138.

72. R. George Wright, 'The High Cost of Rawls' Inegalitarianism', *Western Political Quarterly*, XXX (March 1977), pp. 73-79. Russell Keat and David Miller worry about the 'enormous inequalities' that Rawls's principle allows. 'Understanding Justice', *Political Theory*, II (Feb. 1974), p. 16. And, according to Charles Frankel, 'There is nothing in principle to prevent Mr. Rawls's argument from being used to justify great inequalities. All that would be needed is to show that, on some version of the trickle-down theory, the poor benefit from the advantages offered the rich.' (Actually, it would require that they maximally benefit.) 'The New Egalitarianism and the Old', *Commentary*, LVI (Sept. 1973), p. 56.

73. It may be argued that the possibility of leaving an inheritance to one's offspring is a powerful motivation to contribute to the economic effort. Neither Mill nor Hobhouse were prepared to give a great deal of weight to this argument. See Mill's *Principles of Political Economy*, p. 223; Hobhouse, *Social Justice*, pp. 164 ff.

74. Mill, *Principles of Political Economy*, pp. 218-25; see also pp. 755-56, 887-94.

75. Hobhouse, *Social Justice*, p. 166.

76. Mill, *Principles of Political Economy*, pp. 755-65.

77. Ibid., p. 218.

78. Hobhouse, *Social Justice*, pp. 165-66.

79. Green's position is somewhat different: he thought the principle of property implied inheritance but saw bequest as more problematic. *Political Obligation*, pp. 527-30. See John Herman Randall Jr, 'Idealistic Social Philosophy and Bernard Bosanquet', *Philosophy and Phenomenological Research*, XXVI (1965-66), p. 483. Bosanquet thought that the right to bequest was arguable, though he ultimately favoured it. 'The Principle of Private Property', pp. 311-12.

80. Even if we accept (a), proposition (b) may of course be qualified. See Hal R. Varian, 'Distributive Justice, Welfare Economics and the Theory of Fairness', *Philosophy and Public Affairs*, IV (Spring 1975), pp. 223-47.

81. Wright, 'Rawls' Inegalitarianism', p. 76. See also Lawrence Crocker, 'Equality, Solidarity and Rawls' Maximin', *Philosophy and Public Affairs*, VI (Spring 1977), pp. 262-67.

82. Rawls, *A Theory of Justice*, §§ 80, 81, 82. See also his 'Some Reasons for the Maximin Criterion', *American Economic Review*, LXIV (May 1974), p. 145. Rawls's much-criticised thesis that self-respect turns on one's equal liberty rather than economic position seems consistent with the general tendency of modern liberals to denigrate the importance in life of economic activities and the economic realm.

83. Green, 'An Estimate of the Value and Influence of Works of Fiction in Modern Times' in *Works*, vol. III, p. 42. See §§III.C.3, III.C.6.

84. Green, 'Lecture on the Work to be Done by the New Oxford High School for Boys', in *Works*, vol. III, p. 458.

85. Rawls, *A Theory of Justice*, p. 78. It is not clear how this coheres with the principle of fair equality of opportunity. Ibid., p. 73.

86. Bosanquet described 'the caste system of social stratification' as 'stupid', a term of criticism that he applies to that which is 'unappreciative' of value (§II.B.1). *Some Suggestions in Ethics*, p. 239. Bosanquet appears to see equality of opportunity as allowing a better chance for the great majority to 'level up'. *The Civilization of Christendom*, p. 333. Recent analysis, however, has cast doubt as to whether equality of opportunity induces mobility between classes. See Raymond Boudon, *Education, Opportunity and Social Inequality: Changing Prospects in Western Society* (Wiley, New York, 1973). See also Boudon's 'Review Essay – *A Theory of Justice*', *Contemporary Sociology*, V (March 1976), pp. 102-9. Mill, however, was not entirely in favour of such mobility. *Principles of Political Economy*, pp. 754-55.

87. Greengarten, *Green and Liberal-Democratic Thought*, pp. 92 ff.

88. Rawls, *A Theory of Justice*, p. 225.

89. Ibid., p. 277.

90. Ibid., p. 81. See pp. 61, 73, 79, 158 and 225-26. See also Gutmann, *Liberal Equality*, pp. 138-40; Keat and Miller, 'Understanding Justice', pp. 18 ff.

91. Green, *Political Obligation*, pp. 526-30.

92. Ibid., p. 527. This is a particularly important element in 'Macphersonite' interpretations of Green. See, for example, Greengarten, *Green and Liberal-Democratic Thought*, Chs 5, 6; Philip Hansen, 'T.H. Green and the Moralization of the Market', *Canadian Journal of Political and Social Theory*, I (Winter 1977), pp. 80-104.

93. Bosanquet, 'The Principle of Private Property' in *Aspects of the Social Problem*, p. 314; see also p. 311.

94. Hobhouse, *Sociology and Philosophy*, p. 104.

95. Rawls, *A Theory of Justice*, p. 290.

96. What Mill wrote is that 'the best state for human nature is that in which, while no one is poor, no one desires to be richer, nor has any reason to fear being thrust back by the efforts of others to push themselves forward'. This is not obviously redistributionist; however, he goes on in the following paragraphs to endorse 'legislation favouring equality of fortunes'. *Principles of Political Economy*, pp. 754 ff.

97. Hobhouse, *Social Evolution and Political Theory*, p. 171.

98. See Bosanquet's *The Philosophical Theory of the State*, p. xxxvii, and his *Essays and Addresses*, p. 32.

99. Hobhouse, *Liberalism*, p. 83. For a more general account focusing on Green, see George H. Sabine, *A History of Political Theory* (Harrap, London, 1937), pp. 673 ff.

100. Dewey, *Art as Experience* (Capricorn Books, New York, 1934), p. 343. See also his *Liberalism and Social Action*, p. 88. Charles Frankel, quoting from *Art as Experience*, believes that he 'sounds like a socialist' here. 'John Dewey's Social Philosophy' in Steven M. Cahn, *New Studies in the Philosophy of John Dewey* (University Press of New England, Hanover, N.H., 1977), p. 7.

101. Mill's endorsement of worker co-operatives is famous. See his *Principles of Political Economy*, pp. 768 ff. Somewhat remarkably, Bosanquet cites the same example of worker participation – the house painting venture of M. Leclaire – as does Mill. Indeed, Leclaire is the topic of Bosanquet's essay on 'Two Modern Philanthropists' in his *Essays and Addresses*, pp. 1-23. Bosanquet also argued in

his *Essays and Addresses*, p. 46, that 'of practical Socialism, i.e. of the workman's ownership of the means of production, we cannot have too much'. But see also Bosanquet's *Ideals*, pp. 226-29. Hobhouse notes the possibility of producer co-operatives, but his main concerns lie elsewhere, in consumer co-operatives, trade unions and municipal socialism. See his *Labour Movement*, p. 64, and his *Sociology and Philosophy*, p. 218. Green too appears to endorse consumer co-operatives, *Political Obligation*, p. 530. Rawls only alludes to management by 'worker's councils' (*A Theory of Justice*, p. 280) and has been severely criticised for this lack of attention to industrial democracy. See Kai Neilson, 'On the Very Possibility of a Classless Society: Rawls, Macpherson, and Revisionist Liberalism', *Political Theory*, VI (May 1978), p. 204; Barry Clark and Herbert Gentis, 'Rawlsian Justice and Economic System', *Philosophy and Public Affairs*, VII (Summer 1978), pp. 303, 312 ff.

102. I am grateful to John Kleinig for pressing this point upon me. See also Robert Paul Wolff, *Understanding Rawls* (Princeton University Press, Princeton, 1977), pp. 137 ff.

103. This phrase is drawn from Bosanquet, *Essays and Addresses*, p. 32, and Hobhouse, *Social Justice*, p. 29.

104. Dewey, *Individualism*, p. 122.

105. Gutmann, *Liberal Equality*, p. 207. Gutmann draws here on Carole Pateman, *Participation and Democratic Theory* (Cambridge University Press, Cambridge, 1970), pp. 70-71.

106. Mill, *Principles of Political Economy*, p. 793.

107. Wiles, *Economic Institutions Compared*, p. 129.

108. J.E. Meade, *The Just Economy* (Allen and Unwin, London, 1976), p. 16.

109. Wiles, *Economic Institutions Compared*, p. 134.

110. Ibid., pp. 134-36. See also Chapman, 'Justice, Freedom and Property'. For a more sympathetic treatment see Charles E. Lindblom, *Politics and Markets* (Basic Books, New York, 1977), Ch. 24. For a critical socialist appraisal, see Stuart Holland, *The Socialist Challenge* (Quartet, London, 1976), Chs 9, 10.

111. See my 'Liberal Political Economy'.

112. The next two paragraphs are drawn from John Plamenatz, *Karl Marx's Philosophy of Man* (Clarendon Press, Oxford, 1975), pp. 388-94.

113. According to Dewey, 'The idea that the basic problem can be solved merely by increase of hours of leisure is absurd. Such an idea merely retains the old dualistic division between labor and leisure.' *Art as Experience*, p. 343. Hobhouse, in contrast, seemed to place more importance on increased leisure for manual workers. See *The Labour Movement*, p. 23.

# CONCLUDING REMARKS

Modern liberals have had two great, and related, insights that imply a fundamental reconceptualisation of a liberal social and political order. The first was J.S. Mill's realisation that liberalism's devotion to the individual need not translate into a devotion to a self-interested individualism. In one of his most important early essays, Mill complains that '[m]an is conceived by Bentham as being susceptible of pleasures and pains, and governed in all his conduct partly by the different modifications of self-interest, and the passions commonly classified as selfish, partly by sympathies, or occasionally antipathies, towards other beings.' The problem, as Mill saw it, was that 'here Bentham's conception of human nature stops'.[1] In particular, Mill objects that 'man is never recognised by him as a being capable of pursuing spiritual perfection as an end; of desiring for its own sake, the conformity of his own character to his standard of excellence'.[2] In the end, Mill concludes, Bentham was blind to the notion of 'self-respect'. This, then, points to the first major revision endorsed by modern liberals: viz. a theory of human nature in which the cultivation of individuality replaces self-interested individualism as the critical driving force in man. However, as I indicated in the second chapter, Mill only partially grasps the implications of this new conception of human nature. It is Green who really develops the second insight. If the ultimate natural aim of man is not pursuit of pleasure or self-aggrandisement but, rather, the development of one's nature, the social order can be understood as an essentially co-operative endeavour to promote the development of human nature. Both the doctrines of mutual stimulation and mutual completion of individualities imply this notion of a co-operative commonwealth. Liberalism was thus transformed from a doctrine of competitive individualism to a co-operative pursuit of individuality. We have seen, though, that the break with the older liberalism is by no means complete: neither pursuit of self-interest nor competition is banished. But they become subordinate dimensions of life, acceptable, even desirable, but only if they are kept in their place and do not endanger the co-operative commonwealth.

In contrast to the theories of individuality and social life, the third element of the modern liberal theory of man, community, does not seem to contain these sorts of insights leading to a fundamental reconceptualisation of man and society. The idea of a natural sympathy, so central to the account of fraternity, is by no means absent from traditional liberal theory; indeed, we just saw that Mill acknowledges it to be an element in Bentham's theory of human nature. To be sure, modern liberals stress fraternal sentiments much more than do classical liberals, but that hardly constitutes an innovation. Given all the problems with the idea of a society-wide fraternity, we might well wonder if liberals like Mill, Hobhouse and Rawls have gone astray in their attraction to fraternal community. Indeed, as I argued in §III.E, the claim of the modern liberal theory of man to have reconciled individuality and sociability would be far more convincing without the insistence on fraternal relations. In contradistinction to the ideals of individuality and social life, the ideal of community, especially as articulated through fraternal bonds, seems to harken *back* to a social order in which individualised personalities were by no means dominant. Yet we can understand the attraction of this solidaristic ideal to modern liberals, most of whom were concerned with developing a humane alternative to what they at least perceived as the atomism and harshness of the classical liberal's world. Whatever the reason behind their attraction to communitarian sentiments, however, we have seen throughout Part Two that they play an important part in modern liberal political prescriptions. Fraternal unity provides the basis of arguments for both equality of liberties and limiting the inequality of income and wealth. Without the stress on fraternity the modern liberal theory of man would be conceptually neater and more in accord with the nature of mass industrial society, but it would also be less egalitarian.

Of course, equal rights can be justified by other, apparently far less controversial, arguments than those from human nature. One can well understand Kantian rationalists who strive to deduce principles of political right from the precepts of reason rather than basing them on seemingly precarious psychological claims. But to many in the Anglo-American tradition, the contentious aspect of claims about human nature is compensated for by their richness, for they not only can help yield principles of right, but they can also provide the basis of notions about the good of man and the good of society. Thus, even Rawls, who so stresses his Kantian connections, imports a wide range of assumptions about human nature into his derivation of his principles of justice (§VI.C.2). Indeed, it would seem that sooner or later a political theorist must come to look at human nature. Theories about the political and social good seem inevitably bound up with theories about what man is, what he is capable of being, and how he may be expected to react to different sorts of political and social environments. Despite its pitfalls, theorising about human nature continues to attract political philosophers as it holds out the possibility of designing a political and social order that promotes the good of man.

But a theory of human nature can enter into a political theory in two very different ways. It may merely be used to determine the limits of the politically possible.[3] On this view, rather than being derived from human nature, principles of political right merely have to meet the test of being consistent with the possibilities of human nature. On the more radical view, however, a conception of human nature can be the foundation of a theory of political right or the social good. Modern liberals have utilised their theory of human nature in both ways, but the focus of this book has been on the latter. However, to say that modern liberals have sought to build notions of political right on their theory of human nature is not to assert that unique political or moral conclusions can be derived in any straightforward way from assumptions about human nature.[4] Indeed, I have been particularly concerned here with showing how the general theory can be applied to particular issues in different ways so as to yield different prescriptions. As I stressed in the Introductory, modern liberal theory is not simply a theory of human nature with straightforward deductions of political prescriptions, but the theory of man coupled with typically liberal arguments showing how it endorses equal liberty, democracy and a co-operative economic order. To say that the theory of human nature is the core of modern liberalism is not to claim that all modern liberal positions, or even the most important ones, are simply logical implications of it.

Nevertheless, although my thesis does not entail that modern liberal political prescriptions are simply deductions from the theory of man, it does insist on its fundamental place in modern liberal theory. But if the theory of human nature is so central, one may well wonder if my account of modern liberalism allows any significant political role for modern liberals' ethical theories. As I pointed out in the Introductory, modern liberals have put forward a variety of ethical theories to support their politics: Mill endorsed a form of utilitarianism which, for example, both Green and Rawls explicitly reject, the former favouring a common good morality the latter favouring a social contract/rights ethics. Are these ethical disputes of no importance at all for modern liberal politics? Well, it must be acknowledged that the main thrust of my account is that, indeed, they are not of central importance. I have tried to show in Part Two that modern liberals very often argue in support of liberty, democracy and economic proposals *directly*

*on the basis of their theory of human nature, with little or no re-
ference to their formal ethical theories.* More than that though, a
strong case can be made that the ethical theories themselves rely
largely on the theory of human nature. For example, I argued in
Chapter VI (§C.2) that Rawls imports a wide range of assumptions
about human nature into his 'original position': it would not be going
too far to depict his parties to the original position as searching for
principles of political right that best promote the development of each.
Mill's ethics also relies on the theory of human nature, though the
structure of his argument is different from that of Rawls. In contrast
to Rawls, we may well see Mill's commitment to his formal ethical
theory as logically prior to any assumptions about human nature. But
the utilitarian ethic only yields political prescriptions when conjoined
with a theory about the conditions that promote or retard human
happiness, a theory which we saw is an element of the modern liberal
theory of man (§IV.B.2). So it is only when combined with the theory
of human nature that Mill's utilitarianism produces particular prescriptions. (The theory of human nature is probably even more basic to Mill's
ethics than this analysis suggests, however, as his revision of the nature
of the utilitarian end — from pleasure to happiness — is fairly obviously intended to make the theory more supportive of the development
of higher natures.) It should be even more manifest (especially given
Chapter II) how Green's common good and Hobhouse's harmony
ethics are premised on their theory of human nature. And although it
is by no means clear just how to characterise Dewey's ethics, a reasonable interpretation is that it is devoted to the greatest growth of all, or
at least the greatest number.[5]

My point, then, is that despite their great variety, the formal ethics
of modern liberals all relate back to the core theory of man. All, I
would like to suggest, can be understood as expressions of the developmental ideal. Again, though, no claim is being made here that the
ethical theories are simple derivations from the theory of human nature
and its implied theory of the good of man. Rawls, for example, builds
on the theory of human nature, but in such a way as to yield a deonto-
logical, rights-oriented ethics while, in contrast, Mill integrates it into
his teleological general welfare morality. Real differences thus exist
between the two, differences that derive from their disparate understandings of an adequate ethics. It may well be that these ethical differences will lead them to different prescriptions in certain hard cases.
For example, in cases where the development of one might be sacrificed
to promote the greater development of others, Mill, the utilitarian,

might be more ready to accept the legitimacy of such a sacrifice than a rights theorist like Rawls. To the extent they do differ in these sorts of cases, my account of modern liberal theory is thus limited. However, I have tried to show in this book that the modern liberal theory of man inclines heavily against this sort of sacrifice of the good of some to promote that of others: *its spirit is to emphasise the potential harmony and mutual dependence of individual developments*. It is, I think, for this reason that the political prescriptions of a utilitarian like Mill can converge with those of a rights-theorist such as Rawls. Whether the problem of designing *basic political institutions* is approached with the aim of promoting the general welfare or ensuring the right of each to pursue his plan of life, the modern liberal endorses an equal liberty embedded in a democratic polity and a co-operative economic order. For, ultimately, modern liberals are convinced that the individual and social goods are one: viz. the development of the nature of each. If I am right here, then although both an individual-oriented rights ethics and a collectivity-oriented utilitarian morality can give an ethical expression of the modern liberal developmental ideal, the common good ethics of Green and the harmony morality of Hobhouse are truer to the modern liberal vision. For, while both rights and utilitarian theories allow for it,[6] common good ethics focuses upon and emphasises the ideal of a co-operative community of mutually dependent developing individuals. This, indeed, is the ideal underlying Green's notion of the non-competitive nature of the good of man.

## Notes

1. Mill, 'Bentham' in J.M. Robson (ed.), *Collected Works of John Stuart Mill* (University of Toronto Press, Toronto, 1963), vol. X, p. 94.

2. Ibid., p. 95.

3. See Alan Ryan, 'The Nature of Human Nature in Hobbes and Rousseau' in Jonathan Benthall (ed.), *The Limits of Human Nature* (E.P. Dutton, New York, 1974, p. 13.

4. See Bernard Williams, *Morality: An Introduction to Ethics* (Harper and Row, New York, 1972), pp. 59-67.

5. See John Dewey and James H. Tufts, *Ethics*, rev. edn (Henry Holt, New York, 1932), pp. 272-77, 331-44. See also Robert L. Holmes, 'John Dewey's Social Ethics', *Journal of Value Inquiry*, VII (1973), pp. 274-80. Interpreting Dewey's ethics is difficult as he was so suspicious of general principles. See Charles L. Stevenson, 'Reflections on John Dewey's Ethics', *Proceedings of the Aristotelian Society*, vol. LXII, pp. 77-98; Yeager Hudson, 'Dewey's Criteria of the Worth of any Form of Social Life', *Journal of Social Philosophy*, VII (April 1976), pp. 11-17.

6. For an interesting effort to develop a utilitarian theory concentrating on co-operation, see Donald H. Regan, *Utilitarianism and Co-operation* (Clarendon Press, Oxford, 1980).

# BIBLIOGRAPHY

ALLPORT, GORDON W. 'Dewey's Individual and Social Psychology' in Paul Arthur Schlipp (ed.), *The Philosophy of John Dewey* (Tudor, New York, 1951), pp. 265-90.

ALTHAM, J.E.J. 'Rawls's Difference Principle', *Philosophy*, XLVIII (Jan. 1973), pp. 75-78.

ANSCHUTZ, R.P. *The Philosophy of J.S. Mill* (Clarendon Press, Oxford, 1953).

ARISTOTLE. *The Nicomachean Ethics*, Sir David Ross (trans.) (Oxford University Press, London, 1954).

ARNESON, RICHARD J. 'Mill Versus Paternalism', *Ethics*, XC (July 1980), pp. 470-89.

   'Mill's Doubts About Freedom Under Socialism', *Canadian Journal of Philosophy*, supp. vol. V (1979), pp. 470-89.

ASCH, SOLOMON E. *Social Psychology* (Prentice-Hall, New York, 1952).

ASHLEY, Sir WILLIAM. 'Introduction' in Sir William Ashley (ed.), J.S. Mill's *Principles of Political Economy* (Augustus M. Kelley, Fairfield, N.J., 1976), pp. v-xxxvi.

AUSTIN, JEAN. 'Pleasure and Happiness' in J.B. Schneewind (ed.), *Mill: A Collection of Critical Essays* (Macmillan, London, 1968), pp. 234-50.

BAIN, ALEXANDER. *John Stuart Mill* (Augustus M. Kelley, New York, 1969).

   *The Senses and the Intellect*, 3rd edn (D. Appleton, New York, 1885).

BARBER, BENJAMIN R. 'Justifying Justice' in Norman Daniels (ed.) *Reading Rawls: Critical Studies of* A Theory of Justice (Basic Books, New York, 1974), pp. 292-318.

BARBU, ZEVEDEI. *Democracy and Dictatorship: Their Psychology and Patterns of Life* (Routledge and Kegan Paul, London, 1956).

   *Problems of Historical Psychology* (Routledge and Kegan Paul, London, 1960).

BARKER, ERNEST. *Political Thought in England: 1848 to 1914*, 2nd edn (Oxford University Press, Oxford, 1959).

BARKER, RODNEY. *Political Ideas in Modern Britain* (Methuen, London, 1978).

BARRY, BRIAN. *The Liberal Theory of Justice: A Critical Examination of the Principal Doctrines in* A Theory of Justice, *by John Rawls* (Clarendon Press, Oxford, 1973).

*Political Argument* (Routledge and Kegan Paul, London, 1965).

BATES, STANLEY. 'The Motivation to be Just', *Ethics*, LXXXV (Oct. 1974), pp. 1-17.

BAYLES, MICHAEL. 'Criminal Paternalism' in J. Roland Pennock and John W. Chapman (eds.), *NOMOS XV: The Limits of Law* (Leiber-Atherton, New York, 1974), pp. 174-88.

BELL, DANIEL. 'The Background and Development of Marxian Socialism in the United States' in Donald Egbert and Stow Persons (eds.), *Socialism and American Life* (Princeton University Press, Princeton, 1952), vol. 1, pp. 214-405.

BENN, S.I. 'Freedom, Autonomy and the Concept of a Person' in *Proceedings of the Aristotelian Society* (1976), pp. 109-30.

'Individuality, Autonomy and Community' in Eugene Kamenka (ed.), *Community* (Edward Arnold, London, forthcoming, in the series *Ideas and Ideologies*).

——and GAUS, G.F. 'The Liberal Conception of the Public and Private' in S.I. Benn and G.F. Gaus (eds.), *Conceptions of the Public and Private in Social Life* (Croom Helm, London, forthcoming).

BERLIN, ISAIAH. 'Georges Sorel', *Times Literary Supplement* (31 Dec. 1971), pp. 1617-22.

'John Stuart Mill and the Ends of Life' in his *Four Essays on Liberty* (Oxford University Press, Oxford, 1969), pp. 173-206.

'Two Concepts of Liberty' in his *Four Essays on Liberty*, pp. 118-72.

BERRY, CHRISTOPHER J. 'Property and Possession: Two Replies to Locke — Hume and Hegel' in J. Roland Pennock and John W. Chapman (eds.), *NOMOS XXII: Property* (New York University Press, New York, 1980), pp. 89-100.

BEVERIDGE, Lord WILLIAM. *Voluntary Action: A Report on Methods of Social Advance* (Allen and Unwin, London 1948).

BILLINGS, JOHN R. 'J.S. Mill's Quantity-Quality Distinction', *The Mill Newsletter*, VII (Fall 1971), pp. 6-16.

BLOOM, ALLAN. 'Justice: John Rawls Vs. the Tradition of Political Philosophy', *American Political Science Review*, LXIX (June 1975), pp. 648-62.

BOSANQUET, BERNARD. 'Character and its Bearing on Social Causation' in his edited collection *Aspects of the Social Problem* (Macmillan, London, 1895), pp. 103-17.

*The Civilization of Christendom* (Swan Sonnenschein, London, 1899).

*Essays and Addresses* (Swan Sonnenschein, London, 1891).

'Hegel's Theory of the Political Organism', *Mind*, VII (1898), pp. 1-14.

*Logic* (Clarendon Press, Oxford, 1911).

'The Notion of a General Will', *Mind*, XXIX (1920), pp. 77-81.

*The Philosophical Theory of the State*, 4th edn (Macmillan, London, 1951).

*The Principle of Individuality and Value* (Macmillan, London, 1912).

'The Principle of Private Property' in *Aspects of the Social Problem*, pp. 308-18.

*Psychology of the Moral Self* (Macmillan, London, 1904).

'The Relation of Sociology to Philosophy', *Mind*, VI (1897), pp. 1-8.

'Review of Hobhouse's *Development and Purpose: An Essay Towards a Philosophy of Evolution*', *Mind*, XXII (1913), pp. 383-87.

*Science and Philosophy* (Allen and Unwin, London, 1927).

*Social and International Ideals* (Macmillan, London, 1917).

'Socialism and Natural Selection' in *Aspects of the Social Problem*, pp. 289-307.

*Some Suggestions in Ethics* (Macmillan, London, 1919).

*Three Lectures in Aesthetic* (Macmillan, London, 1915).

*The Value and Destiny of the Individual* (Macmillan, London, 1913).

BOUDON, RAYMOND. *Education, Opportunity and Social Inequality: Changing Prospects in Western Society* (Wiley, New York, 1973).

'Review Essay — *A Theory of Justice*', *Contemporary Sociology*, V (March 1976), pp. 102-9.

BOWERS, DAVID F. 'American Socialism and the Socialist Philosophy of History' in Donald Drew Egbert and Stow Persons (eds.), *Socialism and American Life* (Princeton University Press, Princeton, 1952), vol. I, pp. 409-25.

BRADLEY, F.H. *Ethical Studies*, 2nd edn (Clarendon, Oxford, 1927).

BRETT, G.S. *Brett's History of Psychology*, R.S. Peters (ed. and abridger) (Allen and Unwin, London, 1962).

BRINTON, CRANE. *English Political Thought in the 19th Century* (Harper and Bros., New York, 1962).

BUCHANAN, JAMES M. 'A Contractarian Perspective on Anarchy' in J. Roland Pennock and John W. Chapman (eds.), *NOMOS XIX: Arnarchism* (New York University Press, New York, 1978), pp. 29-42.

BURNS, J.H. 'J.S. Mill and Democracy, 1829-61', *Political Studies*, V (1957), pp. 158-75, 281-94.

CACOULLOS, ANN R. *Thomas Hill Green: Philosopher of Rights* (Twayne, New York, 1974).

CARTER, HUGH. *The Social Theories of L.T. Hobhouse* (Kennikat, Port Washington, N.Y., 1927).

CHAPMAN, JOHN W. 'Justice, Freedom and Property' in J. Roland Pennock and John W. Chapman (eds.), *NOMOS XXII: Property* (New York University Press, New York, 1980), pp. 289-324.

'Political Theory: Logical Structure and Enduring Types' in *L'idée de philosophie politique* (Presses Universitaires de France. Paris, 1965), pp. 57-96.

'Rawls's Theory of Justice', *American Political Science Review*, LXIX (June 1975), pp. 588-93.

'Review — *Law, Legislation and Liberty*', *Journal of Economic Literature*, XVI (March 1978), pp. 96-98.

*Rousseau — Totalitarian or Liberal?* (Columbia University Press, New York, 1956).

'Toward a General Theory of Human Nature and Dynamics' in J. Roland Pennock and John W. Chapman (eds.), *NOMOS XVII: Human Nature in Politics* (New York University Press, New York, 1977), pp. 292-319.

CLARK, BARRY and GENTIS, HERBERT. 'Rawlsian Justice and Economic Systems', *Philosophy and Public Affairs*, VII (Summer 1978), pp. 302-25.

CLARKE, PETER. *Liberals and Social Democrats* (Cambridge University Press, Cambridge, 1978).

COLLINGWOOD, R.G. *An Essay on Philosophical Method* (Clarendon Press, Oxford, 1933).

COLLINI, STEFAN. 'Hobhouse, Bosanquet and the State: Philosophical Idealism and Political Argument in England, 1880-1918', *Past and Present*, LXXII (Aug. 1976), pp. 86-111.

*Liberalism and Sociology: L.T. Hobhouse and Political Argument in England, 1880-1914* (Cambridge University Press, Cambridge, 1979).

CONGER, G.P. *Theories of Macrocosms and Microcosms in the History of Philosophy* (Russell and Russell, New York, 1922).

COPP, DAVID. 'Justice and the Difference Principle', *Canadian Journal of Philosophy*, IV (Dec. 1974), pp. 229-40.

CORK, JIM. 'John Dewey and Karl Marx' in Sidney Hook (ed.), *John Dewey: Philosopher of Science and Freedom* (Dial Press, New York, 1950), pp. 331-50.

CRANSTON, MAURICE. *John Stuart Mill* (Longman's, Green, London, 1958).

CROCKER, LAWRENCE. 'Equality, Solidarity and Rawls' Maximin', *Philosophy and Public Affairs*, VI (Spring 1977), pp. 262-67.

CUSHMAN, ROBERT F. *Cases in Civil Liberties* (Appleton-Century-Crofts, New York, 1968).

D'AGOSTINO, F. 'Mill, Paternalism and Psychiatry', *Australasian Journal of Philosophy* (forthcoming).

DAMICO, ALFONSO J. *Individuality and Community: The Social and Political Thought of John Dewey* (University Presses of Florida, Gainesville, 1978).

DANIELS, NORMAN. 'Equal Liberty and Unequal Worth of Liberty' in Norman Daniels (ed.), *Reading Rawls: Critical Studies of* A Theory of Justice (Basic Books, New York, 1974), pp. 253-81.

DAY, J.P. 'On Liberty and the Real Will', *Philosophy*, XLV (July 1970), pp. 177-92.

DEWEY, JOHN. *Art as Experience* (G.P. Putnam's Sons, New York, 1958).

    *Characters and Events: Popular Essays in Social and Political Philosophy*, Joseph Ratner (ed.) (Henry Holt, New York, 1929).

    *A Common Faith* (Yale University Press, New Haven, 1960).

    'Creative Democracy – The Task Before Us' in *The Philosopher of the Common Man: Essays in Honor of John Dewey* (G.P. Putnam's Sons, New York, 1940), pp. 220-28.

    *Democracy and Education* (Free Press, New York, 1916).

    'Ethics of Democracy' in *The Early Works of John Dewey: 1882-98* (Southern Illinois University Press, Carbondale and Edwardsville, 1967), vol. I, pp. 227-49.

    *Experience and Nature* (Dover, New York, 1958).

    *Freedom and Culture* (Allen and Unwin, London, 1940).

    'From Absolutism to Experimentalism' in Richard J. Bernstein (ed.), *On Experience, Nature and Freedom* (The Liberal Arts Press, New York, 1960), pp. 3-18.

    'Green's Theory of the Moral Motive' in *The Early Works*, vol. III, pp. 155-73.

    *Human Nature and Conduct* (Henry Holt, New York, 1922).

*Individualism — Old and New* (Allen and Unwin, London, 1931).

*Intelligence in the Modern World: John Dewey's Philosophy*, Joseph Ratner (ed.) (Modern Library, New York, 1939).

*Liberalism and Social Action* (G.P. Putnam's Sons, New York, 1935).

*Philosophy and Civilization* (Minton, Balch and Co., New York, 1931).

'The Philosophy of Thomas Hill Green' in *The Early Works*, vol. III, pp. 14-35.

'Philosophies of Freedom' in Bernstein (ed.), *On Experience, Nature and Freedom*, pp. 261-87.

*Problems of Men* (Philosophical Library, New York, 1946).

*Psychology* in *The Early Works*, vol. IV.

*The Public and Its Problems* (Swallow Press, Chicago, 1954).

*The Quest for Certainty* (Allen and Unwin, London, 1930).

*Reconstruction in Philosophy*, enlarged edn (Beacon Press, Boston, 1948).

'Self-Realization and the Moral Ideal' in *The Early Works*, vol. IV, pp. 42-53.

'Time and Individuality' in David Sidorsky (ed.), *John Dewey: The Essential Writings* (Harper and Row, New York, 1977), pp. 134-48.

———— and TUFTS, JAMES H. *Ethics*, rev. edn (Henry Holt, New York, 1932).

DICEY, A.V. *Lectures on the Relation between Law and Public Opinion in England during the Nineteenth Century*, 2nd edn (Macmillan, London, 1919).

DUNCAN, GRAEME. *Marx and Mill: Two Views of Social Conflict and Social Harmony* (Cambridge University Press, Cambridge, 1973).

DURKHEIM, EMILE. *The Division of Labor in Society*, George Simpson (trans.) (Free Press of Glencoe, New York, 1964).

DWORKIN, GERALD. 'Paternalism' in Peter Laslett and James Fishkin (eds.), *Philosophy, Politics and Society*, 5th series (Blackwell, Oxford, 1979), pp. 78-96.

DWORKIN, RONALD. *Taking Rights Seriously* (Harvard University Press, Cambridge, Mass., 1978).

EDWARDS, REM B. *Pleasures and Pains: A Theory of Qualitative Hedonism* (Cornell University Press, Ithaca, 1979).

ERNST, KATHERINE. 'A Comparison of John Dewey's Theory of Valuation and Abraham Maslow's Theory of Value', *Educa-*

*tional Theory*, XXIV (Spring 1974), pp. 130-41.

FAIRBROTHER, W.H. *The Philosophy of Thomas Hill Green* (Methuen, London, 1896).

FEUER, L.S. 'John Stuart Mill as a Sociologist: The Unwritten Ethology' in J.M. Robson and M. Laine (eds.), *James and John Stuart Mill: Papers of the Centenary Conference* (University of Toronto Press, Toronto, 1976), pp. 86-110.

FISK, MILTON. 'History and Reason in Rawls' Moral Theory' in Norman Daniels (ed.), *Reading Rawls: Critical Studies of* A Theory of Justice (Basic Books, New York, 1974), pp. 53-80.

FLYNN, JOHN J. and RUFFINERGO, PIERO. 'Distributive Justice: Some Institutional Implications of Rawls' *A Theory of Justice*', *Utah Law Review* (1975), pp. 123-57.

FRANKEL, CHARLES. 'John Dewey's Social Philosophy' in Steven M. Cahn, *New Studies in the Philosophy of John Dewey* (University Press of New England, Hanover, N.H., 1977), pp. 3-44.

'Justice, Utilitarianism and Rights', *Social Theory and Practice*, III (Spring 1974), pp. 27-46.

'The New Egalitarianism and the Old', *Commentary*, LVI (Sept. 1973), pp. 54-61.

FREDMAN, L.E. and GORDON, B.L.J. 'John Stuart Mill and Socialism', *The Mill Newsletter*, III (Fall 1967), pp. 3-10.

FREEDEN, MICHAEL. *The New Liberalism: An Ideology of Social Reform* (Clarendon Press, Oxford, 1978).

FREUD, SIGMUND. *Civilization and its Discontents*, James Strachy (trans. and ed.) (W.W. Norton, New York, 1962).

*The Ego and the Id*, Joan Riviere (trans.), James Strachy (ed.) (W.W. Norton, New York, 1962).

*A General Introduction to Psychoanalysis*, Joan Riviere (trans.) (Liveright, New York, 1935).

FRIEDMAN, RICHARD B. 'An Introduction to Mill's Theory of Authority' in J.B. Schneewind (ed.), *Mill: A Collection of Critical Essays* (Macmillan, London, 1968), pp. 379-425.

FROEBEL, FRIEDRICH. *The Education of Man*, W.N. Hailman (trans.) (Appleton, New York, 1894).

GARFORTH, F.W. *Educative Democracy: John Stuart Mill on Education in Society* (Oxford University Press, Oxford, 1980).

GAUS, GERALD F. 'Mill's Theory of Moral Rules', *Australasian Journal of Philosophy*, LVII (Sept. 1980), pp. 265-79.

'Public and Private Interests in Liberal Political Economy, Old and New' in S.I. Benn and G.F. Gaus (eds.), *Conceptions of the Public and Private in Social Life* (Croom Helm, London, forthcoming).

———— and CHAPMAN, JOHN W. 'Anarchism and Political Philosophy: An Introduction' in J. Roland Pennock and John W. Chapman (eds.), *NOMOS XIX: Anarchism* (New York University Press, New York, 1978), pp. xvii-xlv.

GEERTZ, CLIFFORD. *The Interpretation of Cultures* (Basic Books, New York, 1973).

GEIGER, GEORGE R. *John Dewey in Perspective* (Oxford University Press, New York, 1958).

GERT, BERNARD and CULVER, CHARLES. 'Paternalistic Behavior', *Philosophy and Public Affairs*, VI (Fall 1976), pp. 45-57.

GEWIRTH, ALAN. *Reason and Morality* (University of Chicago Press, Chicago, 1978).

GINSBERG, MORRIS. 'The Work of L.T. Hobhouse' in J.A. Hobson and Morris Ginsberg (eds.), *L.T. Hobhouse: His Life and Work* (Allen and Unwin, London, 1931), pp. 97-260.

GOLDMAN, ALAN H. 'Rawls's Original Position and the Difference Principle', *Journal of Philosophy*, LXXIII (Dec. 1976), pp. 845-49.

GORDON, PETER and WHITE, JOHN. *Philosophers as Educational Reformers: The Influence of Idealism on British Educational Thought and Practice* (Routledge and Kegan Paul, London, 1979).

GREEN, THOMAS HILL. 'An Estimate of the Value and Influence of Works of Fiction in Modern Times' in R.L. Nettleship (ed.), *Works of Thomas Hill Green* (Longman's, Green, and Co., London, 1889), vol. III, pp. 20-45.

'The Force of Circumstances' in *Works*, vol. III, pp. 3-10.

'Four Lectures on the English Revolution' in *Works*, vol. III, pp. 277-364.

'Fragments of an Address on the Text "The Word is Nigh Thee"' in *Works*, vol. III, pp. 221-29.

'The Influence of Civilisation on Genius' in *Works*, vol. III, pp. 11-19.

'Lecture on Liberal Legislation and Freedom of Contract' in *Works*, vol. III, pp. 365-86.

'Lecture on the Work to be Done by the New Oxford High School for Boys' in *Works*, vol. III, pp. 456-76.

'Lectures on the Philosophy of Kant' in *Works*, vol. II, pp. 1-155.

*Lectures on the Principles of Political Obligation* in *Works*, vol. II, pp. 334-553.

'On the Different Senses of "Freedom" as Applied to Will and to the Moral Progress of Man' in *Works*, vol. II, pp. 307-33.

'Popular Philosophy in its Relation to Life' in *Works*, vol. III, pp. 92-125.

*Prolegomena to Ethics*, A.C. Bradley (ed.) (Clarendon Press, Oxford, 1890).

GREENGARTEN, I.M. *Thomas Hill Green and the Development of Liberal-Democratic Thought* (University of Toronto Press, Toronto, 1981).

GRIFFIN, C.M. 'L.T. Hobhouse and the Idea of Harmony', *Journal of the History of Ideas*, XXXV (Oct.-Dec. 1974), pp. 647-61.

GROTE, JOHN. *An Examination of the Utilitarian Philosophy*, Joseph Bickersteth Mayor (ed.) (Deighton, Bell, and Co., Cambridge, 1870).

GUMBERT, EDGAR B. 'John Dewey and the New Liberalism: Reactions to the U.S.S.R.', *Educational Theory*, XXII (Summer 1972), pp. 344-59.

GUTMANN, AMY. *Liberal Equality* (Cambridge University Press, Cambridge, 1980).

HAKSAR, VINIT. *Equality, Liberty, and Perfectionism* (Oxford University Press, Oxford, 1979).

HALLIDAY, R.J. *John Stuart Mill* (Allen and Unwin, London, 1976).

HAMBURGER, JOSEPH. 'Mill and Tocqueville on Liberty', in John M. Robson and Michael Laine (eds.), *James and John Stuart Mill: Papers of the Centenary Conference* (University of Toronto Press, Toronto, 1976), pp. 111-25.

HAMER, D.A. *Liberal Politics in the Age of Gladstone and Rosebury* (Clarendon Press, Oxford, 1972).

HANSEN, PHILIP. 'T.H. Green and the Moralization of the Market', *Canadian Journal of Political and Social Theory*, I (Winter 1977), pp. 80-105.

HARRINGTON, K.W. 'John Dewey's Ethics and the Classical Conception of Man', *DIOTIMA*, I (1973), pp. 125-48.

HARRIS, ABRAM L. 'John Stuart Mill's Theory of Progress', *Ethics*, LXVI (April 1956), pp. 157-75.

HART, H.L.A. 'Rawls on Liberty and its Priority' in Norman Daniels (ed.), *Reading Rawls: Critical Studies of* A Theory of Justice (Basic Books, New York, 1974), pp. 230-52.

HAYEK, F.A. *The Constitution of Liberty* (Routledge and Kegan Paul, London, 1960).

*Law, Legislation and Liberty*, vol. 2: *The Mirage of Social Justice*

(University of Chicago Press, Chicago, 1976).

*Law, Legislation and Liberty*, vol. 3: *The Political Order of a Free People* (University of Chicago Press, Chicago, 1979).

'Liberalism' in his *New Studies in Philosophy, Politics, Economics and the History of Ideas* (Routledge and Kegan Paul, London, 1978), pp. 119-51.

HEGEL, G.W.F. *Phenomenology of the Spirit*, A.V. Miller (trans.) (Clarendon Press, Oxford, 1977).

HEMINGWAY, JOHN LUTHER. 'The Emergence of an Ethical Liberalism: A Study of Idealist Liberalism from Thomas Hill Green to the Present', unpublished PhD thesis, University of Iowa, 1979.

HOBHOUSE, L.T. *Democracy and Reaction* (T. Fisher Unwin, London, 1904).

*Development and Purpose: An Essay Towards a Philosophy of Evolution* (Macmillan, London, 1913).

*The Elements of Social Justice* (Allen and Unwin, London, 1949).

'The Ethical Basis of Collectivism', *International Journal of Ethics*, VIII (Jan. 1898), pp. 137-56.

*The Labour Movement*, 3rd edn (Harvester, Brighton, 1974).

*Liberalism* (Oxford University Press, Oxford, 1964).

*The Metaphysical Theory of the State* (Allen and Unwin, London, 1926).

*Mind in Evolution*, 3rd edn (Macmillan, London, 1926).

*Morals in Evolution* (Chapman and Hall, London, 1951).

'The Past and the Future: The Influence of Nationalism' in J.A. Hobson and Morris Ginsberg (eds.), *L.T. Hobhouse: His Life and Work* (Allen and Unwin, London, 1931), pp. 325-30.

*The Rational Good: A Study in the Logic of Practice* (Watts, London, 1947).

*Social Development* (Allen and Unwin, London, 1924).

*Social Evolution and Political Theory* (Columbia University Press, New York, 1928).

*Sociology and Philosophy: Centenary Collection of Essays and Articles* (G. Bell and Sons, London, 1966).

HOLLAND, STUART. *The Socialist Challenge* (Quartet, London, 1976).

HOLLIS, MARTIN. 'J.S. Mill's Political Philosophy of Mind', *Philosophy*, XLVII (Oct. 1972), pp. 334-47.

'The Self in Action' in R.S. Peters (ed.), *John Dewey Reconsidered* (Routledge and Kegan Paul, London, 1977), pp. 56-75.

HOLMES, ROBERT L. 'John Dewey's Social Ethics', *Journal of Value Inquiry*, VII (1973), pp. 274-80.

HOLTHOON, F.L. van. *The Road to Utopia: A Study of John Stuart Mill's Social Thought* (Van Gorcum, Assen, 1971).

HOOVER, KENNETH R. 'Liberalism and the Idealist Philosophy of Thomas Hill Green', *Western Political Quarterly*, XXVI (Sept. 1973), pp. 550-65.

HUDSON, YAEGER. 'Dewey's Criteria of the Worth of any Form of Social Life', *Journal of Social Philosophy*, VII (April 1976), pp. 11-17.

IRVING, JOHN A. 'Comments' to Arthur E. Murphy, 'John Dewey and American Liberalism', *Journal of Philosophy*, LVII (1960), pp. 442-50.

KALLEN, HORACE M. '*Individuality, Individualism and John Dewey*', *Antioch Review*, XIX (Fall 1959), pp. 299-314.

KARIER, CLARENCE J. 'John Dewey and the New Liberalism: Reflections and Responses', *History and Education Quarterly*, XV (Winter 1975), pp. 417-43.

KEAT, RUSSELL and MILLER, DAVID. 'Understanding Justice', *Political Theory*, II (Feb. 1974), pp. 3-31.

KELLY, JESSE LANDRUM JR. 'Justice and Utility: The Role of Moral Desert in the Political Writings of John Rawls', unpublished PhD thesis, University of Florida, 1978.

KEYNES, J.M. 'Am I a Liberal?' in his *Essays in Persuasion* (Macmillan, London, 1972), pp. 272-94.

KLEINIG, JOHN. 'Paternalism: What Is at Stake?' Unpublished paper, Research School of Social Sciences, The Australian National University, 1981.

KOCIS, ROBERT A. 'Reason, Development and the Conflict of Human Ends: Sir Isaiah Berlin's Vision of Politics', *American Political Science Review*, LXXIV (March 1980), pp. 38-52.

KOHLBERG, LAWRENCE. 'The Claim to Moral Adequacy of a Highest Stage of Moral Judgment', *The Journal of Philosophy*, LXX (Oct. 1973), pp. 630-46.

LADENSON, ROBERT F. 'Mill's Conception of Individuality', *Social Theory and Practice*, IV (Spring 1977), pp. 167-82.

LAMONT, W.D. *Introduction to Green's Moral Philosophy* (Allen and Unwin, London, 1934).

LAWSON, ALAN. 'John Dewey and the Hope for Reform', *History of Education Quarterly*, XV (Spring 1975), pp. 31-66.

LERNER, RICHARD M. *Concepts and Theories of Human Development* (Addison-Wesley Publishing Co., Reading, Mass., 1976).

LETWIN, SHIRLEY ROBIN. *The Pursuit of Certainty* (Cambridge University Press, Cambridge, 1965).

LEVITT, MORTON. *Freud and Dewey on the Nature of Man* (Philosophical Library, New York, 1960).

LEWIS, H.D. *Freedom and History* (Allen and Unwin, London, 1962).

LICHTMAN, RICHARD. 'The Surface and Substance of Mill's Defense of Freedom', *Social Research*, XXX (1963), pp. 469-94.

LILLEY, IRENE M. 'Introduction' to her *Freidrich Froebel: A Selection from his Writings* (Cambridge University Press, Cambridge, 1967).

LINDBLOM, CHARLES E. *Politics and Markets* (Basic Books, New York, 1977).

LINDSAY, A.D. 'Introduction' to John Stuart Mill, *Utilitarianism, Liberty and Representative Government* (Dent, London, 1910), pp. vii-xxiv.

LIVELY, JACK. *Democracy* (Basil Blackwell, Oxford, 1975).

LOCKE, JOHN. *Some Thoughts Concerning Education* in Peter Gay (ed.), *John Locke on Education* (Teachers College Press, New York, 1964).

LORENZ, KONRAD. *On Aggression*, Marjorie Kerr Wilson (trans.) (Bantam Books, New York, 1971).

LOSMAN, DONALD L. 'J.S. Mill on Alternative Economic Systems', *American Journal of Economics and Sociology*, XXX (Jan. 1971), pp. 85-104.

LYND, HELEN MERRELL. *England in the Eighteen-Eighties* (Oxford University Press, London, 1945).

LYONS, DAVID. 'Mill's Theory of Morality', *Nous*, X (1976), pp. 101-20.

MAC CALLUM, GERALD. 'Negative and Positive Freedom' in Peter Laslett, W.G. Runciman and Quentin Skinner (eds.), *Philosophy, Politics and Society*, 4th series (Basil Blackwell, Oxford, 1972), pp. 174-93.

MAC CUNN, JOHN. *Six Radical Thinkers: Bentham, J.S. Mill, Cobden, Carlyle, Mazzini, T.H. Green* (Edward Arnold, London, 1907).

MAC IVER, R.M. *Community: A Sociological Study*, 3rd edn (Macmillan, London, 1924).

MACPHERSON, C.B. *Democratic Theory: Essays in Retrieval* (Clarendon Press, Oxford, 1973).

'Liberal-Democracy and Property' in his edited collection, *Property: Mainstream and Critical Positions* (University of Toronto Press, Toronto, 1978), pp. 199-207.

*The Life and Times of Liberal Democracy* (Oxford University Press, Oxford, 1977).

'Rawls' Models of Man and Society', *Philosophy of Social Sciences,* III (1973), pp. 341-47.

MANDELBAUM, MAURICE. *History, Man, and Reason* (Baltimore, Johns Hopkins Press, 1971).

'On Interpreting Mill's *Utilitarianism*' in Samuel Gorovitz (ed.), *Mill: Utilitarianism* (Bobbs-Merrill, Indianapolis, 1971), pp. 380-90.

MANNING, D.J. *Liberalism* (Dent, London, 1976).

MANSFIELD, HARVEY. *The Spirit of Liberalism* (Harvard University Press, Cambridge, Mass., 1978).

MARGOLIS, JOSEPH. 'Mill's *Utilitarianism* Again' in Samuel Gorovitz (ed.), *Mill: Utilitarianism* (Bobbs-Merrill, Indianapolis, 1971).

MARTIN, REX. 'A Defence of Mill's Qualitative Hedonism', *Philosophy*, XLVII (April 1972), pp. 140-51.

MC CLOSKEY, H.J. 'Mill's Liberalism', *Philosophical Quarterly*, XIII (1963), pp.

'The Problem of Liberalism', *Review of Metaphysics*, XIX (1965-66), pp. 248-75.

MC CULLOCH, J.R. *Principles of Political Economy* (Adam and Charles Black, Edinburgh, 1864).

MC DONALD, VIRGINIA. 'Rawlsian Contractarianism: Liberal Equality or Inequality?', *Canadian Journal of Philosophy*, III (1977), pp. 71-94.

MC DOUGALL, WILLIAM. *The Group Mind* (Cambridge University Press, Cambridge, 1920).

*An Introduction to Social Psychology*, 22nd edn (Methuen, London, 1931).

MEADE, J.E. *The Just Economy* (Allen and Unwin, London, 1976).

MELDEN, A.I. *Rights and Persons* (Basil Blackwell, Oxford, 1977).

MICHELMAN, FRANK I. 'Constitutional Welfare Rights and *A Theory of Justice*' in Norman Daniels (ed.), *Reading Rawls: Critical Studies of* A Theory of Justice (Basic Books, New York, 1974), pp. 319-47.

MIDGLEY, MARY. *Beast and Man: The Roots of Human Nature* (Methuen, London, 1980).

MILL, JAMES. *Analysis of the Phenomena of the Human Mind*, J.S. Mill (ed.) (Augustus M. Kelley, New York, 1967).

MILL, JOHN STUART. 'Auguste Comte and Positivism' in J.M. Robson (ed.), *The Collected Works of John Stuart Mill* (University of Toronto Press, Toronto, 1963), vol. X, pp. 261-368.

*Autobiography* (Columbia University Press, New York, 1924).

'Bain's Psychology' in his *Dissertations and Discussions* (William V. Spencer, Boston, 1868), vol. IV, pp. 101-56.

'Bentham' in *Collected Works*, vol. X, pp. 75-115.

'Centralisation' in *Collected Works*, vol. XIX, pp. 579-613.

*Chapters on Socialism* in *Collected Works*, vol. V, pp. 703-53.

'Civilization' in *Collected Works*, vol. XVIII, pp. 117-47.

'The Claims of Labour' in *Collected Works*, vol. V, pp. 363-89.

'Coleridge' in *Collected Works*, vol. X, pp. 117-63.

*Considerations on Representative Government* in *Collected Works*, vol. XIX, pp. 371-577.

'De Tocqueville on Democracy in America (II)' in *Collected Works*, vol. XVIII, pp. 153-204.

'Dr Whewell on Moral Philosophy' in *Collected Works*, vol. X, pp. 167-201.

*An Examination of Sir William Hamilton's Philosophy* in *Collected Works*, vol. IX.

'Inaugural Address' in his *Dissertations and Discussions*, vol. IV.

'Nature' in *Collected Works*, vol. X, pp. 373-402.

*On Liberty* in *Collected Works*, vol. XVIII, pp. 213-310.

*Principles of Political Economy* in *Collected Works*, vols. II, III.

'Recent Writers on Reform' in *Collected Works*, vol. XIX, pp. 341-70.

'Sedgwick's Discourse' in *Collected Works*, vol. X, pp. 31-74.

'The Spirit of the Age' in Geraint L. Williams (ed.), *John Stuart Mill on Politics and Society* (Fontana/Collins, Glasgow, 1976), pp. 170-78.

*The Subjection of Women* in Alice S. Rossi (ed.), *Essays on Sex Equality* (University of Chicago Press, Chicago, 1970), pp. 125-242.

*A System of Logic* in *Collected Works*, vols. VII and VIII.

'Thoughts on Parliamentary Reform' in *Collected Works*, vol. XIX, pp. 311-40.

*Utilitarianism* in *Collected Works*, vol. X, pp. 203-59.

'Utility of Religion' in *Collected Works*, vol. X, pp. 403-28.

MILLER, DAVID. 'Democracy and Social Justice' in Pierre Bernbaum, Jack Lively and Geraint Perry (eds.), *Democracy, Consensus and Social Contract* (Sage, Beverly Hills, 1978), pp. 75-100.

*Social Justice* (Clarendon Press, Oxford, 1976).

MILNE, A.J.M. *The Social Philosophy of English Idealism* (Allen and Unwin, London, 1962).

MINOGUE, KENNETH R. 'The Concept of Property and Its Contemporary Significance' in J. Roland Pennock and John W. Chapman (eds.), *NOMOS XXII: Property* (New York University Press, New York, 1980), pp. 3-27.

MONTESQUIEU. *The Spirit of the Laws*, Thomas Nugent (trans.) (Collier Macmillan, London, 1940).

MOORE, G.E. *Principia Ethica* (Cambridge University Press, Cambridge, 1959).

MORRIS, G.R. *Idealist Logic* (Macmillan, London, 1933).

MORROW, JOHN. 'Idealism and Socialism in Britain, 1880-1920', unpublished PhD thesis, York University, Toronto, 1980.

MUELLER, DENNIS C. 'Achieving the Just Polity', *American Economic Review*, LXIV (May 1974), pp. 147-52.

MUIRHEAD, J.H. 'Recent Criticisms of the Idealist Theory of the General Will (II)', *Mind*, XXXIII (July 1924), pp. 233-41.

   *The Service of the State: Four Lectures on the Political Teaching of T.H. Green* (John Murray, London, 1908).

_____(ed.). *Bernard Bosanquet and his Friends* (Allen and Unwin, London, 1935).

MURPHY, ARTHUR E. 'John Dewey and American Liberalism', *Journal of Philosophy*, LVII (1960), pp. 420-36.

MURPHY, JEFFRIE G. 'Incompetence and Paternalism', in his *Retribution, Justice, and Therapy* (Reidel, Boston, 1979), pp. 165-82.

NATHANSON, JEROME. *John Dewey: The Reconstruction of the Democratic Life* (Scribner's, New York, 1951).

NEILL, THOMAS P. *The Rise and Decline of Liberalism* (Bruce Publishing Co., Milwaukee, 1953).

NEILSON, KAI. 'On the Very Possibility of a Classless Society: Rawls, Macpherson, and Revisionist Liberalism', *Political Theory*, VI (May 1978), pp. 191-208.

NEWBURY, DOROTHY JUNE. 'A Search for the Meaning of Discipline in Dewey's Theory of Growth', *Educational Theory*, V (1955), pp. 236-45.

NORTON, DAVID L. *Personal Destinies: A Philosophy of Ethical Individualism* (Princeton University Press, Princeton, 1976).

   'Rawls's *Theory of Justice*: A "Perfectionist" Rejoinder', *Ethics*, LXXXV (Oct. 1974), pp. 50-57.

NOVACK, GEORGE. *Pragmatism versus Marxism* (Pathfinder Press, New York, 1975).

NOZICK, ROBERT. *Anarchy, State and Utopia* (Basic Books, New York, 1974).

OAKESHOTT, MICHAEL. *On Human Conduct* (Clarendon Press, Oxford, 1975).

OWEN, JOHN E. *L.T. Hobhouse: Sociologist* (Nelson, London, 1974).

PASSMORE, JOHN. *A Hundred Years of Philosophy*, 2nd edn (Penguin, Harmondsworth, 1966).

    *The Perfectibility of Man* (Duckworth, London, 1970).

PATEMAN, CAROLE. 'Feminist Critiques of the Public/Private Dichotomy' in S.I. Benn and G.F. Gaus (eds.), *Conceptions of the Public and Private in Social Life* (Croom Helm, London, forthcoming).

    *Participation and Democratic Theory* (Cambridge University Press, Cambridge, 1970).

PENNOCK, J. ROLAND. *Democratic Political Theory* (Princeton University Press, Princeton, 1979).

    *Liberal Democracy: Its Merits and Prospects* (Rinehart and Co., New York, 1950).

    ——— and CHAPMAN, JOHN W. (eds). *NOMOS XI: Voluntary Associations* (Atherton Press, New York, 1969).

    *NOMOS XX: Constitutionalism* (New York University Press, New York, 1979).

PETERS, R.S. *Psychology and Ethical Development* (Allen and Unwin, London, 1974).

PFANNENSTILL, BERTIL. *Bernard Bosanquet's Philosophy of the State: A Historical and Systematical Study* (G.W.K. Gleerup, Lund, 1936).

PIAGET, JEAN. *The Moral Judgment of the Child*, Marjorie Gabain (trans.) (The Free Press, New York, 1965).

PLAMENATZ, JOHN. *Consent, Freedom and Political Obligation*, 2nd edn (Oxford University Press, Oxford, 1968).

    *Democracy and Illusion* (Longman Group, London, 1973).

    *The English Utilitarians* (Basil Blackwell, Oxford, 1949).

    *Karl Marx's Philosophy of Man* (Clarendon Press, Oxford, 1975).

PLANT, RAYMOND; LESSER, HARRY; and TAYLOR-GOOBY, PETER. *Political Philosophy and Social Welfare* (Routledge and Kegan Paul, London, 1980).

PLATO. *The Republic*, Francis MacDonald Cornford (trans.) (Oxford University Press, Oxford, 1941).

PLATTNER, MARC F. 'The Welfare State vs. the Redistributive State', *The Public Interest*, LV (Spring 1979), pp. 28-48.

POIRIER, PHILIP D. 'Introduction' to Hobhouse, *The Labour Movement*, 3rd edn (Harvester Press, Brighton, 1974), pp. vii-xxiv.

POPPER, K.R. *The Open Society and Its Enemies*, vol. I: *The Spell of Plato* (Routledge and Kegan Paul, London, 1966).

PRICHARD, H.A. *Moral Obligation and Duty and Interest* (Oxford University Press, Oxford, 1968).

RAMSEY, PAUL. 'The Idealist View of Moral Evil: Josiah Royce and Bernard Bosanquet', *Philosophy and Phenomenological Research*, VI (June 1946), pp. 554-89.

RANDALL, JOHN HERMAN JR. 'Idealist Social Philosophy and Bernard Bosanquet', *Philosophy and Phenomenological Research*, XXVI (1965-66), pp. 473-502.

RAPHAEL, D.D. 'Fallacies in and about Mill's Utilitarianism', *Philosophy*, XXX (Oct. 1955), pp. 344-51.

RAWLS, JOHN. 'The Basic Structure as Subject' in Alvin I. Goldman and Jaegwon Kim (eds.), *Values and Morals* (D. Reidel, Dordrecht, 1978), pp. 47-71.

'Constitutional Liberty and the Conception of Justice' in Carl J. Friedrich and John W. Chapman (eds.), *NOMOS VI: Justice* (Leiber-Atherton, New York, 1963), pp. 98-125.

'Kantian Constructivism in Moral Theory', *Journal of Philosophy*, LXXVII (Sept. 1980), pp. 515-72.

'Reply to Alexander and Musgrave', *Quarterly Journal of Economics*, LXXXVIII (Nov. 1974), pp. 635-55.

'Social Unity and Primary Goods' in A.K. Sen and Bernard Williams (eds.), *Utilitarianism and Beyond* (Cambridge University Press, Cambridge, 1982), pp. 159-85.

'Some Reasons for the Maximin Criterion', *American Economic Review*, LXIV (May 1974), pp. 141-46.

*A Theory of Justice* (The Belknap Press of Harvard University Press, Cambridge, Mass., 1971).

'A Well-Ordered Society' in Peter Laslett and James Fishkin (eds.), *Philosophy, Politics and Society*, 5th series (Basil Blackwell, Oxford, 1979), pp. 6-20.

REGAN, DONALD H. *Utilitarianism and Co-operation* (Clarendon Press, Oxford, 1980).

RICARDO, DAVID. *On the Principles of Political Economy and Taxation*, Piero Straffa (ed.) (Cambridge University Press, Cambridge, 1951).

RICHARDS, DAVID A.J. 'Free Speech and Obscenity Law: Towards a Moral Theory of the First Amendment', *University of Pennsylvania Law Review*, CXXIII (Nov. 1974), pp. 45-91.

RICHTER, MELVIN. *The Politics of Conscience: T.H. Green and his Age* (Weidenfeld and Nicolson, London, 1964).

RITCHIE, D.G. *Principles of State Interference: Four Essays on the*

*Political Philosophy of Mr Herbert Spencer, J.H. Mill and T.H. Green* (George Allen and Co., 1902).

ROBBINS, Lord. *Political Economy: Past and Present* (Macmillan, London, 1977).

　　*The Theory of Economic Policy in English Classical Political Economy* (Macmillan, London, 1961).

ROBSON, JOHN M. *The Improvement of Mankind: The Social and Political Thought of John Stuart Mill* (University of Toronto Press, Toronto, 1968).

　　'J.S. Mill's Theory of Poetry' in J.B. Schneewind (ed.), *Mill: A Collection of Critical Essays* (Macmillan, London, 1968), pp. 251-79.

ROBSON, WILLIAM A. *Welfare State and Welfare Society: Illusion and Reality* (Allen and Unwin, London, 1976).

ROCKOW, LEWIS. *Contemporary Political Thought in England* (Leonard Press, London, 1925).

RODMAN, JOHN. 'Introduction' to his edited collection *The Political Theory of T.H. Green* (Appleton-Century-Crofts, New York, 1964), pp. 1-40.

　　'What is Living and What is Dead in the Political Philosophy of T.H. Green', *Western Political Quarterly*, XXVI (Sept. 1973), pp. 566-86.

ROTH, ROBERT J. *John Dewey and Self-Realization* (Prentice-Hall, Englewood Cliffs, N.J., 1962).

ROUSSEAU J.-J. *Discourse on the Arts and Sciences* in Roger D. and Judith R. Masters (trans.), *The First and Second Discourses* (St. Martin's Press, New York, 1964).

　　*Discourse on the Origin and Foundations of Inequality Among Men* in *The First and Second Discourses*.

　　*Emile*, Barbara Foxley (trans.) (Dent, London, 1911).

RUGGIERO, GUIDO de. *The History of European Liberalism*, R.G. Collingwood (trans.) (Oxford University Press, London, 1927).

RYAN, ALAN. *J.S. Mill* (Routledge and Kegan Paul, London, 1974).

　　'The Nature of Human Nature in Hobbes and Rousseau' in Jonathan Benthall (ed.), *The Limits of Human Nature* (E.P. Dutton and Co., New York, 1974), pp. 3-19.

　　*The Philosophy of John Stuart Mill* (Macmillan, London, 1970).

　　'Two Concepts of Politics and Democracy' in Martin Fleisher (ed.), *Machiavelli and the Nature of Political Thought* (Atheneum Press, New York, 1972), pp. 76-113.

SABINE, GEORGE H. *A History of Political Theory* (Harrap, London, 1937).

SARTORI, GIOVANNI. *Democratic Theory* (Wayne State University Press, Detroit, 1962).

SCHWARTZ, ADINA BETH. 'John Stuart Mill: A Program for Social Philosophy', unpublished PhD thesis, Rockefeller University, New York, 1976.

SCHWARTZ, BERNARD. *The Great Rights of Mankind* (Oxford University Press, New York, 1971).

SCHWARTZ, PEDRO. *The New Political Economy of J.S. Mill* (Weidenfeld and Nicolson, London, 1972).

SEAMAN, JOHN W. 'L.T. Hobhouse and the Theory of "Social Liberalism"', *Canadian Journal of Political Science*, XI (1978), pp. 777-801.

SETH, JAMES. 'The Alleged Fallacies in Mill's *Utilitarianism*', *Philosophical Review*, XVII (Sept. 1908), pp. 468-88.

SHILS, EDWARD. 'The Antinomies of Liberalism' in *The Relevance of Liberalism*, Staff of the Research Institute on International Change (eds.) (Westview Press, Boulder, Colo., 1978), pp. 135-200.

SHUE, HENRY. 'Liberty and Self-Respect', *Ethics*, LXXXV (April 1975), pp. 195-203.

SIDGWICK, HENRY. *Lectures on the Ethics of T.H. Green, Mr Herbert Spencer and J. Martineau* (Macmillan, London, 1902).

    *The Methods of Ethics*, 7th edn (University of Chicago Press, Chicago, 1907).

SIEDENTOP, LARRY. 'Two Liberal Traditions' in Alan Ryan (ed.), *The Idea of Freedom: Essays in Honour of Isaiah Berlin* (Oxford University Press, Oxford, 1979), pp. 154-74.

SIMEC, SOPHIE M. 'Human Nature According to Dewey', *Proceedings of the American Catholic Philosophical Association*, XXIX (1955), pp. 225-34.

SIMON, W.M. (ed.). *French Liberalism, 1789-1848* (Wiley, New York, 1972).

SKINNER, B.F. *About Behaviorism* (Alfred A. Knopf, New York, 1974).

    *Walden Two* (Macmillan, New York, 1962).

SMIRNOFF, GEORGI. *Soviet Man: The Making of a Socialist Type Personality* (Progress Publishers, Moscow, 1973).

SMITH, ADAM. *An Inquiry into the Nature and Causes of the Wealth of Nations*, W.B. Todd (ed.) (Clarendon Press, Oxford, 1976).

SMITH, JOHN E. 'The Value of Community: Dewey and Royce', *Southern Journal of Philosophy*, XII (Winter 1974), pp. 469-79.

SOMJEE, A.H. *The Political Theory of John Dewey* (Teachers College Press, New York, 1968).

SPAHR, MARGARET. 'Mill on Paternalism in Its Place' in Carl J. Freidrich (ed.), *NOMOS IV: Liberty* (Atherton Press, New York, 1962), pp. 162-75.

SPENCER, HERBERT. *Social Statics and Man Versus State* (Williams and Norgate, London, 1892).

SPITZ, DAVID. 'Freedom and Individuality: Mill's *Liberty* in Retrospect' in Carl J. Friedrich (ed.), *NOMOS IV: Liberty* (Atherton Press, New York, 1962), pp. 176-226.

STEPHEN, Sir LESLIE. *The English Utilitarians*, vol. III: *John Stuart Mill* (Augustus M. Kelley, New York, 1968).

STEVENSON, CHARLES L. 'Reflections on John Dewey's Ethics', *Proceedings of the Aristotelian Society* (1962), pp. 77-98.

STEVENSON, LESLIE. *Seven Theories of Human Nature* (Oxford University Press, Oxford, 1974).

STILLMAN, PETER G. 'Property, Freedom and Individuality in Hegel's and Marx's Political Thought' in J. Roland Pennock and John W. Chapman (eds.), *NOMOS XXII: Property* (New York University Press, New York, 1980), pp. 130-67.

TEN, C.L. *Mill on Liberty* (Oxford University Press, Oxford, 1980).

THOMPSON, DENNIS F. *The Democratic Citizen: Social Science and Democratic Theory in the Twentieth Century* (Cambridge University Press, Cambridge, 1970).

*John Stuart Mill and Representative Government* (Princeton University Press, Princeton, 1976).

THUROW, LESTER C. *Generating Inequality: Mechanisms of Distribution in the U.S. Economy* (Basic Books, New York, 1975).

TIGER, LIONEL and FOX, ROBIN. *The Imperial Animal* (Secher and Warburg, London, 1971).

ULAM, ADAM. *Philosophical Foundations of English Socialism* (Harvard University Press, Cambridge, Mass., 1951).

VARIAN, HAL R. 'Distributive Justice, Welfare Economics and the Theory of Fairness', *Philosophy and Public Affairs* IV (Spring 1975), pp. 223-47.

WARD, JAMES. 'J.S. Mill's Science of Ethology', *International Journal of Ethics*, I (July 1891), pp. 446-59.

WATKINS, FREDERICK. *The Political Tradition of the West: A Study in the Development of Modern Liberalism* (Harvard University Press, Cambridge, Mass., 1948).

WATSON, JOHN B. *Behaviorism*, rev. edn (University of Chicago Press, Chicago, 1930).

WEILER, PETER. 'The New Liberalism of L.T. Hobhouse', *Victorian Studies*, XVI (Dec. 1972), pp. 141-61.

WEINSTEIN, W.L. 'The Concept of Liberty in Nineteenth Century English Political Thought', *Political Studies*, XIII (1965), pp. 145-62.

WIKLER, DANIEL. 'Paternalism and the Mildly Retarded', *Philosophy and Public Affairs*, VIII (Summer 1979), pp. 377-92.

WILES, P.J.D. *Economic Institutions Compared* (Wiley, New York, 1977).

WILKINS, BURLEIGH TAYLOR. 'James, Dewey, and Hegelian Idealism', *Journal of History of Ideas*, XVII (June 1956), pp. 332-46.

WILLIAMS, BERNARD. *Morality: An Introduction to Ethics* (Harper and Row, New York, 1972).

WILLIAMS, GERAINT L. 'Introduction' to his edited selection *John Stuart Mill on Politics and Society* (Fontana/Collins, Glasgow, 1976), pp. 9-52.

WILSON, EDWARD O. *On Human Nature* (Harvard University Press, Cambridge, Mass., 1978).

WILSON, R. JACKSON. 'Dewey's Hegelianism', *History of Education Quarterly*, XV (Spring 1975), pp. 87-92.

*In Quest of Community: Social Philosophy in the United States: 1860-1920* (Oxford University Press, Oxford, 1968).

WITTGENSTEIN, LUDWIG. *Philosophical Investigations*, 3rd edn, G.E.M. Anscombe (trans.) (Macmillan, New York, 1958).

WOLFF, ROBERT PAUL. *The Poverty of Liberalism* (Beacon Press, Boston, 1968).

*Understanding Rawls* (Princeton University Press, Princeton, 1977).

WOODS, THOMAS. *Poetry and Philosophy: A Study in the Thought of John Stuart Mill* (Hutchinson, London, 1961).

WRIGHT, GEORG HENRICK von. *The Varieties of Goodness* (Routledge and Kegan Paul, London, 1963).

WRIGHT, R. GEORGE. 'The High Cost of Rawls' Inegalitarianism', *Western Political Quarterly*, XXX (March 1977), pp. 73-79.

# INDEX

The only proper names included in this index are those that appear in the text.

Absolute Idealism, 23ff, 55, 109
  *see also* Idealism
Affection
  contagion thesis, 96-97
  distinguished from sympathy, 89, 95
  encouraging sympathy, 93
  neighbourliness, relation to, 95
  network of, 96
Affective Ties, 88ff, 212
  *see also* Affection, Community, Fraternity, Sympathy
Anarchists, 6, 7, 9, 182
Apathy/Lethargy, 136ff, 142, 148, 167, 175-76, 182
Appercipient Mass, 72ff, 211
Aristocracy, 213, 218
Aristotelian Conception of Development, 43-44, 103
Aristotelian Justice, 188ff
Aristotelian Principle, 26-27, 220
  and discipline/specialisation, 149
  and principle of inclusiveness, 150
  and self-respect, 135-36
Aristotle, 18, 23
Art, 30-32
Artificial Growth, 131
  *see also* Pathologies, Plant Analogy
Asch, Solomon E., 56, 81, 241
Associationism, 32, 118, 123-26, 133
Autonomy, 6, 182, 224

Barbu, Zevedei, 2, 80
Barker, Ernest, 8
Barry, Brian, 101, 236
Behaviourism, 118-19
Bentham, Jeremy, 25, 30, 31, 238, 270, 271
Bequest, 253, 255
Berlin, Isaiah, 163-65, 178
Bill of Rights, 183, 185, 187
Bosanquet, Bernard
  aesthetics, 31

Bosanquet, Bernard (Cont.)
  on arduous satisfactions, 26, 31
  on bad capacities, 142
  on capacities and occupations, 186-87
  charge of Toryism, 3
  on classes, 113
  on coherence and many-sided lives, 39
  on commonality and community, 83
  on community of mankind, 86-87
  conscious unity, 80ff, 210-11
  on containing others, 22ff
  on danger of coercion, 175
  on deliberation and community, 4, 210-11
  on dependency, 249-50
  on development of individual natures, 45
  each-knows-best assumption, 166
  on family and community, 96-98
  general will and democracy, 81ff, 210-11, 214-15
  on Green's theory of development, 29
  and Hegelian interactionism, 120-21
  on human equality, 188
  on identity in difference, 70
  impulse to completion, 55
  impulses, 140
  on inborn gifts, 17, 22
  individuality and absolute idealism, 24
  on individuality and sociability, 107
  individuality as an achievement, 25
  instinct to harmony, 35
  on intellectual freedom, 184
  on leisure, 41
  on life plans, 32ff
  on limiting acquisition, 256
  on market relations, 241